London and the Kingdom Vol. -1

by

Reginald R. Sharpe

London and the Kingdom Vol. -1
by Reginald R. Sharpe

ISBN: 978-93-59393-22-3

Published by

DOUBLE 9 BOOKS

2/13-B, Ansari Road
Daryaganj, New Delhi – 110002
info@double9books.com
www.double9books.com
Tel. 011-40042856

ABOUT THE AUTHOR

Reginald R. Sharpe was an eminent historian who devoted his career to studying London's past and who made important contributions to his discipline. Although not much is known about Sharpe, his writings have greatly influenced how we view the history of this city. Sharpe is widely recognized for his studies and writings on London in the Middle Ages and the Early Modern Era. He spent his whole professional life poring over original documents, manuscripts, and records in search of insights into the city's past. Sharpe is best known for his monumental multi-volume work titled "London and the Kingdom," which details the city's history within the framework of the English kingdom as a whole. This series demonstrates Sharpe's knowledge and comprehension of London's history by providing insightful commentary on the city's political, social, economic, and cultural aspects.

CONTENTS

PREFACE.

Of the numerous works that have been written on London, by which I mean more especially the City of London, few have been devoted to an adequate, if indeed any, consideration of its political importance in the history of the Kingdom. The history of the City is so many-sided that writers have to be content with the study of some particular phase or some special epoch. Thus we have those who have concentrated their efforts to evolving out of the remote past the municipal organization of the City. Their task has been to unfold the origin and institution of the Mayoralty and Shrievalty of London, the division of the City into wards with Aldermen at their head, the development of the various trade and craft guilds, and the respective powers and duties of the Courts of Aldermen and Common Council, and of the Livery of London assembled in their Common Hall. Others have devoted themselves to the study of the ecclesiastical and monastic side of the City's history—its Cathedral, its religious houses, and hundred and more parish churches, which occupied so large an extent of the City's area. The ecclesiastical importance of the City, however, is too often ignored. "We are prone," writes Bishop Stubbs, "in examining into the municipal and mercantile history of London, to forget that it was a very great ecclesiastical centre." Others, again, have confined themselves to depicting the every-day life of the City burgess, his social condition, his commercial pursuits, his amusements; whilst others have been content to perpetuate the memory of streets and houses long since lost to the eye, and thus to keep alive an interest in scenes and places which otherwise would be forgotten.

The political aspect of the City's history has rarely been touched by writers, and yet its geographical position combined with the innate courage and enterprise of its citizens served to give it no small political power and no insignificant place in the history of the Kingdom. This being the case, the Corporation resolved to fill the void, and in view of the year 1889 being the 700th Anniversary of the Mayoralty of London—according to popular tradition—instructed the Library Committee to prepare a work showing "the pre-eminent position occupied by the City of London and the important function it exercised in the shaping and making of England."

It is in accordance with these instructions that this and succeeding volumes have been compiled. As the title of the work has been taken from a chapter in Mr. Loftie's book on London ("Historic Towns" series, chap. ix), so its main features are delineated in that chapter. "It would be interesting"—writes Mr. Loftie—"to go over all the recorded instances in which the City of London interfered directly in the affairs of the Kingdom. Such a survey would be the history of England as seen from the windows of the Guildhall." No words could better describe the character of the work now submitted to the public. It has been compiled mainly from the City's own archives. The City has been allowed to tell its own story. If, therefore, its pages should appear to be too much taken up with accounts of loans advanced by the City to impecunious monarchs or with wearisome repetition of calls for troops to be raised in the City for foreign service, it is because the City's records of the day are chiefly if not wholly concerned with these matters. If, on the other hand, an event which may be rightly deemed of national importance be here omitted, it is because the citizens were little affected thereby, and the City's records are almost, if not altogether, silent on the subject.

The work does not affect to be a critical history so much as a *chronique pour servir*, to which the historical student may have recourse in order to learn what was the attitude taken up by the citizens of London at important crises in the nation's history. He will there see how, in the contest between Stephen and the Empress Matilda, the City of London held as it were the balance; how it helped to overthrow the tyranny of Longchamp, and to wrest from the reluctant John the Great Charter of our liberties; how it was with men and money supplied by the City that Edward III and Henry " were enabled to conquer France, and how in after years the London trained bands raised the siege of Gloucester and turned the tide of the Civil War in favour of Parliament. He will not fail to note the significant fact that before Monk put into execution his plan for restoring Charles II to the Crown, the taciturn general—little given to opening his mind to anyone—deemed it advisable to take up his abode in the City in order to first test the feelings of the inhabitants as to whether the Restoration would be acceptable to them or not. He will see that the citizens of London have at times been bold of speech even in the presence of their sovereign when the cause of justice and the liberty of the subject were at stake, and that they did not hesitate to suffer for their opinions; that, vat many of the most critical periods of our history, the influence of London and its Lord Mayors has turned the scale in favour of those liberties of which we are so justly proudv; and that had the entreaties of the City been listened to by the King and his ministers, the American Colonies would never have been lost to England.

There are two Appendices to the work; one comprising copies from the City's Records of letters, early proclamations and documents of special interest to which reference is made in the text; the other consisting of a more complete list of the City's representatives in Parliament from the earliest times than has yet been printed, supplemented as it has been by returns to writs recorded in the City's archives and (apparently) no where else. The returns for the City in the Blue Books published in 1878 and 1879 are very imperfect.

R. R. S.

THE GUILDHALL, LONDON,
April, 1894.

CHAPTER I.

The greatness of London. How far due to its geographical position.

The wealth and importance of the City of London are due to a variety of causes, of which its geographical position must certainly be esteemed not the least. The value of such a noble river as the Thames was scarcely over-estimated by the citizens when, as the story goes, they expressed to King James their comparative indifference to his threatened removal of himself, his court and parliament, from London, if only their river remained to them. The mouth of the Thames is the most convenient port on the westernmost boundary of the European seaboard, and ships would often run in to replenish their tanks with the sweet water for which it was once famous. 1

After the fall of the Western Empire (A.D. 476), commercial enterprise sprang up among the free towns of Italy. The carrying trade of the world's merchandise became centred for a time in Venice, and that town led the way in spreading the principles of commerce along the shores of the Mediterranean, being closely followed by Genoa, Florence, and Pisa. The tide, which then set westward, and continued its course beyond the Pillars of Hercules, was met in later years by another stream of commerce from the shores of the Baltic. 2 Small wonder, then, if the City of London was quick to profit by the continuous stream of traffic passing and repassing its very door, and vindicated its title to be called—as the Venerable Bede had in very early days called it the Emporium of the World. 3

But if London's prosperity were solely due to its geographical position, we should look for the same unrivalled pre-eminence in commerce in towns like Liverpool or Bristol, which possess similar local advantages; whilst, if royal favour or court gaieties could make cities great, we should have surely expected Winchester, Warwick, York, or Stafford to have outstripped London in political and commercial greatness, for these were the residences of the rulers of Mercia, Northumbria, and Wessex, and the scenes of witena-gemóts long before London could boast of similar favours. Yet none of these equals London in extent, population, wealth, or political importance.

The tenure of the City of London compared with other boroughs.

We must therefore look for other causes of London's pre-eminence, and among these, we may reckon the fact that the City has never been subject to any over-lord except the king. It never formed a portion of the king's demesne (*dominium*), but has ever been held by its burgesses as tenants *in capite* by burgage (free socage) tenure. Other towns like Bristol, Plymouth, Beverley, or Durham, were subject to over-lords, ecclesiastical or lay, in the person of archbishop, bishop, abbot, baron or peer of the realm, who kept in their own hands many of the privileges which in the more favoured City of London were enjoyed by the municipal authorities.

In the early part of the twelfth century, the town of Leicester, for instance, was divided into four parts, one of which was in the king's demesne, whilst the rest were held by three distinct over-lords. In course of time, the whole of the shares fell into the hands of Count Robert of Meulan, who left the town in demesne to the Earls of Leicester and his descendants; and to this day the borough bears on its shield the arms of the Bellomonts. 4 The town of Birmingham is said, in like manner, to bear the arms of the barons of that name; the town of Cardiff, those of the De Clares; and Manchester, those of the Byrons. Instances might be multiplied. But the arms of the City of London and of free boroughs, like Winchester, Oxford, and Exeter, are referable to no over-lord, although the borough of Southwark still bears traces in its heraldic shield of its former ecclesiastical connection.

The powers of an over-lord.

The influence of an over-lord for good or evil, over those subject to his authority, was immense. Take for instance, Sheffield, which was subject, in the reign of Elizabeth, to the Earl of Shrewsbury. The cutlery trade, even in those days, was the main-stay of the town, and yet the earl could make and unmake the rules and ordinances which governed the Cutlers' Company, and could claim one half of the fines imposed on its members. 5

When, during the reign of Charles II, nearly every municipal borough in the kingdom was forced to surrender its charter to the king, the citizens of Durham surrendered theirs to the Bishop, who, to the intense horror of a contemporary writer, reserved to himself and his successors in the See the power of approving and confirming the mayor, aldermen, recorder, and common council of that city. 6

London under the Roman Empire.

The commercial greatness of London can be traced back to the time of the Roman occupation of Britain. From being little more than a stockaded fort, situate at a point on the river's bank which admitted of an easy passage by ferry across to Southwark, London prospered under the protection afforded to its traders by the presence of the Roman legions, but it never in those days became the capital of the province. Although a flourishing centre of commerce in the middle of the first century of the Christian era, it was not deemed of sufficient importance by Suetonius, the Roman general, to run the risk of defending against Boadicea, 7 and although thought worthy of the title of Augusta—a name bestowed only on towns of exceptional standing—the Romans did not hesitate to leave both town and province to their fate as soon as danger threatened them nearer home.

Roman highways.

For military no less than for commercial purposes—and the Roman occupation of Britain was mainly a military one—good roads were essential, and these the Romans excelled in making. It is remarkable that in the Itinerary of Antoninus Pius, London figures either as the starting point or as the terminus to nearly one-half of the routes described in the portion relating to Britain. 8 The name of one and only one of these Roman highways survives in the city at the present day, and then only in its Teutonic and not Roman form—the Watling or "Wathelinga" Street, the street which led from Kent through the city of London to Chester and York, and thence by two branches to Carlisle and the neighbourhood of Newcastle. The Ermin Street, another Roman road with a Teutonic name, led from London to Lincoln, with branches to Doncaster and York, but its name no longer survives in the city.

London bridge and the city wall.

The same reasons that led the Romans to establish good roads throughout the country led them also to erect a bridge across the river from London to Southwark, and in later years to enclose the city with a wall. To the building of the bridge, which probably took place in the early years of the Roman occupation, London owed much of its youthful prosperity; whenever any accident happened to the bridge the damage was always promptly repaired. Not so with the walls of the city. They were allowed to fall into decay until the prudence and military genius of the great Alfred caused them to be repaired as a bulwark against the onslaughts of the Danes.

The departure of the Roman legions, and its consequences.

"Britain had been occupied by the Romans, but had not become Roman," 9 and the scanty and superficial civilization which the Britons had received from the Roman occupation was obliterated by the calamities which followed the northern invasions of the fifth and following centuries. A Christian city, as Augusta had probably been, not a vestige of a Christian church of the Roman period has come down to us. 10 It quickly lapsed into paganism. Its very name disappears, and with it the names of its streets, its traditions and its customs. Its inhabitants forgot the Latin tongue, and the memories of 400 years were clean wiped out. There remains to us of the present day nothing to remind us of London under the Roman empire, save a fragment of a wall, a milestone, a few coins and statuettes, and some articles of personal ornament or domestic use—little more in fact, than what may be seen in the Museum attached to the Guildhall Library. The long subjection to Roman rule had one disastrous effect. It enervated the people and left them powerless to cope with those enemies who, as soon as the iron hand of the Roman legions was removed, came forth from their hiding places to harry the land.

Appeal to Rome for aid against the Picts and Scots. A. D. 446.

Thus it was that when the Picts and Scots again broke loose from their northern fastnesses and threatened London as they had done before (A.D. 368), they once more appealed for aid to the Roman emperor, by whose assistance the marauders had formerly been driven back. But times were different in 446 to what they had been in 368. The Roman empire was itself threatened with an invasion of the Goths, and the emperor had his hands too full to allow him to lend a favourable ear to the "groans of the Britons." 11

Meeting with refusal, the Britons call in the Saxons.

Compelled to seek assistance elsewhere, the Britons invited a tribe of warriors, ever ready to let their services for hire, from the North Sea, to lend them their aid. The foreigners came in answer to the invitation, they saw, they conquered; and then they refused to leave an island the fertility of which they appreciated no less than they despised the slothfulness of its inhabitants. 12 They turned their weapons against their employers, and utterly routed them at Crayford, driving them to take refuge within the walls of London.

The battle of the "Creegan Ford." A.D. 457.

"A.D. 457 (456). This year Hengist and Æsc [Eric or Ash] his son fought against the Britons at a place called Creegan-Ford [Crayford] and there slew four thousand men, and the Britons then forsook Kent, and in great terror fled to London." 13 So runs the Anglo-Saxon chronicle, and this is the sole piece of information concerning London it vouchsafes us for one hundred and fifty years following the departure of the Romans. The information, scant as it is, serves to show that London had not quite become a deserted city, nor had yet been devastated as others had been by the enemy. Its walls still served to afford shelter to the terrified refugees.

London, the metropolis of the East Saxons.

When next we read of her, she is in the possession of the East Saxons. How they came there is a matter for conjecture. It is possible that with the whole of the surrounding counties in the hands of the enemy, the Londoners were driven from their city to seek means of subsistence elsewhere, and that when the East Saxons took possession of it, they found houses and streets deserted. Little relishing a life within a town, they probably did not make a long stay, and, on their departure, the former inhabitants returned and the city slowly recovered its wonted appearance, as the country around became more settled.

Mellitus, the first Bishop of London, A.D. 604.

Christianity in the country had revived, and London was now to receive its first bishop. It is the year 604. "This year," writes the chronicler, "Augustine hallowed two bishops, Mellitus and Justus; Mellitus he sent to preach baptism to the East Saxons, whose king was called Seberht, son of Ricula, the sister of Ethelbert whom Ethelbert had there set as king. And Ethelbert gave to Mellitus a bishop's see at London." This passage is remarkable for two reasons: — (1) as shewing us that London was at this time situate in Essex, the kingdom of the East Saxons, and (2) that Seberht was but a *roi fainéant*, enjoying no real independence in spite of his dignity as ruler of the East Saxons and nominal master of London, his uncle Ethelbert, king of the Cantii, exercising a hegemony over "all the nations of the English as far as the Humber." 14

Hence it is that London is spoken of by some as being the *metropolis* of the East Saxons, 15 and by others as being the principal city of the Cantii; 16 the fact being that, though locally situate in Essex, it was deemed the political capital of that kingdom which for the time being happened to be paramount.

St. Paul's Cathedral founded by Ethelbert.

After the death of Seberht, the Londoners became dissatisfied with their bishop and drove him out. Mellitus became in course of time Archbishop of Canterbury, whilst the Londoners again relapsed into paganism. 17 Not only was the erection of a cathedral in the city due to Ethelbert, but it was also at his instigation, if not with his treasure, that Seberht, the "wealthy sub-king of London," was, as is believed, induced to found the Abbey of Westminster. 18

The rival Cities of London and Winchester.

When the Saxon kingdoms became united under Egbert and he became *rex totius Britanniæ* (A.D. 827), London began to take a more prominent place among the cities of the kingdom, notwithstanding its having been three times destroyed by fire between 674 and 801. 19 It became more often the seat of the royal residence, and the scene of witena-gemóts; nevertheless it was not the seat of government, much less the capital. Then and for a long time to come it had a formidable rival in Winchester, the chief town of Egbert's own kingdom of Wessex. To Winchester that king proceeded in triumph after completing the union of the Saxon kingdoms, and thither he summoned his vassals to hear himself proclaimed their overlord. From Winchester, Alfred, too, promulgated his new code of Wessex law—a part of the famous *Domboc*, a copy of which is said to have been at one time preserved among the archives of the City of London 20—and the Easter gemót, no matter where the other gemóts of the year were held, was nearly always held at Winchester. When it came to a question of trade regulation, then London took precedence of Winchester. "Let one measure and one weight pass, such as is observed at London and at Winchester," 21 enacted King Edgar, whose system of legislation was marked with so much success that "Edgar's Law" was referred to by posterity as to the old constitution of the realm.

London in the hands of the Danes.

In the meantime, the country had been invaded by a fresh enemy, and the same atrocities which the Briton had suffered at the hands of the Saxon, the Saxon was made to suffer at the hands of the Dane. London suffered with the rest of the kingdom. In 839 we read of a "great slaughter" there; 22 in 851 the city was in the hands of the enemy, and continued to remain at the mercy of the Danes, so much so, in fact, that in 872 we find the Danish army taking up winter quarters within its walls, as in a city that was their own. 23

The Treaty of Wedmore, A.D. 878.

It was now, when the clouds were darkest, that Alfred, brother of King Ethelred, appeared on the scene, and after more than one signal success by land and sea, concluded the treaty of Wedmore (A.D. 878) 24 by which a vast tract of land bounded by an imaginary line drawn from the Thames along the river Lea to Bedford, and thence along the Roman Watling Street to the Welsh border, was ceded to the enemy under the name of *Danelagh*. The treaty, although it curtailed the Kingdom of Wessex, and left London itself at the mercy of the Danes, was followed by a period of comparative tranquillity, which allowed Alfred time to make preparations for a fresh struggle that was to wrest from the enemy the land they had won.

The Danes expelled from London.

The Danes, like the Angles and the Jutes before them, set little store by fortifications and walled towns, preferring always to defend themselves by combat in open field, and the Roman wall of the City was allowed to fall still further into decay. In the eyes of Alfred on the other hand, London, with its surrounding wall, was a place of the first importance, and one to be acquired and kept at all hazards. At length he achieved the object of his ambition and succeeded in driving out the Danes, (A.D. 883 or 884). 25

Alfred "restores" London, 886-887.

Whilst the enemy directed their attention to further conquests in France and Belgium, Alfred bent his energies towards repairing the City walls and building a citadel for his defence—"the germ of that tower which was to be first the dwelling place of Kings, and then the scene of the martyrdom of their victims." 26 To his foresight in this respect was it due that the city of London was never again taken by open assault, but successfully repelled all attacks whilst the surrounding country was often devastated.

Nor did Alfred confine his attention solely to strengthening the city against attacks of enemies without or to making it more habitable. He also laid the foundation of an internal Government analagous to that established in the Shires. Under the year A.D. 886, the Anglo-Saxon Chronicle 27 records that "King Ælfred restored London; and all the Anglo race turned to him that were not in bondage of the Danish men; and he then committed the burgh to "the keeping of the aldorman Æthelred." In course of time the analogy between shire and city organization became more close. Where the former had its Shiremote, the latter had its Folkmote, meeting in St. Paul's Churchyard by summons of the great bell. The County Court found its co-relative in the Husting Court of the City; the Hundred Court in the City Wardmote. 28

An attack of the Danes in the absence of Alfred gallantly repelled by the Citizens, A.D. 894.

For the next ten years Alfred busied himself founding a navy and establishing order in different parts of the country, but in 896 he was compelled to hasten to London from the west of England to assist in the repulse of another attack of the Danes. Two years before (894) the Danes had threatened London, having established a fortification at Beamfleate or South Benfleet, in Essex, whence they harried the surrounding country. The Londoners on that occasion joined that part of the army which Alfred had left behind in an attack upon the fort, which they not only succeeded in taking, but they "took all that there was within, as well money as women and children, and brought all to London; and all the ships they either broke in pieces or burned, or brought to London or to Rochester." 29 Nor was this all: Hasting's wife and his two sons had been made prisoners, but were chivalrously restored by Alfred.

Successful strategy of Alfred against the Danes, A.D. 896.

The Danes, however, were not to be daunted by defeat nor moved from their purpose by the generous conduct of Alfred. In 896 they again appeared. This time they erected a work on the sea, twenty miles above London. Alfred made a reconnaissance and closed up the river so that they found it impossible to bring out their ships. 30 They therefore abandoned their vessels and escaped across country, and "the men of London" writes the chronicler, "brought away the ships, and all those which they could not bring off they broke up, and those that were *stalworth* they brought into London." 31

The London "frith-gild" under Athelstan, 925-940.

The principle of each man becoming responsible to the Government for the good behaviour of the neighbour, involved in the system of frankpledge which Alfred established throughout the whole of his kingdom, subject to his rule, was carried a step further by the citizens of London at a later date. Under Athelstan (A.D. 925-940) we find them banding together and forming an association for mutual defence of life and property, and thus assisting the executive in the maintenance of law and order. A complete code of ordinances, regulating this "frith" or peace gild, as it was called, drawn up by the bishops and reeves of the burgh, and confirmed by the members on oath, is still preserved to us. 32

First mention of a Guildhall in London.

The enactments are chiefly directed against thieves, the measures to be taken to bring them to justice, and the penalties to be imposed on them, the formation of a common fund for the pursuit of thieves, and for making good to members any loss they may have sustained. So far, the gild undertook duties of a public character, such as are found incorporated among other laws of the kingdom, but it had, incidentally, also its social and religious side. When the ruling members met in their gild-hall, 33 which they did once a month, "if they could and had leisure," they enjoyed a refection with ale-drinking or "byt-filling."

The "frith-guild," something more than a mere friendly society.

Some writers see in the "frith-gild" of Athelstan's day, nothing more than a mere "friendly society," meeting together once a month, to drink their beer and consult about matters of mutual insurance and other topics of more or less social and religious character. 34 But there is evidence to show that the tie which united members of a "frith-gild" was stronger and more solemn than any which binds the members of a friendly society or voluntary association. The punishment of one who was guilty of breaking his "frith" was practically banishment or death. Such a one, in Athelstan's time, was ordered to abjure the country, which probably meant no more than that he was to leave his burgh or perhaps the shire in which he dwelt, but if ever he returned, he might be treated as a thief taken "hand-habbende" or one taken with stolen goods upon him, in other words, "with the mainour." 35 A thief so taken might lawfully be killed by the first man who met him, and the slayer was, according to the code of the "frith-gild," "to be twelve pence the better for the deed." 36 Under these circumstances, it is more reasonable to suppose, that the "frith-gild" was not so much a voluntary association as one imposed upon members of the community by some public authority. 37

Encouragement given to London merchants.

The commercial supremacy of London, not only over Winchester but over every other town in the kingdom, now becomes more distinct, for when Athelstan appointed moneyers or minters throughout the country, he assigned eight (the largest number of all) to London, whilst for Winchester he appointed only six, other towns being provided with but one or at most two. 38 The king, moreover, showed his predilection for London by erecting a mansion house for himself within the city's walls.

The encouragement which Athelstan gave to commercial enterprise by enacting, that any merchant who undertook successfully three voyages across the high seas at his own cost (if not in his own vessel) should rank as a thane, 39 must have affected the London burgess more than those of any other town.

Return of the Danes *temp.* Ethelred the Unready, 991-994.

Under Ethelred II, surnamed the "Unready" or "redeless" from his indifference to the "rede" or council of his advisers, the city would again have fallen into the hands of the Danes, but for the personal courage displayed by its inhabitants and the protection which, by Alfred's foresight, the walls were able to afford them. In 994, Olaf and Sweyn sailed up the Thames with a large fleet and threatened to burn London. Obstinate fighting took place, but the enemy, we are told, "sustained more harm and evil than they ever deemed that any townsman could do to them, for the Holy Mother of God, on that day, manifested her mercy to the townsmen and delivered them from their foes." 40

The first payment of Danegelt, 991.

Matters might not have been so bad had not the king already committed the fatal error of attempting to secure peace by buying off the enemy. In 991, he had, with the consent of his witan, raised the sum of £10,000 with which he had bribed the Danish host. This was the origin of the tax known as Danegelt, which in after years became one of the chief financial resources of the Crown and continued almost uninterruptedly down to the reign of Henry II. The effect of the bribe was naturally enough to induce the enemy to make further depredations whenever in want of money; and accordingly, a Danish fleet threatened London the very next year (992) and again in 994. On this last occasion, the same wretched expedient was resorted to, and the Danes were again bought off.

The massacre of Danes 13th Nov., 1002.

Nor was cowardice the only charge of which Ethelred was guilty. To this must be added treachery and murder. In the year 1002, when he married the daughter of the Duke of Normandy, hoping thereby to win the Duke's friendship and to close the harbours on the French coast against Sweyn, Ethelred issued secret orders for a massacre of all Danes found in England. In this massacre, which took place on the Festival of St. Brice (13th Nov.), perished Gunhild, sister of Sweyn. Under these circumstances, it can scarcely be wondered at, that thenceforth the Danish invasions became more frequent, more systematic, and more extensive than ever.

For four years they continued their depredations "cruelly marking every shire in Wessex with burning and with harrying." Then they were again bought off with a sum of £36,000, and two years' respite (1007-8) was gained. 41 It was a respite and no more. As soon as they had spent their money, they came again, and in 1009 made several assaults on London— "They often fought against the town of London, but to God be praise that it yet stands sound, and they have ever fared ill." 42 Every year they struck deeper into the heart of the country, and carried their plundering expeditions from Wessex into Mercia and East Anglia.

The murder of Abp. Alphage, 1012.

In 1011 Canterbury was taken and sacked, Alphage, the Archbishop, being made prisoner, and carried away by the Danish fleet to Greenwich. Finding it impossible to extort a ransom, they brutally murdered him (19th May, 1012), in one of their drunken moods, pelting him in their open court or "husting" with bones and skulls of oxen. 43 The worthy prelate's corpse was allowed to be removed to London where it was reverently interred in St. Paul's. A few years later, Cnut caused it to be transferred with due solemnity to the Archbishop's own metropolitan church of Canterbury.

Sweyn again attacks London, A.D. 1013.

In the following year, Sweyn was so successful in reducing the Northumbrians and the inhabitants of the five boroughs, 44 as well as the towns of Winchester and Oxford, taking hostages from each as he went, that he thought he might venture once more to attack London itself; hoping for better success than had attended him on previous occasions. He was the more anxious to capture London, because Ethelred himself was there, but he again met with such determined resistance, and so many of his followers were drowned in the Thames that for the fourth time he had to beat a retreat. 45

London submits.

Leaving London for a while, Sweyn proceeded to conquer that part of England which still held out against him, and having accomplished his purpose, was again preparing to attack the one city which had baffled all his attempts to capture, when the Londoners themselves, finding further opposition hopeless, offered their submission and left Ethelred to take care of himself. 46 This he did by betaking himself to Normandy, where he remained until Sweyn's death in the following year (3rd Feb., 1014).

Election of Cnut, 1014.

Upon this event taking place, the crews of the Danish fleet assumed the right of disposing of the English crown, and elected Sweyn's son, Cnut, to be king. The English, however, compelled as they had been by superior strength to submit to the father, were in no mood to accept without a struggle the sovereignty of his son. The whole of the Witan at once declared in favour of sending for Ethelred, with the assurance "that no lord was dearer than their natural lord," if only he would promise to govern them more justly than before. 47 Ethelred sent word by Edmund his son that "he would be to them a kind lord, and amend all the things which they eschewed, and all the things should be forgiven which had been done or said to him, on condition that they all, unanimously and without treachery, would turn to him." Pledges were given and taken on either side, and thenceforth a Danish king was to be looked upon as an outlaw. 48

Ethelred returns to London.

When Ethelred arrived in England, he was accompanied according to an Icelandic Saga, 49 by King Olaf, of Norway, who assisted him in expelling the Danes from Southwark, and gaining an entrance into the city. The manner in which this was carried out, is thus described. A small knot of Danes occupied a stronghold in the City, whilst others were in possession of Southwark. Between the two lay London Bridge—a wooden bridge, "so broad that two waggons could pass each other upon it"—fortified by barricades, towers, and parapets, and manned by Danes. Ethelred was naturally very anxious to get possession of the bridge, and a meeting of chiefs was summoned to consult how it could be done. Olaf promised to lay his fleet alongside the bridge if the English would do the same. This was agreed upon. Having covered in the decks of the vessels with a wooden roof to protect the crew and fighting men, Olaf succeeded in rowing light up to the bridge and laying cables round its piers. This done, he caused his ships to head down stream and the crews to row their hardest. The result was that the piles were loosened and the bridge, heavily weighted by the Danes who were fighting upon it, gave way. Many were thrown into the river, whilst others made good their retreat to Southwark, which was soon afterwards stormed and taken. This incident in connection with Ethelred's return formed the subject of more than one Scandinavian poem, of which the following may serve as a specimen:—

> "London Bridge is broken down—
> Gold is won and bright renown.
> Shields resounding,
> War-horns sounding,
> Hildur shouting in the din!
> Arrows singing,
> Mail-coats ringing—
> Odin makes our Olaf win!"

Drives Cnut out of England.

For a short while after his return Ethelred displayed a spirit of patriotism and courage beyond any he had hitherto shown. He succeeded in surprising and defeating the Danes in that district of Lincolnshire known as Lindsey, and drove Cnut to take refuge in his ships, and eventually to sail away to Denmark. 50

Return of Cnut, A.D. 1015.

It was not long before he again appeared; he was then, however, to meet in the field Ethelred's son, Edmund, whose valour had gained for him the name of Ironside. This spirited youth, forming a striking contrast to the weak and pusillanimous character of his father, had collected a force to withstand the enemy, but the men refused to fight unless Ethelred came with them, and unless they had "the support of the citizens of London." 51 A message was therefore sent to him at London to take the field with such a force as he could gather. Father and son thereupon joined forces; but the king was in ill-health, and it wanted but a whisper of treachery to send him back to the security of London's walls. Thither, too, marched Cnut, but before he arrived Ethelred had died (23rd April, 1016). 52 The late king was buried in St. Paul's. 53

The laws of Ethelred regulating foreign trade.

The city of London had by this time attained a position higher than it had ever reached before. "We cannot as yet call it the capital of the kingdom, but its geographical position made one of the chief bulwarks of the land, and in no part of the realm do we find the inhabitants outdoing the patriotism and courage of its valiant citizens." 54 Under Edgar the foreign trade with the city had increased to such an extent that Ethelred, his son, deemed it time to draw up a code of laws to regulate the customs to be paid by the merchants of France and Flanders as well as by the "emperor's men," the fore-runners of those "easterling" merchants, who, from their headquarters in the Steel-yard at Dowgate, subsequently became known as merchants of the Steel-yard. 55

Among the multitude of foreigners that in after-years thronged the streets of the city bartering pepper and spices from the far east, gloves and cloth, vinegar and wine, in exchange for the rural products of the country, might be seen the now much hated but afterwards much favoured Dane. 56 The Dane was again master of all England, except London, and Ethelred's kingdom, before the close of his reign, was confined within the narrow limits of the city's walls; "that true-hearted city was once more the bulwark of England, the centre of every patriotic hope, the special object of every hostile attack." 57

Election of Edmund Ironside by the Londoners, 1016.

At Ethelred's death the Witan who were in London united with the inhabitants of the city in choosing Edmund as his successor. This is the first recorded instance of the Londoners having taken a direct part in the election of a king. Cnut disputed Edmund's right to the crown, and proceeded to attack the city. He sailed up the Thames with his fleet, but being unable to pass the bridge, he dug a canal on the south side of the river, whereby he was enabled to carry his ships above bridge, and so invest the city along the whole length of the riverside. To complete the investment, and so prevent any of the inhabitants escaping either by land or water, he ditched the city round, so that none could pass in or out. 58

Cnut's attempts on London frustrated.

This, as well as two other attempts made by Cnut within a few weeks of each other to capture London by siege, were frustrated by the determined opposition of the citizens. 59 "Almighty God saved it," as the chronicler piously remarks. 60

Victory of the Danes at Assandun, 1016.

Nor was Cnut more successful in the field, being worsted in no less than five pitched battles against Edmund, until by the treachery of Edmund's brother-in-law, Eadric, alderman of Mercia, he succeeded at last in vanquishing the English army on the memorable field of Assandun. 61

Agreement between Edmund and Cnut for partition of the kingdom.

After this Edmund reluctantly consented to a conference and a division of the kingdom. The meeting took place at Olney, and there it was agreed that Edmund should retain his crown, and rule over all England south of the Thames, together with East Anglia, Essex and London, whilst Cnut should enjoy the rest of the kingdom. "The citizens, beneath whose walls the power of Cnut and his father had been so often shattered, now made peace with the Danish host. As usual, money was paid to them, and they were allowed to winter as friends within the unconquered city." 62

Cnut king of all England, 1016-1035.

The partition of the kingdom between Edmund and Cnut had scarcely been agreed upon before the former unexpectedly died (30th Nov., 1016) and Cnut became master of London and king of all England. His rule was mild, beneficent and just, recognising no distinction between Dane and Englishman, and throughout his long reign of nearly twenty years the citizens of London enjoyed that perfect peace so necessary for the successful exercise of their commercial pursuits.

Election of Cnut's Successors. 1183.

At the election of Cnut's successor which took place at Oxford in 1035, the Londoners again played an important part. This time, however, it was not the "burhwaru or burgesses" of the City who attended the gemót which had been summoned for the purpose of election, but "lithsmen" of London.

The lithsmen of London attend gemót at Oxford.

As to who these "lithsmen" were, and how they came to represent the City (if indeed they represented the City at all) on this important occasion much controversy has arisen. To some they appear as nothing more than the "nautic multitude" or "sea-faring men" of London. 63 On the other hand, there are those who hold that they were merchants who had achieved thane right under the provisions of Athelstan's day already mentioned; 64 whilst there are still others who are inclined to look upon them as so many commercial travellers who had made their way to Oxford by river in the ordinary course of business, and who happened by good fortune to have been in that city at the time of a great political crisis. 65 The truth probably lies somewhere between these extremes. The "lithsmen" may not themselves have been thanes, although they are recorded as having been at Oxford with almost all the thanes north of the Thames; 66 but that they were something more than mere watermen, such as we shall see joining with the apprentices of London at important political crises, and that they were acting more or less as representatives of the Londoners who had already acquired a predominant voice in such matters, seems beyond doubt.

Londoners desire for peace above all things.

During the next thirty years London took no prominent part in the affairs of the country, content if only allowed to have leisure to mind its own business. The desire for peace is the key-note to the action of the citizens of London at every important crisis. Without peace, commerce became paralyzed. Peace could be best secured by a strong government, and such a government, whether in the person of a king or protector could count upon their support. "For it they were ready to devote their money and their lives, for commerce, the child of opportunity, brought wealth; wealth power; and power led independence in its train." The quarrels of the half-brothers, Harold and Harthacnut, the attempt by one or both of the sons of Ethelred and Emma to recover their father's kingdom, and the question of the innocence or guilt of Earl Godwine in connection with the murder of one of them, affected the citizens of London only so far as such disturbances were likely to impede the traffic of the Thames or to make it dangerous for them to convey their merchandise along the highways of the country.

Revival of Danegelt, A.D., 1040.

The payment of Danegelt at the accession of Harthacnut (A.D. 1040), 67 probably touched the feelings, as it certainly did the pockets, of the Londoners, more than any other event which happened during this period.

London the recognised capital, *temp.* Edward, Confessor.

Upon the sudden death of Harthacnut (A.D. 1042), who died in a fit "as he stood at his drink," 68 the choice of the whole nation fell on Edward, his half-brother—"before the king buried were, all folk chose Edward to king at London." 69 The share that the Londoners took in this particular election is not so clear as in other cases. Nevertheless, the importance of the citizens was daily growing, and by the time of the accession of Edward the Confessor, the City was recognised as the capital of the kingdom, the chief seat for the administration of the law, and the place where the king usually resided. 70

Gemóts held in London.

In early Saxon times the witan had met in any town where the king happened at the time to be; and although theoretically every freeman had a right to attend its meetings, practically the citizens of the town wherein the gemót happened at the time to be held, enjoyed an advantage over freemen coming from a distance. Alfred ordained that the witan should meet in London for purposes of legislation twice a year. 71 Athelstan, Edmund and Edgar had held gemóts in London, the last mentioned king holding a great gemót (*mycel gemót*) in St. Paul's Church in 973.

London declares for Godwine, 1052.

During the reign of Edward the Confessor, at least six meetings of the witan took place in London; the more important of these being held in 1051 and the following year. By the gemót of 1051, which partook of the nature of a court-martial, Earl Godwine was condemned to banishment; but before a twelve-month had elapsed, he was welcomed back at a great assembly or *mycel gemót* held in the open air without the walls of London. 72 The nation had become disatisfied owing to the king's increasing favour to Norman strangers, but the earl desired to learn how stood the City of London towards him, and for this purpose made a stay at Southwark. He was soon satisfied on this point. "The townsfolk of the great city were not a whit behind their brethren of Kent and Sussex in their zeal for the national cause. The spirit which had beaten back Swend and Cnut, the spirit which was in after times to make London ever the stronghold of English freedom, the spirit which made its citizens foremost in the patriot armies alike of the thirteenth and of the seventeenth centuries, was now as warm in the hearts of those gallant burghers as in any earlier or later age. With a voice all but unanimous, the citizens declared in favour of the deliverer; a few votes only, the votes, it may be, of strangers or of courtiers, were given against the emphatic resolution, that what the earl would the city would." 73 Having secured the favour of London his cause was secure. That the citizens heartily welcomed the earl, going forth in a body to meet him on his arrival, we learn also from another source; 74 although, one at least of the ancient chroniclers strongly hints that the favour of the citizens had been obtained by bribes and promises. 75 The earl's return was marked by decrees of outlawry against the king's foreign favourites, whose malign influence he had endeavoured formerly to counteract, and who had proved themselves strong enough to procure the banishment of himself and family.

The dedication of Westminster Abbey, A.D. 1065.

The last gemót held under Edward was one specially summoned to meet at Westminster at the close of the year 1065, for the purpose of witnessing the dedication of the new abbey church which the king loved so well and to which his remains were so shortly afterwards to be carried.

Death of Edward the Confessor.

He died at the opening of the year, and the same witan who had attended his obsequies elected Harold, the late Earl Godwine's son, as his successor. This election, however, was doomed to be overthrown by the powerful sword of William the Norman.

CHAPTER II.

The landing of William, and Battle of Senlac, 1066.

As soon as the news of Harold's coronation reached William of Normandy, he claimed the crown which Edward the Confessor had promised him. According to every principle of succession recognised in England, at the time, he had no right to the crown whatever. When the Norman invader landed at Pevensey, Harold was at York, having recently succeeded in defeating his brother Tostig, the deposed Earl of Northumbria, who, with the assistance of Harold Hardrada, had attacked the northern earls, Edwine and Morkere. On hearing of the Duke's landing, Harold hastened to London. A general muster of forces was there ordered, and Edwine and Morkere, who were bound to Harold by family tie—the King having married their sister—were bidden to march southward with the whole force of their earldoms. But neither gratitude for their late deliverance at the hands of their brother-in-law, nor family affection, could hurry the steps of these earls, and they arrived too late. The battle of Senlac, better known as the battle of Hastings, had been won and lost (14th Oct., 1066), the Norman was conqueror, and Harold had perished. For a second time within twelve months the English throne was vacant. 76

The times were too critical to hold a formal gemót for the election of a successor to the throne; but the citizens of London and the sailors or "butsecarls" (whom it is difficult not to associate with the "lithsmen" of former days) showed a marked predilection in favour of Edgar the Atheling, grandson of Edmund Ironside, and the sole survivor of the old royal line. The Archbishop, too, as well as the northern earls, were in his favour, but the latter soon withdrew to their respective earldoms and left London and the Atheling to their fate. 77 Thus, "the patriotic zeal of the men of London was thwarted by the base secession of the northern traitors."

William's March to London.

After waiting awhile at Hastings for the country to make voluntary submission, and finding that homagers did not come in, William proceeded to make a further display of force. In this he betrayed no haste, but made his way through Kent in leisurely fashion, receiving on his way the submission of Winchester and Canterbury, using no more force than was absolutely necessary, and endeavouring to allay all fears, until at length he reached the suburbs of London. 78

He had been astute enough to give out that he came not to claim a crown, but only a right to be put in nomination for it. To the mind of the Londoner, such quibbling failed to commend itself, and the citizens lost no time in putting their city into a posture of defence, determined not to surrender it without a blow.

Sets fire to Southwark in hopes of terrifying the citizens.

Upon William's arrival in Southwark, the citizens sallied forth. They were, however, beaten back after a sharp skirmish, and compelled to seek shelter again within their city's walls. William hesitated to make a direct attack upon the city, but hoped by setting fire to Southwark to strike terror into the inhabitants and bring them to a voluntary surrender. He failed in his object; the city still held out, and William next resorted to diplomacy.

Negotiations between William and the City.

The ruling spirit within the city at that time was Ansgar or Esegar the "Staller" under whom, as Sheriff of Middlesex, the citizens had marched out to fight around the royal standard at Hastings. He had been carried wounded from the field, and was now borne hither and thither on a litter, encouraging the citizens to make a stout defence of their city. To him, it is said, William sent a private message from Berkhampstead, asking only that the Conqueror's right to the crown of England might be acknowledged and nothing more, the real power of the kingdom might remain with Ansgar if he so willed. Determined not to be outwitted by the Norman, Ansgar (so the story goes) summoned a meeting of the eldermen (*natu majores*) of the City—the forerunners of the later aldermen—and proposed a feigned submission which might stave off immediate danger. The proposal was accepted and a messenger despatched. William pretended to accept the terms offered, and at the same time so worked upon the messenger with fair promises and gifts that on his return he converted his fellow citizens and induced them by representations of the Conqueror's friendly intentions and of the hopelessness of resistance, to make their submission to him, and to throw over the young Atheling.

London submits to the Conqueror.

Whatever poetic tinge there may be about the story as told by Guy of Amiens, it is certain that the citizens came to the same resolution, in effect, as that described by the poet, nor could they well have done otherwise. The whole of the country for miles around London, had already tendered submission or been forced into it. The city had become completely isolated, and sooner or later its inhabitants must have been starved out. There was, moreover, a strong foreign element within its walls. 79 Norman followers of Edward the Confessor were ever at hand to counsel submission. London submitted, the citizens accepting the rule of the Norman Conqueror as they had formerly accepted that of Cnut the Dane, "from necessity." An embassy was despatched to Berkhampstead, comprising the Archbishop of York, the young Atheling, the earls Edwine and Morkere, and "all the best men of London," to render homage and give hostages, 80 and thus it was, that within three months of his landing, William was acknowledged as the lawfully elected King of England, and, as such, he crowned himself at Westminster, promising to govern the nation as well as any king before him if they would be faithful to him.

His charter to the citizens of London.

The conciliatory spirit of William towards the Londoners is seen in the favourable terms he was ready to concede them. Soon after his coronation— the precise date cannot be determined—he granted them a charter, 81 by which he clearly declared his purpose not to reduce the citizens to a state of dependent vassalage, but to establish them in all the rights and privileges they had hitherto enjoyed.

The charter, rendered into modern English, runs as follows:—

"William, King, greets William, Bishop, and Gosfregdh, Portreeve, and all the burgesses within London, French and English, friendly. And I give you to know that I will that ye be all those laws worthy that ye were in King Eadward's day. 82 And I will that every child be his father's heir after his father's day and I will not suffer that any man offer you any wrong. God keep you."

The terms of the charter are worthy of study. They are primarily remarkable as indicating that the City of London was, at the time, subject to a government which combined the secular authority of the port-reeve with the ecclesiastical authority of the bishop. It was said, indeed, to have been greatly due to the latter's intercession that the charter was granted at all, and, in this belief, the mayor and aldermen were long accustomed to pay a solemn visit to the bishop's tomb in St. Paul's church, there to hear a *De profundis* on the day when the new mayor took his oath of office before the Barons of the Exchequer. 83

The office of port-reeve.

As regards the port-reeve—the *port-gerefa, i.e.,* reeve of the port or town of London 84—the nature and extent of his duties and authority, much uncertainty exists. Whilst, in many respects, his position in a borough was analogous no doubt to the shire-reeve or sheriff of a county, there were, on the other hand, duties belonging to and exercised by the one which were not exercised by the other. Thus, for instance, the port-reeve, unlike the sheriff, exercised no judicial functions in a criminal court, nor presided over court-leets in the city as the sheriff did in his county by *turn*, the latter being held independently by the alderman of each ward. 85

The foreign element already existing in the City.

Its increase after the Conquest.

The charter makes no new grant.

In the next place the charter brings prominently to our notice the fact that there was already existing within the City's walls a strong Norman element, existing side by side with the older English burgesses, which the Conqueror did well not to ignore. The descendants of the foreign merchants from France and Normandy, for whose protection Ethelred had legislated more than half a century before, had continued to carry on their commercial intercourse with the Londoners, and were looking forward to a freer interchange of merchandise now that the two countries were under one sovereign. Their expectation was justified. No sooner had London submitted to the Norman Conqueror than, we are told, "many of the citizens of Rouen and Caen passed over thither, preferring to be dwellers in that city, inasmuch as it was fitter for their trading, and better stored with the merchandise in which they were wont to traffic." 86 But by far the most important clause in the charter is that which places the citizens of London in the same position respecting the law of the land as they enjoyed in the days of their late king, Edward the Confessor. Here there is distinct evidence that the Conqueror had come "neither to destroy, nor to found, but to continue." 87 The charter granted nothing new; it only ratified and set the royal seal 88 to the rights and privileges of the citizens already in existence.

William's other charter granting the sheriffwick of London.

It is recorded that William granted another charter to the citizens of London, vesting in them the City and Sheriffwick of London, and this charter the citizens proffered as evidence of their rights over the cloister and church of St. Martin le Grand, when those rights were challenged in the reign of Henry VI. 89 This charter has since been lost.

The strong government of William.

The compact thus made between London and the Conqueror was faithfully kept by both parties. Having ascended the English throne by the aid of the citizens of London, William, unlike many of his successors, was careful not to infringe the terms of their charter, whilst the citizens on the other hand continued loyal to their accepted king, and lent him assistance to put down insurgents in other parts of the kingdom. The fortress which William erected within their city's walls did not disturb their equanimity. It was sufficient for them that, under the Conqueror's rule, the country was once more peaceful, so peaceful that, according to the chronicler, a young maiden could travel the length of England without being injured or robbed. 90

"Doomsday" Book completed.

The close of the reign of William the First witnessed the completion of "Doomsday," or survey of the kingdom, which he had ordered to be made for fiscal purposes. For some reason not explained, neither London nor Winchester—the two capitals, so to speak, of the kingdom—were included in this survey. It may be that the importance of these boroughs, their wealth and population, necessitated some special method of procedure; but this does not account for the omission of Northumberland, Cumberland, Westmorland, and Durham, from the survey. We know that Winchester was afterwards surveyed, but no steps in the same direction were ever taken . with respect to London. The survey was not effected without disturbances, owing to the inquisitorial power vested in the commissioners appointed to carry it out.

Death of William the Conqueror, and accession of his son, 1087.

William died whilst on a visit to his duchy of Normandy, and "he who was before a powerful king, and lord of many a land, had then of all his land, only a portion of seven feet." 91 the same which, to this day, holds his mortal remains in the Abbey at Caen. He was succeeded by William his son. The death of the father and accession of his son was marked by fire, pestilence, and famine. 92

St. Paul's destroyed by fire, 1087.

A fire destroyed St. Paul's and the greater part of the City. Maurice, Bishop of London, at once set to work to rebuild the Cathedral on a larger and more magnificent scale, erecting the edifice upon arches in a manner little known in England at that time, but long practised in France. The Norman Conquest was already working for good. Not only the style of architecture, but the very stone used in re-building St. Paul's came from France, the famous quarries of Caen being utilised for the purpose. 93

There was already in the city, one church built after the same manner, and on that account called St. Mary of Arches or "le Bow." The object of setting churches and other buildings upon vaults was to guard against fire. Whatever defence against fire this method of building may have afforded, it was certainly no defence against wind. In 1091, the roof of St. Mary-le-Bow was clean blown off, huge baulks of timber, 26 feet long, being driven into the ground with such force that scarce 4 feet of them could be seen. 94

The Tower strengthened and the bridge repaired, 1097.

The reign of the new king was one of oppression. Nevertheless, he continued to secure that protection for life and property which his father had so successfully achieved, so that a man "who had confidence in himself" and was "aught," could travel the length and breadth of the land unhurt, "with his bosom full of gold." 95 He also had an eye for the protection of the city, and the advancement of its commerce, surrounding the Tower of London by a wall, and repairing the bridge which had been nearly washed away by a flood. 96

Election of Henry I by the Witan at Winchester, 1100.

On the 2nd August, 1100, the Red King met his death suddenly in the New Forest, and the next day was buried at Winchester. According to a previous agreement, the crown should have immediately devolved upon his brother Robert. Crowns, however, were not to be thus disposed of; they fell only to those ready and strong enough to seize them. Robert was far away on a crusade. His younger brother Henry was on the spot, and upon him fell the choice of such of the witan as happened to be in or near Winchester at the time of the late king's death. 97

Their choice confirmed by the City of London.

The two days that elapsed before his coronation at Westminster (5th August), the king-elect spent in London, where by his easy and eloquent manner, as well as by fair promises, he succeeded in winning the inhabitants over to his cause, to the rejection of the claims of Robert. The election, or perhaps we should rather say, the selection of Henry by the witan at Winchester, was thus approved and confirmed by the whole realm (*regni universitas*), in the city of London.

The choice was made however on one condition, viz.:—that Henry should restore to his subjects their ancient liberties and customs enjoyed in the days of Edward the Confessor. 98 The charter thus obtained served as an exemplar for the great charter of liberties which was to be subsequently wrung from King John.

Henry's charter to the City of London.

Another charter was granted by the new king—a charter to the citizens of London—granted, as some have thought, soon after his accession, and by way of recognition of the services they had rendered him towards obtaining the crown. This however appears to be a mistake. There is reason for supposing that this charter was not granted until at least thirty years after he was seated on the throne. 99

The main features of the charter.

The chief features of the grant 100 were that the citizens were thenceforth to be allowed to hold Middlesex to farm at a rent of £300 a year, and to appoint from among themselves whom they would to be sheriff over it; they were further to be allowed to appoint their own justiciar to hold pleas of the crown, and no other justiciar should exercise authority over them; they were not to be forced to plead without the city's walls; they were to be exempt from scot and lot and of all payments in respect of Danegelt and murder; they were to be allowed to purge themselves after the English fashion of making oath and not after the Norman fashion by wager of battle; their goods were to be free of all manner of customs, toll, passage and lestage; their husting court might sit once a week; and lastly, they might resort to "withernam" or reprisal in cases where their goods had been unlawfully seized.

The grant of Middlesex to ferm, and choice of sheriff.

Touching the true import of this grant of Middlesex to the citizens at a yearly rent, with the right of appointing their own sheriff over it, no less than the identity of the justiciar whom they were to be allowed to choose for themselves for the purpose of hearing pleas of the crown within the city, much divergence of opinion exists. Some believe that the government of the city was hereby separated from that of the shire wherein it was situate, and that the right of appointing their own justiciar which the citizens obtained by this charter was the right of electing a sheriff for the city of London in the place of the non-elective ancient port-reeve. Others deny that the charter introduced the shire organization into the government of the city, and believe the justiciar and sheriff to have been distinct officials. 101 The latter appear to hold the more plausible view. Putting aside the so-called charter of William the First, granting to the citizens in express terms *civitatem et vice-comitatum Londoniæ*, as wanting in corroboration, a solution of the difficulty may be found if we consider (1) that the city received a shire organization and became in itself to all intents and purposes a county as soon as it came to be governed by a port-reeve, if not as soon as an alderman had been set over it by Alfred; (2) that the duties of the shrievalty in respect of the county of the city of London were at this time performed either by a port-reeve or by one or more officers, known subsequently as sheriffs, and (3) that for the right of executing these duties no rent or ferm was ever demanded or paid. 102

If this be a correct view of the matter, it would appear that the effect of Henry's grant of Middlesex to the citizens to farm, and of the appointment of a sheriff over it of their own choice, was not so much to render the city independent of the shire, as to make the shire subject to the city. It must be borne in mind that no sheriff (or sheriffs) has ever been elected by the citizens for Middlesex alone, the duties appertaining to the sheriff-wick of Middlesex having always been performed by the sheriffs of the city for the time being. 103 Hence it is that the shrievalty of London and Middlesex is often spoken of as the shrievalty of "London" alone, and the shrievalty of "Middlesex" alone (the same officers executing the duties of both shrievalties) and the *firma* of £300 paid for the shrievalty of Middlesex alone is sometimes described as the *firma* of "London," sometimes of "Middlesex," and sometimes of "London and Middlesex." 104

The citizens' right to elect their own Justiciar.

The right of electing their own justiciar granted to the citizens by Henry resolves itself into little more than a confirmation of the right to elect their own sheriffs. 105 Just as sheriffs are known to have held pleas of the crown in the counties up to the time of the Great Charter (although their duties were modified by Henry I, and again by Henry II, when he appointed Justices in eyre) so in the city of London, no one, except the sheriffs of London could hold pleas of the crown, and an attempt made by the Barons in 1258 to introduce a justiciar into the Guildhall was persistently challenged by the citizens. 106

Even those who stedfastly maintain that in the country the sheriff and justiciar grew up to be two distinct officers, the one representing local interest and the other imperial, are willing to allow that in the city of London such distinction was evanescent. The office of justiciar in the city was twice granted *eo nomine* to Geoffrey de Mandeville, Earl of Essex, and it is twice mentioned as having been held by one named Gervase, who (there is reason to believe) is identical with Gervase de Cornhill, a Sheriff of London in 1155 and 1156; but the office became extinct at the accession of Henry II. 107

London and the election of Stephen, 1135

The events which followed Henry's decease afford us another instance of the futility of all attempts at this early period to settle the succession to the crown before the throne was actually vacant. The King's nephew, Stephen of Blois, and the nobility of England had sworn to accept the King's daughter Matilda, wife of Geoffery of Anjou, as their sovereign on the death of her father; yet when that event took place in 1135, Stephen, in spite of his oath, claimed the crown as nearest male heir of the Conqueror's blood. 108

There was no doubt of his popularity, whilst Matilda on the other hand injured her cause by marrying an Angevin. On the continent a bitter feud existed between Norman and Angevin; in England the Norman had steadily increased in favour, and England's crown was Stephen's if he had courage enough to seize it.

Landing on the Kentish coast, his first reception was far from encouraging. Canterbury and Dover, held by the Earl of Gloucester, refused to acknowledge him and closed their gates on his approach. Undismayed by these rebuffs, Stephen pushed on to London, where he was welcomed by every token of good will. The Londoners had been no party to the agreement to recognise Matilda as Henry's successor; they had become accustomed to exercising a right of sharing in the choice of a king who should reign over them, and they now chose Stephen. "It was their right, their special privilege," said they, "on the occasion of the king's decease, to provide another in his place." 109 There was no time to be lost, the country was in danger, Stephen was at hand, sent to them, as they believed, by the goodness of Providence. They could not do better than elect him: and elected he was by the assembled aldermen or eldermen (*majores natu*) of the City.

Such is the story of Stephen's election as given by the author of the "Gesta Stephani," one who wrote as an eye-witness of what took place, but whose statements cannot always be taken as those of an independent chronicler of events. Informal as this election may have been, it marks an important epoch in the annals of London. Thenceforth the city assumes a pre-eminent position and exercises a predominant influence in the public affairs of the kingdom. 110

Coronation of Stephen, December, 1135.

From London Stephen went down to Winchester, where he was heartily welcomed by his brother Henry, recently appointed papal legate. Next to London, it was important that Stephen should secure Winchester, and now that London had spoken, the citizens of Winchester no longer hesitated to throw in their lot with the king. Winchester secured, and Stephen put in possession of the royal castle and treasury, he returned to London, where all doubts as to the validity or invalidity of his election were set at rest by the ceremony of coronation (Dec. 1135).

A great Council held in London, April, 1136.

In the spring of the following year (April 1136), a brilliant council of the clergy and magnates of the realm was held in London, 111 reminding one of the Easter courts of the days of the Conqueror which latterly had been shorn of much of their splendour. The occasion was one for introducing the new king to his subjects as well as for confirming the liberties of the church, and Stephen may have taken special care to surround it with exceptional splendour as a set off against the meagreness which had characterised the recent ceremony of his coronation. 112

Arrival of the Empress Matilda in England. 1139.

In the meanwhile the injured Matilda appealed to Rome, but only with the result that her rival received formal recognition from the Pope. Three years later (1139) she landed in England accompanied by her brother, the Earl of Gloucester. She soon obtained a following, more especially in the west; and Winchester—the seat of the royal residence of the queens of England since the time when Ethelred presented the city as a "morning gift" to his consort at their marriage—became her headquarters and rallying point for her supporters, whilst London served in the same way for Stephen.

Attempted negotiations between Stephen and Matilda, May, 1140.

After nine months of sieges and counter sieges, marches and counter marches, in which neither party could claim any decided success, Stephen, as was his wont, withdrew to London and shut himself up in the Tower, with only a single bishop, and he a foreigner, in his train. Whilst safe behind the walls of that stronghold, negotiations were opened between him and the empress for a peaceful settlement of their respective claims (May, 1140), Henry of Winchester acting as intermediary between the rival parties. 113 The negotiations ended without effecting the desired result.

Matilda formally acknowledged "Lady of England," 1141.

Matters assumed an entirely different aspect when Stephen was made prisoner at Lincoln in the following year (2nd Feb., 1141). Henry of Winchester forsook his rôle of arbitrator, and entered into a formal compact with the empress who arrived before Winchester with the laurels of her recent success yet fresh, agreeing to receive her as "Lady of England," (*Domina Angliæ*) and promising her the allegiance of himself and his followers so long as she would keep her oath and allow him a free hand in ecclesiastical matters. 114

A synod at Winchester, 7th April, 1141.

This compact was entered into on the 2nd March, and on the following day the empress was received with solemn pomp into Winchester Cathedral. It remained for the compact to be ratified. For this purpose an ecclesiastical synod was summoned to sit at Winchester on the 7th April. The day was spent by the legate holding informal communications with the bishops, abbots, and archdeacons who were in attendance, and who then for the first time in England's history claimed the right not only of consecration, but of election of the sovereign. 115

On the 8th April, Henry in a long speech announced to the assembled clergy the result of the conclave of the previous day. He extolled the good government of the late king who before his death had caused fealty to be sworn to his daughter, the empress. The delay of the empress in coming to England (he said) had been the cause of Stephen's election. The latter had forfeited all claim to the crown by his bad government, and God's judgment had been pronounced against him. Lest therefore, the nation should suffer for want of a sovereign, he, as legate, had summoned them together, and by them the empress had been elected Lady of England. The speech was received with unanimous applause, those to whom the election did not commend itself being wise enough to hold their tongue.

The Londoners summoned to attend the synod.

But there was another element to be considered before Matilda's new title could be assured. What would the Londoners who had taken the initiative in setting Stephen on the throne, and still owed to them their allegiance, say to it? The legate had foreseen the difficulty that might arise if the citizens, whom he described as very princes of the realm, by reason of the greatness of their city (*qui sunt quasi optimates pro magnitudine civitatis in Anglia*), could not be won over. He had, therefore, sent a special safe conduct for their attendance, so he informed the meeting after the applause which followed his speech had died away, and he expected them to arrive on the following day. If they pleased they would adjourn till then.

They arrive and request the king's release, 9th April, 1141.

The next day (9th April) the Londoners arrived, as the legate had foretold, and were ushered before the council. They had been sent, they said, by the so called "commune" of London; and their purpose was not to enter into debate, but only to beg for the release of their lord, the king. 116 The statement was supported by all the barons then present who had entered the commune of the city 117 and met with the approval of the archbishop and all the clergy in attendance. Their solicitations, however, proved of no avail. The legate replied with the same arguments he had used the day before, adding that it ill became the Londoners who were regarded as nobles (*quasi proceres*) in the land to foster those who had basely deserted their king on the field of battle, and who only curried favour with the citizens in order to fleece them of their money.

Their request backed up by a letter from the Queen.

Here an interruption took place. A messenger presented to the legate a paper from Stephen's queen to read to the council. Henry took the paper, and after scanning its contents, refused to communicate them to the meeting. The messenger, however, not to be thus foiled, himself made known the contents of the paper. These were, in effect, an exhortation by the queen to the clergy, and more especially to the legate himself, to restore Stephen to liberty. The legate, however, returned the same answer as before, and the meeting broke up, the Londoners promising to communicate the decision of the council to their brethren at home, and to do their best to obtain their support.

The Londoners after much hesitation receive the Empress into their city, June, 1141.

The next two months were occupied by the empress and her supporters in preparing the way for her admission into the city, the inhabitants of which, had as yet shown but little disposition towards her. But however great their inclination may have been to Stephen, they at length found themselves forced to transfer their allegiance and to offer, for a time at least, a politic submission to the empress. Accordingly, a deputation went out to meet her at St. Albans (May 1141), and arrange terms on which the city should surrender. 118

More delay took place; and it was not until shortly before midsummer (1141), that she entered the city. Her stay was brief. She treated the inhabitants as vanquished foes, 119 extorted large sums of money, 120 and haughtily refused to observe the laws of Edward the Confessor they valued so much, preferring those of the late king, her father. 121

The Empress forced to leave the city.

The consequence was that, within a few days of her arrival in London, the inhabitants rose in revolt, drove her out of the city 122 and attacked the Tower, of which Geoffrey de Mandeville was constable, as his father William had been before him. 123

Geoffrey de Mandeville, Earl of Essex, and Constable of the Tower, won over by the Empress.

This Geoffrey de Mandeville had been recently created Earl of Essex by Stephen, in the hope and expectation that the fortress over which Geoffrey was governor, would be held secure for the royal cause. The newly fledged earl, however, was one who ever fought for his own hand, and was ready to sell his fortress and sword to the highest bidder. The few days that the empress was in the city, afforded her an opportunity of risking a trial to win over the earl from his allegiance. To this end she offered to confirm him in his earldom and to continue him in his office of Constable of the Tower, conferred upon him by Stephen; in addition to which, she was ready to allow him to enjoy lands of the rent of £100 a year, a license to fortify his castles, and the posts of sheriff and justiciar throughout his earldom. The bait was too tempting for the earl not to accept; and a charter to the above effect was drawn up and executed. 124

Forsakes the Empress for the Queen.

Scarcely had the fickle earl consented to throw in his lot with the empress before she had to flee the city. The departure of the empress was quickly followed by the arrival of her namesake, Matilda, the valiant queen of the captured Stephen; and again the earl proved false to his allegiance and actively supported the queen in concert with the citizens. 125

Capture of Winchester, and release of Stephen, Sept., 1141.

With his aid 126 and the aid of the Londoners, 127 the queen was enabled to reduce Winchester and to effect the liberation of her husband by exchanging the Earl of Gloucester, brother of the empress, for the captured king.

His second charter to Mandeville.

After being solemnly crowned, for the second time, 128 at Canterbury, Stephen issued a second charter (about Christmas time, 1141), 129 to Geoffrey de Mandeville, confirming and augmenting the previous grant by the empress. Instead of sheriff and justiciar of his own county of Essex merely, he is now made sheriff and justiciar of London and Middlesex, as well as of Hertfordshire.

London holds the balance between the rival powers.

But even these great concessions failed to secure the earl's fidelity to the king. Again he broke away from his allegiance and planned a revolt in favour of the empress who recompensed him with still greater dignities and possessions than any yet bestowed. This second charter of the empress, 130 is remarkable for a clause in which she promises never to make terms with the Londoners without the earl's consent, "because they are his mortal foes." 131 But the plans of the earl were doomed to be frustrated. The empress, tired of the struggle, soon ceased to be dangerous, and eventually withdrew to the continent, and Stephen was left free to deal with the rebel earl alone. With the assistance of the Londoners, who throughout the long period of civil dissension, were generally to be found on the winning side, and held as it were the balance between the rival powers, Stephen managed after considerable bloodshed to capture the fortifications erected by the Earl at Farringdon. 132

Arrest of the earl, his freebooting life and death, September, 1143.

The earl was subsequently treacherously arrested and made to give up his castles. Thenceforth his life was that of a marauding freebooter, until, fatally wounded at the siege of Burwell, he expired in September, 1143.

Arrival of Henry of Anjou in England, 1153

Notwithstanding the absence of the empress and the death of the faithless earl, a desultory kind of war continued to be carried on for the next ten years on behalf of Henry of Anjou, son of the empress. In 1153 that prince arrived in England to fight his own battles and maintain his right to the crown, which the king had already attempted to transfer to the head of his own son Eustace. This attempt had been foiled by the refusal of the bishops, at the instigation of the pope, to perform the ceremony. The sudden death of Eustace made the king more ready to enter into negotiations for effecting a peaceful settlement.

Peace concluded between Stephen and Henry at Winchester, November, 1153.

Henry conducted to London.

A compromise was accordingly effected at Winchester, 133 whereby Stephen was to remain in undisputed possession of the throne for life, and after his death was to be succeeded by Henry. The news that at last an end had come to the troubles which for nineteen years had disturbed the country, was received with universal joy, and Henry, conducted to London by the king himself, was welcomed in a manner befitting one who was now the recognised heir to the crown. 134

CHAPTER III.

Fitz-Stephen's description of London.

Both London and Winchester had been laid in ashes during Stephen's reign, the former by a conflagration—which took place in 1136, again destroying St. Paul's and extending from London Bridge to the church of St. Clement Danes—the latter by the burning missiles used in the conflict between Stephen and the empress in 1141. Winchester never recovered her position, and London was left without a rival. Fitz-Stephen, who wrote an account of the city as it stood in the reign of Henry II, describes it as holding its head higher than all others; its fame was wider known; its wealth and merchandise extended further than any other; it was the capital of the kingdom (*regni Anglorum sedes*). 135

Thomas of London.

It was through the mediation of an intimate friend and fellow citizen of Fitz-Stephen that Archbishop Theobald had invited Henry of Anjou over from France in 1153. Thomas of London, better known as Thomas Becket, although of foreign descent, was born in the heart of the city, having first seen the light in the house of Gilbert, his father, some time Portreeve of London, situate in Cheapside on a site now occupied by the hall and chapel of the Mercers' Chapel. Having been ordained a deacon of the Church, he became in course of time clerk or chaplain to the archbishop. Vigorous and active as he was, Thomas soon made his influence felt, and it was owing to his suggestion (so it is said 136) that the bishops had declined to be a party to the coronation of Eustace during Stephen's lifetime.

On the accession of Henry, Thomas passed from the service of the archbishop, then advanced in years, to the service of the young king. He was raised to the dignity of chancellor, and became one of the king's most trusted advisers. By their united efforts order was once again restored throughout the kingdom. The great barons, who had established themselves in castles erected without royal licence, were brought into subjection to the crown and compelled to pull down their walls. Upon the death of the archbishop, Thomas was appointed to the vacant See (1162). From that day forward the friendship between king and archbishop began to wane. Henry found that all his attempts to establish order in his kingdom were thwarted by exemptions claimed by the archbishop on behalf of the clergy. He found that allegiance to the Crown was divided with allegiance to the Pope, and this state of things was likely to continue so long as the archbishop lived. Becket's end is familiar to us all. His memory was long cherished by the citizens of London, who made many a pilgrimage to the scene of his martyrdom and left many an offering on his tomb in the cathedral of Canterbury. It is hard to say for which of the two, the father or the son, the citizens entertained the greater reverence. For many years after his death it was the custom for the Mayor of the City for the time being, upon entering into office, to meet the aldermen at the church of St. Thomas of Acon—a church which had been erected and endowed in honour of the murdered archbishop by his sister Agnes, wife of Thomas Fitz-Theobald of Helles 137—and thence to proceed to the tomb of Gilbert Becket, the father, in St. Paul's churchyard, there to say a *De profundis*; after which both mayor and aldermen returned to the church of St. Thomas, and, each having made an offering of two pence, returned to his own home. 138 St. Thomas's Hospital, in Southwark, was originally dedicated to the murdered archbishop, but after its dissolution and subsequent restoration as one of the Royal Hospitals, its patron saint was no longer Thomas the Martyr, but Thomas the Apostle.

Charter of Henry II to the City of London.

Whilst the king and his chancellor were busy settling the kingdom, establishing a uniform administration of justice and system of revenue, and not only renewing but extending the form of government which had been instituted by Henry I, the citizens of London, availing themselves of the security afforded by a strong government, redoubled their energy in following commercial pursuits and succeeded in raising the city, as Fitz-Stephen has told us, to a pitch of prosperity far exceeding that of any other city in the world.

They obtained a charter from Henry, 139 although of a more limited character than that granted to them by his grandfather. The later charter, for instance, although in the main lines following the older charter, makes no mention of Middlesex being let to ferm nor of any appointment of sheriff or justiciar being vested in the citizens. It appears as if Henry was determined to bring the citizens no less than the barons of the realm within more direct and immediate subservience to the crown. The concession made by the king's grandfather had been ignored by Stephen and the empress Matilda, each of whom in turn had granted the shrievalty of London and Middlesex to the Earl of Essex. For a time the appointment of sheriffs was lost to the citizens. Throughout the reigns of Henry II and his successor they were appointed by the crown. Richard's charter to the citizens makes no mention of the sheriffwick, nor is it mentioned in the first charter granted by John.

When it was restored to the citizens (A.D. 1199), by John's second charter, the office of sheriff of London had lost much of its importance owing to the introduction of the communal system of municipal government under a mayor.

The Inquest of sheriffs, 1170.

In the meantime the sheriffs of the counties, who had by reason of Henry's administrative reforms, risen to be officers of greater importance and wider jurisdiction, and who had taken advantage of their positions to oppress the people during the king's prolonged absence abroad, were also made to feel the power of the crown. A blow struck at the sheriffs was calculated to weaken the nobility and the larger landowners—the class from which it had been the custom hitherto to select these officers. Henry saw the advantage to be gained, and on his return to England in 1170 deposed most of the sheriffs and ordered a strict enquiry to be made, as to the extortions they had committed in his absence. Their places were filled for the most part by men of lower rank, and therefore likely to be more submissive. Some, however, were reinstated and became more cruel and extortionate than ever. 140

The revolt of the barons, 1174.

The last fifteen years of Henry's life were full of domestic trouble. He had always found it an easier matter to rule his kingdom than his household. His sons were for ever thwarting his will and quarrelling with each other. It was his desire to secure the succession to the crown for his eldest son Henry, and to this end he had caused him to be crowned by the Archbishop of York (14th June, 1170), who was thereupon declared excommunicated by his brother of Canterbury. The son began to clamour for his inheritance whilst his father still lived, and appealed in 1173 to the French king, whose daughter he had married, to assist him in his unholy enterprise. Whilst Henry was engaged in defending his crown against his own son on the continent, the great barons of England rose in insurrection, and the king was obliged to hasten home, where he arrived in July, 1174. The rebellion was quickly put down, and the strife between king and nobles for a time ceased.

Disturbances in the city, 1174-1177.

In the city there were occasional disturbances caused by the younger nobility—the young bloods of the city 141—who infested the streets at night, broke into the houses of the rich and committed every kind of excess. In 1177 the brother of the Earl of Ferrers was waylaid and killed, and for some time the streets were unsafe at night. The chronicler records a singular outrage perpetrated three years before, by these sprigs of nobility. They forcibly entered the house of a wealthy citizen whose name has not come down to us, he is simply styled the *pater-familias*. Of his courage we are left in no doubt, for we are told that he slipt on a coat of mail, armed his household, and awaited the attack. He had not long to wait. The leader of the band—one Andrew Bucquinte soon made his appearance, and was met by a pan of hot coals. Swords were drawn on both sides and *pater-familias*, whose coat of mail served him well, succeeded in cutting off the right hand of his assailant. Upon the cry of thieves being raised, the delinquents took to their heels, leaving their leader a prisoner. The next day, being brought before the king's justiciar, he informed against his companions. This cowardly action on the part of Bucquinte led to many of them being taken, and among them one who is described by the chronicler as the noblest and wealthiest of London citizens, but to whom the chronicler gives no other name than "John, the old man" (*Johannes Senex*). An offer was made to John to prove his innocence by what was known as the ordeal by water, 142 but the offer was declined, and he was eventually hanged. The whole story looks suspicious.

The last days of Henry II. 1177-1189.

Having settled the succession of the crown of England upon his eldest son, the king put his second son, Richard, into possession of the Duchy of Aquitaine, and provided for his third son, Geoffrey, by marriage with the heiress of Brittany. There was yet another son, John, who was too young to be provided for just now, and who being without any territory, assigned to him, acquired the name of Lackland. Both Richard and Geoffrey had taken the part of their brother Henry in 1173, and in 1177 the three brothers were again quarrelling with their father and with each other. After the deaths of Henry and Geoffrey, the quarrel was taken up by the surviving brothers, Richard and John.

In all these—more or less—petty wars with his sons, the king had always to deal with the ruler of France. At last, in 1189, the loss of Le Mans—his own birth-place—and the unexpected discovery that his youngest and best beloved son, John, had turned traitor towards him, left the king nothing to live for, and after a few days suffering he died, ill and worn out, at Chinon.

Accession of Richard I, and administration of Longchamp, 1189-1190.

Richard had scarcely succeeded to the throne, before he set out on a crusade, leaving the government of his country in the hands of William Longchamp, Bishop of Ely, as chancellor. 143 With him was associated in the government, Hugh de Puiset, or Pudsey, Bishop of Durham, but Longchamp soon got the supreme control of affairs into his own hands, and commenced to act in the most tyrannical fashion. He increased the security of the Tower of London, which had been committed to his charge, by surrounding it with a moat, 144 and having got himself nominated papal legate, made a progress through the country committing the greatest extortion. 145

Longchamp opposed by Prince John, 1191.

Arrival of Longchamp in London; the citizens divided, 7th October, 1191.

Report of the Chancellor's conduct having reached the ears of Richard, he despatched the Archbishop of Rouen to England with a new commission, but the worthy prelate on arrival (April, 1191), was afraid to present the commission, preferring to let matters take their course. 146 Already a fierce rivalry had sprung up between the chancellor and John, the king's brother, who, for purposes of his own, had espoused the cause of the oppressed. Popular feeling at length became so strong, that Longchamp feared to meet John and the bishops, and, instead of going to Reading, where his attendance was required, he hastened to London. Arriving there (7 Oct.), he called the citizens together in the Guildhall, and prayed them to uphold the King against John, whom he denounced as aiming plainly at the Crown. The leading men in the city at the time were Richard Fitz-Reiner and Henry de Cornhill. These took opposite sides, the former favouring John, whilst the latter took the side of the chancellor. 147 John's party proving the stronger of the two, Longchamp thought it safest to seek refuge in the Tower. 148

John admitted into the city.

As soon as John found that the chancellor had gone to London instead of Reading, he too hastened thither. On his arrival he was welcomed and hospitably entertained by Richard Fitz-Reiner who gave him to understand on what terms he might expect the support of the city. 149 As to terms, John was ready to accede to any that might be proposed.

A meeting of barons and citizens in St. Paul's, 8 Oct., 1191.

Longchamp deposed and John recognised as head of the kingdom.

The next day (8 Oct.), a meeting of the barons of the realm, as well as of the citizens of London, was convened in St. Paul's Church, to consider the conduct of the chancellor, and it was thereupon decided that Longchamp should be deposed from office. The story, as told by different chroniclers, 150 varies in some particulars, but the main features are the same in all. The king's minister was set aside, John was recognised as the head of the kingdom, and new appointments made to judicial, fiscal, and military offices. The Archbishop of Rouen, who attended the council, seeing the turn affairs had taken, no longer hesitated to produce the letters under the king's sign manual appointing a new commission for the government of the kingdom.

John grants or confirms to the citizens their commune.

The same day that witnessed the fall of Longchamp was also a memorable one in the annals of the City of London; for immediately after judgment had been passed on the chancellor, John and the assembled barons granted to the citizens "their commune," swearing to preserve untouched the dignities of the city during the king's pleasure. The citizens on their part swore fealty to King Richard, and declared their readiness to accept John as successor to the throne in the event of his brother dying childless. 151

Change of name from port-reeve to mayor.

This is the first public recognition of the citizens of London as a body corporate; but so far from granting to them something new, the very words *their* commune (*communam suam*) imply a commune of which they were *de facto*, if not *de jure* already in enjoyment. How long the commune may have been in existence, unauthorised by the crown, cannot be determined; but that the term *communio* in connection with the city's organization was known half a century before, we have already seen; 152 and, according to the opinion of Giraldus Cambrensis, there is no valid distinction between the words *communio, communa* and *communia*. 153 Bishop Stubbs, however, hesitates to translate *communio* as "commune," the latter being essentially a French term for a particular form of municipal government. He prefers to render it "commonalty," "fraternity," or "franchise," although he goes so far as to allow that the term "suggests that the communal idea was already in existence as a basis of civic organization" in Stephen's reign, an idea which became fully developed in the succeeding reign. 154 He is also in favour of dating the foundation of the *communa* in London from this grant by John and the barons, 155 and in this view he is supported by Richard of Devizes, who distinctly states that the *communia* of London was instituted on that occasion, and that it was of such a character that neither King Richard nor Henry his father would have conceded it for a million marks of silver, and that a *communia* was in fact everything that was bad. It puffed up the people, it threatened the kingdom, and it emasculated the priesthood. 156

Change of name from port-reeve to mayor.

With the change from a shire organization to that of a French *commune*, whenever that happened to take place, there took place also a change in the chief governor of the city. The head of the city was no longer a Saxon "port-reeve" but a French "mayor," the former officer continuing in all probability to perform the duties of a port-reeve or sheriff of a town in a modified form. From the time when this "civic revolution" 157 occurred, down to the present day, the sheriff's position has always been one of secondary importance, being himself subordinate to the mayor.

When did the change take place?

The earliest mention of a mayor of London in a formal document is said to occur in a writ of the reign of Henry II. 158 The popular opinion, however, is that a change in the name of the chief magistrate of the City of London took place at the accession of Richard I. What gave rise to this belief is hard to say, but it is not improbable that it arose from a statement to be found in an early manuscript record still preserved among the archives of the Corporation, and known as the *Liber de Antiquis Legibus*. 159 The original portion of this manuscript purports to be a chronicle of mayors and sheriffs from 1188 down to 1273, noticing briefly the chief events in each year, and referring to a few particulars relative to the year 1274.

After naming the sheriffs who were appointed at Michaelmas, A.D. 1188, "the first year of the reign of King Richard," 160 it goes on to say that "in the same year Henry Fitz-Eylwin of Londenestane was made mayor of London, who was the first mayor of the city, and continued to be such mayor to the end of his life, that is to say, for nearly five and twenty years." That Henry Fitz-Eylwin was mayor in the first year of Richard's reign is stated no less than three times in the chronicle. 161

Arnald Fitz-Thedmar, the compiler of the *Liber de Antiquis*.

The compiler of the chronicle is supposed to have been Arnald or Arnulf Fitz-Thedmar, 162 an Alderman of London, although it is not known over which ward he presided. Particulars of his life are given in the volume itself, from which we gather that he was a grandson on the mother's side of Arnald de Grevingge 163 a citizen of Cologne; that his father's name was Thedmar, a native of Bremen; that he was born on the vigil of St. Lawrence [10 August] A.D. 1201, his mother being forewarned of the circumstances that would attend his birth in a manner familiar to biblical readers; that he was deprived of his aldermanry by the king, but was afterwards restored; that he became supporter of the king against Simon de Montfort and the barons, and that he was among those whom Thomas Fitz-Thomas, the leader of the democratic party and his followers, had "intended to slay" on the very day that news reached London of the battle of Evesham, which crushed the hopes of Montfort and his supporters. The date of his death cannot be precisely determined, but there can be but little doubt that it took place early in the third year of the reign of Edward the First, inasmuch as his will was proved and enrolled in the Court of Husting, London, held on Monday, the morrow of the Feast of St. Scolastica [10 Feb.] of that year (A.D. 1274-5). 164

Setting aside the statement—namely that mention is made of a mayor of London, in a document of the reign of Henry II—as wanting corroboration, the first instance known at the present day of any such official being named in a formal document occurs in 1193 when the Mayor of London appears among those who were appointed treasurers of Richard's ransom. 165

The title of Mayor, first mentioned in a Royal Charter of 1202.

Richard's first charter to the City (23 April, 1194) 166 granted a few weeks after his return from abroad makes no mention of a mayor, nor does the title occur in any royal charter affecting the City until the year 1202, when John attempted to suppress the guild of weavers "at the request of our mayor and citizens of London." A few years later when John was ready to do anything and everything to avoid signing the Great Charter which the barons were forcing on him, he made a bid for the favour of the citizens by granting them the right to elect annually a mayor, and thus their autonomy was rendered complete.

Richard's return from captivity, March, 1194.

When Richard recovered his liberty and returned to England he was heartily welcomed by all except his brother John. One of his first acts was to visit the City and return thanks for his safety at St. Paul's. 167 The City was on this occasion made to look its brightest, and the display of wealth astonished the foreigners in the King's suite, who had been led to believe that England had been brought to the lowest stage of poverty by payment of the King's ransom. 168

Is crowned for the second time.

The custom of the Mayor assisting the Chief Butler at coronation banquets.

In order to wipe out the stain of his imprisonment, he thought fit to go through the ceremony of coronation for the second time. His first coronation had taken place at Westminster (3 Sept., 1189,) soon after his accession, and the citizens of London had duly performed a service at the coronation banquet—a service which even in those days was recognised as an "ancient service"—namely, that of assisting the chief butler, for which the mayor was customarily presented with a gold cup and ewer. The citizens of the rival city of Winchester performed on this occasion the lesser service of attending to the viands. 169

The second coronation taking place at Winchester and not at Westminster, the burgesses of the former city put in a claim to the more honourable service over the heads of the citizens of London, and the latter only succeeded in establishing their superior claim by a judicious bribe of 200 marks. 170

Heavy taxation.

Richard was ever in want of money, and cared little by what means it was raised. He declared himself ready to sell London itself if a purchaser could be found. 171 The tax of Danegelt, from which the citizens of London had been specially exempted by charter of Henry I, and which had ceased to be exacted under Henry II, mainly through the interposition of Thomas of London, was practically revived under a new name. The charter already mentioned as having been granted to the citizens by Richard after his return from captivity was probably purchased, for one of the king's regular methods of raising money was a lavish distribution of charters to boroughs, not from any love he had for municipal government, but in order to put money in his purse. As soon as Richard had collected all the money he could raise in England, he again left the country, never to return.

The rising in the city under Longbeard. 1196.

The pressure of taxation weighed heavily on the poor, and occasioned a rising in the city under the leadership of William Fitz-Osbert. The cry was that the rich were spared whilst the poor were called upon to pay everything. 172 Accounts of the commotion differ according as the writer favoured the autocratic or democratic side. One chronicler, for instance, finds fault with Fitz-Osbert's personal appearance, imputing his inordinate length of beard—he was known as "Longbeard"—to his desire for conspicuousness, and declares him to have been actuated by base motives. 173

Others describe him as a wealthy citizen of the best family, and yet as one who ever upheld the cause of the poor against the king's extortions. 174 Whatever may have been the true character of the man and the real motive of his action, it is certain that he had a large following. When Hubert Walter, the justiciar, sent to arrest him, "Longbeard" took refuge in the church of St. Mary-le-Bow. Thither he was followed by the king's officers—described by a not impartial chronicler as men devoid of truth and piety and enemies of the poor. 175—who with the aid of fire and faggot soon compelled him to surrender. On his way to the Tower, he was struck at and wounded by one whose father (it was said) he had formerly killed; 176 but this again may or may not be the whole truth. A few days later he and a number of his associates were hanged. 177

Richard's so-called second charter ordering the removal of wears in the Thames, 14 July, 1197.

Two years before his death at Chaluz, Richard, with the view of aiding commerce, caused the wears in the Thames to be removed, and forbade his wardens of the Tower to demand any more the toll that had been accustomed. The writ to this effect was dated from the Island of Andely or

Les Andelys on the Seine, the 14th July, 1197, in the neighbourhood of that fortress which Richard had erected, and of which he was so proud—the Château Gaillard or "Saucy Castle," as he jestingly called it. The reputation which the castle enjoyed for impregnability under Richard, was lost under his successor on the throne.

First mention of a deliberative municipal body in the city, 1200.

Soon after John's accession we find what appears to be the first mention of a court of aldermen as a deliberative body. In the year 1200, writes Thedmar (himself an alderman), "were chosen five and twenty of the more discreet men of the city, and sworn to take counsel on behalf of the city, together with the mayor." 178 Just as in the constitution of the realm, the House of Lords can claim a greater antiquity than the House of Commons, so in the city—described by Lord Coke as *epitome totius regni*—the establishment of a court of aldermen preceded that of the common council.

The council held at St. Paul's, 25th Aug., 1213.

When, after thirteen years of misgovernment, during which John had enraged the barons and excited general discontent by endless impositions, matters were brought to a climax by his submission to the pope, it was in the city of London that the first steps were taken by his subjects to recover their lost liberty. On the 25th August, 1213, a meeting of the clergy and barons was held in the church of St. Paul; a memorable meeting, and one that has been described as "a true parliament of the realm, though no king presided in it." 179 Stephen Langton, whose appointment as Archbishop of Canterbury had so raised John's ire, took the lead and produced to the assembly a copy of the Charter of Liberties, granted by Henry I, when that king undertook to put an end to the tyranny of William Rufus. If the barons so pleased, it might (he said) serve as a precedent. The charter having been then and there deliberately read, the barons unanimously declared that for such liberties they were ready to fight, and, if necessary, to die. 180

The clergy and people who had hitherto supported the king against the barons, having now engaged themselves to assist the barons against the tyranny of the king, John found himself with but one friend in the world, and that was the Pope. "Innocent's view of the situation was very simple," writes Dr. Gardiner, "John was to obey the Pope, and all John's subjects were to obey John." Within a few weeks of the council being held at St. Paul's, the same sacred edifice witnessed the formality of affixing a golden *bulla* to the deed—the detestable deed (*carta detestabilis*)—whereby John had in May last resigned the crown of England to the papal legate, and received it again as the Pope's feudatory. 181

Meeting of the barons at Bury St. Edmunds, 1214.

In the following year (1214), whilst the king was abroad, the barons met again at Bury St. Edmunds, and solemnly swore that if John any longer delayed restoring the laws and liberties of Henry the First, they would make war upon him. It was arranged that after Christmas they should go in a body and demand their rights, and that in the meantime they should provide themselves with horses and arms, with the view of bringing force to bear, in case of refusal. 182 The citizens at the same time took the opportunity of strengthening their defences by digging a foss on the further side of the city wall. 183

Open hostility between John and the barons, 1215.

Christmas came and a meeting between John and the barons took place in London at what was then known as the "New" Temple. The result, however, was unsatisfactory, and both parties prepared for an appeal to force, the barons choosing as their leader Robert Fitz-Walter, whom they dubbed "Marshal of the army of God and of Holy Church." 184

Robert Fitz-Walter, castellain of London.

This Fitz-Walter was Baron of Dunmow in Essex, the owner of Baynard's Castle in the City of London, and lord of a soke, which embraced the whole of the parish known as St. Andrew Castle Baynard. He moreover enjoyed the dignity of castellain and chief bannerer or banneret of London. The rights and privileges attaching to his soke and to his official position in time of peace were considerable, to judge from a claim to them put forward by his grandson in the year 1303. Upon making his appearance in the Court of Husting at the Guildhall, it was the duty of the Mayor, or other official holding the court, to rise and meet him and place him by his side. Again, if any traitor were taken within his soke or jurisdiction, it was his right to sentence him to death, the manner of death being that the convicted person should be tied to a post in the Thames at the Wood Wharf, and remain there during two tides and two ebbs. 185

In later years, however, upon an enquiry being held by the Justiciars of the Iter (a° 14 Edward II, a.d. 1321), the claimant was obliged to acknowledge that he had disposed of Baynard's Castle in the time of Edward I, but had especially reserved to himself all rights attaching to the castle and barony, although he very considerately declared his willingness to forego the right and title enjoyed by his ancestor of drowning traitors at Wood Wharf. 186

Duties of the castellain of the City in time of war.

But it was in time of war that Fitz-Walter achieved for himself the greatest power and dignity. It then became the duty of the castellain to proceed to the great gate of St. Paul's attended by nineteen other knights, mounted and caparisoned, and having his banner, emblazoned with his arms, displayed before him. Immediately upon his arrival, the mayor, aldermen, and sheriffs, who awaited him, issued solemnly forth from the church, all arrayed in arms, the mayor bearing in his hand the city banner, the ground of which was bright vermilion or gules, with a figure of St. Paul, in gold, thereon, the head, feet, and hands of the saint being silver or argent, and in his right hand a sword. 187 The castellain, advancing to meet the mayor, informed him that he had come to do the service which the city had a right to demand at his hands, and thereupon the mayor placed the city's banner in his hands, and then, attending him back to the gate, presented him with a charger of the value of £20, its saddle emblazoned with the arms of Fitz-Walter, and its housing of cendal or silk, similarly enriched.

A sum of £20 was at the same time handed to Fitz-Walter's chamberlain to defray the day's expenses. Having mounted his charger, he bids the Mayor to choose a Marshal of the host of the City of London; and this being done, the communal or "mote-bell" is set ringing, and the whole party proceed to the Priory of Holy Trinity at Aldgate. There they dismount, and entering the Priory, concert measures together for the defence of the city. There is one other point worthy of remark, touching the office of chief banneret, and that is that on the occasion of any siege undertaken by the London forces, the castellain was to receive as his fee the niggardly sum of one hundred shillings for his trouble, and no more.

Feud between Fitz-Walter and King John.

It is not improbable that Fitz-Walter's election as leader of the remonstrant barons was in some measure due to his official position in the city. It is also probable, as Mr. Riley has pointed out, that the unopposed admission of the barons into the city, on the 24th May, 1215, may have been facilitated by Fitz-Walter's connexion, as castellain, with the Priory of Holy Trinity, situate in the vicinity.

But there were other reasons for selecting Fitz-Walter as their leader at this juncture. If the story be true, Fitz-Walter had good reason to be bitterly hostile to King John, for having caused his fair daughter Maude or Matilda to be poisoned, after having unsuccessfully made an attempt upon her chastity. 188 This is not the only crime of the kind laid to the charge of this monarch, 189 and there appears to be too much reason for believing most of the charges against him to be true. It is certain that Fitz-Walter was one of the first to entertain designs against John, and that he and Eustace de Vesci, on whose family the king is said to have put a similar affront, were forced to escape to France. The story how Fitz-Walter attracted John's notice by his prowess at a tournament in which he was engaged on the side of the French, and was restored to the King's favour and his own estates, is familiar to all.

The Barons admitted into the City, May, 1215.

After a feeble attempt to capture Northampton, the barons, with Fitz-Walter at their head, accepted an invitation from the citizens of London to enter the city. They made their entry through Aldgate. 190

The concession which John had recently made to the citizens, viz.:— the right of annually electing their own mayor 191—had failed to secure their allegiance. The city became thenceforth the headquarters of the barons, 192 and the adhesion of the Londoners was followed by so great a defection from the King's party (including among others that of Henry de Cornhill), that he was left without any power of resistance. 193

The city and Magna Carta, 15th June, 1215.

The citizens met their reward for fidelity to the barons when John was brought to bay at Runnymede. In drafting the articles of the Great Charter the barons, mindful of their trusty allies, made provision for the preservation of the city's liberties, and the names of Fitz-Walter and of the mayor of the city appear among those who were specially appointed to see that the terms of the charter were strictly carried out. 194

By way of further security for the fulfilment of the articles of the charter the barons demanded and obtained the custody of the City of London, including the Tower, and they reserved to themselves the right of making war upon the king if he failed to keep his word. For a year or more the barons remained in the city, having entered into a mutual compact with the inhabitants to make no terms with the king without the consent of both parties. 195

Open war between John and the barons.

The right of resistance thus established was soon to be carried into execution. Before the year was out, John had broken faith, and was besieging Rochester with the aid of mercenaries. An attempt to raise the siege failed, owing to the timidity (not to say cowardice) of Fitz-Walter, who, like the rest of the barons, was inclined to be indolent so soon as the struggle with the king was thought to have ended. 196

London under an interdict.

The Pope supported his vassal king. For a second time during John's reign London was placed under an interdict. The first occasion was in 1208, when the whole of England was put under an interdict, and for six years the nation was deprived of all religious rites saving the sacraments of baptism and extreme unction. 197 It was then the object of Innocent to stir up resistance against John by inflicting sufferings on the people, now his purpose was to punish the people for having risen against John.

The arrival of the Dauphin, May, 1216.

Death of John, 19th October, 1216.

The barons saw no other course open to them but to invite Louis the Dauphin to come and undertake the government of the kingdom in the place of John. On the 21st May, 1216, Louis landed at Sandwich and came to London, where he was welcomed by the barons. Both barons and citizens paid him homage, whilst he, on his part, swore to restore to them their rights, to maintain such laws of the realm as were good, and to abolish those (if any) that were bad. 198 Suspicion, however, had been aroused against Louis by the confession of a French nobleman who had come over in his train, and who had solemnly declared on his deathbed that his master had sworn when once on the throne of England to banish all John's enemies. 199 Just when matters seemed to be approaching a crisis and the barons were wavering in their allegiance, John died (19th October, 1216).

CHAPTER IV.

The barons desert Louis.

Although London remained faithful to Louis after John's death, the barons began to desert him, one by one (*quasi stillatim*), 200 and to transfer their allegiance to John's eldest son, a boy of nine years of age, who had been crowned at Gloucester soon after his father's death, the disturbed state of the country not allowing of his coming to London for the ceremony. 201

Defeat of Louis at Lincoln, 20th May, 1217.

After his defeat at Lincoln (20th May, 1217), by William the Marshal, Earl of Pembroke, one of Henry's guardians, Louis beat a hasty retreat to London and wrote to his father, the French king, to send him military assistance, for without it he could neither fight nor get out of the country.

Fitz-Walter and Muntfichet made prisoners.

Among the prisoners taken at Lincoln were Robert Fitz-Walter, and a neighbour of his in the ward of Castle Baynard, Richard de Muntfichet, who, like Fitz-Walter, had also suffered banishment in 1213. The tower or castle of Muntfichet lay a little to the west of Baynard's Castle, and was made over in 1276 by Gregory de Rokesle, the mayor, and citizens of London to the Archbishop of Canterbury, for the purpose of erecting a new house for the Dominican or Black Friars, in place of their old house in Holborn. 202 We hear little of Fitz-Walter after this, beyond the facts that he soon afterwards obtained his freedom, that he went on a crusade, and continued a loyal subject to Henry until his death in 1235. He is said to have been in the habit of wearing a precious stone suspended from his neck by way of a charm, which at his last moments he asked his wife to remove in order that he might die the easier. 203

London invested by the Earl Marshal.

A French fleet which had been despatched in answer to Louis was defeated off Dover by Hubert de Burgh, who had gallantly held that town for John, and continued to hold it now for Henry. London itself was invested by the Marshal, and threatened with starvation; but before matters came to extremes, Louis intimated his willingness to come to terms. 204

Treaty of Lambeth, 11th Sept., 1217.

A meeting was held on the 11th of September (some say at Kingston, 205 others at Staines 206), and a peace concluded. 207 Louis swore fealty to the Pope and the Roman Church, for which he was absolved from the ban of excommunication that had been passed on him, and surrendered all the castles and towns he had taken during the war. He, further, promised to use his influence to obtain the restoration to England of the possessions that had been lost beyond the sea.

Departure of Louis after borrowing a sum of money from the citizens.

Henry, on his part, swore to preserve to the barons and the rest of the kingdom, all those liberties which they had succeeded in obtaining from John. Everything being thus amicably settled, Louis went to London, and, after borrowing a large sum of money from his former trusty supporters, betook himself back to his native country. 208 The general pardon which was granted by the young king extended to the Londoners, who became reconciled and received back their lands, 209 but did not extend to the clergy, who were left to the tender mercy of the papal legate.

Attempt by Constantine Fitz-Athulf or Olaf, to raise a cry in favour of Louis, 1222.

For some years to come there remained a party in the city who cherished the memory of Louis, and the cry of "Mountjoy!" the war-cry of the French king—was sufficient to cause a riot as late as 1222, when Constantine Fitz-Athulf or Olaf, an ex-sheriff of London, raised the cry at a tournament, in order to test the feeling of the populace towards Louis. Any serious results that might have arisen were promptly prevented by Hubert de Burgh, the justiciar, who very quickly sought out the ringleader, and incontinently caused him and two of his followers to be hanged at the Elms in Smithfield. Whilst the halter was round his neck, Fitz-Athulf offered 15,000 marks of silver for his life. The offer was declined. He was not to be allowed another chance of stirring up sedition in the city. 210

A more circumstantial account of this event is given us by another chronicler, 211 who relates that the wrestling match which took place on the festival of Saint James (25th July),—the same as that mentioned by Matthew Paris—was held at Queen Matilda's hospital in the suburbs, 212 and was a match between the citizens of London and those outside; that victory declared itself in favour of the Londoners, and that their opponents, and among them the steward of the Abbot of Westminster, thereupon left in high dudgeon. With thoughts of revenge in their hearts, the latter caused invitations to be issued for another match to be held at Westminster, on the following feast of Saint Peter ad Vincula (1st August).

It was at this second and later match that the trouble began. The steward was not content with collecting the most powerful athletes he could find, but caused them to seize weapons and to attack the defenceless citizens who had come to take part in the games. The Londoners hurried home, bleeding with wounds, and immediately took counsel as to what was best to be done. Serlo, the mercer, who had held the office of mayor of the city for the past five years, and was of a peaceable disposition, suggested referring the matter to the abbot; and it was then that Constantine, who had a large following, advocated an attack upon the houses of the abbot and of his steward. No sooner said than done, and many houses had already suffered before the justiciar appeared upon the scene with a large force. As to the seizure of Constantine and his subsequent execution, the chroniclers agree.

Constantine's fellow citizens were very indignant at the indecent haste with which the justiciar had caused his execution to be carried out, and did not fail to bring the matter up in judgment against him, when, some ten years later, Hubert de Burgh himself fell into disgrace. 213 The result was, that the justiciar took refuge in the Priory of Merton. When the citizens received the king's orders to follow him there, and to take him dead or alive, they obeyed with unconcealed joy. They allowed little time to elapse, but set out at once, 20,000 strong, ready to tear him limb from limb; but luckily they were stopped in time by another message from the king, and Hubert obtained a respite. 214

The foreign element in the country.

At the time of Constantine's execution, there was real danger to be anticipated from raising the cry in favour of any foreigner. The land was already swarming with foreigners, and in that very year (viz. 1222), the archbishop had been under the necessity of summoning a council of bishops and nobles to be held in London, owing to dissensions that had arisen between the Earl of Chester, William of Salisbury, the king's uncle, and Hubert de Burgh, and to a rumour that had got abroad, that foreigners were inciting the Earl of Chester to raise an insurrection. 215

A few years later, the country was over-run by a brood of Italian usurers who battened on the inhabitants, reducing many to beggary. When attempts were made to rid the city of these pests, they sheltered themselves under the protection of the Pope. 216

Throughout the reign of Henry III, there was one continuous struggle against foreign dominion, either secular or ecclesiastical. In this struggle, none took a more active part than the citizens of London, and "when [in 1247], the nobles, clergy, and people of England put forth their famous letter denouncing the wrongs which England suffered at the hands of the Roman bishop, it was with the seal of the city of London, as the centre of national life that the national protest was made." 217

The city's struggle against encroachment by the king.

Side by side with this struggle another was being carried on, a struggle for the liberty of the subject against the tyranny and rapacity of the king. More especially was this the case with the city. Henry was for ever invading the rights and liberties of the citizens. Thus in 1239, he insisted upon their admitting to the shrievalty one who had already been dismissed from that office for irregular conduct, and because they refused to forego their chartered right of election and to appoint the king's nominee, the city was deprived of a mayor for three months and more. 218

The city "taken into the king's hand" on the most frivolous pretences.

The substitution of a *custos* or warden appointed by the king for a mayor elected by the citizens, and of bailiffs for sheriffs,—a procedure known as "taking the city into the king's hands,"—was frequently resorted to both by Henry and his successors, and notably by Edward I, in whose reign the city was deprived of its mayor, and remained under government of a *custos* for thirteen consecutive years (1285-1298). 219

Any pretext was sufficient for Henry's purpose. If the citizens harboured a foreigner without warrant, not only was the city taken into the king's hand, but the citizens were fined £1,000, 220 a sum equal to at least £20,000 at the present day. A widow brings an action for a third part of her late husband's goods in addition to her dower. The case goes against her in the Court of Husting, and is heard on appeal before the king's justiciar sitting at St. Martin's-le-Grand. The verdict is not set aside, but some flaw is discovered in the mode of procedure; the explanation of the citizens is deemed insufficient, and the mayor and sheriffs are forthwith deposed, to be reinstated only on the understanding that they will so far forego their chartered right—viz.: of not impleading nor being impleaded without the walls of their city—as to consent to attend the king's court at Westminster, where finally, and after considerable delay, they are acquitted. 221

Take another instance. The king had shown an interest in the Abbey Church of Westminster, and had caused a new chapel to be built in 1220, he himself laying the first stone. Thirty years later, or thereabouts, he made certain concessions to the Abbot of Westminster—what they were we are not told—but it is certain that they, in some way or other, infringed the rights of the citizens of London in the County of Middlesex. The king promised to compensate them for the loss they would sustain; but failing to get their consent by fair promises, he resorted to his favourite measure of taking the city into his own hands. For fifteen years the dispute between the citizens and the Abbot as to their respective rights in the County of Middlesex was kept alive, and was at last determined by a verdict given by the barons of the exchequer, which completely justified 222 the attitude taken up by the citizens of London.

Money extorted from the Jews as well as the citizens for payment of the king's tradesmen.

In 1230 he extorted a large sum of money from the citizens at a time when he was meditating an expedition to the continent for the purpose of recovering lost possessions. The citizens, however, were not the only sufferers. The religious houses were heavily mulcted, as were also the Jews, who, whether they would or not, were made to give up one third of their chattels. 223 Again in 1244, the citizens of London and the Jews were made to open their purse-strings that the king might the better be able to pay his wine merchant, his wax chandler, and his tailor; but even then his creditors were not paid in full. 224

Only once does it appear that the king's conscience pricked him for the extortions he was continually practising on the citizens. This was in 1250, when he called the citizens together at Westminster, and begged their forgiveness for all trespasses, extortions of goods and victuals under the name of "prises," and for forced loans or talliages. Seeing no other way out of it, the citizens acceded to his request. 225 As recently as the previous year (1249) he had exacted from them a sum of £2,000. 226

The coronation of king and queen, 1236.

Henry had been crowned at Gloucester soon after his accession. 227 Nevertheless he was again crowned—this time in London in 1236, after his marriage with Eleanor of Provence. The city excelled itself in doing honour to the king and queen as they passed on their way to Westminster: but the joy of the citizens was damped by the king refusing to allow Andrew Bukerel the mayor to perform the customary service of assisting the chief butler at the coronation banquet. It was not a time for raising questions of etiquette, so the mayor pocketed the affront, preferring to settle the question of the city's rights at some more convenient time, rather than damp the general joy of the company by pressing his claim. 228

The king's custom of formally taking leave of his citizens before going abroad.

Yet, notwithstanding his manifestly unjust treatment of the citizens of London, and the cynical contempt with which he looked upon their ancient claim to the title of "barons," he usually went through the formality of taking leave of them at Paul's Cross or at Westminster, before crossing the sea to Gascony 229 and was not above making use of them when compelled to sell his plate and jewels to satisfy his debts. In 1252, he even went so far as to grant them a charter of liberties, but for this concession the citizens had to pay 500 marks. 230

The Mad Parliament, 11th June, 1258.

It is scarcely to be wondered at if, when the crisis arrived, and king and barons found themselves in avowed hostility, the citizens of London joined the popular cause. By the month of June, 1258, the barons had gained their first victory over Henry. He was forced to accept the Provisions of Oxford, passed by the Mad Parliament, 231 as it came to be called in derision. The Tower of London was transferred to the custody of the barons, and they were for the future to appoint the justiciar. Towards the end of July, a deputation from the barons waited upon the mayor and citizens to learn if they approved of the agreement that had been made with the king. 232

The Citizens throw in their lot with the Barons.

The mayor, aldermen, and citizens, after a hasty consultation, gave their assent, but with the reservation "saving unto them all their liberties and customs," and the city's common seal was set to the so-called "charter" which the deputation had brought.

Hugh Bigod the baron's justiciar in the city, 1258.

It was not long before the city discovered that the barons were as little likely to respect its liberties as the king himself. Hugh Bigod, whom they had appointed justiciar gave offence by the way he exercised his office. In spite of all remonstrance he insisted upon sitting at the Guildhall to hear pleas, a jurisdiction which belonged exclusively to the sheriffs. He summoned the bakers of the city to appear before him, and those who were convicted of selling bread under weight he punished, in a way that was not in conformity with city usage. 233

The king takes leave of the citizens. November, 1259.

In November of the following year (1259), Henry took occasion of his departure for the continent to make some popular concessions to the citizens. He appeared at a Folkmote, which was being held at Paul's Cross, and, before taking leave, he announced that in future the citizens should be allowed to plead their own cases (without employing legal aid) in all the courts of the city, excepting in pleas of the crown, pleas of land, and of wrongful distress. On the same day John Mansel who had been one of the king's justiciars in 1257, when the city was "taken into the king's hand," and Fitz-Thedmar had been indicted and deprived of his aldermanry for upholding the privileges of the citizens 234 — publicly acknowledged on the king's behalf the injustice of Fitz-Thedmar's indictment, and announced that Henry not only recalled him to favour, but commanded that he should be restored to his former position. 235

The king's return from abroad, April, 1260.

During the king's absence abroad, the barons' cause was materially strengthened by the support afforded Simon de Montfort, Earl of Leicester, by the king's son. Upon hearing of the defection of his son, Henry hurried back to England. A consultation took place in the city as to the attitude which the citizens ought to take up, with the result that when Henry appeared (April, 1260), both he and the Earl of Gloucester were admitted into the city, whilst the Earl of Leicester and "Sir Edward," as the chronicler styles the king's son, had to find accommodation in the suburbs. 236

Henry was now master of the situation. The city was his, and he determined that it should remain so. Strict watch was kept over the gates, which for the most part, were kept shut night and day in order to prevent surprise. Every inhabitant of the age of twelve years and upwards was called upon to take an oath of allegiance before the alderman of his ward, and those of maturer age were bound to provide themselves with arms. The king, who now ruled again in his own way, stirred the anger of the barons, by presuming to appoint Philip Basset, his chief justiciar, without first asking their assent; and the barons retaliated by removing the king's sheriffs, and appointing "wardens of the counties" in their stead. 237 In June 1261, Henry produced a Bull of Alexander IV, annulling the Provisions of Oxford, and freeing him from his oath. 238

The king summoned to observe the Provisions of Oxford. 1263.

For eighteen months the king reigned supreme. The barons could do nothing, and the Earl of Leicester, finding their cause hopeless, withdrew in August (1261) to France, and remained there until the spring of 1263, when he returned as the unquestioned head of the baronial party, to take up arms against the king. The citizens professed loyalty to Henry, who was residing in the Tower, and bound themselves by oath to acknowledge his son Edward as heir to the crown. 239 At Whitsuntide, the barons sent a letter to the king requiring him to observe the Provisions of Oxford, and shortly afterwards, addressed another letter to the citizens "desiring to be certified by them whether they would observe the said ordinances and statutes made to the honour of God in fealty to his lordship the king, and to his advantage of all the realm, or would, in preference, adhere to those who wished to infringe the same." 240

Arrangements made between the king, the barons, and the city, July, 1263.

Before sending a reply, the citizens had an interview with the king in the Tower, to whom they showed the barons' letter. The result was, that Henry availed himself of their services to mediate between him and the barons. A deputation of citizens accordingly travelled to Dover, where an understanding was arrived at between the hostile parties. The citizens were prepared to support the barons, subject to their fealty to the king and saving their own liberties; whilst the king promised to dismiss his foreign supporters—the real cause of all the mischief. Hugh le Despenser, whom Henry had deposed, was again installed justiciar of all England in the Tower; and the king and his family left the city for Westminster, the day after the barons entered it. "Thus was a league made between the barons and the citizens with this reservation—'saving fealty to his lordship the king.'" 241

Organization of the Craft Guilds under Fitz-Thomas the Mayor. 1262.

Whilst the commons of England were thus winning their way to liberty, the commons of the city were engaged in a similar struggle with the aristocratic element of the municipal government. The craft guilds cried out against the exclusiveness of the more wealthy and aristocratic trade guilds, the members of which monopolized the city's rule. They found an able champion of their cause in the person of Thomas Fitz-Thomas, the mayor for the time being (1261-1265). The mayor's action in the matter disgusted Fitz-Thedmar, the city alderman and chronicler, who complains that he "so pampered the city populace," that they styled themselves the "commons of the city," and had obtained the first voice in the city. The mayor would ask them their will as to whether this or that thing should be done; and if they answered "ya" "ya," it was done, without consulting the aldermen or chief citizens, whose very existence was ignored. 242 It is not surprising that, under a mayor so thoroughly in sympathy with the people, opportunity was taken by the citizens to rectify abuses from which they had so long suffered. Their trade had been prejudiced by the number of foreigners which the king had introduced into the city, and accordingly we read of an attack made on the houses of some French merchants. Rights of way which had been stopped up, were again opened, and where land had been illegally built upon, the buildings were abated.

The chronicler complains of the populace acting "like so many justices itinerant." It was in vain that the king addressed a letter to the mayor and citizens, setting forth that the dissensions between himself and the barons had been settled, and commanding his peace to be kept as well within the city as without. 243

The movement favoured by the barons.

The popular movement received every encouragement from the barons. Let those who were disaffected put their complaints into writing, and the barons would see that the matter was duly laid before the king, and that the city's liberties were not diminished. Fortified with such promises, the mayor set to work at once to organize the craft guilds. Ordinances were drawn up "abominations" Fitz-Thedmar calls them 244 for the amelioration of the members, and everything was done that could be done to better their condition.

The queen insulted by the citizens, 13th July, 1263.

A few days before Henry and the barons had concluded a temporary peace, the citizens had been greatly excited by an action of the king's son. Henry was, as usual, in want of money, and had failed to raise a loan in the city. His son came to his assistance and seized the money and jewels lying at the Temple (29th June). The citizens were so exasperated at this high-handed proceeding on the part of the prince that they vented their spleen on the queen, and pelted her with mud and stones, calling her all kinds of opprobrious names, as she attempted to pass in her barge under London Bridge on her way from the Tower to Windsor. (13th July). 245

Such conduct very naturally incensed the king and his son against the citizens. Henry was angry with them, moreover, for having admitted the barons contrary to his express orders. 246 It is not surprising, therefore, that when Fitz-Thomas presented himself before the Barons of the Exchequer to be admitted to the mayoralty for the third year in succession, they refused to admit him by the king's orders, Henry "being for many reasons greatly moved to anger against the city." 247

The Mise of Amiens. 23rd Jan., 1264

Before the end of the year (1263), both king and barons agreed to submit to the arbitration of the King of France. The award known as the Mise of Amien—from the place whence it was issue—which Louis made on the 23rd Jan., 1264, proved of so one-sided a character that the barons had no alternative but to reject it. However unjustifiable such repudiation on the part of the barons may have been from a moral point of view, it was a matter of necessity. Many of them, moreover, including those of the Cinque Ports, as well as the Londoners, and nearly all the middle class of England, had not been parties to the arbitration, and therefore, were not pledged to accept the award. 248

League between the citizens of London and the barons.

The citizens and the barons now entered into solemn covenant to stand by each other "saving however their fealty to the king." A constable and a marshal were appointed to command the city force, which was to stand prepared night and day to muster at the sound of the great bell of St. Paul's. The manor of Isleworth, belonging to Richard, King of the Romans, the king's brother, was laid waste, and Rochester besieged, but, disturbances again breaking out at home, Leicester had to hurry back to restore order and prevent the city being betrayed to the king's son. 249

The Battle of Lewes, 14th May, 1264.

In May the earl set out again with a force of Londoners 250 to meet the king, who was threatening the Cinque Ports. In the early morning of the 14th he came upon the royal army at Lewes. Prince Edward himself led the charge against the Londoners—he had not forgotten the insult they had recently offered to his mother—and succeeded in driving them off the field. They scarcely indeed awaited his onslaught, so unpractised in warfare had they become of recent years, but turned their backs and sped away towards London, followed in hot pursuit by Edward. When he returned he found that, owing to his absence, the day was lost, and that his father and brother had been made prisoners. 251 In spite of his own success, he also had to surrender.

The Mise of Lewes.

The barons returned to the city in triumph, bringing the king and Richard, king of the Romans, in their train. Edward had been placed in custody in Dover Castle, pending negotiations. Henry was lodged in the Bishop's Palace, whilst Richard was committed to the Tower. An agreement was drawn up which secured the safety of the king, and left all matters of dispute to be again referred to arbitration. 252 This treaty formed the basis of a new system of government, and led to the institution of Simon de Montfort's famous Parliament.

The short respite—for it proved to be no more—from civil war was welcomed by the Londoners. The city had been drained of a large part of its population in order to increase the Earl of Leicester's army, and business had been seriously disturbed. For the past year no Court of Husting had been held, and therefore no wills or testaments had received probate; whilst all pleas of land, except trespass, had to stand over until the country became more settled. 253

Meeting of Simon de Montfort's Parliament, 20th Jan., 1265.

The parliament which Leicester summoned to meet on the 20th January, 1265, marked a new era in parliamentary representation. It was the first parliament in which the merchant and the trader were invited to take their seats beside the baron and bishop. Not only were the shires to send up two representatives, but each borough and town were to be similarly privileged. 254

Terms of reconciliation between king and barons were arranged, and once more the mayor and aldermen did fealty to Henry in person in St. Paul's church. Fitz-Thomas, who for the fourth time was mayor, was determined to lose nothing of his character for independence; "My lord," said he, when taking the oath, so long as you are willing to be to us a good king and lord, we will be to you faithful and true." 255

Jealousy between the Earls of Leicester and Gloucester.

Peace was not destined to last long. Dissensions quickly broke out between Gilbert, Earl of Gloucester, and Simon de Montfort, owing in a great measure to jealousy. Gloucester insisted that the Mise of Lewes and the Provisions of Oxford had not been properly observed, hinting unmistakably at the foreign birth and extraction of his rival. Endeavours were made to arrange matters by arbitration, but in vain; and by Whitsuntide the two earls were in open hostility. Gloucester was joined by Edward, who had succeeded by a ruse in escaping from Hereford, where he was detained in honourable captivity. 256

The Battle of Evesham, 4th August, 1265.

With their combined forces they fell on Earl Simon at Evesham and utterly defeated him (4 Aug.). Simon himself was killed, and his body barbarously mutilated. 257 The king, who was in the earl's camp, only saved himself by crying out in time "I am Henry of Winchester, your king." Whilst the battle was raging the city was visited with a terrible thunderstorm—an evil omen of the future.

If credit be given to every statement made by the city alderman and chronicler, Fitz-Thedmar, we must believe that the battle of Evesham took place just in time to prevent a wholesale massacre of the best and foremost men of the city, including the chronicler himself, which was being contrived by the mayor, the popular Thomas Fitz-Thomas, the no less popular Thomas de Piwelesdon or Puleston, and others. 258

The city taken into the king's hands from 1265 to 1270.

The citizens of London were soon to experience the change that had taken place in the state of affairs. The day after Michaelmas, the mayor and citizens proceeded to Westminster to present the new sheriffs to the Barons of the Exchequer; but finding no one there, they returned home. The truth was that the king had resorted to his favourite measure of taking the city into his own hands for its adherence to the late Earl of Leicester; and for five years it so remained, being governed by a *custos* or warden appointed by the king, in the place of a mayor elected by the citizens. 259

Threat of the king to subdue the city by force.

There had been some talk of the king meditating an attack upon the city, and treating its inhabitants as avowed enemies. 260 The very threat of such a proceeding was sufficient to throw the city into the utmost state of confusion. Some there were "fools and evil-minded persons," as our chronicler describes them—who favoured resisting force by force; but the "most discreet men" of the city, and those who had joined the Earl under compulsion, would have none of it, preferring to solicit the king's favour through the mediation of men of the religious orders. Henry still remained unmoved, and the fear of the citizens increased to such an extent that it was finally resolved that the citizens as a body should make humble submission to the king; and that the same should be forwarded to him at Windsor under the common seal of the city. Whilst the deputation bearing this document was on its way it was met by Sir Roger de Leiburn, who turned it back on the ground that he himself was on his way to the city for the express purpose of arranging terms of submission. 261

Fitz-Thomas and others summoned to Windsor.

That night Sir Roger lodged at the Tower, and the next morning he went to Barking Church, on the confines of the city, 262 where he was met by the mayor and a "countless multitude" of the citizens. The advice he had to give the citizens was that if they wished to be reconciled to the king, they would have to submit their lives and property unreservedly to his will. Letters patent were drawn up to that effect under the common seal, and taken by Sir Roger himself to Windsor. The citizens had not long to wait for an answer. The king's first demand was the removal of the posts and chains which had been set up in the streets as a means of defence. His next was that the mayor—his old antagonist Fitz-Thomas—and the principal men of the city should come in person to him at Windsor, under letters of safe conduct. Trusting to the royal word, the mayor and about forty of the more substantial men of the city proceeded to Windsor, there to await a conference with the king. To their great surprise, the whole of the party were made to pass the night in the Castle keep. They were practically treated as prisoners.

The fate of Fitz-Thomas unknown.

Some regained their liberty, but of Fitz-Thomas nothing more is heard. From the time that he entered Windsor Castle, he disappears from public view. That he was alive in May, 1266, at least in the belief of his fellow-citizens, is shown by their cry for the release of him and his companions "who are at Windleshores." They would again have made him Mayor, if they could have had their own way. "We will have no one for mayor" (they cried) "save only Thomas Fitz-Thomas." 263

The city taken into the king's hand, 1265.

In the meantime the king had himself gone to London and confiscated the property of more than sixty of the citizens, driving them out of their house and home. Hugh Fitz-Otes, the Constable of the Tower, had been appointed warden of the city in the place of the imprisoned mayor; bailiffs had been substituted for sheriffs, and the citizens made to pay a fine of 20,000 marks. Then, and only then, did the king consent to grant their pardon. 264

London Bridge bestowed on the queen.

Queen Eleanor, who had interceded for the Londoners, 265 was presented by the king with the custody of London Bridge, the issues and profits of which she was allowed to enjoy. She allowed the bridge, however, to fall into such decay, that she thought she could not do better than restore it to its rightful owners. This she accordingly did in 1271, but soon afterwards changed her mind, and again took the bridge into her charge. 266

The Earl of Gloucester master of the city, April, 1267.

At Easter, 1267, the Earl of Gloucester, who had constituted himself the avowed champion of those who had suffered forfeiture, and become "disinherited" for the part they had taken with the Earl of Leicester, sought admission to the city. The citizens hesitated to receive him within their gates, although according to some, he was armed with letters patent of the king addressed to the citizens on his behalf. 267 Under pretence of holding a conference with the papal legate at the Church of Holy Trinity, Aldgate, he gained admission for himself and followers: and there he remained, having made himself master of the city's gates. 268 Thereupon many citizens left the city, fearing the wrath of the king, and once more the city was in the hands of the populace. The leading citizens were placed under a guard; the aldermen and bailiffs were deposed to make way for the earl's own supporters, and, for better security, a covered way of timber was made from the city to the Tower. 269

Whatever may have been the actual part played by the legate in admitting the disinherited into the city, he soon showed his dissatisfaction at the state of things within its walls, by leaving the Tower, to join the king at Ham, and placing the disinherited—"the enemies of the king"—under an interdict. 270

Terms arranged between Gloucester and the king, 16th June, 1267.

At length the king and the Earl of Gloucester came to terms (16 June). The earl was to have his property restored to him, and the city was to be forgiven all trespasses committed against the king since the time that the earl made his sojourn within its walls. The earl gave surety in 10,000 marks for keeping the peace, and the citizens paid the king of the Romans 1,000 marks for damages they had committed three years before in his manor of Isleworth. 271 Not a word about the imprisoned mayor, Fitz-Thomas!

Charter of Henry III, 26th March, 1268.

The king's letters patent granting forgiveness to the citizens for harbouring the Earl of Gloucester 272 were followed in the spring of the following year by another charter to the city. 273 But inasmuch as this charter did not restore the mayoralty, the citizens had little cause to be thankful and looked upon it as only an instalment of favours to come.

The city recovers its rights to elect mayor and sheriffs, 1270.

Towards the end of this year or early in the next (1269), the city was committed by the king to his son Edward, who ruled it by deputy, Sir Hugh Fitz-Otes being again appointed Constable of the Tower, and warden of the city. 274 It was through the good offices of the prince, that the citizens eventually recovered the right to elect their mayor, so long withheld. "About the same time, that is to say, Pentecost, 1270," writes Fitz-Thedmar, "at the instance of Sir Edward, his lordship the king granted unto the citizens that they might have a mayor from among themselves in such form as they were wont to elect him." 275

The sheriff's ferm increased to £400.

He further allowed them to choose two sheriffs who should discharge the duties of sheriff, (*qui tenerent vicecomitatem*) of the City and Middlesex, as formerly; but instead of the yearly ferm of £300 in pure silver (*sterlingorum blancorum*), formerly paid for Middlesex, they were thenceforth to pay an annual rent of £400 in money counted (*sterlingorum computatorum*.) 276

Election of John Adrian, Mayor, 1270.

The citizens lost no time in exercising their recovered rights. Their choice fell upon John Adrian for the mayoralty, whilst Philip le Taillour and Walter le Poter were elected sheriffs. After they had been severally admitted into office—the mayor before the king himself on Wednesday, the 16th July, and the sheriffs at the Exchequer two days later—the king restored the city's charters, and the citizens acknowledged the royal favour by a gift of 100 marks to the king, and 500 marks to Prince Edward, who had proved so good a friend to them, and who was about to set out for the Holy Land. 277

Election of Hervy, 1272, disputed.

Adrian was succeeded in the mayoralty by Walter Hervy, who had already served as sheriff or bailiff on two occasions, once by royal appointment. He made himself so popular with the "commons" of the city during his year of office, that when October, 1272, came round and the aldermen and more "discreet" citizens were in favour of electing Philip le Taillour as his successor, the commons or "mob of the city"—as the chronicler prefers to style them—cried out, "Nay, nay, we will have no one for mayor but Walter Hervi." 278

Appeal made by both parties to the king's council.

The aldermen finding themselves in a minority, appealed to the king and council at Westminster. Hervy did the same, being accompanied to Westminster by a large number of supporters, who took the opportunity of the aldermen laying their case before the council to insist loudly, as they waited in the adjacent hall, upon their own right of election and their choice of Hervy. It was feared that the noise might disturb the king who was confined to his bed with what proved to be his last illness. All parties was therefore dismissed, injunction being laid upon Hervy not to appear again with such a following, but to come with only ten or a dozen supporters at the most.

The king's illness and death, 16th November, 1272.

Hervy paid no heed to this warning, but continued to present himself at Westminster every day for a fortnight, accompanied by his supporters in full force, expecting an answer to be given by the council. At length the council resolved to submit the whole question to arbitration, the city in the meanwhile being placed in the custody of a warden. Before the arbitrators got to work, the king died (16 Nov.), and rather than the city should continue to be disturbed at such a crisis, the aldermen agreed to a compromise, and Hervy was allowed to be mayor for one year more. 279

CHAPTER V.

Fitz-Thedmar's prejudice against Hervy.

Although the aldermen had been prevailed upon to give their assent to Hervy's election to the mayoralty, his democratic tendencies made him an object of dislike, more especially to Fitz-Thomas. When, therefore, that chronicler records that throughout Hervy's year of office he did not allow any pleading in the Husting for Pleas of Land except very rarely, for the reason that the mayor himself was defendant in a suit brought against him by Isabella Bukerel, 280 we hesitate to place implicit belief in his statement. 281 We are inclined, moreover, to give less credit to anything that Fitz-Thedmar may say against the mayor when we bear in mind that the former had a personal grievance against the latter. 282

Hervy's so-called "charter" to the guilds.

Hervy was a worthy successor to Fitz-Thomas, and, under his government, the craft guilds improved their position. Fresh ordinances for the regulation of various crafts were drawn up, and to these the mayor, on his own responsibility, attached the city seal. 283 When Hervy's year of office expired—these so-called "charters" were called in question as having been unauthorised by the aldermen of the city and as tending to favour the richer members of the guilds to the prejudice of the poorer. After a "wordy and most abusive dispute" carried on in the Guildhall between the ex-mayor and Gregory de Rokesley who acted as spokesman for the body of aldermen, Hervy left the hall and summoned the craft-guilds to meet him in Cheapside. There he told them that it was the wish of Henry le Galeys (or Waleys) the mayor and others to infringe their charters, but that if they could stand by him he would maintain those charters in all their integrity.

Fearing lest a riot might follow, the chancellor—Walter de Merton, through whose mediation Hervy had been at last accepted as mayor by the aldermen—ordered his arrest. This was on the 20th December, 1273. Hervy was, accordingly, attached but released on bail, and early in the following January (1274), his charters were duly examined in the Husting before all the people, and declared void. Thenceforth, every man was to enjoy the utmost freedom in following his calling, always provided that his work was good and lawful. 284

Dispute between Hervy and the Mayor, 1274.

When the mayor removed certain butchers' and fishmongers' stalls from Cheapside, in order that the main thoroughfare of the city might present a creditable appearance to the king on his return from abroad, the owners of the stalls, who complained of being disturbed in their freeholds — "having given to the sheriff a great sum of money for the same" — found a champion in Hervy. Their cause was pleaded at the Guildhall, and such "a wordy strife" arose between Hervy and the mayor, that the session had to be broken up, and Hervy's conduct was reported to the king's council. The next day, upon the resumption of the session, a certain roll was produced and publicly read, in which "the presumptuous acts and injuries, of most notorious character" which Hervy was alleged to have committed during his mayoralty were set forth at length.

Charges against Hervy for acts done during his mayoralty.

Is discharged from his aldermanry.

The charges against him were eight in number, of which some at least appear to be in the last degree frivolous. He had on a certain occasion borne false witness; he had failed on another occasion to attend at Westminster upon a summons; he had failed to observe all the assizes made by the aldermen and had allowed ale to be sold in his ward for three halfpence a gallon; he had taken bribes for allowing corn and wine to be taken out of the city for sale, and he had misappropriated a sum of money which had been raised for a special purpose. Such was the general run of the charges brought against him, in addition to which were the charges of having permitted the guilds to make new statutes to their own advantage and to the loss of the city and all the realm, as already narrated, and of having procured "certain persons of the city, of Stebney, of Stratford, and of Hakeneye" to make an unjust complaint against the mayor, "who had warranty sufficient for what he had done, namely, the council of his lordship the king." This last charge had reference to the recent removal of tradesmen's stalls from Chepe. No defence appears to have been allowed Hervy. The charges were read, and he was then and there declared to be "judicially degraded from his aldermanry and for ever excluded from the council of the city"; a precept being at the same time issued for the immediate election of a successor, to be presented at the next court. 285

The after-results of the policy of Hervy and Fitz-Thomas.

From this time forward nothing more is heard of Hervy. The same cloud envelopes his later history, that gathered round the last years of his predecessor and political tutor Thomas Fitz-Thomas. The misfortune of both of these men was that they lived before their age. Their works bore fruit long after they had departed. The trade or craft guilds, as distinguished from the more wealthy and influential mercantile guilds, eventually played an important part in the city. Under Edward II, no stranger could obtain the freedom of the city (without which, he could do little or nothing), unless he became a member of one of these guilds, or sought the suffrages of the commonalty of the city, before admission to the freedom in the Court of Husting. 286

The normal and more expeditious way of obtaining the freedom was thus through a guild. If Hervy or Fitz-Thomas lived till the year 1319, when the Ordinances just cited received the king's sanction, he must have felt that the struggle he had made to raise the lesser guilds had not been in vain. The mercantile element in the city, which had formerly overcome the aristocratic element, 287 in its turn gave way to the numerical superiority and influence of the craft and manufacturing element. Hence it was that in 1376—when the number of trade or craft guilds in the city compared with the larger mercantile guilds was as forty to eight—the guilds succeeded in wresting for a while from the wards the right of electing members of the city's council. 288

Arrival of Edward I, in London, 18th August, 1274.

In the meantime, King Edward I, arrived in London (18th August, 1274), where he was heartily welcomed by the citizens, 289 and was crowned the following day. He had expected to have returned much earlier, and had addressed a letter to the mayor, sheriffs, and commonalty of the City of London, eighteen months before, informing them of his purposed speedy return, and of his wishes that they should endeavour to preserve the peace of the realm. 290 He was, however, detained in France.

Edward's hereditary right to the crown clearly acknowledged.

Edward's right to succeed his father was never disputed. For the first time in the annals of England, a new king commences to reign immediately after the death of his predecessor. *Le Roi est mort, vive le Roi!* Within a week of his father's decease, a writ was issued, in which the hereditary right of succession was distinctly asserted as forming Edward's title to the crown. 291

Four citizens to be sent to confer with Edward at Paris, 3rd April, 1274.

Before setting sail for England, Edward despatched a letter (3rd April), "to his well-beloved, the mayor, barons, and reputable men of London," thanking them for the preparations he understood they were making for the ceremony of his coronation, and bidding them send a deputation of four of the more discreet of the citizens, to him at Paris, for the purpose of a special conference. 292

The object of the conference.

The difficulty which gave rise to this conference and to the signal mark of distinction bestowed upon the citizens of London, proved to be of a commercial character, and, as such, one upon which the opinions of the leading merchants of London would be of especial value. Ever since the year 1270, the commercial relationship between England and Flanders had been strained. The Countess of Flanders had thought fit to lay hands upon the wool and other merchandise belonging to English merchants found within her dominions, and to appropriate the same to her own use. Edward's predecessor on the throne had thereupon issued a writ to the mayor and sheriffs of London, forbidding in future the export of wool to any parts beyond sea whatsoever, 293 but this measure not having the desired effect, he shortly afterwards had recourse to reprisals.

On the 28th June, 1270, a writ had been issued to the same parties ordering them to seize the goods of all Flemings, Hainaulters, and other subjects of the Countess, for the purpose of satisfying the claims of English merchants; and all subjects of the Countess, except those workmen who had received express permission to come to England for the purpose of making cloth, and those who had taken to themselves English wives, and had obtained a domicile in this country, were to quit the realm by a certain date. 294 Those Flemings who neglected this injunction were to be seized and kept in custody until further orders, and the same measures were to be taken with those who harboured them. In the meantime, an inquisition was ordered to be made as to the amount and value of the goods seized by the Countess, and the English merchants were to lodge their respective claims for compensation.

Interruption of trade between England and Flanders.

The interruption of trade between England—at that time the chief wool-exporting country in the world—and Flanders where the cloth-working industry especially flourished, caused much tribulation; and the King of France, the Duke of Brabant, and other foreign potentates, whose subjects began to feel the effect of this commercial disturbance, addressed letters to the King of England, requesting that their merchants might enter his realm and stay, and traffic there as formerly. They had never offended the King or his people; the Countess of Flanders was the sole offender, and she alone ought to be punished. The matter having received due consideration, the embargo on the export of wool was taken off with respect to all countries, except Flanders, with the proviso that no wool should be exported out of the kingdom without special license from the king. 295

By the month of October, 1271, the inquisitors, who had been appointed to appraise the goods and chattels of Flemings in England, were able to report to parliament that their value amounted to £8,000 "together with the king's debt," whilst the value of merchandise belonging to English merchants and seized by the countess amounted to £7,000, besides chattels of other merchants. Parliament again sat in January of the new year to consider the claims of English merchants, when those whose goods had been taken in Flanders, "and the Londoners more especially," appeared in person. Each stated the amount of his loss and the amount of goods belonging to Flemings which he had in hand, and a balance was struck. An inquisition was, at the same time, taken in each of the city wards, as to the number of merchants who bought, sold, exchanged, or harboured the goods of persons belonging to the dominion of the Countess; and also as to who had taken wools out of England to the parts beyond the sea, contrary to the king's prohibition. 296 Many Flemings, still lurking in the city, were arrested, and only liberated on condition they abjured the realm so long as the dispute between England and Flanders should continue. Nearly six months elapsed before any further steps were taken by either party in the strife. The Countess then showed signs of giving way. Envoys from her arrived in England. She was willing to make satisfaction to all English merchants for the losses they had sustained, but this was to be subject to the condition that the king should bind himself to discharge certain alleged debts, which had been the cause of all the mischief from the outset, within a fixed time. In the event of the king failing to discharge these claims, the justice of which he never recognised, the Countess was to be allowed to distrain all persons coming into her country from England by their bodies and their goods, until satisfaction should be made for arrears. This haughty message only made matters worse. The king and his council became indignant, and contemptuously dismissed the envoys, commanding them to leave England within three days on peril of life and limb. 297

Writ for the expulsion of all Flemings, 8th Sept., 1273.

Time went on; Henry died, and before his son Edward arrived in England from the Holy Land to take up the reins of government, his chancellor, Walter de Merton, had caused a proclamation to be made throughout the city, forbidding any Fleming to enter the kingdom, under penalty of forfeiture of person and goods. The proclamation was more than ordinarily stringent, for it went on to say that if perchance any individual had received special permission from the late king to sojourn and to trade within the realm, such permission was no longer to hold good, but the foreigner was to pack up his merchandise, collect his debts, and leave the country by Christmas, 1273, at the latest. 298

Negotiations opened with Edward at Paris for peace with Flanders.

The Countess had probably hoped that a change of monarch on the English throne would have favoured her cause. This proclamation was sufficient to show her the character of the king with whom she had in future to deal, and destroyed any hope she may have entertained in this direction. She therefore took the opportunity of Edward's passing through Paris to London, to open negotiations for the purpose of restoring peace between England and Flanders; and it was to assist the king in conducting these negotiations, that he had summoned a deputation of citizens of London to meet him at Paris.

Particulars of the four citizens sent to confer with the king at Paris.

The choice of the citizens fell upon Henry le Waleys, their mayor for the time being, one who was known almost as well in France as in the city of London, if we may judge from the fact of his filling the office of Mayor of Bordeaux in the following year. With him were chosen Gregory de Rokesley who, besides being a large dealer in wool, was also a goldsmith and financier, and as such was shortly to be appointed master of the exchange throughout England; 299 John Horn, whose name bespeaks his Flemish origin, 300 and who may on that account have been appointed, as one who was intimate with both sides of the question under discussion; and Luke de Batencurt, also of foreign extraction, who was one of the Sheriffs of London this same year.

Peace concluded between England and Flanders, July, 1274.

These four accordingly set out to confer with the king at Paris, having previously seen to the appointment of wardens over the city, and of magistrates to determine complaints which might arise at the fair to be held at St. Botolph's, or Boston, in Lincolnshire, during their absence. 301 The deputation were absent a month. On the 19th July, Gregory de Rokesle and certain others whose names are not mentioned again set out in compliance with orders received from the king; the object of their journey being, as we are expressly told, to treat of peace between the king and the Countess of Flanders at Montreuil. 302 A month later Edward himself was in England.

Strong Government of the city under Edward I.

The king ruled the city, as indeed he ruled the rest of the kingdom, with a strong hand. Londoners had already experienced the force of his arm and his ability in the field, when he scattered them at Lewes; they were now to experience the benefit of his powers of organization in time of peace. Fitz-

Thedmar's chronicle now fails us, but we have a new source of information in the letter books 303 of the Corporation.

The necessity for an immediate supply of money.

The first and the most pressing difficulty which presented itself to Edward, was the re-organization of finance. Without money the barons could not be kept within legitimate bounds. Having won their cause against the usurpations of the crown, they began to turn their arms upon each other, and it required Edward's strong hand not only to impose order upon his unruly nobles, but also, to bring Scotland and Wales into submission. The country was flooded with clipt coin. This was called in, and new money minted at the Tower, under the supervision of Gregory de Rokesley as Master of the Exchange. 304 Parliament made large grants to the king; and he further increased his resources by imposing knighthood upon all freeholders of estates worth £20 a year. 305 When the Welsh war was renewed in 1282, the city sent him 6,000 marks by the hands of Waleys and Rokesley. 306

The so-called Parliament at Shrewsbury. 1283.

In 1283 an extraordinary assembly—styled a parliament by some chroniclers—was summoned to meet at Shrewsbury to attend the trial of David, brother of Llewelyn, Prince of Wales. To this so-called parliament the city sent no less than six representatives, viz.: Henry le Waleys, the mayor, Gregory de Rokesley, Philip Cissor, or the tailor, Ralph Crepyn, Joce le Acatour, or merchant, and John de Gisors. 307 Their names are worthy of record, inasmuch as they are the first known representatives of the city in any assembly deserving the name of a parliament, the names of those attending Simon de Montfort's parliament not having been transmitted to us. David was convicted and barbarously executed, his head being afterwards carried to London, and set up on the Tower, where his brother's head, with a mock crown of ivy, had recently been placed. 308

Ralph Crepyn and Laurence Duket.

Of Ralph Crepyn, one of the city's representatives at Shrewsbury, a tragic story is told. Meeting, one day, Laurence Duket, his rival in the affections of a woman known as "Alice atte Bowe," the two came to blows, and Crepyn was wounded. The affray took place in Cheapside, and Duket, fearing he had killed his man, sought sanctuary in Bow Church. Crepyn's friends, hearing of the matter, followed and having killed Duket, disposed of their victim's body in such a way as to suggest suicide. It so happened, however, that the sacrilegious murder had been witnessed by a boy who informed against the culprits and no less than sixteen persons were hanged for the part they had taken in it. Alice, herself, was condemned to be burnt alive as being the chief instigator of the murder; others, including Ralph Crepyn, were sent to the Tower, and only released on payment of heavy fines. 309 The church was placed under interdict, the doors and windows being filled with thorns until purification had been duly made. Duket's remains, which had been interred as those of a suicide, were afterwards taken up and received the rights of Christian burial in Bow Churchyard.

Legislative enactments of 1285.

The year 1285 was a memorable one both for London and the kingdom. It witnessed the passing of two important statutes. In the first place the statute *De Donis* legalised the principle of tying up real estate, so as to descend, in an exclusive perpetual line; in other words, it sanctioned entails, and its effect is still experienced at the present day in every ordinary settlement of land. In the next place the Assise of Arms of Henry II was improved so as to secure for the king a national support in the time of danger. In every hundred and franchise each man's armour was to be viewed twice a year; and defaults reported to the king "who would find a remedy." The gates of walled towns were to be closed from sun-set to sun-rise, and watch and ward were to be kept as strictly as in times past, "that is to wit, from the day of the Ascension until the day of S. Michael, in every city by six men at every gate; in every borough, twelve men; every town, six or four, according to the number of the inhabitants of the town, and they shall watch the town continually all night from the sun-setting unto the sun-rising." 310 Three years previous to the passing of this statute the mayor, alderman and chamberlain had made very similar provisions for the keeping of the City of London, the city's gates, and the river Thames. 311

The justiciars at the Tower, 1285

For the city, the year was a memorable one, owing to the suspension of its franchise. The circumstances which caused the loss of its liberties for a period of thirteen years (1285-1298) were these. The king's justiciars were sitting at the Tower, where the mayor, sheriffs, and aldermen of the city had been summoned to attend. Owing to some informality in the summons, Gregory de Rokesley, the Mayor, declined to attend in his official capacity, but formally "deposed himself" at the Church of All Hallows Barking— the limit of the city jurisdiction— by handing the city's seal to Stephen Aswy or Eswy, a brother alderman. On entering the chamber where sat the justiciars, the mayor excused his unofficial appearance on the ground of insufficient notice. This was not what the justiciars had been accustomed to. On the contrary, the citizens had usually shown studied respect towards the justiciars whenever they came to the Tower for the purpose of holding pleas of the crown.

The customary procedure when the citizens waited on the justices at the Tower.

The rules of procedure on such occasions are fully set out in the city's "Liber Albus," 312 and they contain, curiously enough, a provision expressly made for cases where the full notice of forty days had not been given. In such an event the prescribed rule was to send some of their more discreet citizens to the king and his council to ask for the appointment of another day. Whether Rokesley had taken this step before resorting to the measures he did we are not told. It was also the custom on such occasions for the citizens to gather at Barking Church, clothed in their best apparel, and thence proceed in a body to the Tower. A deputation was appointed — selected members of the common council — who should also proceed to the Tower for the purpose of giving an official welcome to the justiciars on behalf of the citizens. It was not thought to be in any way derogatory to secure the goodwill of the king's justiciars by making ample presents. It had been done time out of mind. The sheriffs and aldermen were to attend with their respective sergeants and beadles, the benches at the Tower were to be examined beforehand and necessary repairs carried out, all shops were to be closed and no business transacted during the session. In a word, everything was to be done that could add to the dignity of the justiciars and the solemnity of the occasion. In contrast with all this, Rokesley's conduct was indeed strange, and leads us to suppose that his action was caused by some other and stronger reason than the mere omission to give the usual notice of the coming of the king's justiciars.

The city declared to be taken into the king's hand.

Be this as it may, the king's treasurer, who may possibly have been forewarned of what was about to take place, at once decided what course to take. He declared the city to be there and then taken into the king's hands, on the pretext that it was found to be without a mayor, and he summoned the citizens to appear on the morrow before the king at Westminster. When the morrow came, the citizens duly appeared, and about eighty of them were detained. Those who accompanied Rokesley to Barking Church on the previous day were confined in the Tower, but after a few days they were all set at liberty, with the exception of Stephen Aswy, who was removed in custody to Windsor. 313

For thirteen years the city governed by a *custos* instead of a mayor.

The king appointed Ralph de Sandwich *custos* or warden of the city, enjoining him at the same time to observe the liberties and customs of the citizens, and for the next thirteen years (1285-1298) the city continued to be governed by a warden in the person of Sandwich or of John le Breton, whilst the sheriffs were sometimes appointed by the Exchequer and sometimes chosen by the citizens. 314

Both the king and the city in straits for money, 1289-1290.

In May, 1286, the king went to Gascony, leaving the country in charge of his nephew, Edmund, Earl of Cornwall, and did not return until August, 1289. He was then in sore straits for money, as was so often the case with him, and was glad of a present of £1,000 which the citizens offered by way of courtesy (*curialitas*). The money was ordered (14th October) to be levied by poll, 315 but many of the inhabitants were so poor that they could only find pledges for future payment, and these pledges were afterwards sold for what they would fetch. 316 A twelve-month later (October, 1290) when Edward visited London, he was fain to be content with the smaller sum of 1,000 marks. 317

The king's difficulties increased by the expulsion of the Jews, 1290.

The expulsion of the Jews in 1290 increased Edward's difficulties, for on them he chiefly depended for replenishing his empty exchequer. Their expulsion was not so much his own wish as the wish of his subjects, who, being largely in debt to the Jews, regarded them as cruel tyrants. The nation soon discovered that it had made a mistake in thus getting rid of its creditors, for in the absence of the Jews, Edward was compelled to resort to the Lombard merchants. It may possibly have been owing to some monetary transactions between them that the king was solicitous of getting a life interest in the city's Small Beam made over to.a lady known as Jacobina la Lumbard. No particulars are known of this lady, but to judge from her name she probably came of a family of money-lenders, and if so, the king's action in writing from Berwick (28th June, 1291) to the warden and aldermen of the city—at a time when he was completely in the hands of the Italian goldsmiths and money-lenders—soliciting for her a more or less lucrative post is easily intelligible. 318 The king's request was refused, notwithstanding the city being at the time in charge of a *custos* of his own choice instead of a mayor elected by the citizens themselves. Such requests produced friction between the king and the city, and the former's financial relations with the foreign merchants were fraught with danger to himself and to his son. 319

Edward's domestic troubles of 1290.

Edward's anxiety was in the meanwhile increased by domestic troubles. In 1290 he suffered a bitter disappointment by the death of a Scottish princess who was affianced to his son, the Prince of Wales, and thus a much-cherished plan for establishing friendly relations between the two countries was frustrated. But this disappointment was quickly cast in the shade by the more severe affliction he suffered in the loss of his wife. In November Queen Eleanor died. Her corpse was brought from Lincoln to Westminster, and the bereaved husband ordered a memorial cross to be set up at each place where her body rested. One of these crosses was erected at the west end of Cheapside. After the Reformation the images with which the cross was ornamented, like the image of Becket set over the gate of the Mercers' Chapel, roused the anger of the iconoclast, who took delight in defacing them.

Seizure of treasure in monastries and churches, 1294.

Time only increased the king's pecuniary difficulties. In February, 1292, all freeholders of land of the annual value of £40 were ordered to receive knighthood, and in the following January the estates of defaulters were seized by the king's orders. 320 In June, 1294, war was declared against France. Money must be had. Every monastery and every church throughout England was ransacked for treasure, and the sum of £2,000, found in St. Paul's Church, was appropriated for the public service. 321 The dean was seized with a fit (*subita percussus passione*) and died in the king's presence. 322

The city furnishes ships and men for the defence of the coast 1295, 1296.

Instead of invading France, Edward found his own shores devastated by a French fleet, whilst at the same time his hands were full with fresh difficulties from Scotland and Wales. In the summer of 1295, the city furnished the king with three ships, the cost being defrayed by a tax of twopence in the pound charged on chattels and merchandise. John le Breton, then warden, advanced the sum of £40, which the aldermen and six men of each ward undertook to repay. 323 In the following year (1296) the city agreed, after some little hesitation, to furnish forty men with caparisoned horses, and fifty arbalesters for the defence of the south coast, under the king's son, Edward of Carnarvon. 324

The subjection of Scotland, 1296.

Edward again turned his attention to Scotland, and, having succeeded in reducing Balliol to submission, he carried off from Scone the stone which legend identifies with Jacob's pillow, and on which the Scottish kings had from time immemorial been crowned, 325 By Edward's order the stone was enclosed in a stately seat, and placed in Westminster Abbey, where it has since served as the coronation chair of English sovereigns.

The parliament of Bury St. Edmund's, 3rd Nov., 1296.

From Berwick Edward issued (26 Aug., 1296,) writs for a Parliament to meet at Bury St. Edmund's, in the following November. The constitution of this Parliament was the same as that which had met at Westminster in November of the previous year (1295) and which was intended to serve as a model parliament, a pattern for all future national assemblies. The city was represented by two aldermen, namely, Sir Stephen Aswy, or Eswy, who had been confined in Windsor Castle ten years before for his conduct towards the king's justiciars at the Tower, and Sir William de Hereford. 326 From this time forward down to the present day we have little difficulty in discovering from one source or another the names of the city's representatives in successive parliaments. Edward, of course, wanted money. The barons and knights increased their former grants; so also did the burgesses. The clergy, on the other hand, declared themselves unable to make any grant at all in the face of a papal prohibition, 327 and the king was at last driven to seize the lay fees of the clergy of the province of Canterbury. In the spring of the following year he proceeded to seize all the wool of the country, paying for it by tallies, and to levy a supply of provisions on the counties. The act was only justifiable on the plea of necessity, and led to measures being taken to prevent its repetition. 328

Edward's altercation with Roger Bigod, Feb., 1297.

It was an easier matter for Edward to raise money than to get the barons to accompany him abroad. To leave them behind was to risk the peace of the country. He therefore spared no efforts to persuade them to join in a projected expedition, and when persuasion failed tried threats. It was his desire that the barons should go to Gascony, whilst he took the command in Flanders. This was not at all to the taste of the barons, who declined to go abroad, except in the personal retinue of the king himself. "With you, O king," said Roger Bigod, "I will gladly go; as belongs to me by hereditary right, I will go in front of the host, before your face;" but without the king he positively declined to move. "By God, earl," cried the king, fairly roused by the obstinacy of his vassal, "you shall either go or hang;" to which the earl replied, with equal determination, "By the same token, O king, I will neither go nor hang." 329

Nothing daunted, the king issued writs (15 May) for a military levy of the whole kingdom for service abroad, to meet at London on the 7th July, a measure as unconstitutional as the seizure of wool and the levying of taxes without the assent of Parliament. On the day appointed, the barons, who had received a large accession of strength from the great vassals, appeared with their forces at St. Paul's; but instead of complying with the king's demands—or rather requests, for the king had altered his tone—they prepared a list of their grievances.

The "Confirmatio Cartarum," Oct. 1297.

With difficulty civil war was avoided, and in August Edward set sail for Flanders. No sooner was his back turned, than the barons and the Londoners made common cause in insisting upon a confirmation and amplification of their charters. 330 Prince Edward, the king's son, who had been appointed regent in his father's absence, granted all that was asked, and on the 10th October (1297), the *Confirmatio Cartarum*, as it was called, was issued in the king's name. 331 Thenceforth, no customs duties were to be exacted without the consent of parliament.

The mayoralty restored to the city, 11th April, 1298.

In view of the king's return to England in March (1298), the warden of the city, Sir John Breton, the aldermen, and a deputation from the wards met together and resolved that every inhabitant of the city, citizen and stranger, should pay to the king's collectors the sum of sixpence in the pound of all their goods up to £100. 332 In the following month Edward issued letters patent (11th April), restoring to the citizens their franchises and the right of again electing their mayor. 333 The choice of the citizens fell upon Henry le Waleys, who was duly admitted by the Barons of the Exchequer after presentation to the king. 334

Suppression of the Scottish rising under Wallace, 1298, 1304.

In the summer Edward marched to Scotland for the purpose of putting down the rising under Wallace. An account of the battle of Falkirk, fought on the 22nd July, was conveyed to the mayor, aldermen, and "barons" of London, by letter from Walter Langton, Bishop of Lichfield and Coventry, or, as he was then styled, Bishop of Chester, who wrote as an eye-witness, if not indeed as a partaker in that day's work. 335 It was the first battle of any consequence in which the English long-bow was brought into prominence. Edward's victory was complete. The enemy's loss was great, the number that perished, according to the bishop's information, being two hundred men-at-arms and twenty thousand foot soldiers. Edward was unable, however, to follow up his success for want of supplies, and so retreated. In 1304, he again marched northward, notwithstanding the defection of many nobles. He had previously resorted once more to the questionable practice of talliaging the city of London, 336 levying from the citizens the fifteenth penny of their moveable goods and the tenth penny of their rents. 337 The campaign was eminently successful. Sterling surrendered after a siege of two months, and Wallace himself shortly afterwards fell into his hands, having refused the terms of an amnesty which Edward had generously offered.

Wallace brought to London, 22 Aug., 1305.

He was carried to London, where a crowd of men and women flocked out to meet one, of whose gigantic stature and feats of strength they had heard so much. He was lodged in the house of William de Leyre, an alderman of the city, situate in the parish of All Hallows at the Hay or All Hallows the Great. Having been tried at Westminster and condemned to death on charges of treason, sacrilege and robbery, he was hanged, drawn, and quartered, and his head set up on London Bridge. 338

Knighthood conferred on John le Blound, the mayor, and others, May 1306.

No sooner was Wallace disposed of than another claimant to the Scottish crown appeared in the person of Bruce. Before Edward took the field against the new foe, he conferred knighthood upon his son and nearly three hundred others, including John le Blound the mayor. The number of knights within the small compass of the city was reckoned at that time to be not less than a thousand. 339 Knighthood, as we have seen, was one of the means Edward resorted to for raising money, and on this occasion the citizens of London are said to have made him a free gift of £2,000, in recognition of the honour bestowed on their mayor. 340

Death of the king, 7th July, 1307.

In the summer of 1307, Edward set out to execute the vow of vengeance against Bruce that he had made on the occasion of the knighthood of his son, but the hand of death was upon him, and before lie reached the Scottish border he died (7th July).

CHAPTER VI.

The accession of Edward II.

The new king's character, differing as it did so much from that of his father, was not one to commend itself to the citizens of London. With them he never became a favourite. The bold and determined character of Queen Isabel, the very antipodes of her husband, was more to their liking, and throughout the contests that ensued between them, the citizens steadily supported her cause. At her first appearance, as a bride, in the city, the streets were compared with the New Jerusalem, so rich were they in appearance; 341 whilst at the coronation ceremony, which took place a month later (25th February, 1308), she and her husband were escorted by the mayor and aldermen in their most gorgeous robes, quartered with the arms of England and France, and were served at the banquet as custom commanded. 342

The king's foreign favourites.

But even thus early in Edward of Carnarvon's reign the presence of foreigners—to whom the king was even more addicted than his father—was likely to prove a source of trouble; and it was necessary to make special proclamations forbidding the carrying of arms on the day of the coronation and enjoining respect for foreigners attending the ceremony. 343 The king's foreign favourites proved his ruin, and contributed in no small degree to the eventual defection of the city. They were for ever desiring some favour of the citizens. At one time it was Piers de Gavestone who wanted a post for his "valet"; 344 at another it was Hugh le Despenser who desired (and obtained) a lease of the Small Beam for a friend. 345 The friend only held the Beam for little more than six months, and then, at the urgent request of the queen herself, it was given to another. 346

The Ordainers and their work, 1308-1311.

The barons were especially irritated at being supplanted by the king's favourites, and in 1308 succeeded in getting Edward to send Gaveston out of England. In the following year, however, he was recalled, and the barons became so exasperated that in 1310, when the king summoned an assembly of bishops and barons, the latter appeared, contrary to orders, in full military array. The king could not do otherwise than submit to their dictation. Ordainers were appointed from among the barons for the purpose of drawing up ordinances for the government of the kingdom. These ordinances were promulgated in their complete form in 1311, when they received the sanction of a parliament assembled at the House of the Black Friars, in the month of August, and were afterwards publicly proclaimed in St. Paul's Churchyard, 347 special precautions being taken at the time to safeguard the gates of the city by night and day. 348 Gaveston was condemned to banishment for life.

The City's gift of 1,000 marks to assist the king against Scotland, March, 1311.

In the meantime, whilst the Ordainers were engaged on their work, Edward had put himself at the head of his army and marched against the Scots, who were rapidly gaining ground under Bruce. He remained on the border until July, 1311, trying every means to raise money. In March of that year the city sent him one thousand marks, by the hands of Roger le Palmere and William de Flete, the mayor, Richer de Refham, contributing no less than one hundred pounds of the whole sum. The money was despatched on horseback, tied up in baskets covered with matting and bound with cords, and the cost of every particular is set out in the city's records. 349

Richer de Refham, Mayor, 1310-1311.

Refham was a mayor of the popular type. He had already suffered deprivation of his aldermanry for some reason or another, but was reinstated in 1302. 350 No sooner was he chosen mayor than he caused a collection to be made of the ancient liberties and customs of the city, from the books and rolls preserved in the city's Chamber, and having assembled the aldermen and best men of the city, he caused them to be publicly read. This having been done, he next proceeded to ask the assembly if it was their will that these ancient customs and liberties, which had so often been infringed by the removal of mayors and sheriffs, should be for the future maintained. Their answer being given unanimously in the affirmative, he at once took steps to obtain the king's writ of confirmation, and caused them to be proclaimed throughout the city. He made a perambulation of the city and abated all nuisances and encroachments. He went further than this. For some time past the streets had been rendered unsafe to pass after dark by bands of rioters who at that day were known by the *sobriquet* of "roreres." A few years later, the same class went under the name of "riffleres." They were the precursors of the "Muns," the "Tityre Tus," the "Hectors," and the "Scourers,"—dynasties of tyrants, as Macaulay styles them, which domineered over the streets of London, soon after the Restoration, and at a later period were superseded by the "Nickers," the "Hawcubites," and the still more dreaded "Mohawks," of Queen Anne's reign. By whatever name they happened at the time to be known, their practice was the same, viz.:— assault and robbery of peaceful citizens whose business or pleasure carried them abroad after sundown.

During Refham's mayoralty, a raid was made on all common nightwalkers, "bruisers" (*pugnatores*), common "roreres," *wagabunds* and others, and many were committed to prison, to the great relief of the more peaceably disposed. 351

His strictness and impartiality were such as to raise up enemies, and an excuse was found for removing him not only from the office of mayor, but once again from his aldermanry. 352 On this point, however, the city archives are altogether silent, they only record the appointment of his successor to the mayoralty chair at the usual time and in the usual manner.

The fall of Gaveston.

In January, 1312, the king returned to the north, and as soon as he had arrived at York ignored the ordinance touching Gaveston, and instead of sending his favourite into exile, received him into favour and restored his forfeited estates. Foreseeing the storm that he would have to meet from the barons, the king wrote from Knaresborough (9th Jan.) to Refham's successor, John de Gisors, enjoining him to put the city into a state of defence, and not allow armed men to enter on any pretext whatever. 353 On the 21st he wrote again, not only to the mayor, but to nineteen leading men of the city, exhorting them to hold the city for him. 354 Other letters followed in quick succession—on the 24th and 31st January and the 8th February—all couched in similar terms. 355 When, however, he saw how hopeless his case was, Edward sent word to the mayor and sheriffs that the barons might be admitted provided the city was still held for the king. Accordingly the barons were admitted without bloodshed, and held consultation at St. Paul's as to what was best to be done. 356 Gaveston's days were numbered. On the 12th June he was forced to surrender unconditionally to the Earl of Warwick, and that day week was beheaded without the semblance of a trial. 357

The influence he had exercised over the king had been remarkable from their youth. The son of a Gascon knight, he had been brought up with Edward as his foster brother and playfellow, and in course of time the strong will of the favourite gained a complete mastery over the weaker will of the prince. But his arrogant behaviour soon raised such a storm among the nobles at Court that he was forced to leave England. When Edward succeeded to the throne, one of his first acts was to recall Gaveston, to whom he gave his own niece in marriage, after having bestowed upon him the Earldom of Cornwall. The king seemed never tired of heaping wealth upon his friend. Among other things, he bestowed upon his favourite (28th Aug., 1309) the sum of 100 shillings payable out of the rent of £50 due from the citizens of London for Oueenhithe, to be held by him, his wife, and the heirs of their bodies. 358

Both of them had friends and enemies in common. As Prince of Wales, Edward had made an attempt to encroach upon some woods belonging to Walter Langton, Bishop of Chester. This caused a breach between father and son, and the prince was banished from Court for a whole half-year. Gaveston also bore the same bishop a grudge, for it was owing in a great measure to Langton's influence as treasurer to Edward I that he was in the first instance forced into exile. When the prince succeeded his father, there came a day of retribution for the bishop; his property was handed over to Gaveston, and he himself carried prisoner from castle to castle by the now all powerful favourite. A proclamation was also issued at the instance of Gaveston, inviting complaints against the bishop. 359

Parliament at London. August, 1312.

Edward had purposed holding a parliament at Lincoln towards the end of July, 1312, but the turn that affairs had taken induced him to change his mind, and he summoned it to meet at Westminster. 360 It was important that he should secure the city, if possible, in his favour. In this he was successful; so that when the barons appeared to threaten London, having arrived with a large force at Ware, they found the city's gates strongly guarded. 361

The birth of a prince, 13 Nov., 1312.

In November (1312), the queen gave birth to a son, who afterwards ascended the throne as Edward III. Isabel herself informed the citizens of the auspicious event by letter sent by the hands of John de Falaise, her "taillur." 362 The news had already reached the city, however, before the queen's own messenger arrived, and he signified his disappointment at being forestalled by declining to accept a sum of £10 and a silver cup of 32 ozs., which the city offered him by way of gratuity, as being inadequate to his deserts. As nothing further is recorded of the matter, it is probable that the offended tailor had reason to repent of his folly. For more than a week the city was given up to merry-making, in honour of the birth of an heir to the crown. The conduits ran with wine; a solemn mass was sung at St. Paul's, and the mayor and aldermen rode in state to Westminster, accompanied by members of the fraternities of drapers, mercers, and vintners of London, in their respective liveries, to make offering, returning to dine at the Guildhall, which was hung with tapestry as befitted the occasion.

The question of the king's rights to talliage the city, 1312-1314.

After the death of Gaveston, his old enemy Walter Langton again found favour and resumed his office as treasurer. The city had little reason to be gratified at his return to power; for it was by his advice that the king in December of this year (1312), issued orders for a talliage, which the great towns, and especially London, objected to pay. Early in the following January (1313), the mayor and aldermen were summoned to attend the royal council, sitting at the house of the White Friars. The question was there put to them—would they make fine for the talliage, or be assessed by poll on their rents and chattels? Before making answer, the mayor and aldermen desired to consult the commons of the city. An adjournment accordingly took place for that purpose. When next the mayor and aldermen appeared before the council, they resisted the talliage on the following grounds: 363—In the first place, because, although the king might talliage cities and boroughs that were of his demesne, he could not, as they understood, talliage the City of London, which enjoyed exemption from such an imposition by charter. In the next place, there were prelates and barons, besides citizens, who enjoyed rents and tenements in the city, and their consent would first have to be obtained before the municipal authorities could levy such a tax. Thirdly, the citizens held the city by grant of former kings, at a fee ferm for all services payable into the exchequer, and on that account ought not to be talliaged. Under these circumstances the council was asked to delay the talliage until Parliament should meet.

This request the king and council expressed themselves as ready to comply with on condition that the city made an immediate advance of 2,000 marks. The city refused, and the king's assessors appeared at the Guildhall, and read their commission. They were on the point of commencing work, when the city obtained a respite until the meeting of Parliament by a loan of £1,000. More than eighteen months elapsed, and at last a Parliament was summoned to meet at York (Sept. 1314); but the country was in such a disturbed state, owing to the renewal of the war with Scotland, that the talliage question was not discussed. Nevertheless the king's officers appeared again in the city to make an assessment, and again they were bought off by another loan of £400. The king took the money and broke his word, and the record of pledges taken from citizens for "arrears of divers talliages and not redeemed," is significant of the hardship inflicted by this illegal exaction on a large number of inhabitants of the city. 364

The renewal of the war with Scotland, 1314.

Out of this sum of £400, nearly one-half (£178 3s. 4d.), was allowed the city for the purpose of furnishing the king with a contingent of 120 arbalesters, fully equipped for the defence of Berwick. Edward had been defeated by the Scots at Bannockburn (24 June, 1314), and Berwick was threatened. On the 21st November, Edward wrote from Northampton, asking for 300 arbalesters if the city could provide so many; but the city could do no more than furnish him with 120. 365 The fall of Berwick was only postponed. In 1318 the great border fortress against Scotland was captured by Bruce. Edward was forced soon afterwards to come to terms with the Earl of Lancaster and the barons with whom he had so long been in avowed antagonism, and a general pacification ensued, which received the sanction of Parliament sitting at York in November. 366 On the 4th December, the king sent home the foot soldiers which the city had furnished, with a letter of thanks for the aid they had afforded him. They were immediately paid off and disbanded. 367

Dissension in the city, 1318-1319.

It was not long before the king and Lancaster were preparing to join forces for the recovery of Berwick. In the meantime, the Barons of the Exchequer appeared at the Guildhall (25th February, 1319), and summoned the mayor, sheriffs and aldermen to answer for certain trespasses. Several holders of office, and among them Edmund le Lorimer, Gaoler of Newgate, for whom Hugh le Despenser had solicited the Small Beam, were deposed: a proceeding which gave rise to much bickering between mayor, aldermen and commons. Disputes, moreover, had arisen in the city touching the election and removal of the mayor, sheriffs and aldermen of the city, which required some pressure from the Earl Marshal and other of the king's ministers, sitting in the Chapter-house of St. Paul's, before peace could be restored. 368

Articles for the better government of the city confirmed by the king, 8th June, 1319.

According to the writer of the French Chronicle, to which reference has frequently been made, 369 the dissension in the city was mainly attributable to John de Wengrave, the mayor. The citizens had lately been busy drawing up certain "points" for a new charter. Wengrave, who was at the time, or until quite recently, the city's Recorder, had contrived, in 1318, to force himself into the mayoralty having served as mayor the two years preceding—"against the will of the commons." He had shown no little opposition to the "points" of the proposed charter, possibly because one of the points precluded the mayor, for the time being, from drawing or hearing pleas, saving only "those pleas which, as mayor, he ought to hear, according to the custom of the city." 370 If this received the king's approval, Wengrave's occupation as Recorder, at least so long as he was mayor, was gone. However this may be, the mayor's opposition was rendered futile, and the articles were confirmed by the king's letters patent.

371 Their main feature has already been alluded to; thenceforth the direct way to the civic franchise was to be through membership of one of the civic guilds. A foreigner or stranger, not a member of a guild, could only obtain it by appealing to the full body of citizens before admission through the Court of Husting. Conscious of their newly acquired importance, the guilds began to array themselves in liveries, and "a good time was about to begin." 372 Edward did not give his assent to these articles without receiving a *quid pro quo*. The citizens were mulcted in a sum of £1,000 before the king's seal was set to the letters patent. 373 They did not mind this so much as they did the annoyance caused by the king's justiciars eighteen months later.

The Iter at the Tower of 1321.

Early in 1321 commenced a memorable Iter at the Tower which lasted twenty-four weeks and three days. No such Iter had been held before, although the last Iter held in 1275 had been a remarkable one for the courageous conduct of Gregory de Rokesle, the mayor. This was to surpass every other session of Pleas of the Crown in its powers of inquisition, and was destined to draw off many a would-be loyal citizen from the king's side. Its professed object was to examine into unlawful "colligations, confederations, and conventions by oaths," which were known (or supposed) to have been formed in the city. 374 The following particulars of its proceedings are gathered from an account preserved in the city's records and supervised, if not compiled, by Andrew Horn, the city's Chamberlain, an able lawyer who was employed as Counsel for the city during at least a portion of the Iter. 375 The annoyance caused by this Iter, the general stoppage of trade and commerce, the hindrance of municipal business, is realised when we consider that for six months not only the mayor, sheriffs and aldermen for the time being, but everyone who had filled any office in the city since the holding of the last Iter—a period of nearly half a century— as well as twelve representatives from each ward, were called upon to be in constant attendance. All charters were to be produced, and persons who had grievances of any kind were invited to appear. Great commotion prevailed among the citizens upon receiving the king's writ, and they at once addressed themselves to examining the procedure followed at former Iters. It is probable, as Mr. Riley suggests, that for this purpose they had resort to the "Ordinances of the Iter" already mentioned as set out in the city's Liber Albus. 376 When the dreaded day arrived and the justiciars had taken their seat at the Tower, the mayor and aldermen, who, according to custom, as already seen in Rokesley's day, were assembled at the church of All Hallows Barking, sent a deputation to welcome them, and to make a formal request for a safe conduct to the citizens on entering the Tower. This favour being granted, the king's commission was read.

Complaint of negligence of duty by the sheriffs.

The opening of the Iter did not augur well for the city. Fault was found, at the outset, by Geoffrey le Scrop, the king's sergeant-pleader, because the sheriffs had not attended so promptly as they should have done. The excuse that they had only acted according to custom in waiting for the grant of a safe conduct was held unsatisfactory, and nothing would please him but that the city should be at once taken into the king's hand. 377

The city claims to record its custom by mouth of the Recorder.

Again, when the citizens claimed to record their liberties and customs by word of mouth without being compelled to reduce them into writing, as the justices had ordered, the only reply they got was that they did so at their own peril. 378 Three days were consumed in preliminary discussion of points of etiquette and questions of minor importance.

the 4th day of the Iter.

On the fourth day the mayor and citizens put in their claim of liberties, which they supported by various charters. 379 The justiciars desired answers on three points, which were duly made, 380 and matters seemed to be getting forward when there arrived orders from the king that the justiciars should enquire as to the ancient right of the aldermen to record their liberties orally in the king's courts. Having heard what the citizens had to say on this point, the justiciars were instructed to withhold their judgment; and this and other questions touching the liberties of the city were to be postponed for future determination. 381

The 9th day of the Iter.

On the ninth day of the Iter, a long schedule, containing over 100 articles upon which the Crown desired information, was delivered to each ward of the city. 382 Days and weeks were consumed in considering various presentments, besides private suits and pleas of the Crown. Suits were determined in the Great Hall of the Tower facing the Thames, whilst pleas of the Crown were heard in the Lesser Hall, beneath the eastern tower. The justiciars occasionally protracted their sittings till dusk, much to the disgust of the citizens, whose business was necessarily at a stand-still, and as yet no indictments had been made. 383 These were to come.

Indictment against a late mayor.

On the thirty-fourth day of the Iter, John de Gisors was indicted for having during his mayoralty (1311-1313), admitted a felon to the freedom of the city, and fraudulently altered the date of his admission. The question of criminality turned upon this date. Had the felony been committed before or after admission? The accused declared in his defence that admission to the freedom had taken place before the felony; a jury, however, came to the opposite conclusion, and not only found that admission had taken place after an indictment for the felony, but that the mayor at the time was aware of the indictment. The judges therefore ordered Gisors into custody. He was soon afterwards released on bail, but not without paying a fine of 100 marks. 384

The city taken into the king's hand.

A similar indictment against his son Anketin, as having participated in his father's offence, failed. Within a week of Gisors's indictment, the mayor for the time being, Nicholas de Farndon, was deposed, and the city placed in the hands of Sir Robert de Kendale, the king's commissioner. 385

Adjournment of the Iter over Easter.

For nine weeks in succession the citizens had suffered from the inconveniences of the Iter, when a brief adjournment over Easter took place. In the meantime, an assay was held at the Guildhall of the new weights and measures which Walter Stapleton, Bishop of Exeter, had, in his capacity as the king's treasurer, caused to be issued throughout the country. One result of the trial was that whilst the city's weight of eight marks was discovered to be slightly deficient, the city's bushel was found to be more true than the king's.

Sudden change in the attitude of the judges after Easter.

After Easter the sittings of the justiciars were resumed. A great change, however, had come over them during the recess. They no longer behaved "like lions eager for their prey; on the contrary, they had become very lambs." 386 The reason for this sudden change, we are told, was the insurrection in Wales, under the Earl of Hereford, the king's brother-in-law.

Andrew Horn appears as counsel for the City.

The chief questions discussed before the justices were the right of the weavers of London to hold their guild, and the right of the fishmongers of Fish-wharf to sell their fish at their wharf by retail instead of on their vessels or at the city markets. The claim of the fishmongers was opposed by Andrew Horn, himself a fishmonger by trade, as well as an eminent lawyer, who acted on this occasion as leading counsel for the City.

The indictment brought against the Constable of the Tower.

When Whitsuntide was approaching, an indictment was brought by the city wards against their old enemy John de Crombwelle, the Constable of the Tower. He had already made himself obnoxious to the citizens by attempting to enclose a portion of the city's lands; 387 and now he was accused of seizing a small vessel laden with tiles, and converting the same to his own use, and further, with taking bribes for allowing unauthorised "kidels" to remain in the Thames. The judges, having heard what he had to say in defence, postponed the further hearing until after Trinity Sunday (14th June). In the meantime, the citizens had the gratification of seeing the constable removed from office, for allowing the Tower to fall into such a dilapidated state, that the rain came in upon the queen's bed, while giving birth to a daughter, afterwards known as Joanna of the Tower, 388 and destined to become the wife of David the Second, King of Scotland.

The Iter brought to a sudden termination. 4 July, 1321.

On the judges resuming their sittings after Trinity Sunday, they sat no longer in the Great Hall or the Lesser Hall, "as well by reason of the queen being in childbed there, as already mentioned, as of the fortifying of the Tower, through fear of the Earl of Hereford and his accomplices, who were in insurrection on every side." Temporary buildings had to be found for them. A fortnight later there were signs of the Iter being brought to an abrupt termination, the citizens having represented that they could not possibly keep proper watch and ward owing to disturbances consequent to the holding of the Iter; 389 and within a week, viz., on 4th July, it was actually closed.

The mayoralty restored to the city.

It was the bursting of the storm which had long been gathering against the king's new favourites, the Despensers, father and son, that caused the sudden termination of the Iter, and it was the fear lest he should lose the support of the city against Lancaster and his allies that caused the king quickly to restore to the citizens their Mayor. Hamo de Chigwell took the place of the deposed Farndon. 390

The City promises to support the king, July, 1321.

Within a few hours of the closing of the Iter Chigwell and the aldermen were summoned to Westminster to say whether they would be willing to support the king and to preserve the city of London to his use in his contest with the barons. Edward and his council received for answer that the mayor and his brethren "were unwilling to refuse the safe keeping of the city," but would keep it for the king and his heirs. They were thereupon enjoined to prepare a scheme for its defence for submission to the king's council, and this was accordingly done. 391

Letter from the Earl of Hereford and the City's reply.

The city was, however, wavering in its support; Chigwell did his best to hold the balance between king and baron, and to hold a middle course, avoiding offence as far as was possible to one side and the other. After the lapse of a few days, a letter came from the Earl of Hereford, addressed to the mayor, sheriffs, aldermen and commonalty of the city, asking for an interview. It was then decided, after due deliberation in the Court of Husting, to ask Edward's advice on the matter before returning an answer. At first the king was disinclined to allow the interview, but when the lords approached nearer London, and resistance would have been hopeless, he gave way, and a deputation was appointed to meet the lords at the Earl of Lancaster's house in Holborn. To them the earl explained the aim and object of himself and his confederates. They were desirous of nothing so much as the good of the realm and the overthrow of the Despensers, father and son, who led the king astray and had caused the Iter to be held at the Tower in order to injure the city. Having listened to the earl's statement, the recorder, on behalf of the deputation, asked for a few days' delay in order to consult with the mayor and commonalty. The matter was laid before an assembly which comprised representatives from each ward (30th July), and again it was resolved to ask the king's advice. At length a reply was sent to the lords to the effect that the citizens would neither aid the Despensers nor oppose the lords, but the city would in the meantime be strongly guarded for the preservation of order. With this the lords were satisfied. 392

Terms arranged between the king and the lords, 14 August.

A fortnight later (14th August) the king, moved by the intercession of the Earl of Pembroke, the bishops, and his queen, yielded to the lords, and an agreement between them was reduced to writing and publicly read in Westminster Hall. 393

Chigwell continued in the mayoralty.

Chigwell's conduct throughout met with so much favour from the citizens as well as from the king that when the latter issued letters patent 394 granting a free election of a mayor in October of this year, it was decided to continue Chigwell in office without a fresh election. 395

The queen insulted by Lady Badlesmere.

Such popularity as the king had for a time achieved by his concession to the demands of the lords, however unwillingly made, was enhanced by another circumstance. An insult had been offered to the queen by Lady Badlesmere, who had refused to admit her into her castle at Ledes, co. Kent, when on her way to Canterbury. The queen was naturally indignant, and the unexpected energy displayed by Edward in avenging the insult gave fresh strength to his cause. With the assistance of a contingent sent by the citizens of London, the king beseiged the castle, and, having taken it, hanged the governor. 396 Sir Bartholomew de Badlesmere, the owner of the castle, was afterwards taken and put to death at Canterbury.

Attempt to issue a "charter of service."

Elated with his success, the king forthwith proceeded to issue "a charter of service" — *i.e.*, a charter binding the citizens to serve him in future wars — which he wished the good people of London to have sealed, "but the people of the city would not accede to it for all that the king could do." 397 In the place of this charter, however, he was induced to grant the citizens one of a diametrically opposite nature, whereby it was provided that the aids granted by the citizens upon this occasion should not be prejudicial to the mayor and citizens, nor be looked upon as establishing a precedent. 398

The Londoners at Boroughbridge, 16 March, 1322.

Having thus secured an acknowledgment of their rights, the citizens were ready enough to waive them when occasion required. The battle of Boroughbridge (16 March, 1322) was won for the king by the aid of Londoners. We know, at least, that when he started from London at the close of 1321 he was accompanied by five hundred men at arms from the city, and one hundred and twenty more were sent after him on the 3rd March. 399

The character of the citizen soldier in the field.

The Londoners were by no means to be despised in the field. Froissart describes them as being very dangerous when once their blood was up, and slaughter on the battle field only gave them fresh courage. 400 A late writer 401 who was pleased to describe the city's military force as "an army of drapers' apprentices and journeymen tailors, with common councilmen for captains and aldermen for colonels," gave it credit, nevertheless, for natural courage, which, combined with befitting equipment and martial discipline, rendered the force a valuable ally and a formidable enemy.

Defeat and execution of the Earl of Lancaster, March, 1322.

The Earl of Lancaster, who was made prisoner at Boroughbridge, and afterwards executed before his own castle at Pomfret, had come to be a great favourite with the Londoners, in whose eyes he appeared as the champion of the oppressed against the strong. His memory was long cherished in the city, and miracles were believed to have taken place — the crooked made straight, the blind receiving sight and the deaf hearing — before the tablet he had set up in St. Paul's commemorative of the king's submission to the Ordinances. Edward ordered the removal of the tablet, but it was again set up as soon as all power had passed from his hands. 402

Edward again despotic, 1322-1323.

Edward, again a free ruler, lost no time in revoking these Ordinances. The elder Despenser he raised to the earldom of Winchester. 403 This was in May, 1322; a year later (April, 1323), he deposed Chigwell, who had again been re-elected to the mayoralty in the previous October, and put in his place Nicholas de Farndon, 404 thus reversing the order of things in 1321, when Farndon had been deposed and his place taken by Chigwell.

The deposed mayor, however, was ordered to keep close attendance on the Court, as were also three other London citizens, viz.: Hamo Godchep, Edmund Lambyn, and Roger le Palmere; and in the following November he recovered his position, 405 and held it for the rest of Edward's reign.

Escape of Roger Mortimer from the Tower. Aug. 1323.

The king's triumph was destined to be short-lived. In August, 1323, Roger Mortimer, a favourite of the queen, effected his escape from the Tower, where he had lain prisoner since January, 1322. The divided feeling of the citizens which had been more or less apparent since the year of the great Iter, now began to assert itself. Mortimer's escape had taken place with the connivance, if not active assistance, of a leading citizen, Richard de Betoyne, and he took sanctuary on the property of another leading citizen, John Gisors. 406 In November the citizens thought fit to close their gates, to prevent surprise. 407

A feud between the Weavers and the Goldsmiths, 1324.

In the following year (1324), a quarrel broke out between two of the city guilds, the weavers and the goldsmiths. Fights took place in the streets and lives were lost. 408 How far, if at all, such a quarrel had any political significance it is difficult to say, but it is not unlikely, at a time when the guilds were winning their way to chartered rights, that occasionally their members took sides in the political struggle that was then being carried on.

Departure of the queen for France, 9 March, 1324.

Edward, in the meanwhile, was threatened with war by France, unless he consented to cross the sea and do homage to the French king for the possessions he held in that country. This the Despensers dared not allow him to do. A compromise was therefore effected. Queen Isabel, who was not sorry for an opportunity of quitting the side of a husband who had seized all her property, removed her household, and put her on board wages at twenty shillings a day, 409 undertook, with the king's assent, to revisit her home and to bring about a settlement. Accordingly, on the 9th March, 410 1324, she crossed over to France, where she was afterwards joined by Mortimer and her son.

Her return to England, 24 September, 1326.

Once on the continent, the queen threw off the mask, and immediately began to concert measures against the king and the Despensers. By negotiating a marriage for her son with the daughter of the Count of Hainault, she contrived to raise supporters in England, whilst by her affected humility and sorrow, displayed by wearing simple apparel as one that mourned for her husband, she won the sympathy of all who beheld her. 411 The king, on the other hand, publicly forbade any one holding correspondence with her, caused provisions to be laid up in the Tower in case of emergency, and prepared a fleet to prevent her landing.

The City lost to Edward.

It was all in vain. The majority of the citizens had made up their mind to give him no more support. On the 24th September, 1326, Isabel, in spite of all precautions, effected a landing near Harwich; and Edward, as soon as he was made aware of her arrival in England, took fright and left London for the west. The queen, who was accompanied by her son and her "gentle Mortimer," gave out that she came as an avenger of Earl Thomas, whose memory was yet green in the minds of the citizens, and as the enemy of the Despensers. 412 Adherents quickly came in from all sides, and with these she leisurely (*quasi peregrinando*) followed up the king. 413

In the meantime a letter had been despatched to the city in her name and that of her son, desiring its assistance in destroying "the enemies of the land." To this letter, we are told, no answer was sent "through fear of the king." Another letter was therefore sent to the same effect, in which Hugh Despenser was especially named as one to be destroyed, and an immediate answer was requested. 414 This letter was affixed to the cross in Cheapside and copies circulated through the city.

On the 15th October, the city broke out into open rebellion. The mayor and other leading men had gone to the house of the Blackfriars to meet the Bishops of London and Exeter. The mob, now fairly roused by the queen's second letter, hurried thither and forced them to return to the Guildhall, the timid Chigwell "crying mercy with clasped hands," and promising to grant all they required. A proclamation was made shortly afterwards to the effect that "the enemies to the king and the queen and their son" should depart the city. 415

The murder of Bishop Stapleton, 15 October, 1326.

One unfortunate man, John le Marchall, suspected of being employed by Hugh Despenser as a spy, was seized and incontinently beheaded in Cheapside. The mob, having tasted blood, hastened to sack the house of Walter Stapleton, Bishop of Exeter, who as Edward's treasurer, had confiscated the queen's property. It so happened, that the bishop himself, attended by two esquires, was riding towards the city intending to have his midday meal at his house in Old Dean's Lane (now Warwick Lane), before proceeding to the Tower. Hearing cries of "Traitor!" he guessed that something was wrong, and made for sanctuary in St. Paul's. He was caught, however, just as he was about to enter the north door, dragged from his horse, carried to Chepe, and there put to death in the same way as John le Marchall had been executed a short hour before. 416

The bishop's two attendant esquires also perished at the hands of the mob. Their bodies were allowed to lie stark naked all that day in the middle of Chepe. The head of the bishop was sent to the queen at Gloucester, 417 but his corpse was reverently carried into St. Paul's after vespers by the canons and vicars of the cathedral. It was not allowed, however, to remain there long; for hearing that the bishop had died under sentence of excommunication, the authorities caused it to be removed to the church of St. Clement Danes, near which stood the bishop's new manor house of which we are reminded at the present day by Exeter Hall. The parish church was in the gift of the Bishop of Exeter for the time being, and John Mugg, then rector, owed his preferment to Stapleton. He was, therefore, guilty of gross ingratitude when he refused to take in the corpse of his patron, or to allow it the rites of burial. Certain poor women had more compassion; they at least cast a piece of old cloth over the corpse for decency's sake and buried it out of sight, although without any attempt to make a grave and "without any office of priest or clerk." Thus, it remained till the following month of February, when it was disinterred and taken to Exeter. The treatment of Bishop Stapleton caused other prelates to look to themselves, and many of them, including the primate himself, began to make overtures of submission to Queen Isabel.

After the Bishop's murder there was no pretence of government in the city. The mob did exactly as they liked. They sacked the houses of Baldock, the Chancellor, and carried off the treasure he had laid up in St. Paul's. The property of the Earl of Arundel, recently executed at Hereford, which lay in the Priory of Holy Trinity, Aldgate, shared the same fate. The banking house of the Bardi, containing the wealth accumulated by the younger Despenser, was sacked under cover of night. The Tower was entered, the prisoners set free, and new officers appointed. 418 All this was done in the face of a proclamation, calling upon the citizens to sink their differences and to settle their disputes by lawful means. 419

The queen confirms to the citizens their right to elect their mayor, Nov., 1326.

Betoyne elected mayor.

When the Feast of St. Simon and Jude again came round, and Chigwell's term of office expired by efflux of time, no election of a successor took place, but on the 15th November, the Bishop of Winchester paid a visit to the Guildhall, where, after receiving the freedom of the city, and swearing "to live and die with them in the cause, and to maintain the franchise," he presented a letter from the queen, permitting the citizens freely to elect their mayor as in the days before the Iter of 1321, for since that time no mayor had been elected, save only by the king's favour. 420 They at once elected Richard de Betoyne, whom the queen had that day appointed Warden of the Tower, conjointly with John de Gisors. 421 Thus were these two aldermen recompensed for the assistance they had rendered Mortimer in his escape from the Tower.

Public declaration in favour of the queen and the City's rights. 13 Jan., 1327.

On the 13th January, 1327—exactly one week before the king met his wretched end in Berkeley Castle—Mortimer came to the Guildhall with a large company including the Archbishop of Canterbury and several bishops, and one and all made oath to maintain the cause of the queen and of her son, and to preserve the liberties of the City of London. This was solemnly done in the presence of the mayor, the chamberlain, Andrew Horn, and a vast concourse of citizens. The Archbishop, who had offended many of the citizens by annulling the decree of exile passed against the Despensers in 1321, now sought their favour by the public offer of a gift to the commonalty of 50 tuns of wine. 422

CHAPTER VII.

Edward's charter to the city, 6 March, 1327.

Edward III was only fourteen years of age when he succeeded to the throne. For the first three years of his reign the government of the country was practically in the hands of Mortimer, his mother's paramour; and it was no doubt by his advice and that of the queen-mother that the young king rewarded the citizens of London, who had shown him so much favour, by granting them not only a general pardon 423 for offences committed since he set foot in England in September, 1326, but also a charter confirming and enlarging their ancient liberties. 424

This latter charter, which has been held to be of the force of an Act of Parliament, 425 established (among other things) the ferm of the Sheriffwick of London and Middlesex at the original sum of £300 per annum, instead of the increased rental of £400 which had been paid since 1270; 426 it appointed the mayor one of the justices at the gaol delivery of Newgate, as well as the king's escheator of felon's goods within the city; it gave the citizens the right of devising real estate within the city; it restored to them all the privileges they had enjoyed before the memorable Iter of the last reign; and granted to them a monopoly of markets within a circuit of seven miles of the city. 427 These two charters—the charter of pardon and the charter of liberties—together with another charter 428 releasing the citizens from all debts due to the late king, were publicly read and explained in English to the citizens assembled at the Guildhall by Andrew Horn, the Chamberlain, on the 9th March. 429

The City sends a contingent to assist the king against the Scots.

Scarcely was he knighted and crowned king before necessity compelled him to take the field against the Scots. The Londoners were, as usual, called upon to supply a contingent towards the forces which had been ordered to assemble at Newcastle-upon-Tyne. 430 They responded to the king's appeal by sending 100 horsemen fully equipped, each one supplied with the sum of 100 shillings at least for expenses, and a further contingent of 100 foot-men. They made their rendezvous at West Smithfield, whence they proceeded to "la Barnette." 431

This act not to be made a precedent.

Whilst furnishing this aid to the king the citizens were anxious that their liberality should not be misconstrued, or tend to establish a precedent in derogation of their chartered privileges. Their fears on this score were set at rest by the receipt of letters patent from the king declaring that their proceedings on this occasion should not be to their prejudice. 432

The City's representatives at the Parliament at Lincoln, Sept., 1327.

A parliament held in September, at Lincoln, in which the citizens were represented by Benedict de Fulsham and Robert de Kelseye, 433 granted the king an aid of a twentieth to defray expenses; and Hamo de Chigwell, among others, was appointed by the king to collect the tax from the citizens. 434

Petition against removing the courts and the exchequer to York.

The City's representatives were accompanied to Lincoln by the mayor, Richard de Betoyne, who was the bearer of letters under the seal of the commonalty addressed to the king, the queen, and members of the king's council praying that the courts of King's Bench and Exchequer might not be removed from Westminster to York. 435 The removal was inconvenient to the city merchants, whatever advantage might accrue to those dwelling in the north of England. Negotiations between the City and the king on this subject were protracted for some weeks; the king at length promising that the courts should return to Westminster as soon as the country was in a more settled state. 436

Peace with Scotland, 1328.

The campaign against the Scots brought little credit to either side, and terminated in a treaty, the terms of which were for the most part arranged by Mortimer and the queen-mother. One of the articles of peace stipulated for the surrender of all proofs of the subjection of Scotland; and accordingly the abbot of Westminster received orders to deliver up the stone of Scone to the Sheriffs of London for transmission to Isabel, who was in the north. 437 This the abbot refused to do—"for reasons touching God and the church,"—without further instructions from the king and his council. 438

When negotiations were opened in 1363 for the union of the kingdoms of England and Scotland, it was proposed that Edward should be crowned king at Scone on the royal seat (*siége roial*) which he should cause to be returned from England. These negotiations, however, fell through, and the stone remains in Westminster Abbey to this day. 439

The treaty which had been arranged at Edinburgh (17 March, 1328), was afterwards confirmed by a Parliament held at Northampton, in which the city was represented by Richard de Betoyne and Robert de Kelseye. 440

The revolt of the Earl of Lancaster, Oct., 1328.

When the terms of this treaty of Northampton (as it was called) came to be fully understood, the nation began to realise the measure of disgrace which they involved, and Mortimer and the queen became the objects of bitter hatred. Henry, Earl of Lancaster, the king's nominal guardian, had grown weary of his false position, and of serving only as Mortimer's tool. Determined to throw off the yoke, he refused to attend a parliament which met at Salisbury in October (1328), 441 unless certain changes in the government and in the king's household were first made. In the meantime, Bishop Stratford of Winchester and Thomas, Lord Wake, two of his supporters, had paid a visit to the city and had endeavoured to rouse the citizens to action. The king, hearing of this, wrote to the municipal authorities for an explanation. They frankly acknowledged, in reply, that the bishop had been in the city for the purpose of discussing the ill state of affairs, and themselves expressed a hope, amid vows of the utmost loyalty, that the king would redress the grievances under which the nation suffered. 442

The earl's letter to the City, 5 Nov., 1328.

Instead of attending the parliament at Salisbury, the earl marched in full force to Winchester. On the 5th November he wrote to the citizens from Hungerford, to the effect that he had made known to parliament his honourable intentions, but had received no reply; that the parliament had been adjourned to London; that he had been informed of certain matters about which he could not write, but which the bearer would communicate to them; and he concluded with assuring them that he desired nothing so much as the king's honour and the welfare of the kingdom, and declaring his implicit confidence in their loyalty. 443

The election of John de Grantham, mayor, in place of Chigwell.

The mayor of the city at this time was John de Grantham. His election had taken place but recently, and was the result of a compromise. Chigwell, who had again been chosen mayor at the expiration of Betoyne's year of office in 1327, was a decided favourite with the citizens, notwithstanding a certain want of firmness of character, and he was again put up as a candidate for the mayoralty in October, 1328. He had enemies, of course. Towards the close of his last mayoralty he was ill-advised enough to sit in judgment upon a brother alderman on a charge of having abused him two years previously. During the troublous times of 1326, John de Cotun, alderman of Walbrook ward, was alleged to have described Chigwell, who was then mayor, as "the vilest worm that had been in the city for twenty years," adding that the city would know no peace so long as Chigwell was alive, and that it would be a blessing if he lost his head. 444 After some hard swearing on both sides, leading to the discovery of bad blood existing between the informer and the alderman, the charge was dismissed.

At the outset it appeared that Chigwell's reelection was assured; but the city as well as the country was in a disturbed state, and political reasons may have led to an endeavour to force another candidate in the person of Benedict de Fulsham over his head. Be that as it may, it is certain that when Chigwell's name was proposed to the assembled citizens at the Guildhall, the cry was raised of "Fulsham! Fulsham!" So high did party spirit run, that the election had to be postponed, and eventually it was thought best that both candidates should be withdrawn. This having been done, the choice of the electors fell on John de Grantham, a pepperer. 445

The king desires a deputation from the city to meet him at Windsor, Nov., 1328.

On the 8th November the new mayor despatched a letter to the king, expressing the joy of the city at the news of a proposed visit, and the prospect of the next parliament being held in London. His majesty might be assured of the city's loyalty. 446 Four days later (12 November), Edward despatched a messenger from Reading with a letter to John de Grantham, bidding him cause a deputation to be nominated for the purpose of proceeding to Windsor. The messenger arrived late on Sunday evening, and the deputation was to be at Windsor on the following Tuesday. A meeting was therefore summoned on Monday, when six aldermen and six commoners were nominated to meet the king. On Thursday the deputation returned and reported the result of the interview. It appears that Edward had complained to the deputation of armed men having left the city to join the earl at Winchester. He was also desirous to know if the city was in a proper state of defence and the king's peace preserved therein. On these points the mayor endeavoured to satisfy him by letter of the 18th November. As to armed men having left the city for Winchester, his majesty was informed that none had so left with the knowledge of the municipal authorities, and if any should be found to have done so, they would most assuredly be punished. 447

The king pays a short visit to London, Dec., 1328.

Early in December the king and queen came to London, accompanied by the queen-mother and Mortimer, and took up their quarters at Westminster. The whole of the city went forth to welcome them, and they were made the recipients of valuable gifts. Their stay, however, lasted but one short week. 448

The king's letter from Gloucester to the Mayor, &c., of London. 16 Dec., 1328.

By the 16th the king was at Gloucester, where he wrote to the Mayor of London, enclosing a copy of particulars of all that had passed between himself and the Earl of Lancaster—the charges made by the earl and his own replies—in order, as he said, that the citizens might judge for themselves of the rights of the quarrel between them. These particulars, the mayor was desired to have publicly read at the Guildhall. 449 This was accordingly done (20 Dec.), in the presence of some of the earl's supporters, who took the opportunity of explaining the earl's position. 450

The bishops and barons in the city.

Whilst notifying the king that his wishes had been complied with, the mayor and commonalty besought him that all measures of hostility between himself and the barons might be suspended until parliament should meet. The city became the headquarters of the dissatisfied bishops and nobles. The Sunday before Christmas, the pulpit in St. Paul's was occupied by the primate, who was equally anxious with the civic authorities that matters should be left to be adjusted by parliament. 451

Failure of Lancaster to raise a confederation against the king. 2 Jan., 1329.

The barons in the city, in the meanwhile, awaited the arrival of the Earl of Lancaster. On New Year's day he came, and on the 2nd January (1329) a conference of bishops and barons took place at St. Paul's. 452 The futility of an attempt to form a confederation soon became apparent. The city stood fast to the king; some of the barons wavered, and nothing was left to Lancaster but to make the best terms he could. Edward had already offered pardon to all who should submit before the 7th January, with certain exceptions. 453

Trial at the Guildhall of those implicated with Lancaster. Feb., 1329.

Now that the king, or rather, we should say, Mortimer, was once more master of the situation, the citizens who had favoured the constitutional party became the objects of retribution. On Sunday, the 22nd January (1329), the mayor and twenty-four citizens were ordered to meet the king at St. Albans. They returned on the following Thursday with instructions to see if the city was prepared to punish those who had favoured Lancaster. No sooner were the king's wishes made known, than an enquiry was at once set on foot. On Wednesday (1st February), the deputation returned to the king, who was then at Windsor, to report the sense of the city; and on the following

Sunday (4th February), the king's justices commenced to sit at the Guildhall for the trial of those implicated in the late abortive attempt to overthrow Mortimer. Three days were consumed in preliminary proceedings; and it was not until Wednesday (8th February) that the real business of the session commenced. By that time the king himself had come to London, and had taken up his headquarters at the Tower, having passed through the city accompanied by his consort, the queen-mother, and many of the nobility. 454 It does not appear that Mortimer came with them.

Trial of Hamo de Chigwell, 13 Feb., 1329.

Among those who were brought to trial at the Guildhall was Chigwell. He was accused of being implicated in the abduction of the Abbot of Bury St. Edmunds, and of feloniously receiving two silver basins as his share of the plunder. Being convicted, he claimed the benefit of clergy, and the Bishop of London, after some delay, was allowed to take possession of him on the ground that he was a clerk. His life was thus saved and he was conveyed to the episcopal prison amid general regret, although, as we have already seen, he was not a universal favourite. "Many said, he is a good man; others, nay, but he deceiveth the people." 455 He was kept for some months in honourable confinement at the bishop's manor of Orset, co. Essex, and early in 1330 was admitted to purgation. Thus encouraged, he hastened once more to return to the city. He was still popular with a large body of the citizens, who, on hearing of his approach, flocked to meet him, his re-entry into the city being made to resemble a triumphal progress. Both Isabel and her son were seized with alarm; and a writ was forthwith issued for his arrest. 456 He was, however, forewarned, and able to make his escape. Little is known of his subsequent career; Stow places his death in or about 1328, but this must be a mistake. By his will dated 1332, he left some real estate in the city to the dean and chapter of St. Paul's Cathedral for the maintenance of a chantry. 457

Execution of Mortimer, 29 Nov., 1330.

Mortimer's vengeance was not confined to a few leading citizens. Lancaster's life was spared, but he was mulcted in a heavy fine. Many of his associates took refuge in flight. The Earl of Kent, the king's uncle, was shortly afterwards charged with treason, into which he had been drawn by the subtlety of Mortimer, and made to pay the penalty with his head. This, more than anything else, opened the king's eyes to Mortimer's true character, and at length (Oct., 1339,) he caused him to be privily seized in the castle of Nottingham. 458 Thence he was carried to London, and hanged at the Elms in Smithfield.

The queen retires into privacy.

Queen Isabel, who witnessed the seizure of her favourite and whose prayers to spare the "gentle Mortimer" were of no avail, was made to disgorge much of the wealth she had acquired during her supremacy, and was put on an allowance. The rest of her life, a period of nearly thirty years, she spent in retirement. Before her death 459 she gave the sum of forty shillings to the Abbess and Minoresses of Aldgate of the Order of St. Clare, for the purpose of purchasing for themselves two pittances or doles on the anniversaries of the decease of her husband the late king and of Sir John de Eltham his son. 460 The removal of Mortimer corresponded very closely with the king's coming of age. He was now eighteen years old, and thenceforth he "ruled as well as reigned."

Increase of trade with Flanders.

The king's marriage with Philippa of Hainault, which had taken place at York on the 30th January, 1328, had been popular with the city 461 as tending to open up trade with Flanders. Hitherto nearly all the wool produced by this country had been sent to Flanders for manufacture, the export trade being so large that the king is said to have received more than £30,000 in a single year from duties levied on this commodity alone. 462 We have already seen how, in order to punish the Countess of Flanders for injuries inflicted upon English merchants, the king's grandfather resorted, in 1270, to the expedient of forbidding all export of wool to her country. 463 The misery which her half-starved people were then compelled to suffer soon induced the Countess to come to terms. It was also in no small measure owing to the fear of a similar stoppage by the intervention of the French fleet, that the Flemings laid aside their neutrality in 1339, and openly assisted Edward in his war with France.

The establishment of staples in England.

Towards the close of the last reign the "staples" or market towns for the sale of certain commodities, but more especially of wool, had been removed from the continent and established at various places in England, Ireland and Wales. 464 London was one of those places. No wool was to be exported abroad until it had remained at one or another of the staples for a period of forty days. This rule appears however to have been relaxed by Edward II, in favour of all staple towns but London; merchants being allowed to remove their goods from other staples after a stay of only fifteen days. The London merchants, therefore, were under the disadvantage of finding the market always forestalled. Edward III had not long been on the throne before they took the opportunity of submitting this hardship not only to the king, but also to the queen-mother, and prayed that the relaxation of the rule touching the forty days with respect to other staples might be withdrawn. 465 Their prayer, however, would seem to have had but little effect, for within a week of the petition to the king we find that monarch issuing an order to the collector of customs on wool, leather and wool-fells in the port of London, to enforce the delay of forty days before goods could be removed. 466

A new tax on wool, leather, and wool-fells.

Nor was this the only grievance that the London merchants had. In order to raise money to put down the rebellion of the Scots which had broken out soon after his accession, he had recourse to an extra tax upon wool, leather, and wool-fells. The money thus raised was to be considered a loan, receipts being given to the merchants under the king's seal, known as "Coket," and the merchants in return were to be allowed absolute free trade from the 2nd July, 1327, the date of the writ, up to the following Christmas. 467 The Londoners objected altogether to this impost, on the grounds that they had never been consulted on the matter, and had never given their assent. 468

A compromise was subsequently effected. In consideration of the good service which the citizens of London had already done to the king in times past, and for the good service which they were prepared to render again in the future, they were released of arrears of the tax due from 2nd July to the 23rd September, provided they were willing to pay it for the remainder of the term. 469 After Christmas the restrictions upon free trade were again enforced. 470

Proposal to remove the Staple to the continent, Feb., 1328.

On the 11th December (1327), Edward issued a writ 471 to the Sheriffs of London to choose two representatives to attend on behalf of the citizens at a parliament to be held at York, on Sunday next after the Feast of the Purification (2 Feb., 1328). Instead, however, of sending only two members as directed, the citizens appear on this occasion to have sent no less than four, viz.: Richard de Betoyne, Robert de Kelseye, John de Grantham, and John Priour the Younger. 472

One of the questions to be determined was the advisability of again removing the Staple from England to the continent. On this question, there appears to have arisen some difference of opinion among the city representatives. Betoyne, who had formerly enjoyed the office of Mayor of the Staple beyond the seas, favoured a return to the old order of things, whilst his colleagues were opposed to any such proceeding. Notification of Betoyne's disagreement with his colleagues was made to the mayor and commonalty of the City by letter from the mayor and commonalty of York, to which reply was made that Betoyne's action was entirely unauthorised. 473 A letter was sent the same day to Betoyne himself, enjoining him to do nothing in the matter opposed to the wish of the commonalty of London

474; and another to Betoyne's colleagues informing them of the City's action, and bidding them to exert themselves to the utmost to keep the Staple in England. 475

The account of Betoyne's difference with his colleagues, as related in the letter from the City of York, was subsequently found to require considerable modification, when a letter was received by the Mayor of London from two of his colleagues, Grantham and Priour. 476 Their account of what had actually taken place was to the effect that Betoyne had been publicly requested by a number of representatives from various towns, assembled in the Chapter House at York, to resign his mayoralty (of the Staple) and to deliver up the charters which had been acquired at no little expense. Betoyne replied that the charters were in the possession of John de Charleton, 477 who refused to give them up, but that he had himself, four years since, caused a transcript of the charters to be made, which he was prepared to give up to them if they so wished. Thereupon, there suddenly appeared upon the scene the Mayor of York, hand in hand with John de Charleton himself, and followed by a number of burgesses of York. The appearance of John de Charleton was eminently distasteful to Betoyne, and he got up and left the room, declining to take any further part in the discussion so long as Charleton was present. That was practically all that had occurred, and the writers expressed themselves as much hurt if anything more than this had been reported from the mayor and commonalty of York, for in their opinion Betoyne had never shown himself otherwise than diligent in his duty. The letter concluded with a report of general news, the chief item being the announcement of the death of the King of France, and the writers expressed a wish that the same publicity might be given to their letter as was given to the letter received from the Mayor of York.

Betoyne's own account of his disagreement with his colleagues.

Betoyne on the same day sent home his own account of what had taken place at York. 478 It agrees in the main with the account sent by his colleagues, but contains some particulars of interest not mentioned in the latter. He relates how he had been asked to retire from the Mayoralty of the Staple beyond the seas, and to give up the charters and other muniments which the several towns had obtained at considerable cost. To this he had replied that many charters he had left behind on the continent, but he had brought over with him the charters of the franchises of the staples which had been purchased of the late king. These were in the hands of John de Charleton, who refused to give them up. He had himself, however, gone to Dover in the eighteenth year of Edward II, when the king himself was there, and had caused a duplicate of the charters to be made, which he had expressed his readiness to show them. He encloses a copy. As a proof of the bad feeling (*la malencolye*) which the burgesses of York entertained towards him, he proceeds to relate how the Mayor of York, maliciously and without any warning, had appeared at the assembly with four or five of his suite, accompanied by John de Charleton, clothed in the mayor's livery, and by a crowd of citizens, to the terror of the assembled merchants. Thereupon, Bretoyne had declared that he would not sit nor remain where Charleton was, and had left the meeting; for, said he, he would never make peace with Charleton except with the assent of the Mayor and Commonalty of London. He concluded by asking that his character might not be allowed to suffer by anything which the Mayor of York may have written. By a postscript he informs the Mayor of London, that on the eve of the Purification (the day fixed for the re-assembly of parliament) the Mayor of York had come to his hostel, accompanied by many others, and had accused him of having come to the city for the express purpose of annoying their fellow-burgess John de Charleton, which he had denied. This insult, he is advised, touches not only himself, but the Corporation of London whose representative he was.

Betoyne's action approved by the citizens, 19 Feb., 1328.

Both these letters were laid before the commonalty of London assembled at the Guildhall on the 19th February, when Betoyne's action was approved, and on the following day a letter was addressed to him to that effect. The Mayor and Commonalty of York received also a missive in which their late conduct to Betoyne was severely criticised. 479 Betoyne's recent services were recognized by the grant, at his own request, of a handsome coverlet furred with minever, in part payment of his expenses incurred in attending the parliament at York. 480

Temporary abolition of Staples. Aug., 1328.

The king, finding that the opposition to the removal of the staple displayed not only by London but by York, Winchester, Bristol and Lincoln was too great to be overcome, abolished staples altogether (August, 1328), and re-established free-trade. 481 He even invited Flemish weavers to settle in England so as to give a stimulus to the manufacture of woollen fabrics. These he took under his special protection, 482 for the native looked askance upon all foreigners, traders or craftsmen.

England and France, 1329-1331

One of the last political acts of Mortimer had been to send Edward over to France to do homage to Philip of Valois, the new king, for his possessions in that country. This homage Edward paid in 1329, but subject to certain reservations. 483 In 1330 he was making preparations for war, and took the opportunity of the presence of Stephen de Abyndone and John de Caustone, the City's representatives in the parliament held that year at Westminster, to ask them what assistance the City would be likely to afford him. The City members asked leave to consult the commonalty on the matter. Eventually the sum of 1,000 marks was offered, a sum so trifling that Edward consented to accept it only as a free gift, and plainly intimated that he looked for more substantial aid in the future. 484

In July, he summoned the mayor and twenty-four of the leading citizens to attend him at Woodstock. The mayor (Simon de Swanlonde) would have had them excused on the ground of the disturbed state of the city, but the king was not to be denied. Substitutes were appointed for the mayor during his absence, and he and seven aldermen and sixteen commoners went to Woodstock, where they gave assurances of the City's loyalty. 485 In 1331, after Mortimer's fall, when Edward was his own master, lie again visited France, and a peace was concluded between the two kings. 486

The war with Scotland, 1332-1335.

From 1332 to 1335 the king was chiefly occupied with Scotland. It was part of the policy of Philip of Valois to encourage disturbance in the north of England, as a means of recovering his lost possessions in France. 487 The period of four years during which peace had been assured by Edward with Scotland by the treaty of Northampton had now elapsed, 488 and active operations on both sides re-commenced. In 1334 the city voted 1,000 marks, afterwards raised to 1,200, for raising 100 horsemen and as many men-at-arms to assist the king for a period of forty days. 489

A spy was also despatched to Normandy and Brabant to see how matters were going there, and gifts were made to the courts of Juliers and Namur to secure their favour. The parliament which sat at York in May, 1335, 490 having decided in favour of a fresh expedition to Scotland, 491 the king sent orders to the City to hold its forces in readiness to march under the leadership of two of its aldermen, John de Pulteney and Reginald de Conduit. 492 A commission to seize ships in the port of London to the king's use, resulted in the detention of six ships. 493

Preparations for war with France, 1337.

At length, the friendly attitude which Philip of Valois had taken up towards Scotland, much to Edward's prejudice, determined the latter to go in person to France for the purpose, not only of defending his possessions there, but also of enforcing his claim to the French crown. The year 1337 was devoted to active preparations for the struggle. The City of London, in spite of its franchise, was called upon to furnish 500 men at arms, and to send them to Portsmouth by Whitsuntide. 494 The date was subsequently altered to Trinity Sunday. 495 The king took occasion to find fault with the city's dilatoriness in executing his demands, as well as with the physique of the men that were being supplied. At the request of the mayor, Sir John de Pulteney (he had recently received the honour of knighthood 496), the number of men to be furnished was reduced to 200, the rest to be supplied on further notice. 497

Charter, 26 March, 1337.

When Parliament met in London in February, the City made presents of money to the king, the queen, the chancellor, the treasurer, and others, 498 for no other purpose apparently, but to win their favour. In the following month the City obtained a charter declaring its liberties and customs to be unaffected by the recent statute establishing free trade, 499 when presents in money or kind were again made to the officers of state. 500

The services of John de Pulteney, Mayor.

The services which the mayor had done the city in the work of obtaining this charter were acknowledged by a gift of two silver basins and the sum of £20 from his fellow citizens. 501 It was by Pulteney's influence that the king consented to allow a sum of 1,000 marks to be taken into account at a future assessment for a fifteenth, instead of insisting upon its being a free gift from the citizens. 502

The king monopolises the wool of the country.

In March, 1337, a statute forbade the importation of wool, as a preliminary to the imposition of an additional custom, and in the following year parliament granted the king half the wool of the kingdom. 503 The Londoners having no wool of their own, paid a composition, 504 and were often reduced to sore straits. Thus in April, 1339, an assessment had to be made in the several wards of the City to discharge a debt to the king of 1,000 marks. The men of Aldersgate ward refused to pay their quota of £9. A precept was thereupon issued to the sheriffs to levy the larger sum of £16 10s., on the lands, tenements, goods, and chattels of the ward, and pay the same into the Chamber of the Guildhall by a certain day. 505 The citizens of London, and the nation generally, would the more willingly have borne these exactions if any adequate good had resulted from them. But Edward's first campaign resulted in nothing more than the assumption by him of the name and arms of the King of France, at a cost of £300,000. 506

Naval and military preparations in the City.

Among the ships which had been prepared for the king's expedition to France, three were known as "La Jonette," of London; "La Cogge," of All Hallows; and "La Sainte Marie Cogge." The last mentioned belonged to William Haunsard, 507 an ex-sheriff of London, who subsequently did signal service in the great naval battle of Sluys. Prior to the king's departure, measures were taken for the safe custody of the city during his absence. 508 The City had difficulties in raising a contingent of soldiers, for many of the best men had joined the retinue of nobles, and all that could be mustered amounted to no more than 100 men, viz: 40 men-at-arms, and 60 archers. 509

The city put into a posture of defence after the king's departure, July, 1338.

After the king's departure (12 July, 1338) the City laid in provisions for transmission abroad, 500 quarters of corn and 100 carcases of oxen to be salted down. In addition to which it purchased 1,000 horseshoes and 30,000 nails. 510 In October steps were taken to protect London from attack by sea and land. Piles were driven into the bed of the river to prevent the approach of a hostile fleet; the wharves were "bretasched" with boards, and springalds set at different gates and posterns. 511

Orders for city to provide more ships and men, Feb., 1339.

In February, 1339, the citizens received the king's orders to furnish four ships with 300 men, and four scummars 512 with 160 men, victualled for three months, to proceed to Winchester. Upon some demur being made to this demand, the number of ships was reduced to two, well equipped with men and arms. Pursuant to these orders each ward was assessed for the purpose of levying 110 men armed with haketon, plates, bacinet with aventail, and gloves of plate; and sixty men armed with only haketon and bacinet. The pay of the men was to be threepence a day each for two months. The vessels were to be joined by ships from various other ports, and proceed to sea in charge of Sir William Trussel by the middle of March to intercept, if possible, the enemy's fleet. 513

A threatened invasion up the Thames, Easter, 1339.

By Easter time the danger appeared more imminent, and the mayor and aldermen met hurriedly in the Guildhall, on Easter Sunday afternoon after dinner. An immediate attack up the Thames was expected. The mayor and aldermen agreed to take it in turns to watch the river night and day. On the following Wednesday, each alderman was ordered to enquire as to the number of arbalesters, archers, and men capable of bearing arms in his ward. A number of carpenters were sworn on the same day to safe-guard the engines of war laid up in the new house near Petywales. 514 This new house appears to have been known as "La Bretaske," and was used for storing springalds, quarels, and other war material. 515

Implements of war stored at the Guildhall.

At this period there were kept in the chamber of the Guildhall six instruments called "gonnes," which were made of latten, a metal closely resembling brass, five "teleres" or stocks for supporting the guns, four cwt. and a half of pellets of lead, and thirty-two pounds of gunpowder by way of ammunition. 516 The mention of "teleres" and the small amount of ammunition favours the assumption that the instruments were rather hand-guns than heavy pieces, as has been supposed. 517 A "telere" or tiller was a common name for the stock of a cross-bow, 518 and the earliest hand-guns or fire-arms known consisted of a simple tube of metal with touch-hole, fixed on a straight stick or shaft, which when used was passed under the arm so as to afford a better grip of the weapon.

The king's return, Feb., 1340.

The danger blew over, and before the close of the year the king was expected to return to England. 519 He did not return however before February, 1340, having intimated his intention to the mayor of London, by letter from Sluys, dated Sunday the 20th. 520 Notwithstanding his long absence, he had accomplished little or nothing.

A City loan of £5,000.

He had come to the end of his resources and was in want of money to carry on the war. The City was asked to lend him £20,000. It offered 5,000 marks. This was contemptuously refused, and the municipal authorities were bidden to re-consider the matter, or in the alternative to furnish the king with the names of the wealthier inhabitants of the City. At length the City agreed to advance the sum of £5,000 for a fixed period, and this offer the king was fain to accept. 521 At the close of 1339, the chief towns of Flanders had entered into an offensive and defensive alliance with Edward, and an arrangement was made for paying the sum of £1,500 out of the £5,000 to Jacques van Arteveldt, the king's agent at Bruges. 522 Three aldermen and nine commoners were appointed to make the necessary assessment for the loan, for the repayment of which John de Pulteney was one of the king's sureties. 523

The king again sets sail, June, 1340.

Provided with this and other money supplied by parliament, Edward again set out for the continent (June, 1340). With him went a contingent of 283 men-at-arms, furnished by the City, 140 of them being drawn from that part of the city which lay on the east side of Walbrook, and 143 from the western side. It had been intended to raise 300 men, and the better class of citizens had been called upon to supply each a quota, or in default to serve in person; but eleven had failed in their duty and, on that account, had been fined 50 shillings each, whilst six others, making up the deficit, had set out in the retinue of Henry Darcy, the late mayor. 524

The battle of Sluys, 24 June, 1340.

The names of the transport ships and the number of men-at-arms supplied by each city, the number of mariners and serving-men (*garzouns*), which were about to take part in the great battle fought off Sluys (24 June), are on record. 525 Although the French fleet was superior to his own in numbers and equipment, Edward did not hesitate to attack. The struggle was long and severe, lasting from noon on one day until six o'clock the next morning. If any one person was more conspicuous for valour on that occasion than another, it was William Haunsard, an ex-sheriff of London, who came with "a ship of London" and "did much good." 526

An account of the battle was despatched by the king to his son the Prince Regent, dated from his ship, the "Cogg Thomas," the 28th June. 527

CHAPTER VIII.

The king's unexpected return, 30 Nov., 1340.

It was one of the conditions of the Flemish alliance, mentioned at the close of the last chapter, that the campaign of 1340 should open with the siege of Tournay, and it was with this object specially in view that Edward had set out from England. After his brilliant victory over the French fleet which opposed his passage Edward marched upon Tournay. Its siege, however, proved fruitless, and, disappointed and money-less, he slipt back again to England and made his appearance unexpectedly one morning at the Tower 528 (30 Nov.).

Dismisses ministers and orders an enquiry as to collection of revenue.

The justices at the Tower, March-April. 1341.

The king attributed the failure of the war to the remissness of his ministers in sending money and supplies. Scarcely had he landed before he sent for the chancellor, the treasurer, and other ministers who were in London, and not only dismissed them from office, but ordered them each into separate confinement. John de Pulteney was one of those made to feel the king's anger, and he was relegated to the castle of Somerton, but as soon as Edward's irritability had passed off he and others obtained their freedom. 529 A searching enquiry was instituted in the spring of the following year (1341) as to the way in which the king's revenues had been collected in the city. Objection was raised to the judges holding their session within the city and they sat at the Tower. Great tumult prevailed, and the citizens refused to answer any questions until the judges had formally acknowledged the City's liberties. A special fund was raised for the purpose of defending the City's rights. 530 From the 5th March to the 17th March the justices sat, and then an adjournment was made until the 16th April. On resumption of the session another adjournment immediately took place owing to parliament sitting at Westminster, and when the judges should have again sat, the Iter was suddenly determined by order of the king. 531 The king showed much annoyance at the attitude taken up by the citizens, or at least by a certain portion of them, with respect to this enquiry, and endeavoured to procure the names of the ringleaders. 532 Failing in this, and not wishing to make an enemy of the city on which he largely depended for resources to carry out his military measures, he bestowed a general pardon on the citizens, and promised that no Iter should be held at the Tower for a period of seven years. 533

Charter to the city, dated 26 March, 1341.

As a further mark of favour he granted to the City, soon after the abrupt termination of the Iter, a charter confirming previous charters; allowing the citizens in express terms to vary customs that might in course of time have become incapable of being put into practice, and declaring the city's liberties not subject to forfeiture through non-user. 534

The city called upon to furnish the king with 26 ships.

In August (1341) the citizens met to consider the question of levying a sum of £2,000, of which 2,000 marks was due to certain citizens in part payment of the £5,000 lent to the king, and 1,000 marks was required for the discharge of the city's own debts. A certain number of aldermen and commoners were at the same time appointed to confer with the king's council touching the sending of ships of war beyond the seas. The result of the interview was made known to the citizens at a meeting held later on in the same month. A further grievous burden (*vehemens onus*) was to be laid upon them; they were called upon to provide no less than twenty-six ships, fully equipped and victualled at their own cost. 535

The king's expedition to Brittany, Oct., 1342.

The ships were probably wanted for conveying forces over to Brittany under the command of Sir Walter de Maunay, in the following year. The king himself made an expedition to that country in October, 1342, having previously succeeded in borrowing the sum of £1,000 from the citizens. He had asked for £2,000, but was fain to be content with the lesser sum, security for repayment of which was demanded and granted. 536

A truce with France for three years.

In March, 1343, Edward returned to England, having made a truce with France for three years. 537 He was beginning to learn the value of the English longbow and the cloth-yard shaft in the field of battle. Hitherto he, like others before him, had placed too much reliance on charges by knights on horseback. What the longbow could effect, under proper management, had been experienced at Falkirk in 1298. It had proved a failure at Bannockburn in 1314 through bad strategy, but at Halidon Hill twenty years later (1333) it was again effective. It was destined soon to work a complete reform in English warfare; and the yeoman and archer were to supersede the noble and knight. The London burgess and apprentice were especially apt with the weapon from constant practice in Finsbury fields. Edward realised the necessity of fostering the martial spirit of the Londoners, and on one occasion (January, 1344) invited the wives of the burgesses to witness a tournament at Windsor, where they were entertained right royally. 538

Renewal of the war in 1345.

Before the expiration of the truce Edward was busy with preparations for a renewal of the war. Four hundred London archers were to be got ready by Midsummer of 1344, as the king was soon to cross the sea; and 100 men-at-arms and 200 horsemen were to be despatched to Portsmouth. 539 In 1345, a royal commission was issued for the seizure for the king's use of all vessels lying in the river. 540 A further contingent of 160 archers was ordered to Sandwich by Whitsuntide, and in August the city received another order for yet more archers. 541 In September, the king informed the mayor by letter that, owing to the defective state of his fleet and the prevalence of contrary winds, he had postponed setting sail for a short time; the civic authorities were to keep their men-at-arms and archers ready to set out the morrow after the receipt of orders to march. 542 Six months elapsed, during which the citizens were kept under arms waiting for orders, when, on the 18th March, 1346, another letter was sent by the king to the effect that he had now fully made up his mind to set sail from Portsmouth a fortnight after Easter. The men-at-arms, the horsemen, and the archers, were to be ready by a certain day on pain of losing life, limb, and property. On the 28th March, the archers mustered in "Totehull" or Tothill Fields, near Westminster. 543

Expedition to France sets sail, 10 July, 1346.

The expedition did not actually sail from Portsmouth until the 10th July, the fleet numbering 1,000 vessels more or less. 544 Previous to his departure, Edward caused proclamation to be made in the city and elsewhere, to the effect that the assessments that had been made throughout the country for the purpose of equipping the expedition, should not be drawn into precedent. 545

News of the king's arrival and success in Normandy, 3 Aug.

On the 3rd August the regent forwarded to the city a copy of a letter he had received from the king, giving an account of his passage to Normandy and of the capture of various towns, and among them of Caen. There he had discovered a document of no little importance. This was none other than an agreement made in 1338, whereby Normandy had bound itself to assist the king of France in his proposed invasion and conquest of England. 546 This document the king transmitted to England by the hands of the Earl of Huntingdon, who was returning invalided, and it was publicly read in St. Paul's Churchyard, with the view of stirring the citizens to fresh exertions in prosecuting the war. The king's own letter was also publicly read in the Husting by the regent's order. 547 The City was exhorted to have in readiness a force to succour the king, if need be. Every effort was made to raise money, and the regent did not hesitate to resort to depreciation of the coinage of the realm in order to help his father. The City made a free gift to the king of 1,000 marks and lent him 2,000 more. 548

The battle of Creçy, 26 Aug., 1346.

On the 26th August the battle of Creçy was won against a force far outnumbering the English army. The victory was due in large measure to the superiority of the English longbow over the crossbow used by the Genoese mercenaries; but it was also a victory of foot soldiers over horsemen. The field of Bannockburn had shown how easy a thing it was for a body of horsemen to crush a body of archers, if allowed to take them in the flank, whilst that of Halidon Hill had more recently taught the king, from personal experience, that archers could turn the tide of battle against any direct attack, however violent. Edward profited by the experience of that day. He not only protected the flank of his archers, but interspersed among them dismounted horsemen with levelled spears, the result being that the French were driven off the field with terrible slaughter.

Siege and surrender of Calais, 1346-1347.

Flushed with victory Edward proceeded to lay siege to Calais. His forces, which had been already greatly reduced on the field of Creçy, suffered a further diminution by desertion. The mayor and sheriffs of London were ordered to seize all deserters, whether knights, esquires, or men of lower order, found in the city, and to take steps for furnishing the king with fresh recruits and store of victuals. 549 By Easter of the following year, the City was called upon to furnish two vessels towards a fleet of 120 large ships, which the council had decided to fit out. All ships found in the port of London were pressed into the king's service. 550

In July (1347) the king was in need of more recruits and provisions. 551 Calais still held out, although both besiegers and besieged were reduced to sore straits. At last it surrendered (4 Aug.). Edward spared the lives of its principal burgesses at the intercession of his queen, but he cleared the town of French inhabitants, and invited Londoners and others to take up their abode there, offering them houses at low rents and other inducements. 552 A truce with Philip was agreed on, and Edward returned home. For a time England was resplendent with the spoils of the French war—"A new sun seemed to shine," wrote Walsingham. 553 Every woman of position went gaily decked with some portion of the plunder of the town of Caen or Calais; cupboards shone with silver plate, and wardrobes were filled with foreign furs and rich drapery of continental workmanship. The golden era was of short duration.

The Black Death, 1348-1349.

In August, 1348, the pestilential scourge, known as the Black Death, 554 appeared in England, and reached London in the following November. The number of victims it carried off in the city has been variously computed, 555 but all conjectures of the kind must be received with caution. All that is known for certain is that the mortality caused a marked increase in the number of beggars, and, at the same time, raised the price of labour and provisions within the city's walls to such a degree that measures had to be taken to remedy both evils. 556 Besides the losses by death, the population of the city and the country generally was sensibly diminished by the flight of numbers of inhabitants to the continent, with the hope of escaping the ravages of the plague. The king's treasury threatened soon to become empty, and the country left defenceless, if this were allowed to go on unchecked; he therefore ordered the sheriffs of London to see that no men-at-arms, strangers or otherwise, left the kingdom, with the exception of well-known merchants or ambassadors, without the king's special order. 557 Pilgrimages to Rome or elsewhere were made an excuse for leaving England, at a time when the king's subjects could ill be spared. The king endeavoured to limit this drain upon the population of the kingdom by allowing none to cross the sea without his special licence. The city authorities having negligently executed his orders in this respect, received a rebuke in October, 1350, and were told to be more strict in their observance for the future. 558

A fresh truce with France, commencing 13 June, 1350.

On the night which ushered in New Year's day, 1350, an abortive attempt had been made by the French to recapture Calais. This ill success rendered Philip the more willing to agree to a further prolongation of the truce with England. Notification of this cessation of hostilities was duly sent to the sheriffs of London. 559 Before the truce had come to an end Philip of Valois had ceased to live, and had been succeeded on the throne of France by John II.

Measures taken for the suppression of piracy, July, 1350.

The city had scarcely recovered from the ravages of the late pestilence, before it was called upon (24 July, 1350) to furnish two ships to assist the king in putting down piracy. These were accordingly fitted out; the ship of Andrew Turk being furnished with 40 men-at-arms and 60 archers, whilst that of Goscelin de Cleve had on board 30 men-at-arms and 40 archers. 560 With their aid, Edward succeeded in utterly defeating a Spanish fleet which had recently inflicted much damage on the Bordeaux wine fleet, and capturing 24 large ships laden with rich merchandise. 561 The citizens had further to submit to a tax on wool and wine, in order to maintain the king's vessels engaged in putting down piracy. 562

Charter relative to the City's gold mace, 10 June, 1354.

In 1354 an exception was made by special charter of the king in favour of the City of London, and its sergeants were permitted to carry maces of gold or silver, or plated with silver, and bearing the royal arms. Ten years before the commons of England had petitioned the king (*inter alia*) not to allow any one to carry maces tipped with silver in city or borough, except the king's own officers. All others were to carry maces tipped with copper only (*virolez de cuevere*), with staves of wood as formerly. The petition was granted saving that the sergeants of the City of London might carry their mace within the liberties of the city and before the mayor in the king's presence. 563 This same year (1354), moreover, the king with the assent of parliament had again forbidden the carrying of gold or silver maces. Thenceforth, maces were to be of iron, brass or tin, or staves tipped with latten, and not to bear representations of the royal arms, but the arms or signs of the city using them. Again exception was made in the case of London; two sergeants of the City as well as of the City of York being permitted to carry gold or silver maces, but they were not to be surmounted with the royal arms. This led to a humble remonstrance from the whole body of the citizens of London, presented to the chancellor and the council by their mayor, Adam Fraunceys, and within a month the charter above mentioned was granted. That the charter originated or authorized the title of "Lord" Mayor, as some have supposed, is extremely improbable.

Renewal of war with France, 1355.

In 1355, all efforts to convert the truce into a final peace having failed, war with France was renewed. Edward was soon called home by fresh troubles in Scotland. Having recovered Berwick, which had been taken by surprise, and formally received the crown of Scotland from Edward Baliol, he prepared to rejoin his son, the Black Prince, in France, and in March, 1356, ordered the city to furnish him with two vessels of war. 564

Battle of Poitiers, 19 Sept., 1356

News of the battle of Poitiers (19 September, 1356), and of the defeat and capture of the French king, was received in the city by letter from the Prince of Wales, dated 22nd October. 565 Again the English longbow, combined with superior tactics, gained the day. The prince, on his return, made a triumphal entry into the city, passing over London Bridge on his way to Westminster, with the captive king and the king's son in his train. 566 The streets were almost impassable for the multitude that thronged them; and for the moment the citizens forgot at what cost to themselves the victory had been gained. A truce—a welcome truce—for two years followed. 567

Grievances of the city laid before the king.

Only a few weeks before the prince's return the citizens had laid before the king a list of their grievances and prayed for redress. 568 They had complained of being charged taxes and talliages in excess of any other of the commons. They had lent the king at Dordrecht no less a sum than £60,000, and had incurred further loss by the discrepancy between the weight for weighing wool at Dordrecht and that of England. They had lent the king further sums of £5,000 and £2,000 on two separate occasions, which had not been repaid. The sum of £40,000 had been advanced to the king's merchants at Calais and elsewhere, and this, together with other sums lent (amounting to over £30,000), was still outstanding to the grievous hurt of many citizens. They had, moreover, been called upon to undergo more charges than others with respect to the king's expeditions to Scotland, Flanders and France, and in providing men-at-arms, archers and ships, in aid of his wars. Nor did their complaints stop here. The king's purveyors had been accustomed to seize the carriages, victuals and merchandise of citizens without offering payment for the same, in direct contravention of the king's first charter to the city. Owing, moreover, to deaths by the plague, so much property had come into mortmain that the city had become impoverished, and one-third part of it rendered void of inhabitants. These points they had desired the king to consider, inasmuch as the city had always been loyal and peaceful, setting an example to the whole country. The petition wound up with the usual complaint against the privileges allowed foreign merchants, and a request that the king would grant them letters patent under the great seal, such as they might show to the purveyors whenever they attempted to take anything without payment. 569

Edward's last invasion of France, 1359-1360.

After the expiration of the truce Edward again set out for France. That country, however, had suffered so much during the last two years at the hands of freebooters, that Edward experienced the greatest difficulty in finding sufficient provisions for his army. Whilst he was traversing France in search of a force with which to try conclusions in the field, a Norman fleet swept down upon the south coast and sacked Winchelsea. The news of this disaster so incensed the king that he determined to march direct on Paris. The Londoners, in the meantime, assisted in fitting out a fleet of eighty vessels, manned with 14,000 men, including archers, in order to wipe out this disgrace, but the enemy contrived to make good their escape. 570

The peace of Bretigny, 1360.

At length Edward was induced to accede to the terms offered by France, and the peace of Bretigny was concluded (8th May, 1360). The terms were very favourable to England, although Edward consented to abandon all claim to the French crown. King John was to be ransomed, but the price set on his release was so high that some years elapsed before the money could be raised, and then only with the assistance of a few of the livery companies of the city, which showed their sympathy with the captured king by contributing to the fund being raised for the purpose of restoring him to liberty. 571 It was John's high sense of honour that kept him in captivity in England until his death in 1364. He had in fact been liberated and allowed to return to France soon after the conclusion of peace, on payment of part of his ransom, hostages being accepted for payment of the remainder. In 1363 one of the hostages broke his pledge and fled, and John, shocked at such perfidy, returned Regulus-like to England. Hence it was that he appears as one of the four kings whom Picard, the mayor, entertained that same year at a banquet, followed by play at dice and hazard. 572

England at peace, 1360-1369.

The citizens now enjoyed a period of leisure which they were not slow to turn to account. The years which followed the peace of Bretigny, until war broke out afresh in 1369, witnessed the re-organisation of many of the trade and craft guilds. Some of these, like the Goldsmiths, the Tailors or Linen-Armourers, and the Skinners, had already obtained charters from Edward soon after his accession, so had also the Fishmongers, although the earliest extant charter of the company is dated 1363. The Vintners date their chartered rights from the same year; the Drapers from 1364; whilst the more ancient company of Weavers obtained a confirmation of their privileges in 1365. Minor guilds, like the Founders, the Plumbers, the Fullers and others, had to content themselves with the recognition of their ordinances by the civic authorities alone between 1364 and 1369.

The king's favour was purchased in 1363 by a gift of nearly £500, to which the livery companies largely contributed. 573 The amount of each subscription varied from half-a-mark to £40, the latter sum being contributed by the Mercers, the Fishmongers, the Drapers, and the Skinners respectively. The Tailors subscribed half that amount, being outdone by the Vintners, who contributed £33 6s. 8d.

The renewal of the war, 1369.

With the renewal of the war, a change comes over the pages of the City's annals. The London bachelor and apprentice is drawn off from his football and hockey, with which he had beguiled his leisure hours, and bidden to devote himself to the more useful pursuits of shooting with arrow or bolt on high days and holidays. 574 Once more we meet with schedules of men-at-arms and archers provided by the City for service abroad, and of assessments made on the City's wards to pay for them. 575 Every inducement in the shape of plunder was held out to volunteers for enlistment, and public proclamation was made to the effect that the spoils of France should belong to the captors themselves. 576

City loans, 1370-1371.

It was an easier matter for the City to provide the king with money than men. In 1370 it advanced a sum of £5,000, 577 and in the following year a further sum of £4,000, and more was subscribed by the wealthier citizens, among whom were William Walworth, who contributed over £200, Adam Fr4unceys, Simon de Mordon, and others. 578

New form of taxation, 1371.

Still the expenses of the war exceeded the supply of money, and resort was had to a new form of taxation, by which it was hoped that a sum of £50,000 might be realised. By order of parliament, made in March, 1371, the sum of 22s. 3d. was to be levied on every parish in the kingdom, the number of parishes being reckoned as amounting to 40,000. It soon became apparent that the number of existing parishes throughout the country had been grossly miscalculated. There were not more than 9,000, and the amount of assessment had to be proportionately raised. It was necessary to summon a council at Westminster in June, to remedy the miscalculation that had been made in March. Half of the representatives of the late parliament were summoned to meet the king, and among them two of the city's members, Bartholomew Frestlyng and John Philipot—"the first Englishman who has left behind him the reputation of a financier." 579 The mistake was rectified, the charge of 22s. 3d. was raised to 116s. and the city was called upon to raise over £600. 580

In the meantime the civic authorities had, in answer to the king's writ, 581 prepared a return of the number of parish churches, chapels and prebends within the city. 582 It was found that within the city and suburbs there were 106 parish churches 583 and thirty prebends, but only two of the latter were within the liberties. There was also the free chapel of St. Martin's-le-Grand, which embraced eleven prebends, all within the liberty of the city, and there were, moreover, two other chapels within the liberty. Besides these (the return stated) there were none other.

The city as an ecclesiastical centre.

The bare fact that there existed over 100 parishes, each with its parish church, within so small an area as that covered by the city and its suburbs, is of itself sufficient to remind us that, besides having a municipal and commercial history, the city also possesses an ecclesiastical. The church of St. Paul, the largest foundation in the city, with its resident canons exercising magnificent hospitality, was a centre to which London looked as a mother, although it was not strictly speaking the metropolitan cathedral. That title properly applies to the Minster at Canterbury; but the church of Canterbury being in the hands of a monastic chapter left St. Paul's at the head of the secular clergy of southern England. 584 Besides the hundred and more churches there were monastic establishments and colleges which covered a good fourth part of the whole city. The collegiate church of St. Martin's-le-Grand almost rivalled its neighbour the cathedral church itself in the area of its precinct. The houses of the Black Friars and Grey Friars in the west were only equalled by those belonging to the Augustine and Crossed Friars towards the east; while the Priory of St. Bartholomew found a counterpart in the Priory of Holy Trinity. The church was everywhere and ruled everything, and its influence manifests itself nowhere more strongly than in the number of ecclesiastical topics which fill the pages of early chronicles in connection with London. 585

The prosecution of the war, 1371-1375.

The war brought little credit or advantage in return for outlay. In January, 1371, the Black Prince had returned to England with the glory of former achievements sullied by his massacre at Limoges, and the City of London had made him a present of valuable plate. 586 The conduct of the war was transferred to his eldest surviving brother, John of Gaunt, Duke of Lancaster. In 1372 the king himself set out with the flower of the English nobility, and accompanied by a band of London archers and crossbow men. 587 The expedition, which had for its object the relief of Rochelle, and which is said to have cost no less than £900,000, proved disastrous, and Edward returned after a brief absence. 588 In 1373 the city furnished him with a transport barge called "The Paul of London." The barge when it left London for Southampton was fully supplied with rigging and tackle; nevertheless, on its arrival at the latter port, it was found to be so deficient in equipment that it could not proceed to sea. The only explanation that the master of the barge could give of the matter was that a certain number of anchors and cables had been lost on the voyage. The City paid twenty marks to make up the defects. 589 The year was marked by a campaign under Lancaster which ended in the utmost disaster. The French avoided a general action; the English soldiers deserted, and as the winter came on the troops perished from cold, hunger and disease. By 1374 the French had recovered nearly all of their former possessions. England was tired of the war and of the ceaseless expenditure it involved. It was with no little joy that the Londoners heard, in July, 1375, 590 that peace had been concluded.

Charges against city aldermen, 1376.

In April, 1376, a parliament met, known as the Good Parliament, 591 and before granting supply it demanded an account of former receipts and expenditure. No less than three city aldermen were charged with malversation. Richard Lyons, of Broad Street ward, was convicted with Lord Latimer of embezzling the king's revenue, and sentenced to imprisonment and forfeiture of goods. 592 Adam de Bury, of Langbourn ward, who had twice served the office of mayor, was charged with appropriating money subscribed for the ransom of the French king and fled to Flanders to avoid trial; 593 whilst John Pecche of Walbrook ward was convicted of an extortionate exercise of a monopoly of sweet wines and his patent annulled. All three aldermen were deposed from their aldermanries by order of an assembly of citizens composed of representatives from the various guilds and not from the wards. 594

A new system of election by the guilds, instead of the wards, introduced, 1376.

The guilds, indeed, were now claiming a more direct participation in the government of the city than they had hitherto enjoyed, and their claim had given rise to so much commotion that the king himself threatened to interpose. 595 The threat was not liked, and the citizens hastened to assure him that no disturbance had occurred in the city beyond what proceeded from reasonable debate on an open question, and that to prevent the noise and tumult arising from large assemblies, they had unanimously decided that in future the Common Council should be chosen from the guilds and not otherwise. 596 This reply was sent to the king by the hands of two aldermen—William Walworth and Nicholas Brembre—and six commoners, and the following day (2 August) the king sent another letter accepting the explanation that had been offered, and expressing a hope that the city would be so governed as not to require his personal intervention. 597

Not only was the common council to be selected in future by the guilds, but the guilds were also to elect the mayor and the sheriffs. The aldermen and the commons were to meet together at least once a quarter, 598 and no member of the common council was to serve on inquests, nor be appointed collector or assessor of a talliage. This last provision may have been due to the recent discoveries of malversation, but, however that may be, it was found to work so well that it was more than once re-enacted. 599 These changes in the internal administration of the city were avowedly made by virtue of Edward's charter, which specifically gave the citizens a right to remedy hard or defective customs. 600

The old system of election by wards reverted to in 1384.

The power of the guilds in the matter of elections to the common council was not of long duration. Before ten years had elapsed representation was made that the new system had been forced on the citizens, and in 1384 it was resolved to revert to the old system of election by and from the wards. 601

Proceedings against Alice Perers, the king's mistress, 1376.

Encouraged by the success which had so far attended their efforts of reform, the good parliament next attacked Alice Perers, the king's mistress. Of humble origin, and not even possessing the quality of good looks, this lady, for whom the mediæval chroniclers have scarcely a good word to say, 602 nevertheless gained so complete a mastery over the king as to favour the popular belief that she indulged in magic. At length her barefaced interference in public affairs led to an award against her of banishment and forfeiture. Upon the dissolution of the good parliament (6 July, 1376), and the meeting of a new parliament, elected under the direct influence of the Earl of Lancaster, who once more gained the upper hand now that the Black Prince was dead, Alice Perers was allowed to return. 603 She was again in disgrace soon after Richard's accession, when her property, much of which consisted of real estate in the City, 604 became escheated, and the citizens of London were promised redress for any harm she might have done them. 605 She was afterwards married to Sir William de Windsor, who, in 1376, had got himself into trouble over a disturbance in Whitefriars 606 — a quarter of the city which, under the name of Alsatia, became afterwards notorious for riots, and as the resort of bad characters. Towards the close of 1379 her sentence of banishment, never strictly enforced, was revoked and pardon extended to her and her husband. 607

Charter forbidding free trade to merchant strangers, 4 Dec., 1376.

In December, 1376, the citizens obtained a charter from the king, with the assent of parliament, granting that no strangers (*i.e.* non-freemen) should thenceforth be allowed to sell by retail within the city and suburbs. This had always been considered a grievance, ever since free trade had been granted to merchant strangers by the parliament held at York in 1335.

Hostility between the City and Lancaster.

The last year of Edward's reign was one of serious opposition between the City and the selfish and unprincipled Lancaster. In so far as the duke, with the assistance of Wycliffe, meditated a reform among the higher clergy, he might, if he would, have had the city with him. The citizens, like the great reformer himself, were opposed to the practice of the clergy heaping up riches and intermeddling with political matters. The duke, however, went out of his way to hurt the feelings of the citizens, by proposing to abolish the mayoralty and otherwise encroach upon their liberties. 608 Not content with this he took the occasion when Wycliffe was summoned to appear at St. Paul's (19 Feb., 1377), to offer violence to Courtenay, their bishop. This so incensed the citizens that the meeting broke up in confusion. The next day the mob, now thoroughly roused, hastened to the Savoy where the duke resided. He happened, however, to be dining in the city at the time, with a certain John de Ypre. The company had scarcely sat down to their oysters before a soldier knocked at the door and warned them of the danger. They forthwith jumped up from the table, the duke barking his shins (we are told) in so doing, and, making their way to the riverside, took boat for Kennington, where the duke sought protection in the house of the Princess of Wales. Thanks to the intervention of the bishop, who appeared on the scene, the mob did but little serious harm, beyond ill-using a priest and some of the duke's retainers whom they happened to come across. 609

Interview between the king and the citizens to explain matters.

The civic authorities were naturally anxious as to what the king might say and do in consequence of the outbreak, and desired an interview in order to explain matters. Lancaster was opposed to any such interview taking place. The London mob had seized upon an escutcheon of the duke, displayed in some public thoroughfare, and had reversed it by way of signifying that it was the escutcheon of a traitor. 610 This had particularly raised his anger. Nevertheless, in spite of his efforts to prevent it, an interview was accorded to a deputation from the city, of which John Philipot acted as spokesman. After drawing the king's attention to the threatened attack on the privileges of the city, and the proposed substitution of a "captain" for a mayor, Philipot offered an apology for the late riot. It had taken place, he said, without the cognisance of the civic authorities. Among a large population there were sure to be some bad characters whom it was difficult to restrain, even by the authority of the mayor, when once excited. A mob acted after the manner of a tornado, flying hither and thither, bent on committing havoc at anybody's expense, even its own, but, thank God! the duke had suffered no harm nor had any of his retinue been hurt. The king having listened to the deputation, assured them in reply, that so far from wishing to lessen the privileges of the city, he had a mind to enlarge them. They were not to alarm themselves, but to go home and endeavour to preserve peace. On leaving the presence the deputation met the duke, with whom they interchanged courtesies. 611 In the meanwhile lampoons on the duke were posted in the city. The duke became furious and demanded the excommunication of the authors. The bishops hesitated through fear of the mob, but at last the Bishop of Bangor was induced by representations made to him by leading citizens, who wished it to be known that they did not approve of such libels, to execute the duke's wishes. 612

Another interview with the king at Shene.

The duke was determined to have his revenge, and again the citizens were summoned to appear before the king, who was lying at Shene. This time they did not get off so easily. The mayor, Adam Stable, was removed, and Nicholas Brembre appointed in his place. A fresh election of aldermen took place, 613 and the City did penance for the recent insult to the duke's escutcheon by offering, at the king's confidential suggestion, a wax taper bearing the duke's arms in St. Paul's. Even that did not satisfy him; nay, it was adding insult to injury (he said), for such an act was an honour usually paid to one who was dead! The citizens were in despair, and doubted if anything would satisfy him, short of proclaiming him king. 614

The king's death, 21 June, 1377.

One of the last acts of Edward was to restore the Bishop of Winchester to the temporalities of which he had been deprived by the duke, and this restitution was made at the instance and by the influence of Alice Perers, 615 who within a few weeks robbed her dying paramour of his finger rings and fled. 616

CHAPTER IX.

Reconciliation between Lancaster and the City, 1377.

Shortly after Edward had breathed his last, a deputation from the City waited upon the Prince of Wales at Kennington. John Philipot again acted as spokesman, and after alluding to the loss which the country had recently sustained, and recommending the City of London—the "king's chamber"—to the prince's favour, begged him to assist in effecting a reconciliation with Lancaster. This Richard promised to do, and a few days later the deputation again waited on the young king—this time at Shene, where preparations were being made for the late king's obsequies—and a reconciliation took place, the king kissing each member of the deputation, and promising to be their friend, and to look after the City's interests as if they were his own. 617 Formal announcement of the reconciliation was afterwards made at Westminster, and Peter de la Mare, long a prisoner in Nottingham Castle, was set free, to the great joy of the citizens. 618

The coronation of Richard II, 16 July, 1377.

At the express wish of the citizens, Richard—the "Londoners' king," as the nobles were in the habit of cynically styling the new sovereign, for the reason that he had ascended the throne more by the assistance of the *bourgeois* Londoner than of the nobility 619—took up his quarters at the Tower, whence he proceeded in state to Westminster for his coronation. Great preparations were made in the city to tender his progress through the streets one of exceptional splendour. The claim of the mayor and citizens to assist the chief butler at the banquet was discourteously refused by Robert Belknap, Chief Justice of the Common Pleas, who bluntly told them that they might be of service in washing up the pots and pans. The citizens had their revenge, however. They set up an effigy of the man at a conspicuous arch or tower in Cheapside, in which he appeared to the whole of the procession as it passed on its way to Westminster, in the ignominious attitude of vomiting wine. 620 This was enough; the Londoners gained the day, and were allowed to perform their customary services at the banquet, and the mayor got his gold cup. 621

A city loan and parliamentary supplies, 1377.

Richard was only eleven years of age when raised to the throne. A council was therefore appointed to govern in his name. Neither the Duke of Lancaster nor any other of the king's uncles were elected councillors, and, for a time, John of Gaunt retired into comparative privacy. The task of the council was not easy. The French plundered the coast, 622 and the Scots plundered the borders. Money was sorely needed. The City consented to advance the sum of £5,000 upon the security of the customs of the Port of London and of certain plate and jewels, 623 and when parliament met (13 Oct., 1377) it made a liberal grant of two tenths and two fifteenths, which was to be collected without delay, on the understanding that two treasurers should be appointed to superintend the due application of the money. 624 The two treasurers appointed for this purpose were two citizens of note, namely, William Walworth and John Philipot, of whose financial capability mention has already been made.

Charter granted to the city with the assent of parliament, 4 Dec., 1377.

Before parliament broke up it gave its assent to a new charter to the City. 625 Foreigners (*i.e.* non-freemen) were again forbidden to traffic in the city among themselves by retail, and the City's franchises were confirmed and enlarged. So much importance was attached to this charter that Brembre, the mayor, caused its main provisions to be published throughout the city. 626

The subsidy taken out of the hands of Walworth and Philipot, 1378.

Lancaster soon became tired of playing a subordinate part in the government of the kingdom. As a preliminary step to higher aims, he contrived, after some little opposition, to obtain the removal of the subsidy granted by the last parliament, out of the hands of Walworth and Philipot into his own, although these men had given no cause for suspicion of dishonourable conduct in the execution of their public trust. 627

Patriotic conduct of John Philipot.

The energetic John Philipot soon found other work to do. The English coast had recently become infested with a band of pirates, who, having already made a successful descent upon Scarborough, were now seeking fresh adventures. Philipot fitted out a fleet at his own expense, and putting to sea succeeded in capturing the ringleader, 628 a feat which rendered him so popular as to excite the jealousy of the Duke of Lancaster and other nobles. His fellow citizens showed their appreciation of his character by electing him to succeed Brembre in the mayoralty in October (1378). 629

Factions in the City for and against the Duke of Lancaster, 1378.

The citizens were, however, split up into factions, one party, with Philipot and Brembre at his head, maintaining a stubborn opposition to Lancaster, whilst another, under the leadership of Walworth and John de Northampton, favoured the duke. These factions were continually plotting and counter-plotting one against the other. At Gloucester, to which the duke had brought the parliament in 1378, in the hope of escaping from the interference of the "ribald" Londoners, 630 Brembre was arraigned on a charge of having connived during his recent mayoralty at an attack made on the house of the duke's younger brother, Thomas of Woodstock, Earl of Buckingham, and although he succeeded in proving his innocence, the earl and his party continued to use threats, and Brembre, in order to smooth matters over, consented to be mulcted in 100 marks. When the matter was reported to the Common Council at home (25 Nov.), that body not only signified its approval of his conduct—"knowing for certain that it was for no demerits of his own, but for the preservation of the liberties of the city, and for the extreme love which he bore it, that he had undergone such labours and expenses,"—but recouped him what he had disbursed. 631

The Earl of Buckingham and his partizans withdraw themselves and their custom from the City, 1378.

In course of time the earl and his followers succeeded in persecuting Brembre to a disgraceful death. At present they contented themselves with damaging the trade of the city, so far as they could, by leaving the city *en masse* and withdrawing their custom. The result was so disastrous to the citizens, more especially to the hostel keepers and victuallers, that the civic authorities resolved to win the nobles back to the city by wholesale bribery, and, as the city's "chamber" was empty, a subscription list was set on foot to raise a fund for the purpose. Philipot, the mayor, headed the list with £10, a sum just double that of any other subscriber. Six others, among them being Brembre (the earl's particular enemy) and Walworth, subscribed respectively £5; whilst the rest contributed sums varying from £4 down to five marks, the last mentioned sum being subscribed by Richard "Whytyngdon" of famous memory. 632

Another City loan of £5,000, Feb., 1379.

The grants made to the king by the parliament at Gloucester were soon exhausted by the war, and recourse was had, as usual, to the City. In February, 1379, the mayor and aldermen were sent for to Westminster. They were told that the king's necessities demanded an immediate supply of money, and that the Duke of Lancaster and the rest of the nobility had consented to contribute. What would the City do? After a brief consultation apart, the mayor and aldermen suggested that the usual course should be followed and that they should be allowed to consult the general body of the citizens in the Guildhall. Eventually the City consented to advance another sum of £5,000 on the same security as before, but any tax imposed by parliament at its next session was to be taken as a set off. 633

The poll-tax of 1379.

At the session of parliament held in April and May (1379), the demand for further supply became so urgent that a poll-tax was imposed on a graduated scale according to a man's dignity, ranging from ten marks or £6 1s. 4d. imposed on a duke, to a groat or four pence which the poorest peasant was called upon to pay. The mayor of London, assessed as an earl, was to pay £4; and the aldermen, assessed as barons, £2. The sum thus furnished by the city amounted to less than £700, 634 and the whole amount levied on the country did not exceed £22,000, a sum far short of what had been anticipated.

Renewal of the poll-tax, 1380.

In the following year (1380) there was a recurrence to the old method of raising money, but this proving still insufficient a poll-tax was again resorted to. This time, the smallest sum exacted was not less than three groats, and was payable on everyman, woman and unmarried child, above the age of fifteen, throughout the country. The amount thus raised in the city and liberties was just over £1000. 635 The tax was especially irritating from its inquisitorial character, and led to serious consequences.

The peasants' revolt under Wat Tyler, 1381.

The country was already suffering under a general discontent, when a certain Wat Tyler in Kent struck down a collector of the poll-tax, who attempted in an indecent manner to discover his daughter's age. This was the signal for a revolt of the peasants from one end of England to the other, not only against payment of this particular tax, but against taxes and landlords generally. The men of Essex joined forces with those of Kent on Blackheath, and thence marched on London. With the aid of sympathisers within the City's gates, the effected an entrance on the night of the 12th of June, and made free with the wine cellars of the wealthier class. The next day, the rebels, more mad than drunk (*non tam ebrii quam dementes*), stirred up the populace to make a raid upon the Duke of Lancaster's palace of the Savoy. This they sacked and burnt to the ground. They next vented their wrath upon the Temple, and afterwards upon the house of the Knight's Hospitallers at Clerkenwell. In the meantime reinforcements were gathering in Essex under the leadership of one known as "Jack Straw," and were hurrying to London. At Mile End they were met (14 June) by the young king himself, who set out from the Tower for that purpose, accompanied by a retinue of knights and esquires on horseback, as well as by his mother in a drawn vehicle. The rebels demanded the surrender of all traitors to the king. To this Richard gave his assent, and having done so returned to the city to take up his quarters at the Wardrobe, near Castle Baynard, whilst the rebels, availing themselves of the king's word, hurried off to the Tower. There they found Simon of Sudbury, Archbishop of Canterbury, and he and others were beheaded on Tower Hill. The rest of the day and the whole of the next were given up to plunder and massacre, so that the narrow streets were choked with corpses. Among those who perished at the hands of the rebels was Richard Lyons, the deposed alderman. At length, on the evening of Saturday, the 15th, when the king had ridden to Smithfield accompanied by Walworth, the mayor, and a large retinue in order to discuss matters with Wat Tyler (the Essex men had for the most part returned home), an altercation happened to arise between Tyler and one of the royal suite. Words were about to lead to blows when the mayor himself interposed, and summarily executed the king's order to arrest Tyler by bringing him to the ground by a fatal blow of his dagger. Deprived of their leader the mob became furious, and demanded Walworth's head; the mayor, however, contrived to slip back into the City, whence he quickly returned with such a force that the rioters were surrounded and compelled to submit. The king intervened to prevent further bloodshed, and knighted on the field not only Walworth, but also Nicholas Brembre, John Philipot and Robert Launde. 636 The same day a royal commission was issued to enquire into the late riot and to bring the offenders to account. 637

Orders given for safeguarding the city, 20 June.

Orders were given on the 20th June to each alderman to provide men-at-arms and archers to guard in turns the city's gates, and to see that no armed person entered the city, except those who declared on oath that they were about to join the king's expedition against the rebels. In the meantime, the aldermen were to make returns of all who kept hostels in their several wards. 638 In a list, containing nearly 200 names of divers persons of bad character, who had left the city by reason of the insurrection, 639 there appear the names of two servants of Henry "Grenecobbe." The name is far from common, and we shall not perhaps be far wrong in conjecturing that the owner of it was a relation of William "Gryndecobbe," who led the insurgents against the abbey of St. Albans and compelled the abbot to surrender its charter. 640

Confession made by "Jack Straw."

"Jack Straw," on being brought before the mayor, was induced by promises of masses for the good of his soul, to confess the nature of the intentions of the rioters, which were to use the king's person as a stalking horse for drawing people to their side, and eventually to kill him and all in authority throughout the kingdom. The mendicant friars, who were believed to be at the bottom of the insurrection, 641 were alone to be spared. Wat Tyler was to be made king of Kent, whilst others were to be placed in similar positions over the rest of the counties. The mayor sentenced him to be beheaded. This done, his head was set up on London Bridge, where Wat Tyler's already figured. 642

Revulsion of feeling against the Lollards after the suppression of the peasants' revolt, 1382.

The discontent which had given rise to the peasants' revolt, had been fanned by the attacks made by Wycliffe's "simple priests" upon the rich and idle clergy. The revolt occasioned a bitter feeling among the landlord class against Wycliffe and his followers, and after its suppression the Lollards were made the object of much animadversion. Their preaching was forbidden, 643 and Wycliffe was obliged to retire to his country parsonage, where he continued to labour with his pen for the cause he had so much at heart, until his death in 1384.

Reforms in the city during Northampton's first mayoralty, 1381-1382.

The majority of the citizens favoured the doctrines of Wycliffe and his followers and endeavoured to carry them out. The Duke of Lancaster had no real sympathy with the Lollards; he only wished to make use of them for a political purpose. It was otherwise with the Londoners, and with John de Northampton, a supporter of the duke, who succeeded to the mayoralty soon after the suppression of the revolt. Under Northampton—a man whom even his enemies allowed to be of stern purpose, not truckling to those above him, nor bending to his inferiors, 644—many reforms were carried out, ecclesiastical as well as civil.

The ecclesiastical courts having grossly failed in their duty, the citizens themselves, fearful of God's vengeance if matters were allowed to continue as they were, undertook the work of reform within the city's walls. The fees of the city parsons were cut down. The fee for baptism was not to exceed forty pence, whilst that for marriage was not as a general rule to be more than half a mark. One farthing was all that could be demanded for a mass for the dead, and the priest was bound to give change for a half-penny when requested or forego his fee. 645 Steps were taken at the same time to improve the morality of the city by ridding the streets of lewd women and licentious men. On the occasion of a first offence, culprits of either sex were subjected to the ignominy of having their hair cropt for future identification, and then conducted with rough music through the public thoroughfares, the men to the pillory and the women to the "thewe." After a third conviction, they were made to abjure the City altogether. 646 It was during Northampton's first year of the mayoralty that the citizens succeeded in breaking down the monopoly of the free fish-mongers. A number of "dossers" or baskets for carrying fish were also seized because they were deficient in holding capacity, and on that account were calculated to defraud the purchaser. 647 But, although a mayor in those days exercised, no doubt, greater power in the municipal government than now, we must be careful to avoid the common mistake of attributing to the individuality of the mayor for the time being what was really the action of the citizens as a body corporate.

Northampton re-elected mayor at the king's request, Oct., 1382.

In October, 1382, Northampton was elected mayor for the second time, and Philipot, his rival, either resigned or was deprived of his aldermancy. 648 His re-election was at the king's express wish. On the 6th he wrote to the sheriffs, aldermen and commons of the city intimating that, whilst anxious to leave the citizens free choice in the matter of election of their mayor, he would be personally gratified if their choice fell upon the outgoing mayor. At first Northampton declined re-election, but he afterwards consented to serve another year on receiving a written request from the king. 649 His hesitation was probably due to the factious state of the city. Brembre and Philipot were not his only enemies. Another alderman, Nicholas Exton, of Queenhithe Ward, had recently been removed from his aldermancy for opprobrious words used to Northampton during his first mayoralty. A petition had been laid before the Court of Common Council in August, 1382, when Exton himself being present, and seeing the turn affairs were taking, endeavoured to anticipate the judgment of the court, by himself asking to be exonerated from his office, declaring at the same time that he had offered a large sum of money to be released at his election in the first instance. The court wishing for further time to consider the matter adjourned. At its next meeting a similar petition was again presented, but the court hesitated to pronounce judgment in the absence of Exton, who was summoned to appear at the next Common Council. When the court met again, it was found that Exton had ignored the summons. Judgment was, therefore, pronounced in his absence and he was deprived of his aldermancy. 650

Brembre succeeds Northampton in the mayoralty, Oct., 1383.

At the close of Northampton's second mayoralty (Oct., 1383), his place was taken by his rival, Nicholas Brembre, 651 and a general reversal of the order of things took place. The free-fishmongers recovered their ancient privileges, 652 and the judgment passed upon Exton as well as a similar judgment passed upon another alderman, Adam Carlile, were reversed. 653

Richard's second charter to the City, 26 Nov., 1383.

Soon after Brembre's election the king confirmed the City's liberties by charter, 654 which had the assent of parliament. Two years previously the citizens had besought the newly-married queen to use her interest with Richard to that end. 655 Her good offices, as well as the fact that the City had recently advanced to the king the sum of 4,000 marks, on the security of the royal crown and other things, 656 may have been instrumental in obtaining for the citizens this fresh confirmation of their rights.

Proceedings against Northampton.

In January (1384) Northampton was bound over to keep the peace in the sum of £5,000; 657 but in the following month he was put under arrest (together with his brother, known as Robert "Cumberton," and another), for raising a disturbance in the City, and sent to Corfe Castle. 658 For Northampton's arrest, as well as for the summary execution of a certain John Constantyn, a cordwainer, who had been convicted of taking a leading part in the disturbance, Brembre received a letter of indemnity from the king. 659 The riot had one good effect. It roused public opinion against monopolies and restriction of trade to such an extent, that Richard very soon afterwards caused the city to be opened freely to all foreigners (*i.e.*, non-freemen) wishing to sell fish or other victuals. 660

Trial of Northampton at Reading.

In August (1384) the opinion of each individual member of the Common Council was taken on oath, as to whether it would be to the advantage or disadvantage of the city if Northampton were allowed to return; and it was unanimously found that his return would breed dissension rather than peace and unity. 661 Armed with this *plébiscite* the mayor and a number of citizens, whom the king had summoned by name, attended a council at Reading for the purpose of determining the fate of Northampton. The accused contented himself with objecting to sentence being passed against him in the absence of his patron the Duke of Lancaster. This, however, availed him nothing, and he was sentenced to perpetual imprisonment in Tintagel Castle. 662 Another authority 663 states that the mayor brought with him to the council a man named Thomas Husk or Usk (whose name, by the way, does not appear in the list which the king forwarded to the mayor), who made a number of charges against Northampton. The prisoner so far forgot himself in the royal presence as to call Usk a liar, and to challenge him to a duel. Matters were not improved by Northampton's appeal for delay in passing sentence upon him in the absence of the Duke of Lancaster. Richard flushed crimson with anger at the proposal, declaring that he was ready to sit in judgment upon the duke no less than on Northampton, and forthwith ordered the latter's execution, and the confiscation of his goods. The sentence would have been earned out but for the timely intercession of the queen, who flung herself at her husband's feet and begged for the prisoner's life. The queen's prayer was granted, and Northampton was condemned to perpetual imprisonment and remitted to Corfe Castle. Thence, at the beginning of September, he was removed to the Tower of London, where two of his partisans, John More, one of the sheriffs, and Richard Northbury, recently arrested, were lodged.

Is committed to Tintagel Castle.

The Chief Justice, Tressilian, hesitated to take any steps against the prisoners, one of whom had already been tried and sentenced, asserting that the matter lay within the jurisdiction of the mayor. His scruples, however, on this score were easily set aside, and on the 10th September, each of the prisoners was sentenced to be drawn and hanged. No sooner was sentence passed than the chancellor, Michael de la Pole, entered on the scene, and proclaimed that the king's grace had been extended to the prisoners, that there lives would be spared, but that they would be imprisoned until further favour should be shown them. They were accordingly sent off to various fortresses; Northampton to Tintagel Castle in Cornwall, Northbury to Corfe Castle, and More to Nottingham; and all this arose, says the Chronicler, from the rivalry of fishmongers. 664

Brembre's re-election to the mayoralty, Oct., 1384.

When Brembre sought re-election to the mayoralty in October, 1384, he found a formidable competitor in Nicholas Twyford, with whom he had not always been on the best of terms. It was in 1378, when Twyford was sheriff and Brembre was occupying the mayoralty chair for the first time, that they fell out, the occasion being one of those trade disputes so frequent in the City's annals. A number of goldsmiths and pepperers had come to loggerheads in St. Paul's Churchyard during sermon time, and the mayor had committed one of the ringleaders to the compter. The culprit, however, happened to be, like Twyford, a goldsmith, and was one of his suite. Twyford resented his man being sent to prison, and for his pains got arrested himself. 665 It was felt that the election would be hotly contested and might lead to disturbance. Besides the customary precept issued by the mayor forbidding any to appear who were not specially summoned, 666 the king took the precaution of sending John de Nevill, of Roby, to the Guildhall to see that the election was properly conducted. In spite of all precautions, however, a disturbance took place, and some of the rioters were afterwards bound over to keep the peace. 667 It is said that Brembre himself secreted a body of men in the neighbourhood of the Guildhall, and that when he found the election going against him, he signalled for them, and Twyford's supporters were compelled to flee for safety, and that thus the election was won. 668 Nothing of this appears in the City's Records, where Brembre's re-election is entered in the manner of the day. 669

Renewed efforts to obtain Northampton's release, March, 1386.

In 1385 Brembre was again elected mayor, and continued in office until October, 1386, when he was succeeded by his friend and ally, Nicholas Exton. This was the fourth and last time Brembre was mayor. In the meantime, the Duke of Lancaster and his party had renewed their efforts to effect the release of Northampton and of his fellow prisoners, More and Northbury, on the understanding that they were not to come near the City, and Brembre again took the opinion of the aldermen and commons severally as to the probable effect of the release of the prisoners. This occurred in March, 1386, when it was unanimously resolved that danger would result to the city if Northampton was allowed to come within 100 miles of it. 670 The resolution caused much annoyance to the duke, who characterised it as unreasonable and outrageous, and led to some heated correspondence. 671 It had, however, the desired effect of at least postponing the release of the prisoners. 672

A book of ordinances, known as "Jubilee," burnt by order of mayor, Exton, March, 1387.

A few months after Exton had taken Brembre's place as mayor (Oct., 1386), the new mayor raised a commotion by ordering a book called "Jubilee," which Northampton is supposed to have compiled—or caused to be compiled for the better government of the City, to be publicly burnt in Guildhall yard. 673 The cordwainers of London, staunch supporters of Northampton (the leader of the riot which led to Northampton's arrest in 1384 was a cordwainer), complained to parliament of Exton. The book, said they, " comprised all the good articles pertaining to the good government of the City," which Exton and all the aldermen had sworn to maintain for ever, and now he and his accomplices had burnt it without consent of the commons, to the annihilation of many good liberties, franchises, and customs of the City. 674 The book had already been subjected to revision in June, 1384, when Brembre was mayor; 675 it was now utterly destroyed.

Further efforts to secure Northampton's release, 1387.

In 1387 efforts were again made to secure Northampton's release, and this time with success. On the 17th April Exton reported to the Common Council that Lord Zouche was actually engaged in canvassing the king for the release of Northampton and his allies. The Council thereupon unanimously resolved to send a letter to Lord Zouche, on behalf of the entire commonalty of the City, praying him to desist from his suit, and assuring him of their loyalty to the king even unto death. 676 It also resolved to send a deputation on horseback to the king, who was at "Esthamstede," to ask his favour for the City, and to beg of him not to annul the charters which he had already given to the citizens, more especially as touching the release of the prisoners in question.

Northampton set free, 27 April, 1387.

On the 4th May the Recorder, William Cheyne, reported to the Common Council assembled in the upper chamber of the Guildhall the result of the interview with the king. The deputation had been received most graciously, and the mayor had been particularly successful in his speech, setting forth the dangers that would inevitably ensue, both to the king and to the city, if pardon were granted to Northampton and his friends. The king had replied that he would take good precautions for himself before he granted them their liberty; 677 and with this answer the citizens had to be content. The answer was an evasive one, if it be true, as one authority states, that on the 27th April—the day on which the mayor had informed the citizens of the intervention of Lord Zouche—Northampton had received his pardon and been restored to his property. 678 His friends remained still unsatisfied, and plagued the king for more favourable terms to such a degree that Richard ordered (7 Oct.) proclamation to be made in the city against any further entreaties being made to him on the subject. 679

Letter from the mayor to the king, 5 Oct.

Two days before the order for this proclamation, the king was informed by letter of the nature of a fresh oath of allegiance 680 that had been taken by the mayor, aldermen, and commonalty of the city. He was furthermore exhorted to give credence to what Nicholas Brembre might inform him as to the state and government of the city, since there was no one better informed than Brembre on the subject.

The king's reply, 7 Oct.

To this the king sent a gracious reply. 681 He had learnt with much pleasure from Nicholas Brembre of the allegiance of the citizens, which he trusted would continue, as he would soon have good reason for paying a visit to the city in person. He had heard that the new sheriffs were good and trusty men, and he expressed a hope that at the approaching election of a mayor they would choose one of whom he could approve, otherwise he would decline to receive the mayor-elect at his presentation. He not only forbade any further entreaties to be made to him touching Northampton, More and Northbury, but commissioned enquiry to be made as to their property in the city. He was especially gratified to learn that, in accordance with his request, they had appointed Thomas Usk (the chief witness against Northampton) to the office of under-sheriff, and promised that such appointment should not be drawn into precedent. The citizens were not slow to take the hint about the election of a new mayor, and Exton was continued in office. 682

The Parliament of 1386.

Great discontent had arisen meanwhile in the country at the lavish expenditure of the king, without any apparent result in victories abroad, such as had been gained in the glorious days of his predecessor. A cry for reform and retrenchment was raised, and found a champion in the person of the Duke of Gloucester, the youngest of the king's uncles. At his instigation, the parliament which assembled on the 1st October, 1386, demanded the dismissal of the king's ministers, and read him a lesson on constitutional government which ended in a threat of deposition unless the king should mend his ways. Richard was at the time only twenty-one years of age. In the impetuosity of his youth he is recorded as having contemplated a dastardly attempt upon the life of his uncle, whom he had grown to hate as the cause of all his difficulties. A plan was laid, which is said to have received Brembre's approbation, for beguiling the duke into the city by an invitation to supper, and then and there making away with him, but the duke was forewarned. The chronicler who records Brembre's complicity in this nefarious design against Gloucester's life also relates that Exton, who was mayor, refused to have anything to do with it. 683

Appointment of a Commission of Regency.

The Commission declared illegal.

Richard applies to the City for assistance.

Before the end of the session, parliament had appointed a commission, with Gloucester at its head, to regulate the government of the country and the king's household. This very naturally excited the wrath of the hot-headed king, who immediately set to work to form a party in opposition to the duke. In August of the next year (1387) he obtained a declaration from five of the justices to the effect that the commission was illegal. On the 28th October he sent the Archbishop of York and the Earl of Suffolk into the city to learn whether he could depend upon the support of the citizens. The answer could not have been regarded as unfavourable, for, on the 10th November, the king paid a personal visit to the city and was received with great ceremony. 684 On the following day (11 Nov.) orders were given to the aldermen of the City to assemble the men of their several wards, to see that they were suitably armed according to their rank and estate, and to make a return of the same in due course. 685

The king's advisers charged with treason, 14 Nov.

On the 14th Gloucester formally charged the king's five counsellors—the Archbishop of York, the Duke of Ireland, the Earl of Suffolk, Chief Justice Tressilian and Nicholas Brembre, "the false London knight," with treason. 686 The king retaliated by causing proclamation to be made to the effect that he had taken these same individuals under his own protection, and that no one should harm them save at his own peril. This protection was extended also to the king's uncle, the Duke of Gloucester, and the Earls of Arundel and Warwick, the impeaching parties.

The mayor and aldermen summoned to Windsor, 28 Nov.

On the 28th the mayor and aldermen were summoned to proceed to Windsor forthwith, to consult upon certain matters very weighty (*certeines treschargeauntes matirs*). 687 The City's archives contain no record of what took place at the interview, but it appears that the object of the conference was to ascertain how many men-at-arms the city would be likely to furnish the king at a crisis. The answer given by the mayor was not encouraging; the citizens were merchants and craftsmen, and not soldiers, save for the defence of the city itself; and the mayor straightway asked the king's permission to resign his office. 688

Richard obliged to submit.

Flight of the accused.

Finding that he could not rely on any assistance from the Londoners—whom Walsingham describes as fickle as a reed, siding at one time with the lords and at another time with the king 689—Richard was driven to temporise. He had already promised that in the next parliament his unfortunate advisers should be called to account, but long before parliament met (3 Feb., 1388), four out of the five culprits had made good their escape—at least for a time. Brembre alone was taken. 690 He had anticipated the blow by making over all his property at home and abroad to certain parties by deed, dated the 15th October, 1387, no doubt, upon a secret trust. 691

The lords appellant admitted into the city, Dec., 1387.

Notwithstanding the evident coolness of the citizens towards him, Richard determined to leave Windsor and spend Christmas at the Tower. He would be safer there, and less subject to the dominating influence of the Duke of Gloucester and the Earls of Arundel, Nottingham, Warwick and Derby, who objected to his shaking off the fetters of the commission. As soon as his intention was known, these five lords—who, from having been associated in appealing against Richard's counsellors, were styled "appellant"—hastened to London, and drawing up their forces outside the city's walls, demanded admittance. After some little hesitation, the mayor determined to admit them, defending his action to the king by declaring that they were his true liege men and friends of the realm. 692

The lords at the Guildhall, 18 Jan., 1388.

On the 18th January, 1388, the lords appeared at the Guildhall, accompanied by the Archbishop, the Bishops of Ely, Hereford, Exeter, and others. The Archbishop absolved the citizens of their oaths of allegiance, whilst the Bishop of Ely, the lord treasurer, deprecated any remarks made to the disparagement of the lords. The lords and the bishops had been indicted on an iniquitous charge, and there were some among the citizens who had been similarly indicted, but whether justly or unjustly he (the bishop) could not say. That would be decided by parliament. In the meantime they were ready to assist in settling the trade disputes in the city, for it was absurd for one body of the citizens to attempt to exterminate another. The citizens, however, showed no desire to accept the proffered mediation. 693

Trial of Brembre before parliament, Feb., 1388.

When parliament met (3 Feb.), a formidable indictment of thirty-nine charges was laid against the king's late advisers, of whom Brembre alone appeared. On the 17th February, he was brought up by the constable of the Tower, and was called on to answer off-hand the several charges of treason alleged against him. He prayed for time to take counsel's advice. This being refused, he claimed to support his cause by wager of battle, and immediately the whole company of lords, knights, esquires, and commons, flung down their gages so thick, we are told, that they "seemed like snow on a winter's day." 694 But the lords declared that wager by battle did not lie in such a case. When the trial was resumed on the following day, so much opposition arose between the king, who spoke strongly in Brembre's favour, and the lords, that it was decided to leave the question of the prisoner's guilt or innocence to a commission of lords, who, to the surprise and annoyance of the majority of the nobles, brought in a verdict of not guilty. Brembre was not to be allowed thus to escape. The lords sent for two representatives of the various crafts of the city to depose as to Brembre's guilt; but even so, the lords failed to get any definite verdict. At last they sent for the mayor, recorder, and some of the aldermen (*seniores*) to learn what they had to say about the accused.

Conviction and sentence of death.

One would have thought that with Nicholas Exton, his old friend and ally, to speak up for him, Brembre's life would now at least be saved, even if he were not altogether acquitted. It was not so, however. The mayor and aldermen were asked as to their *opinion* (not as to their knowledge), whether Brembre was cognisant of certain matters, and they gave it as their *opinion* that Brembre was more likely to have been cognisant of them than not. Turning then to the Recorder, the lords asked him how stood the law in such a case? To which he replied, that a man who knew such things as were laid to Brembre's charge, and knowing them failed to reveal them, deserved death. On such evidence as this, Brembre was convicted on the 20th February, and condemned to be executed. 695 He was drawn on a hurdle through the city to Tyburn, showing himself very penitent and earnestly desiring all persons to pray for him. At the last moment he confessed that his conduct towards Northampton had been vile and wicked. Whilst craving pardon of Northampton's son "he was suddenly turned off, and the executioner cutting his throat, he died." 696

Character of Brembre as depicted by Walsingham.

If we are to believe all that Walsingham records of Brembre, the character and conduct of the city alderman and ex-mayor was bad indeed. Besides conniving at the plot laid against Gloucester's life, which involved the grossest breach of hospitality, he is recorded as having lain in wait with an armed force at the Mews near Charing Cross, to intercept and massacre the lords on their way to Westminster, to effect an arrangement with the king, as well as having entertained the idea of cutting the throats of a number of his fellow-citizens, and placing himself at the head of the government of the city, the name of which he proposed changing to that of "Little Troy." 697

Deaths of Tressilian and Uske.

Of Brembre's associates, Tressilian was captured during the trial, torn from the Sanctuary at Westminster, and hanged on the 19th. Another to share the same fate was Thomas Uske, who had been one of the chief witnesses against Northampton. He was sentenced to death by parliament on the 4th March, and died asseverating to the last that he had done Northampton no injury, but that every word he had deposed against him the year before was absolutely true. 698

The proceedings of the "merciless" parliament confirmed by oath.

The lords appellant, who were now complete masters of the situation, insisted upon the proceedings of this "merciless" parliament, as its opponents called it, being ratified by oath administered to prelates, knights, and nobles of the realm, as well as to the mayor, aldermen, and chief burgesses of every town. On the 4th June—the day parliament rose—a writ was issued in Richard's name, enjoining the administration of this oath to those aldermen and citizens of London who had not been present in parliament when the oath was administered there. 699

Party spirit in the city, 1388-1389.

In the meantime the continued jealousy existing among the city guilds — the Mercers, Goldsmiths, Drapers, and others, objecting to Fishmongers and Vintners taking any part in the government of the city on the ground that they were victuallers, and as such forbidden by an ordinance passed when Northampton was mayor to hold any municipal office 700 — had led parliament (14 May) to proclaim free trade throughout the kingdom. 701 A party in the city tried to get parliament to remove Exton from the mayoralty on the ground of his having connived at the curtailment of the City's liberties and franchises. The attempt, however, failed, and he remained in office until succeeded by Nicholas Twyford (Oct., 1388). 702 Although Twyford belonged to the party of Northampton as distinguished from that of Brembre and Exton, his election raised little or no opposition, such as had been anticipated. When he went out of office in October, 1389, however, party strife in the city again showed itself. The majority of the citizens voted William Venour, a grocer, into the mayoralty, but the choice was strongly opposed by the Goldsmiths, the Mercers, and the Drapers, who ran another candidate, one of their own body, Adam Bamme, a goldsmith. 703

The return of Northampton to the city, 1390.

Some months before the close of Twyford's mayoralty, Richard had succeeded in gaining his independence (May, 1389), which he was induced by Lancaster, on his return after a prolonged absence abroad, to exercise at length in favour of Northampton, by permitting him once more to return to London, although only as a stranger. 704 This was in July. In December, letters patent granting him a free pardon were issued, containing no such restriction. 705 His re-appearance in the streets of the city revived the old party spirit, and Adam Bamme, who had succeeded Venour in the mayoralty, found it expedient to forbid all discussion of the rights and the wrongs of the several parties of Northampton and Brembre on pain of imprisonment. 706 Four more years elapsed before Northampton was re-instated in the freedom of the city. 707

Proclamation enforcing knighthood, Feb., 1392.

For some years Richard governed not unwisely. In 1392, however, he quarrelled with the city. Early in that year he called upon every inhabitant, whose property for the last three years was worth £40 in land or rent, to take upon himself the honour of knighthood. The sheriffs, Henry Vanner and John Shadworth, made a return that all tenements and rents in the city were held of the king *in capite* as fee burgage at a fee farm (*ad feodi firmam*); that by reason of the value of tenements varying from time to time, and many of them requiring repair from damage by fire and tempest, their true annual value could not be ascertained, and that, therefore, it was impossible to make a return of those who possessed £40 of land or rent as desired. 708

The mayor summoned to Nottingham, June, 1392.

This answer was anything but agreeable to the king. But he had other cause just now for being offended with the city. Being in want of money, he had offered a valuable jewel to the citizens as security for a loan, and the citizens had excused themselves on the plea that they were not so well off as they used to be, since foreigners had been allowed to enjoy the same privileges in the city as themselves. Having failed in this quarter, the king had resorted to a Lombard, who soon was able to accommodate him; but when the king learnt on enquiry that the money so obtained had been advanced to the Lombard merchant by the very citizens who had refused to lend it to the king himself, his anger knew no bounds, 709 and he summoned John Hende, the mayor, the sheriffs, the aldermen, and twenty-four of the chief citizens 710 of the City to attend him in June, at Nottingham. They accordingly set out on their journey on the 19th June, and arrived in Nottingham on the 23rd; the government of the city being left in the meanwhile in the hands of William Staundon. On the 25th they appeared before the lords of the council, when the chancellor rated them roundly for paying so little attention to the king's writ—the writ touching knighthood—and complained of the defective manner in which the city was governed. 711

The mayor and sheriffs committed to prison, June, 1392.

He thereupon dismissed the mayor from office, committing him to Windsor Castle. The sheriffs were likewise dismissed, one being sent to Odyham Castle, and the other to the Castle of Wallingford. The rest of the citizens were ordered to return home. 712

Sir Edward Dalyngrigge appointed warden of the city, July, 1392.

At nine o'clock in the morning of the 1st July, Sir Edward Dalyngrigge appeared in the Guildhall, and there, before an immense assembly of the commons, read the king's commissions appointing him warden of the city and the king's escheator. The deposed sheriffs were succeeded by Gilbert Maghfeld, or Maunfeld, and Thomas Newton, who remained in office, by the king's appointment, 713 until the end of the year, when they were re-elected, the one by the warden and the other by the citizens. 714 Dalyngrigge was soon afterwards succeeded in the office of warden by Sir Baldwin de Radyngton. 715

The City fined £100,000, July, 1392.

By way of inflicting further punishment upon the citizens, Richard had already removed the King's Bench and Exchequer from London to York; 716 but the removal proved so much more prejudicial to the nation at large than to the City of London that the courts were soon brought back. 717 He would even have waged open war on them had he dared. 718 Instead of proceeding to this extremity, he summoned the aldermen and 400 commoners to Windsor 719 and fined the City £100,000. This was in July (1392). In August the king notified his intention of passing through the city on his way from Shene to Westminster. The citizens embraced the opportunity of giving him a magnificent reception, which the king acknowledged in the following month by restoring to them their liberties and setting free their late mayor and sheriffs. 720 The fine of £100,000 recently imposed, as well as other moneys which the king considered to be due to him from the city, were also remitted. 721

Municipal reforms, 1393.

Once more restored to their liberties, the citizens in the following year (1393), with the assent of parliament, effected a reform in the internal government of the city which the increasing population had rendered necessary. The Ward of Farringdon Within and Without had increased so much in wealth and population that it was deemed advisable to divide it into two parts, each part having its own alderman. Accordingly, in the following March (1394), Drew Barantyn was elected Alderman of Farringdon Within, whilst John Fraunceys was elected for Farringdon Without. A more important reform effected at the same time was the appointment of aldermen for life instead of for a year only. 722

Change of conduct on the part of Richard, 1394-1398.

In the following year (1394) the queen—Anne of Bohemia—died. She had always shown a friendly disposition towards the city, and it was mainly owing to her intercession that Richard had restored its liberties. 723 Her death removed one good influence about Richard, and marks a change of policy or of character. 724 His second marriage in 1396 did not improve matters. In that year the mayor, Adam Bamme, died in office, and instead of allowing the citizens freely to elect a successor, he thrust upon them Richard Whitington. 725 He arrested the Duke of Gloucester and the Earls of Warwick and Arundel, and otherwise behaved so outrageously as to raise doubts as to his sanity. He gave out that he was afraid to appear in public for fear of the Londoners; but this was only a ruse for the purpose of raising money. 726 Like Edward II, he borrowed money from anybody and everybody, and often resorted to unconstitutional measures to fill his purse. He made the nobles and his wealthier subjects sign blank cheques for him to fill up at his pleasure. 727 These cheques, or "charters" as they were called, were afterwards burnt by order of his successor on the throne.

The landing of Henry of Lancaster, July, 1399.

A crisis was fast approaching. The Duke of Hereford, whom the king had banished, and who, on the death of his father "time honoured Lancaster," succeeded to the title early in 1399, was prevailed upon to return to England and strike a blow for the recovery of his inheritance which Richard had seized. Richard, as if infatuated, took this inopportune moment to sail to Ireland. Before setting out he made a last bid for the favour of the citizens by again granting them permission to rule the fish trade according to ancient custom. 728 It was too late; they had already resolved to throw in their lot with Henry of Lancaster.

As soon as Henry had landed at Ravenspur (4th July) a special messenger was despatched to the city with the news. The mayor was in bed, but he hurriedly rose and took steps to proclaim Henry's arrival in England. "Let us apparel ourselves and go and receive the Duke of Lancaster, since we agreed to send for him," was the resolution of those to whom the mayor conveyed the first tidings; and accordingly Drew Barentyn, who had succeeded Whitington in October, 1398, and 500 other citizens, took horse to meet the duke, whom they escorted to the city. The day that Henry entered the city was kept as a holiday, "as though it had been the day for the celebration of Easter."

Richard's surrender and deposition from the crown.

When Richard heard of Henry's landing he hurried back from Ireland. He was met by the duke with a large force, which comprised 1,200 Londoners, fully armed and horsed. 729 Finding resistance hopeless, the king made submission, craving only that he might be protected from the Londoners, who, he was convinced, bore him no good will. He was, in consequence, secretly conveyed to the Tower under cover of night. Articles were drawn up accusing him of misgovernment, and publicly read in the Guildhall. Four of his advisers and supporters, whose names he gave up, hoping to gain favour for himself thereby, were executed at a fishmonger's stall in Cheapside. Sentence of deposition was passed against him, and Lancaster proclaimed king in his stead under the title of King Henry IV.

CHAPTER X.

Doubtful reports as to the late king's death.

The sentence passed on the late king proved his death warrant; his haughty spirit broke down, and he died at Pontefract the following year. According to Henry's account he died of wilful starvation. There were many, however, who believed him to have been put to death by Henry's orders; whilst others, on the contrary, refused to believe his death had actually taken place at all, notwithstanding the fact of the corpse having been purposely exposed to public view throughout its journey from Pontefract to London. 730 This belief that Richard was still alive was fostered by many, and, among others, by William Serle. He had been at one time the late king's chamberlain, and he kept up the delusion of Richard being still in the land of the living, by exhibiting the late king's signet, which had come into his possession. Serle was eventually arrested in the north of England and brought to London, to be executed at Tyburn. 731

The "Trumpington" Conspiracy, 1416-1420.

Sixteen years later (1416), a certain Thomas Warde, called "Trumpyngtone," personated the late king, and a scheme was laid for placing him on the throne with the aid of Sigismund, king of the Romans Sigismund, however, refused to have anything to do with the plot, which was hatched within the city's liberties by Benedict Wolman and Thomas Bekering. The conspiracy having been discovered, its authors were thrown into prison. One died before trial, the other paid the penalty for his rashness with his head. 732 In August, 1420, long after Trumpington was dead, two others, Thomas Cobold and William Bryan, endeavoured still to keep up the delusion in the city. The mayor, Whitington, himself ordered their arrest. Bryan had time to escape from the house of William Norton, a barber given to Lollardry, where he and his fellow conspirator were lodged. Cobold tried to hide himself, but was discovered cunningly concealed in the house, and taken before the mayor and aldermen. Being questioned as to the identity of Trumpington and the late king, he gave an evasive reply, adding, that the question of identity had become immaterial since Trumpington had been dead some time. Cobold was thought to be too dangerous a man to be allowed at large, so he was committed to prison. 733

Proceedings against the Lollards.

In the meantime Wycliffe had died (1384), and Lollardry had become only another name for general discontentment. The clergy made strenuous efforts to suppress the Lollards. Pope Boniface had invoked the assistance of the late king (1395) to destroy these "tares" (*lolium aridum*) that had sprung up amidst the wheat which remained constant to church and king, and called upon the mayor and commonalty of the city to use their interest with Richard to the same end. 734 Besides seeking the support of the commonalty against the powerful nobles, the new king sought the support of the church, and he had not been long on the throne before he issued commissions for search to be made in the city for Lollards, and for the arrest of all preachers found sowing the pestilential seed of Lollardry (*semen pestiferum lollardrie*). 735 Early in 1401 a price was put upon the head of the captain and leader of the sect, Sir John Oldcastle, otherwise known as Lord Cobham. Public proclamation was made in the city, that any one giving information which should lead to his arrest should be rewarded with 500 marks; any one actually arresting or causing him to be arrested should receive double that amount, whilst the citizens and burgesses of any city or borough who should take and produce him before the king, should be for ever quit of all taxes, talliages, tenths, fifteenths and other assessments. 736 Not only were conventicles forbidden, but no one was allowed to visit the ordinary churches after nine o'clock at night or before five o'clock in the morning. 737

The statute of heresy, 1401.

Still the clergy were not satisfied. The ecclesiastical courts could condemn men as heretics, but they had no power to burn them. Accordingly, a statute was passed this year (1401), known as the statute of heresy (*de hæretico comburendo*), authorising the ecclesiastical courts to hand over to the civil powers any heretic refusing to recant, or relapsing after recantation, so that he might pay the penalty of being publicly burnt before the people. 738 It was the first English law passed for the suppression of religious opinion, and its first victim is said to have been one William Sautre, formerly a parish priest of Norfolk. 739

Henry's other troubles.

Henry had other difficulties to face besides opposition from the nobles. France had refused to acknowledge his title to the crown, and demanded the restoration of Richard's widow, a mere child of eleven. The Scots 740 and the Welsh were on the point of engaging in open insurrection. Invasion was imminent; the exchequer was empty, and the Londoners appealed to could offer no more than a paltry loan of 4,000 marks. 741

Supplies granted by parliament in 1404.

As time went on, Henry had to try new methods for raising money. The parliament which met at the opening of 1404, granted the king a 1s. in the pound on all lands, tenements and rents, besides 20s. for every knight's fee. The money so raised was not, however, to be at the disposal of the king's own ministers, but was to be placed in the hands of four officials to be known as treasurers of war (*Guerrarum Thesaurarii*). The names of the treasurers elected for the purpose are given as John Owdeby, clerk, John Hadley, Thomas Knolles, and Richard Merlawe, citizens of London. 742 Three of these were citizens of note. Hadley had already served as mayor in 1393, Knolles had filled the same office in 1399, and was re-elected in 1410, whilst Merlawe was destined to attain that honour both in 1409 and 1417.

More city loans in 1409 & 1412.

It was during Merlawe's first mayoralty that the citizens advanced to the king the sum of 7,000 marks, 743 to enable him to complete the reduction of Wales, which his son, the Prince of Wales, had already nearly accomplished. In 1412 they advanced a further sum of 10,000 marks. 744 At the beginning of that year a commission was addressed by Henry to Robert Chichele, the mayor, brother of the archbishop of the same name, to the sheriffs of the city, to Richard Whitington and Thomas Knolles, the late mayor, instructing them to make a return of the amount of land and tenements held in the city and suburbs, with the view of levying 6s. 8d. on every £20 annual rent by virtue of an act passed by the late parliament. 745 A return was made to the effect that it was very difficult to discover the true value of lands and tenements in the city and suburbs, owing to absence of tenants and dilapidations by fire and water, but that they had caused enquiry to be made, and the names of men, women and other persons (*hominum, feminarum et aliarum personarum*) mentioned in the commission were forwarded by them in the following a, b, c (*in sequenti a, b, c*). What lands and tenements the "men, women and other persons" had elsewhere they had no means of discovering. 746 The schedule, or "a, b, c," is not entered in the City Letter Book, but is to be found among the Exchequer Rolls, preserved at Her Majesty's Public Record 747 Office. The gross rental was returned at £4,220, and the sum paid into the exchequer at 6s. 8d. for every £20, under the provisions of the act amounted to £70 6s. 8d. The mayor and commonalty of the city are credited as possessing lands, tenements and rents of an annual value of no more than £150 9s. 11d., whilst the Bridge House Estate was returned at £148 15s. 3d. Of the livery companies, the Goldsmiths appear as the owners of the largest property, their rental of city property amounting to £46 10s. 1/2d., the Merchant Tailors following them closely with £44 3s. 7d. The Mercers had but a rental of £13 18s. 4d. whilst the Skinners had £18 12s. 8d. Robert Chichele, the mayor, was already a rich man, with an annual rental of £42

19s. 2d., derived from city property, or nearly double the amount (£25) with which Richard Whitington was credited.

Whitington mayor for the third time, 1406.

Whitington had already three times occupied the mayoralty chair; once (in 1396) at the word of a king, and twice (in 1397 and 1406) at the will of his fellow citizens. On the occasion of his third election a solemn mass was for the first time introduced into the proceedings, the mayor, aldermen and a large body of commoners attending the service at the Guildhall Chapel, before proceeding to the election. 748 The custom which then sprang up continues in a modified form to this day, the election of a mayor being always preceded by divine service. Its origin may perhaps be ascribed in some measure to the spirit of Lollardry which, in its best sense, found much favour with the citizens.

The enormous wealth which he succeeded in amassing was bestowed in promoting the cause of education, and in relieving the sufferings of the poor and afflicted. He built a handsome library in the house of the Grey Friars and also the Church of Saint Michael in the "Riole." He is credited by some writers with having purchased and presented to the corporation the advowson of the Church of St. Peter upon Cornhill. But this is probably a mistake arising from the fact of a license in mortmain having been granted by Henry IV to Richard Whitington, John Hende, and others, to convey the manor of Leadenhall, together with the advowsons of the several churches of Saint Peter upon Cornhill and Saint Margaret Patyns, held of the king in free burgage, to the mayor and commonalty of the City of London and their successors. 749

Further proceedings against Oldcastle and the Lollards, 1413.

On the accession of Henry V, Archbishop Arundel, whom Walsingham describes as the most eminent bulwark and indomitable supporter of the church, 750 renewed his attack on the Lollards, and endeavoured to serve Oldcastle with a citation. Failing to accomplish this he caused him to be arrested. The bold defence made by the so-called heretic, when before his judges, gained additional weight from the reputation he enjoyed for high moral character. Nevertheless he was adjudged guilty of the charges brought against him. A formal sentence of excommunication was passed, and he was remitted to the Tower for forty days in the hope that at the expiration of that time he might be found willing to retract. This, however, was not to be.

Meeting of Lollards in St. Giles' Fields, 12 Jan., 1414.

He contrived to make his escape from prison, 751 and shortly afterwards appeared at the head of a number of followers in St. Giles's Fields. Great disappointment was felt at not receiving the assistance that had been expected from city servants and apprentices. According to Walsingham, no less than 5,000 men, comprising masters as well as servants, from the city, were prepared to join the insurgents, had not the king taken precautions to secure the gates. As soon as it was discovered that the young king had made ample preparations to meet attack, the Lollards took to flight. Many, however, failed to make good their escape, and nearly forty paid the penalty of their rashness with their lives. 752 Walsingham was probably misinformed as to the number of the persons who were prepared to assist the Lollards. The fact is that, to the respectable City burgess, Lollardism was a matter of less moment than was the scandalous life led by the chantry priest and other ministers of religion, and this the civic authorities were determined to rectify as far as in them lay. Between the years 1400 and 1440, some sixty clerks in holy orders were taken in adultery and clapt into prison by ward beadles. 753 Nevertheless the clergy, and more especially the chantry priest, continued to live a life of luxury and sloth, oftentimes spending the day in dicing, card playing, cock fighting and frequenting taverns.

The last Statute against the Lollards, 1414.

The recent abortive attempt of Oldcastle gave rise to another Statute against the Lollards, 754 by which the secular power, no longer content with merely carrying into execution the sentences pronounced by ecclesiastical courts, undertook, where necessary, the initiative against heretics. Archbishop Arundel, the determined enemy of the Lollards, had had no hand in framing this Statute—the last that was enacted against them. 755 He had died a few months before parliament met, and had been succeeded by Henry Chichele.

The king's offer of pardon refused by Oldcastle, 1415.

Early in the following year (1415) the king made an offer of pardon to Oldcastle, who was still at large, if he would come in and make submission before Easter. 756 Instead of accepting so generous an offer, Oldcastle busied himself in preparing for another rising to take place as soon as the king should have set sail on his meditated expedition to France. Lollard manifestoes again appeared on the doors of the London churches; whilst Oldcastle himself scoured the country for recruits, to serve under a banner on which the most sacred emblems of the church were depicted. 757

Trial and execution of Cleydon, a Lollard, 1415.

In August (1415) another Lollard, John Cleydone by name, a currier by trade, was tried in St. Paul's Church before the new Archbishop and others, the civic authorities having taken the initiative according to the provisions of the recent Statute, and arrested him on suspicion of being a heretic. The mayor himself was a witness at the trial, and testified as to the nature of certain books found in Cleydon's possession; they were "the worst and the most perverse that ever he did read or see." Walsingham, who styles Cleydon "an inveterate Lollard" (*quidam inveteratus Lollardus*), adds, with his usual acerbity against the entire sect, that the accused had gone so far as to make his own son a priest, and have Mass celebrated by him in his own house on the occasion when his wife should have gone to church, after rising from childbed. 758 Having been convicted of heresy by the ecclesiastical court, the prisoner was again delivered over to the secular authorities for punishment. 759 Both he and his books were burnt. 760

Oldcastle taken and executed, 1417.

Two years later Oldcastle himself was captured in Wales and brought to London. At his trial he publicly declared his belief that Richard II was still alive; he was even fanatic enough to believe that he himself would soon rise again from the dead. 761 He was sentenced to be hanged and burnt on the gallows, a sentence which was carried out in St. Giles's Fields. 762 Lollardry continued to exist, especially in London and the towns, for some years, but it ceased to have any historical or political significance. 763

Preparations for the invasion of France, 1414-1415.

Henry V was resolved to maintain not only the old religion of the days of Edward III, but also the old foreign policy, and in 1414 he commenced making preparations for renewing the claim of his great-grandfather to the crown of France. In 1415 this claim was formally made, and Henry gathered his forces together at Southampton. On the 10th March he informed the civic authorities of his intention of crossing over to France to enforce his claim and of his need of money. On the 14th a brilliant assembly, comprising the king's two brothers, John, Duke of Bedford, and Humphrey, Duke of Gloucester, Edward, Duke of York, the Archbishop of Canterbury, the Bishop of Winchester, and others, met at the Guildhall to consider the matter.

A question of precedence in the city.

A question arose as to order of precedence, and it was arranged that the mayor, as the king's representative in the City, should occupy the centre seat, having the Primate and the Bishop of Winchester on his right, and the Duke of York and the king's brothers on his left. 764 This question having been settled, the meeting, we presume, got to business; but what took place is not recorded in the City's archives. We know, however, that in June the king pledged his jewels to the City for a loan of 10,000 marks, 765 and that on the 1st August—just as he was preparing to set sail—he raised a further loan of 10,000 marks on the security of the customs. 766

The king takes leave of the citizens on Blackheath, June, 1415.

On the 15th June the king, who was then on his way to the coast, took solemn leave of the civic authorities, who had accompanied him to Blackheath. He bade them go home and keep well his "chamber" during his absence abroad, giving them his blessing and saying "Cryste save London." 767 Arriving at Southampton, he there discovered a conspiracy to place the young Earl of March, the legitimate heir of Edward III, on the throne, as soon as he himself should have set sail. The traitors were seized and executed, and the City lost no time in sending the king a letter congratulating him upon his discovery of the plot. 768

The capture of Harfleur, 18 Sept., 1415.

A few days later (12th August) he sailed for France and landed near Harfleur, to which town he laid siege. It offered, however, a stubborn defence, and it was not until the 18th September that the town surrendered. On the 22nd Henry sent a long account of the siege and capture to the mayor and citizens of London, bidding them render humble thanks to Almighty God for this mercy, and expressing a hope of further success in the near future. 769

Volunteers for service in France required, Oct., 1415.

Citizens invited to reside in Harfleur.

Early in October the king caused proclamation to be made in the City, that all and singular knights, esquires and valets who were willing to go with him to Normandy, should present themselves to his uncle Henry, Bishop of Winchester and Treasurer of England, who would pay them their wages. By the same proclamation merchants, victuallers and handicraftmen were invited to take up their residence in the recently captured town of Harfleur, where houses would be assigned to them, and where they should enjoy the same privileges and franchises to which they had always been accustomed. 770

Joy in the city at the news of the battle of Agincourt, Oct., 1415.

The citizens welcome the king on his return from France.

The battle of Agincourt was fought on the 25th October, and news of the joyous victory arrived in England on or before the 28th, on which day— the Feast of St. Simon and St. Jude—Nicholas Wotton, the recently elected mayor, was sworn into office at the Guildhall according to custom. On the following day, therefore, the mayor, aldermen and a large number of the commonalty made a solemn pilgrimage on foot to Westminster, where they first made devout thanksgiving for the victory that had been won, and then proceeded to present the new mayor before the Barons of the Exchequer. Care is taken in the City records to explain that the procession went on this occasion on foot, simply and solely for the purpose of marking their humble thanks to the Almighty and his Saints, and more especially to Edward the Confessor, who lay interred at Westminster, for the joyful news which so unexpectedly had arrived. The journey on foot was not to be drawn into precedent when others succeeded to the mayoralty, nor supplant the riding in state which had been customary on such occasions. 771 The reception given to the king by the Londoners on his return from France, was of so brilliant and varied a character, that one chronicler declares that a description of it would require a special treatise. 772 On the 16th November he landed at Dover and proceeded towards London. On Saturday, the 23rd, the mayor and aldermen and all the companies rode forth in their liveries to meet the king and conduct him and his train of French prisoners through the City to Westminster. On Sunday morning a deputation from the City waited upon Henry and presented him with the sum of £1,000 and two basons of gold worth half that sum. 773

Preparations for another expedition, 1416-1417.

During the next eighteen months succeeding the battle of Agincourt, Henry devoted himself to making preparations at home for renewing active military operations. He had intended at midsummer, 1416, to lead an expedition in person to the relief of Harfleur, but the command was subsequently delegated to his brother, the Duke of Bedford. Proclamation was publicly made in the city by order of the king, dated the 28th May, that all and singular knights, esquires and valets holding any fief or annuity from the king should proceed to Southampton by the 20th June, armed each according to his estate, for the purpose of joining the expedition. 774 In 1417 France was rendered weak by factions, and Henry seized the opportunity for another attack. On the 1st February he issued his writ to the sheriffs of London for a return to be made of the number of men-at-arms and archers the City knights could furnish. 775 In March the mayor, Henry Barton, was made a commissioner for victualling the navy which was to rendezvous at Southampton. 776

City loans, 1417.

In the same month the City advanced the king the sum of 5,000 marks, 777 and in the following June a further sum was advanced by private subscription among the wealthier citizens on the security of a Spanish sword, set in gold and precious stones, of the estimated value of £2,000. The sword was pledged with the subscribers on the understanding that they would not dispose of it before Michaelmas twelve-month. 778

Letter from the king to the City announcing his success, 9 Aug., 1417.

Another letter informing them of the capture of Caen, 5 Sept.

On the 9th August the king addressed a letter to the mayor, sheriffs, aldermen and good folk of the City of London, informing them of his safe arrival in Normandy and of his success in making himself master of the castle of "Touque" without bloodshed. 779 To this the citizens sent a dutiful reply on the 28th day of the same month, assuring the king of the peaceful condition of the city. On the 2nd September an order went forth from the Common Council of the City that each alderman should immediately instruct the constables of his ward to go their rounds and warn all soldiers they might come across, to vacate the City and set out on the king's service before the end of the week on pain of imprisonment. 780 Success continued to attend Henry's arms. On the 5th September he was able to inform the citizens, by letter, 781 of the capture of Caen, excepting only the citadel, and this was to be rendered to him by the 19th day of the same month at the latest, unless relief should have previously arrived for the besieged from the King of France, his son the Dauphin, or the Count of Armagnac, Constable of France. The Duke of Clarence wrote a few days later to the citizens, notifying the extraordinary success which had followed the king. So many towns and fortresses had been taken that the only fear was that there were not sufficient men to keep guard over them. 782

Proclamation by the Duke of Bedford, 18 Oct.

Supplies granted by parliament, Dec, 1417.

In order to keep the English force in Normandy better provided with victuals, the Duke of Bedford, who had been left behind as the king's lieutenant, caused the Sheriffs of London to proclaim that all persons willing and able to ship victuals to France for Henry's use, might do so without paying custom dues on their giving security that the victuals should be sent to Caen and not elsewhere. 783 Bedford, who was learning how to rule a free people—a lesson which, had he been allowed to practice in after years, might have saved the house of Lancaster from utter destruction 784—presided in the parliament, which met in November, 1417. On the 17th December this parliament granted the king two fifteenths and two tenths. No time was lost in taking measures for collecting these supplies, the king's writ appointing commissioners for the City of London being issued the day following. 785

Henry's conquest of Normandy, 1417-1419.

In Paris matters were going on from bad to worse. Whilst the capital of France was at the mercy of a mob, Henry proceeded to lay close siege to Rouen. Frequent proclamation was made in London for reinforcements to join the king, either at Rouen or elsewhere in Normandy. 786 This was in April, 1418, or thereabouts. On the 5th July, the Duke of Clarence informed Richard Merlawe, the mayor, by letter, of the fall of Louviers, and of the expected surrender of Pont de l'Arche, 787 from which latter place the duke wrote. On the 10th August Henry himself wrote to the citizens informing them of his having sat down before Rouen and of the straits his forces were in for lack of victuals and more especially of "drink." He begged them to send as many small vessels as they could, laden with provisions, to Harfleur, whence they could make their way up the Seine to Rouen. 788 In less than a month a reply was sent (8 Sept.) from Gravesend under the seal of the mayoralty, informing Henry that the citizens had been busy brewing ale and beer and purveying wine and other "vitaille," and that they had despatched thirty butts of sweet wine—comprising ten of "Tyre," ten of "Romesey," and ten of "Malvesy"—and 1,000 pipes of ale and beer. With these they had also sent 25,000 cups for the king's "host" to drink out of. 789 In the meantime, the besieged received no such relief from the pains of hunger and thirst, and on the 19th January, 1419, they were compelled to surrender their ancient town. 790 The war continued throughout the year (1419), all attempts at a reconciliation proving abortive. Pointoise fell into Henry's hands; and both Henry and the Duke of Clarence sent word of its capture to London. The duke took the opportunity of asking that the freedom of the City might be conferred on his servant, Roger Tillyngton, a skinner; but the citizens in acknowledging the duke's letter make no reference to his request. 791

The king's letter to the City, 17 Aug., 1419.

On the 17th August the king wrote again to the mayor, aldermen and commons of the City, thanking them for their "kynde and notable prone of an ayde," which they had granted of their own free will, therein setting a good example to others, and prayed them to follow such directions as the Duke of Bedford should give them respecting their proffered assistance. The bearer of this letter having been taken prisoner at Crotoye, a duplicate copy of it was afterwards forwarded from Trie le Chastel on the 12th September. 792

The treaty of Troyes, 20 May. 1420.

The murder of John, Duke of Burgundy, by a partisan of the Dauphin, which took place about this time, induced Duke Philip to come to terms with England in the hope of avenging his father's death; 793 and the French king, finding further resistance hopeless, was content to make peace. By the treaty of Troyes (20 May, 1420), the Dauphin was disinherited in favour of Henry, who was formally recognised as the heir to the French crown, and who agreed to marry Catherine, daughter of Charles VI. 794 The marriage took place on the 3rd June, and on the 14th a solemn procession was made in London and a sermon preached at Paul's Cross in honour of the event. 795

The king's letter to the City, 12 July, 1420.

The mayor's reply, 2 Aug.

On the 12th July Henry addressed a letter from Mant to the corporation of London informing them of his welfare. He had left Paris for Mant in order to relieve the town of Chartres, which was being threatened by the Dauphin. The Duke of Burgundy had joined him and had proved himself "a trusty, lovvng and faithful brother." The king's expedition proved unnecessary, for the Dauphin had raised the siege before his arrival and had gone into Touraine. To this letter a reply was sent under the mayoralty seal on the 2nd August, congratulating Henry upon his success, and assuring him that there was no city on earth more peaceful or better governed than his City of London. 796

The queen's coronation.

On the 26th January, 1421, the Duke of Gloucester, the Guardian of England in the king's absence, ordered the Sheriffs of London to announce that the queen's coronation would take place at Westminster on the third Sunday in Lent. 797 The king and queen landed at Dover with a small retinue on the 1st February, and after a few days' rest at Canterbury, entered the city of London amid tokens of welcome and respect from the laity and clergy. They took up their abode at the Tower, whence they were conducted on the day appointed for the coronation to Westminster by the citizens on foot and on horseback. 798

Henry's last expedition, and death, Aug., 1422.

Henry had not been at home six months before he again left England, never to return. 799 The hopes that he entertained of reforming and governing his possessions in France, and his ambition to have headed, sooner or later, a crusade which should have stayed the progress of the Ottoman and have recovered the sepulchre of Christ, were not destined to be realised. He died at the Bois de Vincennes, near Paris, on the last day of August, 1422, leaving a child nine months old—the unhappy Henry of Windsor who succeeded to the throne as Henry VI. When the body of the late king was brought over from France to be buried at Westminster, the citizens showed it every token of respect in its passage through London. The streets of the city, as well as of the borough of Southwark, were cleaned for the occasion. The mayor, sheriffs, recorder and aldermen, accompanied by the chief burgesses, and clad in white gowns and hoods, went forth to meet the remains of the king they loved so well, as far as St. George's bar in Southwark, and reverently conducted them to St. Paul's Church, where the funeral obsequies were performed. The next day they accompanied the corpse to Westminster, where further ceremonies took place. Representatives of the various wards were told off to line the streets, the solemnity of the occasion being marked by the burning of torches, whilst chaplains stood in the porches of the various churches, clad in their richest copes, with thuribles in their hands, and chanted the *venite* and incensed the royal remains as they passed. The livery companies provided amongst them 211 torches, and to each torch-bearer the city chamberlain gave a gown and hood of white material or "blanket" (*de blanqueto*), at the "cost of the commonalty." 800

CHAPTER XI.

Rivalry between Bedford and Gloucester, 1422.

At the death of Henry V the administration of affairs fell into the hands of his two brothers, John, Duke of Bedford, and Humfrey, Duke of Gloucester. On the 29th September a writ was issued from Windsor, in the name of the infant on whom the crown of England had devolved, summoning four citizens of London to attend a parliament to be held at Westminster at Martinmas, 801 and two days afterwards another was addressed to the sheriffs of London, enjoining them to make proclamation for the keeping the king's peace, and authorising them to arrest and imprison rioters until the king and his council should determine upon their punishment. 802 The precise wishes of the late king as to the respective parts which Bedford and Gloucester were to undertake in the government of the realm are not clearly known, but it is generally thought that he intended the former to govern France, whilst the latter was to act as his vicegerent in England. An attempt to carry out the arrangement was doomed to failure.

As soon as parliament met (9 Nov.) it took into consideration the respective claims of the two dukes. Bedford had already (26 Oct.) despatched a letter from Rouen, addressed to the civic authorities, setting forth his right to the government of the realm, as elder brother of the deceased sovereign and as the party most interested in the succession to the crown. Without mentioning Gloucester by name, he warned the citizens against executing orders derogatory to himself. He professed to do this, not from any ambitious designs of his own, but from a wish to preserve intact the laws, usage and customs of the realm. 803 After some hesitation, parliament resolved to appoint Bedford protector as soon as he should return from France, but that during his absence Gloucester should act for him. 804

An expedition to start for France, 1 March, 1423.

On the 8th February of the new year (1423), the sheriffs of London received orders to make proclamation for all soldiers who were in the king's pay to assemble at Winchelsea by the 1st day of March, as an expedition was to set sail from that port for the purpose of defending the town and castle of Crotoye. The business was pressing and necessitated a repetition of the order to the sheriffs a fortnight later (22 Feb.). 805

Sir John Mortimer.

On the 23rd February William Crowmere, the mayor, William Sevenoke, William Waldene, and John Fray were appointed commissioners to enquire into cases of treason and felony within the city; and two days later they found Sir John Mortimer, who was charged with a treasonable design in favour of the Earl of March, guilty of having broken prison. 806 He was subsequently convicted of treason both by lords and commons, and sentenced to death.

The debts of Henry IV.

On the 5th June (1423) the hearts of the citizens were gladdened with the news that they were likely to be repaid some of the money they had advanced to the king's grandfather. Orders were given for all persons to whom Henry IV was indebted at the time of his decease, and who had not yet received from his executors a moiety of the sums due, to send in their bills and tallies to Sir John Pelham and John Leventhorp, two of the king's executors, sitting at the Priory of Saint Mary, Southwark, by the Monday next after Midsummer-day. 807 We can believe that few orders ever met with readier response from the inhabitants of the city.

Gloucester and Beaufort, 1425-1428.

At home as well as abroad Gloucester soon made enemies; among them was his own uncle, the Chancellor, Henry Beaufort, Bishop of Winchester, a wealthy and ambitious prelate. During Gloucester's absence on the continent, whither he had gone to recover the estates of his newly-married wife, the ill-fated Jacqueline of Hainault, Beaufort garrisoned the Tower with creatures of his own. When Gloucester returned mutual recriminations took place, and the mayor was ordered (29 Oct., 1425) to prevent Beaufort entering the city. A riot ensued in which the citizens took the part of the duke, and the bishop had to take refuge in Southwark. The quarrel was patched up for awhile until Bedford, who was sent for, should arrive to act as arbitrator. 808 He arrived in London on the 10th January, 1426. The citizens, who had more than once been in communication with the duke 809 during his absence abroad, presented him with a pair of basins, silver-gilt, containing 1,000 marks. The gift, however, does not appear to have been so graciously received as it might have been, for a London alderman records that the donors, for all their liberality, "hadde but lytylle thanke." 810

End of the quarrel between Gloucester and Beaufort.

The two brothers had not met since the death of Henry V. After prolonged negotiations, a *modus vivendi* between the parties was arrived at, and Gloucester and the bishop were induced to shake hands. Beaufort left England soon afterwards with the Duke of Bedford, on the plea of making a pilgrimage, and did not return until September, 1428, by which time he had been made a cardinal and appointed papal legate in England. Notwithstanding his legatine authority being unacknowledged by Gloucester and others, the citizens received him on his return "worthily and loyally," riding out to meet him and escorting him into London. 811

Gloucester loses the favour of the citizens.

Gloucester had always been a favourite with the Londoners, until his conduct to his Flemish wife, whom he left behind on the continent to fight her own battles as best as she could, and the undisguised attention he paid to Eleanor Cobham, a lady in his wife's suite, whom he eventually married, estranged their favour. In August, 1424, the Common Council had voted the duke a gift of 500 marks; and two years later—viz., in April, 1426—the citizens raised a sum, variously stated to have been £1,000 and 1,000 marks, for the benefit of his duchess. 812 The female portion of the community were specially incensed against the duke, and a number of women went the length of presenting themselves before parliament in 1427, with a letter complaining of his behaviour towards his wife. In March of the next year (1428) the citizens themselves followed suit, and drew the attention of parliament, through the mouth of John Symond, their Recorder, to the wretched straits to which the duchess had been reduced, as witnessed her own letters. They begged parliament to consider the best means for recovering for her the lands of Hainault, Holland and Zeeland, which had always been places of sure refuge for the English merchant, and the rulers of which had ever been friendly to the king of England. The citizens finally avowed themselves ready to take upon themselves their share in any undertaking the lords and commons of the realm might decide upon. 813

The siege of Orleans, 1428-1429.

In the meantime matters had not gone well with the English in France. In July, 1427, the Earl of Salisbury came over to London for reinforcements. 814 In September of the following year he was able to inform the City of the success that had attended his recruited army. 815 He was then within a short distance of Orleans, before which town he shortly afterwards met his death. Bedford continued the siege, but the town held out until May, 1429, when it was relieved by the Maid from the little village of Domremi, and the English army was compelled to retreat.

Famine in London, 1429.

Whilst Bedford was conducting the siege of Orleans, and Jeanne Darc was meditating how best to relieve the town, the citizens of London were suffering from a severe dearth. At length the Common Council resolved (22 July, 1429) to send agents abroad for the purpose of transmitting all the corn they could lay their hands on to England. The assistance of Bedford, who had by this time been compelled to raise the siege of Orleans, was invoked. 816

Beaufort joins Bedford in France.

Bedford had recently been joined by Beaufort, who had become more than ever an object of hatred to Gloucester, and had lost to a certain extent the goodwill of the nation by the acceptance of a cardinal's hat. He had set out on the 22nd June (1429), carrying with him a small force which he was allowed to raise for the avowed object of prosecuting a Hussite crusade in Bohemia, but which was eventually sent to France. 817 The question of his position in parliament and the council, now that he was a cardinal, was decided by the parliament which met on the 22nd September.

Allowances made to those representing the City in parliament, 1429.

Members of parliament representing the City of London had hitherto been allowed a certain amount of cloth and fur trimming at the City's expense, wherewith to dress themselves and their personal attendants in a manner suitable to the position they held. Those who had from time to time been elected members appear to have abused this privilege—where a yard had been given, they had literally taken an ell—and it was now thought to be high time to take steps to check the abuse in future. Accordingly it was ordained by the mayor and aldermen, on the 12th August of this year (and the ordinance met with the approval of the commoners on the 29th day of the same month), that for the future no alderman elected to attend parliament should take out of the chamber or of the commonalty more than ten yards for gown and cloak, at 15s. the yard, and 100s. for fur if the alderman had already served as mayor, otherwise he was to have no more than five marks. Commoners were to be content with five yards of cloth and 33s. 4d. for fur. Each alderman, moreover, was to be allowed eight yards of cloth at 28 pence a yard for two personal attendants, and each commoner four yards of the same for one attendant, if the parliament was sitting in London or the neighbourhood, and eight yards for two attendants if parliament was sitting in some more remote place, "as was formerly ordained during the mayoralty of John Michell" (1424-5). 818

The coronation of Henry VI, 6 Nov., 1429.

The condition of France necessitated the early coronation of the young king, whose right to the French crown had been established by the Treaty of

Troyes. At his accession to the throne of England Henry VI was but a child of nine months. He was now eight years old. Before he could be crowned King of France, it was necessary that he should first be crowned King of England. Proclamation was accordingly made that he would be crowned on the 6th November following, and that all claims to services should be forthwith laid before the lord steward. 819 Gregory, to whose chronicle we have had frequent occasion to refer, writing as an eye-witness, gives a full account 820 of what took place at the ceremony of coronation in Westminster Abbey, and of the banquet that followed; but omits to mention that the citizens put in their usual claim, in accordance with the above proclamation, to serve the king at the banquet as butler. That the claim was actually made we learn from other sources. 821 We also know that William Estfeld, the recently-elected mayor, received the customary gold cup and ewer used on the occasion, which he afterwards bequeathed to his grandson. 822

Sets out for France, April, 1430.

And is crowned in Paris, Dec., 1431.

In April, 1430, the young king left England for France, and remained abroad for nearly two years. On the 10th November he wrote to the mayor and citizens, urging them to advance him the sum of 10,000 marks, as that sum might do him more ease and service at that particular time than double the amount at another. The letter was dated from Rouen, where the court afterwards established itself for a considerable time. 823 On Sunday, the 12th December, 1431, he made his entry into Paris with great ceremony, and was duly crowned. 824

The citizens welcome him on his return, 1432.

On his return to England early in the following year, he was met by John Welles, the mayor, the aldermen, the sheriffs, and more than 12,000 citizens of London, who rode out on Thursday, the 20th February, as far as Blackheath, and was there presented with the following address:—

> "Sovereign lord as welcome be ye to your noble Roialme of
> Englond, and in especial to your notable Cite London operwise
> called your Chambre, as ever was cristen prince to place or
> people, and of the good and gracioux achevyng of your Coronne of
> Fraunce, we thank hertlich our lord almyghty which of his endles
> mercy sende you grace in yoye and prosperite on us and all your
> other people long for to regne."

The mayor and aldermen present him with a gift of £1,000.

After hearing the address the king rode to Deptford, where he was met by a procession of 120 rectors and curates of the city, in the richest copes, and 500 secular chaplains in the whitest of surplices, with whom were a like number of monks bearing crosses, tapers and incense, and chanting psalms and antiphons in grateful thanks for his safe return. Thence the royal cavalcade passed through Southwark to the city, where pageants appeared at every turn. The fulsome adulation bestowed upon a lad scarcely ten years of age was enough to turn his young brain. Passing through Cornhill and Chepe, the procession eventually reached St. Paul's. There the king dismounted, and being met by the Archbishop of Canterbury and ten other bishops in their pontifical robes, was led by them to the high altar. Prayers were said and the sacred relics kissed. The king then remounted his horse and made his way to his palace of Westminster, the streets being hung with tapestry and the houses thronged to their roofs with crowds of onlookers, and was there allowed a brief day's rest. On the following Saturday a deputation from the city, headed by the mayor and aldermen, went to the palace and presented Henry with £1,000 of the purest gold, in a gold casket, with these words: —

"Most cristen prince the good folk of youre notable Cite of London, otherwise cleped your Chambre, besechen in her most lowely wise that they mowe be recomanded un to yor hynesse, ant þt can like youre noble grace to resceyve this litell yefte yoven with as good will and lovyng hertes as any yefte was yoven to eny erthly prince."

The king having graciously acknowledged the gift, the deputation returned to the city. 825

Gloucester's attacks on Beaufort and Bedford, 1432-1433.

Beaufort, who had returned home in time for the coronation, had again set out for France with the king, and Gloucester took advantage of their absence to renew his attack on his rival. Letters of *præmunire* were drawn up in anticipation of the cardinal's return, and additional offence was given by the seizure of the cardinal's plate and jewels at Dover. On learning of Gloucester's schemes, Beaufort determined to give up a projected visit to Rome, and to return home in time for the opening of parliament (12th May, 1432). 826 He desired to learn why he had been thus "strangely demeened" contrary to his deserts. When parliament met and the cardinal asked who were his accusers, Gloucester held his tongue, and the king expressed his confidence in the cardinal's loyalty. In the following year (1433) Bedford appeared before parliament and announced that he had come home to defend himself against false accusations. He understood that the recent losses that had occurred in France were attributed to his neglect. He desired his accusers, of whom he shrewdly suspected Gloucester to be one, to stand forth and prove their charges. Again there was silence, and the duke, like the cardinal, had to rest satisfied with the king's assurance of loyalty. 827

Financial reform, 1433.

The finances of the country were at this time (1433) in the most deplorable condition. It was necessary to exercise the strictest economy. Bedford was the first to set an example of self-denial by offering to discharge the duties of counsellor at a reduced salary. Gloucester followed his brother's example. The archbishops, the cardinal, and the bishops of Lincoln and Ely agreed to render their services without payment. Parliament showed its good will by voting a fifteenth and tenth, but out of the sum thus realised £4,000 was to be applied to the relief of poor towns. The amount of relief which fell to the share of the poorer wards of the City of London was £76 15s. 6-1/4d., which was apportioned among eighteen wards. The largest sum allotted was £20, which went to Cordwainer Street Ward, whilst Lime Street Ward received the magnificent relief afforded by the odd farthing. 828 The mayor, sheriffs and aldermen were called upon to attend in person before the chancellor, in April, 1434, to make oath that they would duly observe a certain article (*quendam articulum*) which the late parliament had agreed to, but what this article was does not appear in the City's archives. 829

The death of Bedford, 14 Sept., 1435.

Bedford was prevailed upon to remain in England and undertake the office of chief counsellor, but differences again arising between him and Gloucester, which the personal interference of the young king could with difficulty calm, he again set sail for France (June, 1434). His career was fast drawing to an end. Burgundy was intending to desert him as he knew full well, and the knowledge accelerated his end. His death took place at Rouen on the 14th September of the following year (1435). 830

Calais appeals to London for assistance, 27 June, 1436.

With his death England's supremacy in France began to decline, and Henry VI was to lose in that country all or nearly all that had been gained by his doughty predecessor. The defection of Burgundy was followed by the loss of Paris. The chief event of 1436 was the raising of the siege of Calais, which had been invested by the Duke of Burgundy. On the 27th June the mayor and aldermen of Calais, being anxious to get help from the government at home, and finding that according to precedent they could only do so through the mediation of the City of London, addressed a letter to the mayor and aldermen of London imploring them, as the head of "the principal of all the cities of the realm of England," to move the king to send the requisite aid. 831

In answer to this appeal Henry Frowyk, the mayor, consulted the livery companies, and by their advice sent a contingent to the relief of the town. 832 The king, too, had been very urgent that the City should raise a force to oppose "the man who stiled himself Duke of Burgundy and Count of Flanders," whilst he took pains to conciliate such Flemings as were living in the city and were ready to take an oath of allegiance. 833 Gloucester had been appointed captain of Calais for a term of nine years, but before he set sail for its relief the siege had been raised by Edmund Beaufort, Count of Mortain. 834

A tax imposed on aliens, 1439.

An attempt was made in 1439 to bring about a peace, but it failed, and a new tax—a tax upon aliens—had to be imposed for the purpose of raising money in addition to the usual supplies. Every alien householder was called upon to pay sixteen pence, and every alien who was not a householder sixpence, towards the expenses of the country. 835

The penance of Eleanor Cobham, Gloucester's wife, 1441.

The streets of the city have witnessed few sadder sights than the penance inflicted on Eleanor Cobham, at one time the mistress, and afterwards—on the dissolution of his marriage with Jacqueline—the wife of Gloucester. The new duchess was aware that in the event of the king's death her husband was next in succession to the throne, and was inclined to anticipate matters. It was a superstitious age, and the duchess invoked the aid of witchcraft to accomplish her wishes. In 1441 her operations, innocent as they were in themselves, however bad their intent, were discovered, and she was condemned to do public penance followed by imprisonment for life. For three days the wretched lady was made to walk the streets, taper in hand and bare-foot (it was November), in the sight of all the citizens, who were forbidden to show her any respect, but, at the same time, were ordered not to molest her. 836 The latter they were little likely to do. Nay! on each day as she landed at the Temple, at the Swan or at Oueenhithe, the mayor and sheriffs went forth to attend her, accompanied by members of the livery companies. 837 Yet, not a finger did her husband raise in her defence! He either could not or would not save her.

The king's charter to the City, 26 Oct., 1444.

By charter, dated the 26th day of October, 1444, the king confirmed the mayor, recorder and certain aldermen as justices of the peace, and, among other things, granted to the corporation the soil of the Thames within the City's liberties. 838 This grant was not made without some little opposition from the inhabitants of the neighbouring county of Surrey. 839

Henry's marriage with Margaret of Anjou, 22 April, 1445.

The king was now under the influence of William de la Pole, Earl of Suffolk, by whose intervention a truce with France had been concluded on the 28th May of this year (1444), to last until the 1st April, 1446. In order to strengthen the truce, a marriage was arranged between Henry and Margaret of Anjou. The princess came over to England early in the following year, and was married on the 22nd April (1445). The match was not altogether a popular one; nevertheless, when Margaret passed through the city on her way to be crowned at Westminster, she was received "in the most goodly wise, with alle the citezines on horseback ridyng ayenst hir to the Blackheth in blew gownes and rede hodes." 840

Jack Cade's rebellion, 1450.

The truce was renewed, and Suffolk increased in popularity. After the deaths of Gloucester and Cardinal Beaufort, within a few weeks of each other, in 1447, he became the king's chief adviser, and continued to be so until the loss of the French provinces three years later (1450) raised so much opposition against him that the king was compelled to order his banishment. This was not thought a sufficient punishment by his enemies, and he was taken on the high seas and brutally murdered (2 May). After his death an attack was made on his supporters. Again the men of Kent rose in revolt; this time under the leadership of an Irish adventurer—Jack Cade—who called himself Mortimer, and gave out that he was an illegitimate son of the late Earl of March. They mustered on Blackheath 30,000 strong (1 June), and then awaited the king's return from Leicester, where parliament had been sitting. Henry on his arrival sent to learn the reason of the gathering, and in reply received a long list of grievances which the rebels intended to amend. 841 Notwithstanding the boldness of this answer, the king had only to make proclamation that all his true and liege subjects should "a-voyde the fylde," for the whole force to disperse in the course of one night. The danger, indeed, seemed to be over. A week later, however, the royal force met a number of the rebels near Sevenoaks, by whom it was put to rout. Encouraged by this success, the rebels returned and took up their quarters in Southwark. The unhappy king had by this time retired to Kenilworth, notwithstanding the offer made by the citizens of London to stand by him. 842

The city prepares to defend itself.

The city authorities had, in the meantime, taken steps to put the city into a state of defence. A Common Council met on the 8th June, when it decided that an efficient guard should be placed night and day upon all gates, wharves and lanes leading to the Thames. An enclosure recently erected at "le Crane" on the riverside belonging to John Trevillian, was ordered to be abated. Balistic machines (*fundibula*) of all kinds were to be collected on the wharves, whilst the sale of weapons or armour or their removal out of the city was restricted. Lastly, it was agreed to represent to the king the advisability of limiting the number of his nobles coming into the city, owing to the scarcity of provisions. 843 On the 26th June the Common Council again met, and it was then decided to send two mounted men to reconnoitre Cade's position, and to learn, if possible, his movements. 844 Three days later (29 June) orders were given for four men to be selected from each ward to assist the aldermen in preserving the peace. Anyone refusing to do his duty in keeping watch was to be sent to prison. In spite of all precautions, Cade and his followers succeeded in gaining a footing in the city (3 July), their first action being to sack the house of Philip Malpas. 845 Cade himself encouraged rather than restrained the excesses of his men. "Now is Mortimer lord of the City," he cried as he struck with his sword the old Roman mile-stone known as London stone. 846 It is clear that the rebels had friends in the city, otherwise they would never have effected an entrance so easily—"They had othyr men with hem as welle of London as of there owne party." 847 The matter was made the subject of investigation by the Common Council. Evidence was given by Thomas Geffrey, a barber, to the effect that on Friday, the 3rd July, the keys of the bridge had been given up, but by whom he knew not. William Reynold also deposed that Richard Philip, a grocer, had told him that unless the wardens of the bridge opened the gates, the Kentish captain threatened to set fire to the bridge and the city, and that thereupon Thomas Godfrey, a "sporyour," clad in russet, brought the keys and opened the gates. 848

Mock trials held by the rebels at the Guildhall.

On Saturday, the 4th of July, the rebels, who had retired for the night, returned to the city. Robert Horne, alderman of Bridge Ward, who had rendered himself especially obnoxious to the rebels, was made prisoner and sent to Newgate. Sir James Fiennes, the Lord Say, was brought from the Tower to the Guildhall, where the rebels were holding mock trials on those who were unfortunate enough to fall into their hands, and, after a hasty examination, was conveyed to the Standard in Chepe and there executed. His head, together with those of two others who had that day suffered a similar fate, was set up on London Bridge.

Cade apprehended.

By the next evening (Sunday) the citizens had managed to recover their presence of mind, and sallied out at ten o'clock at night, under the leadership of Lord Scales and another, across the bridge. Before they had arrived on the Southwark side of the river they were met by the rebels, and a severe fight took place between the parties on the bridge itself, lasting until eight o'clock the next morning. At last the rebels were defeated, and the city freed from their presence. Offers of pardon were made and accepted, and the rebels dispersed. Cade, however, continued to plunder and ravage the country, until a price having been put upon his head, he was apprehended by the Sheriff of Kent, 849 and died the same night from injuries received at his capture. His head was subsequently set up on London Bridge.

The question of the succession to the throne.

The king had now been married some years, and no heir had appeared. Great uncertainty prevailed as to the right of succession to the throne, and gave rise to much rivalry and mutual mistrust between Richard, Duke of York, who now for the first time becomes a conspicuous figure on the stage, and Edmund Beaufort, recently created Duke of Somerset. Both of them could claim to be the king's nearest kinsmen, both of them being descendants of Edward III, the one tracing his descent, on his father's side, through Edmund Langley, and on his mother's side, through Lionel, Duke of Clarence, whilst the other was the surviving representative of John of Gaunt.

Rivalry between the Dukes of York and Somerset, 1450.

The king's incapacity to govern without a strong minister at his back, as evinced by his conduct during the recent outbreak, induced both of these nobles to throw up their appointments, the one in Ireland and the other in France, and to hasten home. The Duke of York was the first to reach England, and, in spite of measures which had been taken to intercept him, made his way to London. He was anxious in the first place to clear himself of suspicion of having been implicated in Cade's rebellion, 850 and to this end sought and obtained an interview with the king. Having satisfied Henry on this point, he next proceeded to demand the reform of certain abuses in the government. A short session of parliament, which met on the 6th November, opened with an altercation between the rival dukes. On the 1st December Somerset was placed under arrest; and on the following day his lodgings at the Black Friars were broken into and pillaged. An example was made of one of the men convicted of being concerned in the breaking into the Black Friars, and he was beheaded at the Standard in Chepe. The Duke of York made a personal visit to the city, and caused proclamation to be made of the heavy pains and penalties which should follow any attempt at robbery. As a further demonstration against lawlessness, the king himself rode through the city a few days later, accompanied by his lords in full panoply, the route being kept by a line of armed citizens on either side of the way. Alderman Gregory, whose chronicle affords us a vivid picture of contemporary events, and who was called upon to serve the office of mayor of the city the following year, confesses that the procession on this occasion would have been a gay and glorious sight, "if hit hadde ben in Fraunce, but not in Ingelonde," for it boded little good. 851

The Duke of Somerset did not long remain in prison, for immediately after Christmas he was appointed captain of Calais. In 1451 the disasters which followed the English arms in France, when Calais was again threatened, were made an occasion for another attempt by York to crush his rival. He openly avowed his determination to proceed against Somerset, and, joined by the Earl of Devonshire and Lord Cobham, marched to London (Jan., 1452). Henry at once prepared to march against his cousin. The duke had hoped that through the influence of his party within the city, the gates would have been flung open on his approach. In this he was disappointed. The majority of the citizens were still loyal to Henry, and by his orders entrance was denied the duke, who thereupon withdrew to Dartford, whilst the king's forces encamped at Blackheath.

Civil war averted.

For a time civil war was avoided, the king promising that Somerset should be again committed to custody until he should answer such charges as York should bring against him. The king, however, failed to keep his word. Somerset was allowed to remain in power, and York was only allowed his liberty after he had consented to swear public allegiance to the king in St. Paul's Church. Any stronger measures taken against him would probably have provoked disturbance in the city. 852

The king's illness, 1453.

Henry's mind had never been strong, and in the following year (1453) it entirely gave way. In October the queen bore him a son, after eight years of married life, but though the infant was brought to his father, Henry gave no signs of recognising his presence. The illness of the king, and the birth of an heir to the crown, were events which materially affected the fortunes of the Duke of York. In November the civic authorities prepared for emergencies; every citizen was to provide himself with armour, but he was strictly enjoined to be guarded in his conversation, and not to provoke tumult by showing favour to this or that lord. Even a proposal that the mayor and aldermen should pay a visit of respect to the Duke of York was rejected as impolitic at the present juncture. 853

The City again called upon to assist in the defence of Calais, 1453-1454.

Notwithstanding liberal grants made by parliament for the defence of Calais, that town was still in danger. On the 29th November, 1453, a letter was read before the Common Council of the City, emanating from the Lord Welles and the Lord Ryvers, asking for assistance towards putting Calais into a state of defence. Further consideration of the matter was adjourned until the following 4th December. By the 7th day of the same month the Council had consulted the commons, who had declared that owing to their numerous burdens and expenses they could contribute nothing to that end. 854 This did not prevent a further application being made early in 1454, for contributions towards the defence of Calais if that town were besieged. 855 Again the commons were consulted, and again they pleaded the excessive burdens they were already called upon to bear, and the losses they had sustained by seizure of their ships and merchandise by the Duke of Burgundy, rendering them unable for the present to undertake any further charges unless steps were taken for the recovery of their goods. 856 An answer to this effect was accordingly delivered by the Common Sergeant on behalf of the citizens, who declared themselves willing at the same time to bear their share with the rest of the realm. 857 An appeal made in August of the same year (1454), for the sum of £1,200 for the same purpose, met with similar failure. 858

The plea of poverty was no idle one, if we may judge from the fact that when, in November of this year, an assessment of half a fifteenth was made on the city wards, eleven out of twenty-five wards were in default. 859 Between the years 1431 and 1451 the citizens had advanced large sums of money to the king, of which more than £3,000 remained in the latter year due to the city. 860

The Duke of York and his supporters take up their quarters in the city, 1454.

A crisis, in the meanwhile, was fast approaching. The birth of an heir to the throne urged the Duke of York to take prompt action. Although the majority of the nobles were opposed to him, he had on his side the powerful family of the Nevills, having married Cicely Nevill, sister of Richard Nevill, Earl of Salisbury, the head of the family, and father of the still more powerful Earl of Warwick. Towards the end of January (1454) the Duke of York, the Earls of Salisbury and Warwick, and others of the duke's supporters, entered the city, each followed by a large force of retainers fully armed. With them came also York's eldest son, the Earl of March, afterwards King Edward IV. 861

The Common Council were anxious lest the presence of these nobles in the city should lead to a disturbance. A strict neutrality was ordered to be observed both by the mayor and aldermen, as well as by the inhabitants of the city at large. The *waytes*, or watchmen, were ordered to perambulate the streets every night with their minstrels to keep the citizens in good humour (*pro recreacione hominum*), and prevent robbery. Nevertheless, there is evidence to show that disturbances did occasionally arise between the inhabitants and those in the suite of the nobles. 862

The Duke of York nominated protector, 1454.

The king's continued illness necessitated sooner or later the appointment of a regent. For a brief space there seemed a possibility of the regency being claimed by the queen. The City, in the meanwhile, paid court to both parties, the mayor and aldermen one day paying a solemn visit to the queen, attired in their gowns of scarlet, and a few days later paying a similar compliment to the Duke of York. 863 At length the duke was nominated protector (3 April). Some correspondence ensued between the City, the Duke of York, the queen, and the Earl of Salisbury, on what subject we know not, 864 but on the 13th May the mayor and aldermen waited upon the duke to thank him for his favour and goodwill. 865

The first battle of St. Albans, 22 May, 1455.

So long as the king remained an imbecile York was supreme, his rival, Somerset, having been committed to prison at his instigation in December, 1453. Henry, however, soon recovered from his illness, although his convalescence proved of equally short duration, and York's protectorate came to an end. With Henry's restoration came the release of Somerset, and York determined to try conclusions with his rival in the field. At the first battle of St. Albans, fought on the 22nd May, 1455, victory declared for York and Somerset was killed. After the battle York accompanied the king to London and lodged him in the bishop's palace in St. Paul's churchyard. The excitement caused Henry a relapse, and York was for the second time named protector; but in the spring of 1456 he had again to retire upon the king's recovery.

A rising against the Lombards in the city, May, 1456.

Just when the country was settling down to enjoy a period of comparative quiet, there occurred (May, 1456) in the city one of those sudden outbreaks against the "merchant stranger" residing within the city's walls which too often appear in the annals of London. On this occasion the young mercers of the city rose against the Lombards; why or wherefore we are not told. We only know that these foreigners received such bad treatment that they meditated leaving the city in a body and setting up business elsewhere. The fault was not altogether with the citizens, it appears; for two Lombards were ordered to be hanged. 866

The king, who was at the time at Coventry—whither the queen had caused him to be removed, owing to her suspicion that the Londoners were in favour of the Yorkist party—sent for alderman Cantelowe, 867 a mercer, and promptly committed him to Dudley Castle for safe keeping, as having been implicated in the attack on the houses of the Italian merchants.

This outbreak was followed by another "hurlynge" between the mercers of the city and those Lombards who had consented to remain in the city on the understanding that they should be allowed to ply their business without molestation until the council or parliament should determine otherwise. In consequence of this second outbreak no less than 28 mercers were arrested and committed to Windsor Castle. 868

Letter from the king for safe-guarding the city, 3 Sept., 1456.

On the 3rd September, 1456, the king wrote from Lichfield to the Mayor, reminding him of the dangers which had recently threatened the city—"the king's chamber"—the government whereof ought to serve as an example to the rest of the kingdom, and enjoining him that thenceforth he should allow no one to enter the city but such as came peaceably, and with moderate retinue, according to his estate and degree, and should take precautions against gatherings of evil disposed persons which might lead to a breach of the peace. 869

The citizens offer to man and victual ships to punish France, 1457.

Notwithstanding the precautions taken to protect the coast, the French made a descent in 1457, and plundered Sandwich and Fowey, capturing over 30 ships, great and small, and doing much damage. The citizens of London, to whom the protection of their commerce in the "narrow sea," as the channel was then frequently called, was everything, thereupon took counsel among themselves, and made a proposal to the king and to Bishop Waynflete, the chancellor, to find 2,000 men and provisions for certain ships then lying in the Thames, at their own expense, to join an expedition to punish the enemy for their boldness. The king thanked them for their patriotic spirit and gave orders for a naval force to join the city contingent from Hull. 870

A general reconciliation at St. Paul's, 25 March, 1458.

In 1458 Henry tried his hand at effecting a reconciliation between the two rival sections of the nobility, and to this end ordered a great council to meet in St. Paul's on the 27th January. Warwick left his post at Calais, and came over to London to attend the meeting; but he did not arrive until more than a month after the appointed day, and when he came it was with a body of 600 men at his back, "all apparyled in reed jakkettes, with whyte ragged stavis." 871 He took up his quarters within the city, where he found the Duke of York and the Earl of Salisbury. The young Duke of Somerset and other lords, who, like him, had lost their fathers at the battle of St. Albans, were refused an entrance to the city for fear of a breach of the peace, and had to find accommodation outside the city's walls. 872 During the conference the mayor patrolled the streets by day, whilst at night a force of 3,000 men was kept in readiness to assist the aldermen in preserving the king's peace. 873 The times were critical, but at length all ended well. A grand pacification took place in March, and was solemnized by an imposing procession to St. Paul's, in which York led the queen by the hand. The reconciliation thus effected was more apparent than real, and neither party relaxed their efforts to prepare for renewed hostility.

Warwick implicated in a riot, Nov., 1458.

Seeks refuge in the city.

Leaves for Calais.

In August the civic companies were warned against furnishing the confederate lords with any war material, but were to keep their arms and harness at the disposal of the king alone. 874 It wanted very little to kindle the smouldering embers of dissatisfaction into a flame, and this little was soon forthcoming. In November 875 a riot occurred at Westminster, in which the Earl of Warwick was implicated. A yeoman in his suite picked a quarrel with one of the king's servants and wounded him. Thereupon others of the king's household, finding their fellow-servant wounded and his enemy escaped, way-laid the earl and his attendants as they left the council to take barge on the river. By dint of hard hitting, the earl managed to embark and to make his way to the city. But the affray was not without bloodshed, and Warwick found it convenient to withdraw soon afterwards to his post at Calais, which thenceforth became the head-quarters of the disaffected lords.

Riot between citizens and Templars, April, 1459.

In the following April (1459) another affray broke out. This time it was between inhabitants of the city and certain members of the Inns of Court, and the riot was so dangerous as to result in loss of life. The king hearing of this sent for William Tayllour, the alderman of the ward, and kept him in confinement at Windsor until the election of the new mayor, William Hewlyn, in October, by whose intercession he regained his freedom. 876

The battle of Blore Heath, 23 Sept., 1459.

By this time the country was again divided into two hostile camps. A crisis came in September, when the Earl of Salisbury, the king's most inveterate enemy, marched upon Ludlow with a large force. Lord Audley, sent by the queen to arrest him, was defeated by the earl at Blore Heath (23 Sept., 1459). Later on, however, the earl and the Yorkist army were themselves compelled to seek security. The Duke of York took refuge in Ireland, and the Earl of Warwick, who had crossed from France to join his father, returned to Calais, taking the Earl of Salisbury with him.

Parliament at Coventry, 20 Nov., 1459.

On the 9th October the king issued his writ for a parliament to be held at Coventry on the 20th November. The usual writ was sent to the City of London, but the names of the aldermen and commoners elected to represent the citizens do not appear in the City's records. 877 The business of the session was the attainder of the Duke of York and his followers, and judgment was passed upon the duke, the Nevills, father and son, the young Earls of March and Rutland, and others. Two days after the date of this writ, the Common Council decided to send a deputation to wait upon the king and assure him of the City's allegiance and of the steps taken for its safe custody. 878

The king loses favour.

The citizens had previously (Oct., 1459) displayed their willingness to assist the king by a gift of 1,000 marks. 879 This gift must have been the more welcome, inasmuch as Henry's debts had been rapidly on the increase, whilst his creditors remained unpaid. The queen, on the other hand, into whose hands the government of the kingdom had been drawn, was "gaderyng riches innumerable." The imposition of taxes, talliages and fifteenths, whilst harassing the king's subjects, seemed to make him not a whit the richer, the issues and profits being frittered away. They would have forgiven him had he maintained a household in regal style or spent their money on maintaining the country's honour in the field. As matters were, Henry, by misgovernment, was rapidly losing the hearts of his people, and "theyre blessyng was turned in to cursyng." 880

Unconstitutional conduct of the king in issuing commissions to raise an army, Jan., 1460.

A deputation from the City waits upon the king at Northampton.

The City's liberties not to be prejudiced.

On the 14th January, 1460, the king issued a commission to the mayor, aldermen and sheriffs for collecting men-at-arms and archers to resist the *late* Duke of York and the *late* Earls of March, Warwick, Salisbury and Rutland. 881 Similar commissions were addressed to every township, 882 and did much harm to the royal cause, now tottering to its fall, as being unconstitutional. They formed the subject of one of the set of articles of complaint drawn up by the Earls of March, Warwick and Salisbury, and addressed by them, on behalf of themselves and the Duke of York, to the archbishop and the commons of England. 883 Such commissions the lords declared to be an imposition which, if continued, would be "the heaviest charge and worst example that ever grew in England." The city authorities appear to have rested their opposition to the king's commission, not so much on the grounds that they were unwilling to raise a force for his assistance, as that a demand for military aid in such a form might derogate from the city's franchise and liberties. A deputation, consisting of two aldermen, Thomas Urswyk, the Recorder, and one of the under-sheriffs, was sent to Northampton to wait upon the king and council and to explain the views of the citizens in that respect. The interview was of a satisfactory character; and the deputation returned bearing a gracious letter from the king declaring that the City's franchise and liberties should in no way be prejudiced by the commission. 884

Military precautions taken by the City, Feb., 1460.

The citizens deemed it time to look to their own safety, and place their city into a better posture of defence. The master and wardens of the livery companies were exhorted (14 Feb., 1460), on account of the disturbed state of the kingdom, to raise contributions towards the purchase of accoutrements for the safeguard of the city. 885 The king himself was shortly coming into the city, and measures were taken (28 Feb.) for placing a proper guard over the several gates. 886 On the 11th May the masters and wardens were summoned, on behalf of the king, to appear before the mayor and aldermen at the Guildhall, to hear a royal proclamation read touching the preservation of the king's peace. 887

Landing of the confederate earls.

The Yorkist Earls of Salisbury, Warwick and March, encouraged by the reports of the state of affairs in England, at length made up their minds to return and strike a blow for the recovery of their estates, which had become forfeited to the king. They set sail from Calais (26 June), and landing at Sandwich made their way without opposition through Kent to London.

The Common Council determine to oppose their entrance to the city, 27 June, 1460.

On the 27th June, by which time news of their arrival must have reached the city, a Common Council was held, when the commoners who were present solemnly promised to stand by the mayor and aldermen in safeguarding the city, and resist with all their might the rebels against the lord the king who were about to enter the city contrary to the king's orders. The civic companies somewhat tardily gave their adhesion to the royal cause, and agreed to defend the city. The gates were ordered to be manned, and no one was to be allowed to enter without first saying who and what he was. Strict enquiry was to be made as to the character of strangers residing within each of their wards. 888 On the following day the Common Council met again and gave orders that the drawbridge of London Bridge should be always kept down, so that victuallers and others might have ready access to the City, but the gateway on the drawbridge was to be kept closed, whilst *le wikett* was to be constantly open. A strict watch was to be kept on the new tower 889 above the bridge by men-at-arms stationed there, who should also be ready to let down *le port Colyce* when occasion required. 890

Meeting of Common Council on Sunday, 29 June.

A deputation, moreover, was appointed to set out to meet the Earls of March and Warwick on their way to Northampton, for the purpose of inducing them, if possible, to turn aside and not approach the city. The members were instructed to inform the lords of the king's commands to the citizens to hold the city for him, and to oppose the lords' entry under heavy penalty. This instruction to the deputation was given, we are told, with the approval of the Archbishop of Canterbury, the Bishops of Norwich, Ely and Exeter, and of the Prior of St. John's, Clerkenwell. The mayor, aldermen and commonalty agreed to stand by any terms which the deputation might be compelled to make. They had not taken this step without first consulting the Lords Scales and Hungerford, and Sir Edmund Hampden, who held the Tower of London for King Henry. The bridge gate was ordered to be closed between nine and ten o'clock on the night of the 28th, and to remain closed till the morning. Even the portcullis was to be kept down if necessary, whilst the mayor and sheriffs, with a certain number of armed men, patrolled the city, and the aldermen kept watch in their several wards. 891 Notwithstanding the next day being Sunday, the critical state of affairs necessitated a meeting of the Common Council. It was then agreed that if any messenger should arrive from Warwick, no communication should be held with him. Special watches were appointed for the bridge and for Billingsgate by night and day, and so anxious were the authorities to avail themselves of the service of every abled citizen on that Sunday, that no one was allowed to attend Divine Service at St. Paul's. 892

The Yorkist earls admitted into the city, 2 July, 1460.

Up to this point the citizens had shown themselves loyal to Henry. They now began to waver. Early in the morning of the 30th June the mayor and aldermen appear to have changed their minds. The earls had sent them a letter and they resolved to receive it. The contents of this letter are not recorded. On the following day (1 July) another communication from the earls was received. Here again we are left in the dark as to its purport—the City's journals at this period being very imperfect,—we only know that they declined to accede to the request to keep at a distance from London, for the very next day (2 July) they were admitted into the city. 893

The Tower holds out.

The city was thus lost to the king; but the Tower still held out, and no amount of eloquence on the part of certain doctors of divinity, whom the Common Council had appointed to try and arrange matters so as to avoid bloodshed, would induce Lord Scales and his companions to surrender it, although the garrison was hard pressed for victuals. 894 Nothing was left but to starve them out, and this the Earl of Salisbury proceeded to do, with the aid of the citizens and the boatmen on the river, by whom the Tower was strictly invested by land and water. The Common Council appear to have felt some qualms of conscience in joining in this proceeding, for they caused it to be recorded—as if by way of excuse for their action—that "there seemed to be no other way of preserving the city." 895 A resolution, moreover, that each alderman should subscribe the sum of £5 towards raising a force to intercept victuals on their way to the Tower was rescinded. 896

The Tower surrendered, 19 July.

Murder of Lord Scales.

By the 10th July matters had become so serious with the beleaguered garrison, that a letter was sent to the Common Council, signed by the Earl of Kendal, Lord Scales, Lord Hungerford, Lord Lovell and Sir Edmund Hampden, asking why war was thus being made upon them. To this the Council replied that the lords had brought it upon themselves by firing on the citizens in the first instance, and taking provisions from them without payment. 897 At last the garrison could hold out no longer, and the Tower was surrendered (19th July). Lord Scales endeavoured to take sanctuary at Westminster, but was seized by river boatmen and barbarously murdered. 898

Battle of Northampton, 10 July, 1460.

Meanwhile the Duke of York had managed to raise a sum of money in the city; 899 the battle of Northampton had been won and lost (10th July), and Henry had been brought a prisoner to London (16th July). On the same day that the king arrived in London, the mayor, aldermen and commonalty of the City entered into an agreement, under the Common Seal, to abide by any arrangement made between the Earl of Salisbury and the beleaguered lords in the Tower for the surrender of that stronghold. 900

Measures for restoring confidence in the city.

On the 21st July the king, or the Earl of Warwick, in his name, attempted to restore quiet in the city by promising that those who had offended against the king's highness and the common weal of the realm, and had been committed to the Tower, should forthwith receive ample justice. In the meantime all conventicles, assemblies or congregations in breach of the peace were strictly forbidden, and every man was exhorted to repair to his own house, and wait upon his lord or master in whose service he might happen to be. 901

Parliament of 7 Oct., 1460.

The Duke of York's claim to the throne allowed.

The Livery Companies declare their allegiance to the king.

In October the Duke of York attended parliament and boldly asserted his right to the throne. After hearing arguments for and against his claim, parliament arrived at a compromise by which the reversion of the crown was settled on the duke, and to this the king himself was forced to give his assent. 902 It was otherwise with the proud and defiant Queen Margaret. She was determined to acquiesce in no such arrangement. Whilst she was collecting a force in the north, wherewith to strike one blow for the crown of which her son appeared likely to be robbed, the mayor and aldermen held an extraordinary meeting of the wardens of the livery companies. The king wished to be assured of the temper of the citizens. Would they as a body support him and his council, protect his royal person, and defend the city against those who were raising disturbances in divers parts of the realm? To each and all of these questions the wardens are recorded as having given satisfactory replies, and it was then and there agreed that each alderman should make enquiry as to the number of strangers residing in his ward, and the reasons for their being in the city. Watch was to be kept by night in every ward, a lantern hung outside every dwelling-house, and the city's gates were to be closed every night and guarded by men-at-arms. 903 Although these measures were avowedly taken on behalf of King Henry, they were, in reality, so many precautions for securing the government in the hands of his rival the Duke of York.

The battle of Wakefield, 29 Dec., 1460.

The struggle which hitherto had been between two unequal sections of the nobility, each avowing its loyalty to the king, now became a struggle between the two rival Houses of Lancaster and York. Richard, Duke of York, did not live to enjoy the crown, his right to the reversion of which had recently been acknowledged by parliament. Just as the year was drawing to a close he met his death at Wakefield in the first clash with the House of Lancaster, and his head in mockery was set up on one of the city's gates from which he derived his ducal title.

"Off with his head, and set it on York's gates;
So York may overlook the town of York."

The second battle of St. Albans, 17 Feb., 1461.

When Henry was once restored to liberty and to his queen, after the second battle of St. Albans (17 Feb., 1461), York's son, Edward, Earl of March, who became by his father's death heir to the crown, was immediately proclaimed traitor in the city. 904 The queen wished for victuals to be sent from the city to her forces at St. Albans, but the carts were seized before they left the city by a mob which refused to let them go in spite of the mayor's entreaties and threats. Margaret's army consisted for the most part of rude northern followers who threatened to sack the city if once allowed within its walls, and the majority of the inhabitants were unwilling to supply the queen with provisions until she had removed her half-disciplined force to a distance from London. With a civilized army at her back it might have been possible for Margaret to have gained a footing in the city. 905 As matters stood, she deemed it best to accede to the request thus made to her, and to draw off her army.

The Earls of March and Warwick admitted into the city, Feb., 1461.

It was a fatal mistake, for it gave time for Edward and Warwick to join forces and march on London. The civic authorities, finding how hopeless it was to place further dependence upon Henry, and desiring above all things a stronger government than they could look for under the king, now surrendered the city to his opponents. They had not forsaken the king—he had forsaken them. They would no more of him.

"He that had Londyn for sake,
Wolde no more to hem take." 906

Edward's claim to the crown recognised, 1 March, 1461.

On the 1st March the chancellor called a general assembly of the citizens at Clerkenwell, and explained to them the title by which Edward, Duke of York, laid claim to the crown. 907 His title was thereupon acknowledged with universal applause, and on the 4th he proceeded to Westminster Palace, accompanied by many of the nobility and commons of the realm, 908 and was there proclaimed king by the name of Edward IV.

CHAPTER XII.

The accession of King Edward IV, March, 1461.

The new king made himself very popular with the citizens. He was not less a favourite with them because he joined their ranks and became a trader like themselves, or because he took a wife from among his own subjects and made her a sharer of his crown. At the coronations, both of Edward and his queen, which took place after an interval of three years, the City was fully represented, and its claim to services at the king's coronation banquet duly acknowledged. 909 At the latter ceremony no less than four citizens, among them being Ralph Josselyn, the mayor, were created Knights of the Bath. 910 The citizens had previously shown their respect to Elizabeth Woodville by riding forth to meet her and escorting her to the Tower on her first arrival to London, and by presenting her with a gift of 1,000 marks or £750. 911

Edward's first charter to the city, 26 Aug., 1461.

If the young and handsome prince who now ascended the throne occasionally carried his familiarity with the wives of city burgesses beyond the limits of strict propriety, much could be forgotten and forgiven for the readiness he showed to confirm and enlarge the City's privileges and to foster the trade of the country. Before he had been on the throne many months he granted the citizens, by charter, the right of package and scavage, as well as the office of gauger of wines. 912

Second charter of Edward IV, 25 March, 1462.

In the following March (1462) he confirmed the charter granted to the City by Henry IV, whereby the citizens obtained the right of taking toll and custom at Billingsgate, Smithfield and elsewhere, as well as the right of *tronage* or weighing wool at the Tron. 913

City Loans, 1462.

In August, 1462 Calais was again in danger, and the king wanted money. The Earl of Worcester and others of the council were sent into the city to ask for a loan of £3,400. After considering the matter, the civic authorities agreed to lend him £1,000. The money was to be raised by assessment on the wards, but Dowgate ward being at the time very poor, was not to be pressed.

914 In the following October the City again came to the king's assistance with a further loan of 2,000 marks, 915 and on the 9th November the City obtained (in return, shall we say?) a charter confirming its jurisdiction over the Borough of Southwark, 916 originally granted by Edward III. Again, the coincidence of a charter granted by the king to the City, with a loan or gift from the City to the king, is remarkable.

The king's reception in the city on his return from the North, Feb., 1463.

When Edward returned in February, 1463, from the North, where he had succeeded with the assistance afforded him by the Londoners in re-capturing most of the castles which the restless Margaret had taken, the City resolved to give him a befitting reception. Preparations were made for the mayor, aldermen and commons to ride forth to meet him in their finest liveries, but the king having expressed his intention of coming from Shene to the city by water, the citizens went to meet him in their barges, with all the pomp and ceremony of a Lord Mayor's day. 917

Estrangement of Warwick, 1464-1468.

Edward now gave himself up to a life of luxury and pleasure. In 1464 he married the young widow of Sir John Grey, better known by her maiden name of Elizabeth Woodville. His marriage to her gave offence to the nobility, more especially to the Earl of Warwick, who was planning at the time a match with France or Burgundy, and to whom the news of the marriage with one so beneath the king in point of dignity came as an unpleasant surprise. The earl was still more offended when he learnt that the young king had secretly effected a marriage treaty between his sister Margaret (whom Warwick had destined for one of the French princes) and the Duke of Burgundy. These matrimonial alliances, combined with the inordinate favour Edward displayed towards his wife's family, led to an estrangement between the king and his powerful subject.

Alliance between England and Burgundy, 1468.

The proposed alliance with Burgundy was far from being distasteful to the merchants of the city, inasmuch as it was likely to open up trade with those states of the Low Countries which the Burgundian dukes had consolidated as a barrier against France. When the Princess Margaret was about to start (June, 1468) for her future husband's dominions, the mayor and aldermen of London testified their appreciation of the alliance by presenting her with a pair of silver gilt dishes, weighing 19 lbs. 8 oz., besides the sum of £100 in gold, by way of a wedding gift. 918

Renewal of the civil war, 1469.

Disgusted with the king's unhandsome conduct towards him, Warwick found an ally in Clarence, the king's brother, gave him one of his daughters in marriage, and even encouraged him to hope for the succession to the crown. Edward's extravagant and luxurious life had lost him much of his popularity. He had ceased, moreover, to possess the goodwill of the citizens for having allowed the arrest of Sir Thomas Cooke or Coke, 919 an alderman of the city, on a false charge of treason. Notwithstanding his acquittal, Cooke had been committed to prison and only regained his liberty on payment of an extortionate fine to the king and queen. 920 Warwick and Clarence made use of the general discontent that prevailed to further their own designs, and the civil war was renewed. The City endeavoured to steer a middle course. In June (1469) it lent the king the sum of £200, but in the following month it lent Warwick and Clarence just five times that amount on the sole security of some jewels of little value. 921 In May, 1470, when there seemed little hope of the jewels being redeemed, as Warwick and Clarence had been obliged to flee to France, the Common Council entertained the thought of selling them for what they were worth. The sale did not take place, however, but they were kept some in the "Treasury," and some in the custody of William Taillour, late mayor, on the express understanding that he was not to be held responsible in the event of their being stolen or taken by force. 922 In February, 1471, when the wheel of fortune had once more placed Henry VI on the throne from which he had been driven by Edward, and Warwick and Clarence were again in power, the mayor and aldermen caused it to be placed on record that the loan on the jewels had been made by agreement of the whole court, with the assistance of certain commoners who had been called in to contribute. What their object was in so doing is not clear. Perhaps they felt some qualms as to what Edward might say or do in respect of the loan, should he again return to power. They, at the same time, extended the time for the repayment of the loan, at the desire of the dukes of Clarence and Warwick. If the jewels were not redeemed by Whitsuntide at the latest, they were to be sold. 923

Flight of Edward and restoration of Henry VI, Oct., 1470.

Whilst Warwick and Clarence were in France in 1470, they concerted measures with Queen Margaret for effecting another revolution. By September matters were ready for execution. On the 13th Warwick landed in England; and before the end of the month the Kentish men so threatened the City and Westminster, that the newly-elected sheriffs had to be escorted by an armed force in order to be sworn in at the Exchequer, whilst a constant patrol was kept in the streets. 924 On the 1st October it was made known in the city that the king had taken flight. His queen took sanctuary at Westminster, leaving the Tower in the hands of the mayor and aldermen and members of the council of Warwick and Clarence. The unfortunate Henry was quickly removed from the wretched cell in which he had so long been confined to a commodious and handsomely furnished apartment which the queen herself, being *enceinte* at the time, purposed occupying when she should be brought to bed. A garrison was placed in the Tower by order of the Common Council, sitting, for safety's sake, in the church of St. Stephen, Walbrook. On the 5th October Archbishop Nevill, Warwick's brother, entered the city with a strong force and relieved the civic authorities of the custody of the Tower, and on the following day Warwick himself appeared, accompanied by Clarence and a large following, and removed Henry from the Tower to the Bishop of London's palace. 925 Two days later (9 Oct.) he obtained from the Common Council the sum of £1,000 for the defence of his stronghold, Calais, besides a loan of £100 from the aldermen of the city for his own private use. 926 On the 18th the Earl of Worcester, Edward's constable and minister of his cruelties, 927 was beheaded on Tower Hill, the ground being kept by the Sheriffs of London and a contingent from the several wards. 928

Sir Thomas Cooke or Coke, late alderman.

In November Henry was made to hold a parliament, and Sir Thomas Cooke, the deposed alderman, lost no time in presenting a bill for the restoration of his lands, which had been seized by the queen's father, Lord Rivers. He would probably have been successful had fortune continued to favour King Henry, for, besides being a member of parliament, he was, writes Fabyan (a brother alderman), "a man of great boldnesse in speche, and well spoken and syngulerly wytted and well reasoned." 929 John Stokton had recently been elected mayor, but there is reason for believing that he, like other aldermen, preferred Edward on the throne, licentious and extravagant as he was, to an imbecile like Henry. He fell ill, or, as Fabyan puts it, feigned sickness and took to his bed, and Cooke assumed the duties of the mayoralty. At Edward's restoration Cooke had to seek refuge in France, but he was taken at sea before he could reach the continent. The same fate might have awaited Stokton had he shown himself less cautious at that critical time.

Edward recovers the throne, April, 1471.

That the aldermen and the better class of citizens favoured Edward, is shown by the ease with which he effected an entry into the city when he returned to England in the spring of the following year (1471). The gates, we are told, were opened to him by Urswyk, the Recorder, and certain aldermen (their names are not mentioned), who took advantage of the inhabitants being at dinner to let in Edward. 930 Two days later, having recruited his forces, Edward marched out of the city, with Henry in his train, to meet Warwick. He encountered him on Easter Day (14 April) at Barnet, and totally defeated him, both the earl and his brother being left dead on the field. By this time Margaret had landed with a fresh army; but a crushing defeat inflicted upon her at Tewkesbury (4 May) left Edward once more master of the kingdom.

The Kentish rising under "bastard" Fauconberg, May, 1471.

Attack made on the City.

For a short time the city lay in some peril whilst Edward was engaged with Warwick and Margaret. The men of Kent again became troublesome. They affected not to believe that Warwick had actually fallen at Barnet. Under the leadership of Thomas Fauconberg or Falconbridge, generally spoken of as the "bastard," being a natural son of William Nevill, first Lord Fauconberg, Earl of Kent, they marched to London, with the intention of releasing Henry from confinement and placing him again on the throne. Fauconberg, who had been made a freeman of the City in 1454, 931 assumed the title of captain of King Henry's people in Kent, and on the 8th May wrote from Sittingbourne to inform the inhabitants of the city that he had undertaken the cause of Henry against the "usurper" Edward, and to ask to be allowed to pass through the city with his followers, whom he promised to hold in restraint and prevent doing any mischief. He had written to the mayor and aldermen to the same effect, and had desired to have a reply sent to him at Blackheath by a certain day and hour. To this letter the mayor and aldermen sent an answer on the following day, to the effect that when Edward left the city, after the battle of Barnet, to follow the movements of Margaret and endeavour to bring about an action before she could completely rally her forces, he had charged them on their allegiance to hold the city of London for him, and for none other. For that reason they dared not, neither would they, suffer him to pass through the city. They hesitated to accept his assurance as to the peaceable behaviour of his followers, judging from past experience. As for the statement he had caused to be published, that he held a commission as captain of the Navy of England and men of war by sea and land under the Earl of Warwick, whom he still supposed to be alive, they assured him that the earl was dead, and that his corpse, as well as the corpse of Montague, the earl's brother, had been exposed to view for two days in St. Paul's. They gave him the names of some of the chief men who had fallen at Tewkesbury, obtained, they assured him, not from hearsay but from eye-witnesses—special war correspondents, whom the City had despatched for the express purpose of reporting on the state of the field, and they concluded by exhorting him to do as they themselves had done, and to acknowledge Edward IV as the rightful king. They would even plead for royal favour on his behalf, but as to letting him and his host pass through the city, that was out of the question. 932 Having despatched this answer to Fauconberg, the civic fathers at once set to work to fortify the river's bank from Castle Baynard to the Tower, where lay the rebels' fleet. On Sunday, the 12th May, the Kentish men tried to force London Bridge and set fire to some beer-houses near Saint Katherine's Hospital. The attack was renewed on the following Tuesday, whilst portions of the rebel force, amounting it was said to 5,000 persons, were told off to try and force the gates of Aldgate and Bishopsgate. There, however, they were repulsed, and nearly 300 of them met their death, either in actual fight or in their endeavours to get on board their boats at Blackwall. Urswyk, the city's Recorder, as well as Robert Basset, alderman of Aldgate Ward, showed conspicuous valour in the fight which took place in that quarter. 933 The city was never again troubled by Fauconberg. After much wandering he was taken prisoner at Southampton, and thence conveyed to Middleham, in Yorkshire, where he was beheaded. His head was afterwards sent to London and set up on London Bridge, "looking into Kentward." 934

Edward's return to London, and death of Henry VI, May, 1471.

On the night after Edward's return 935 in triumph to London, Henry VI ended his life in the Tower, murdered, in all probability, at the instance of the Duke of Gloucester, the king's brother, afterwards King Richard III. His remains lay in state at St. Paul's and at the Blackfriars a short while, and were then carried to Chertsey to be buried. 936 Edward distributed honours among his supporters in the city with a lavish hand. Not only did the Lord Mayor—the cautious Stokton—receive the honour of knighthood, but the aldermen 937 besides, whilst the city's doughty Recorder was soon afterwards raised to be Baron of the Exchequer. The City was so pleased with its Recorder that it voted him a pipe of wine annually, but the gift was not to be drawn into precedent. 938

Birth of Edward V.

The rest of Edward's reign was undisturbed by any attempt to unseat the new dynasty, and his position was rendered the more secure by the birth of a son (afterwards Edward V) in the sanctuary of Westminster, whither his wife Elizabeth had fled for refuge. Before the young Prince of Wales was five years old he received the honour of knighthood at Westminster. The mayor and aldermen went to meet him on his way from the city to Westminster on that occasion, clad in scarlet robes, whilst the streets from Bishopsgate to Saint Paul's were thronged with the commons in their livery. 939

The invasion of France, 1475.

Edward was now free to carry out his foreign policy. Parliament voted supplies to enable him to make war with France, but these were not sufficient, and he had recourse to a system of "benevolences" or free gifts, which few, however, dared to refuse. On the 30th May, 1475, he left the Bishop of London's palace in St. Paul's Church-yard, and, passing through Cheapside to London Bridge, took boat to Greenwich for the purpose of crossing over to France. The livery companies turned out to do him honour. 940 The expedition ended without a blow, Edward allowing himself to be bought off with a sum of 75,000 crowns paid down and a pension of 50,000 more. On his return he was met at Blackheath by the mayor and aldermen in scarlet gowns, with their servants in gowns of "musterdevilers," accompanied by more than 600 members of the companies in gowns of bright murrey. 941

Edward and the citizens.

By resorting again to benevolences and exacting money from the City in return for charters, Edward avoided the necessity of summoning parliament between the years 1478 and 1483. On the 25th May, 1481, the king granted the City a general pardon, 942 and in the following month the City returned the compliment by a loan of 5,000 marks. 943 This loan was not only repaid, but the king in the next year extended his hospitality to the City by giving a large number of citizens a day's hunting in Waltham forest, and afterwards regaling them and their wives with venison and wine. 944

A famine threatened, 1482.

The close of the year 1482 witnessed such a dearth of cereals that the exportation of wheat or other grain was absolutely forbidden. It was feared that a famine might arise in the City of London, so vast had its population become, both from the influx of nobles who had taken up their quarters within its walls as well as of strangers from foreign lands. Merchants were therefore encouraged to send their grain to London by a promise that it should not be intercepted by the king's purveyors. 945

Edward's last parliament, 1483.

The names of the City's representatives who attended the parliament which met in January, 1483, are not recorded, but we have the names of four aldermen and five commoners, who were appointed in the previous month of December to confer with the City members on matters affecting the City. 946 In addition to parliamentary grants of a fifteenth and tenth, and a renewal of the tax on aliens, the citizens agreed to lend the king the sum of £2,000, each alderman to lay down 50 marks and 80 commoners to subscribe £15 a piece. 947 Some difficulty was experienced in raising the money, and the names of eleven persons who had refused to contribute were forwarded to the king. 948 A little more than a month elapsed and Edward was dead.

Preparations for the coronation of Edward V.

The coronation of the young prince who now succeeded to his father's throne, only to occupy it however for a few weeks, was fixed to take place on the first Sunday in May; and on the 19th April the City was busy making arrangements for the prince's reception. It was decided that the mayor and aldermen should ride forth to meet the king, clad in gowns of scarlet, their attendants being provided with gowns of the colour of lion's-foot (*pied de lyon*), at the public cost. Five sergeants-at-mace belonging to the mayor, and nineteen sergeants-at-mace in the service of the sheriffs, were also to ride out to meet the king, clad in gowns of the last-mentioned colour. The sword-bearer was to be provided with a gown of murrey, and a deputation from the civic guilds, to the number of 410 persons, clad in gowns of the same colour, was to join the cavalcade. 949 On the 14th May they rode out to Hornsey, where they met the prince and his uncle, the Duke of Gloucester, and escorted them to the city. The duke was the same day appointed Protector, to the great disappointment of the queen, who again took sanctuary at Westminster. She was induced shortly afterwards to give up possession of her younger son, the Duke of York, and he and Prince Edward were lodged in the Tower by order of Gloucester, who took up his quarters at Crosby Palace, the mansion house of Sir John Crosby, in Bishopsgate Street.

Although preparations had been made for the coronation, and the City had appointed representatives from the livery companies to assist the chief butler at the banquet 950 according to custom, that ceremony never took place. Gloucester feared that if once the young king was crowned, the project which he had already begun to entertain of transferring the crown to his own head would be less capable of realization. Although he took an oath of allegiance to the new king, 951 it was not long before he determined to feel the pulse of the citizens as to their feelings towards himself as a claimant of the crown.

Shaw's sermon at Paul's Cross, Sunday, 22 June, 1483.

In order to do this he called to his assistance Dr. Shaw, an eminent preacher, whose brother, Sir Edmund Shaa, or Shaw, happened to be mayor at the time. Acting upon instructions from Gloucester, Shaw preached a sermon at Paul's Cross on Sunday, the 22nd June (1483), in which he charged the late king with bigamy, Edward IV having, as he declared, made a contract of marriage with one of his mistresses before he married Elizabeth Woodville, and this being the case the late king's children by her were illegitimate, and Gloucester was the rightful heir to the throne. It was arranged that at this point in his discourse Gloucester himself should appear on the scene, coming up, as if by chance, from his lodgings at Castle Baynard.

By some mischance the duke failed to appear at the proper moment, and the effect was lost. The citizens sat stolidly silent, not a single cry being raised in favour of Gloucester.

The Duke of Buckingham at the Guildhall, 24 June, 1483.

Nothing daunted by this dismal failure, Gloucester made another and more successful attempt to win over the citizens. On the following Tuesday (24 June) he sent the Duke of Buckingham to harangue the citizens at the Guildhall. The duke began by reminding his hearers of the danger to which their wives and daughters had been exposed under the late king; of the undue influence exercised at court by Jane Shore, 952 one only of a number of respectable women whom Edward, he said, had seduced; of the excessive taxes and illegal extortions by way of "benevolences" they had recently suffered, and of the cruel treatment of their own alderman, Cooke. He then went on to repeat the remarks of Dr. Shaw touching the illegitimacy of the princes, and spoke of the dangers of having a boy king on the throne, concluding by saying that although it were doubtful if Gloucester would accept the crown if asked, he would certainly be greatly influenced by any request proceeding from the "worshipful citizens of the metropolis of the kingdom." 953 Buckingham's eloquence was lost on the citizens, who were as little influenced by what their new Recorder, Thomas Fitz-William, had to say on the matter. At length the duke lost patience and plainly told them that the matter lay entirely with the lords and commons, and that the assent of the citizens, however desirable in itself, was not a necessity. By this time the back of the hall was packed with Gloucester's partisans, so that when Buckingham put the question pointedly to the assembly—would they have the Protector assume the crown?—a cry of assent arose from this quarter and was taken up by a few lads and apprentices. This was enough; the voice of the few was accepted as the voice of the many, and the citizens were bidden to attend on the morrow to petition Gloucester to accept the crown.

The deposition of Edward V, 26 June, 1483.

Accordingly, on the morrow, a deputation from the city waited on the Duke of Gloucester at Baynard's Castle and invited him to accept the crown. After a considerable show of affected reluctance, Richard assented, and, having assented, lost no time in carrying out his pre-conceived purpose. The very next day he hastened to Westminster and, seating himself on the throne, declared himself king by inheritance and election.

The coronation of Richard III, 6 July, 1433.

On the 6th July the last Angevin king that reigned over England was crowned—crowned with his wife Anne, widow of Prince Edward, killed at Tewkesbury, but after the battle not in it, and of whose blood Richard himself is thought to have been guilty. The City accepted the position and made the new king and queen a present of £1,000; two-thirds for the king and the remainder for the queen. The money was raised in the city by way of a fifteenth; the poor were not to be called upon to contribute, and the gift was not to form a precedent. 954 The claim of the mayor and citizens to assist the chief butler at the coronation banquet was made and allowed, 955 the king, sitting crowned in *le Whitehawle*, presented to the mayor and aldermen who were present on that occasion a gold cup set with pearls and precious stones, to be used by the commonalty at public entertainments in the Guildhall. 956 Concerning this cup there is the following curious entry made in the City's Records, under date 13th July, 1486, when Hugh Brice was mayor:— 957

"Item it is aggreed this day by the Court that where Hugh Brice Mair of this Citie, hathe in his Kepyng a Cuppe of gold, garneised with perle and precious stone of the gifte of Richard, late in dede and not of right, Kyng of Englond, which gifte was to thuse of the Cominaltie of the said Citee, that if the saide Cuppe be stolen or taken away by thevys oute of his possession, or elles by the casualtie of Fire hereafter it shall hapne the same Cuppe to be brent or lost, that the same Hugh Brice hereafter shall not be hurt or impeched therfore."

This extract is interesting as showing that the coronation cup presented to the mayor of the City by way of *honorarium* was, at this period at least, looked upon as a gift made to the City's use, and that the mayor could not claim it as his own perquisite, as mayors had been in the habit of doing in days gone by, and as they continued to do afterwards. William Estfeld, who, as mayor, attended the coronation of Henry VI (6 Nov., 1429), and received the customary gold cup and ewer, appropriated the gift to his own use, and, as we have already mentioned, bequeathed them to his grandson.

Rebellion of the Duke of Buckingham, 1483.

His execution, 2 Nov.

Richard had scarcely been seated three months on the throne before the Duke of Buckingham, who had been rewarded for his late services by being appointed lord high constable, was in open rebellion, and Henry, Earl of Richmond, long an exile in France, was meditating an invasion.

Buckingham's conspiracy proved a failure, and he paid for his rashness with his head. The Earl of Richmond was detained in France by stress of weather, and danger from that quarter was averted at least for a time.

The king's reception in the city, Nov., 1483.

Bold speech of the Londoners.

On Richard's return to London after putting down his enemies, he was welcomed by over 400 members of the various civic companies, who rode out to meet him in gowns of murrey. 958 His policy was one of conciliation, and he lent a ready ear to a Petition which the citizens presented to him setting forth the wrongs which they had suffered: "We be determined" said the citizens in forcible language, "rather to adventure and to commit us to the peril of our lives and jeopardy of death, than to live in such thraldom and bondage as we have lived some time heretofore, oppressed and injured by extortions and new impositions against the laws of God and man, and the liberty and laws of this realm wherein every Englishman is inherited." 959

Richard's Parliament, Jan., 1484.

Richard met this appeal by summoning parliament to meet in January (1484), when various acts were passed affecting the trade and commerce of the city and the country, and among them one which forbade aliens keeping any foreign apprentices or workpeople to assist them in their occupation, and otherwise imposed great restrictions upon the merchant stranger. 960 This statute was scarcely less welcome to the citizens of London than that which declared the practice of exacting money under the guise of benevolences to be unconstitutional. 961

Expected invasion of Henry of Richmond, 1484.

In the summer he was welcomed wherever he went, yet he knew that danger threatened. Richmond was preparing for an invasion and the nobles were not to be trusted. The citizens, too, were aware of the danger, and had in the early part of the year appointed a joint committee of aldermen and commoners to survey the city's ordnance, and to supply guns and gunpowder in place of that which had recently been destroyed by a fire. 962 In August they had promised Richard a loan of £2,400, each alderman contributing £100; 963 and in the following November the mayor and aldermen rode out to Kennington to meet him and escort him to the Wardrobe, near Blackfriars. 964

Richard defeated and slain at Bosworth, 22 Aug., 1485.

Matters became more serious as time went on. In June, 1485, the City advanced another sum of £2,000 to assist Richard against the "rebels," who were daily expected to land in England. 965 Extraordinary precautions were taken to guard the city. 966 At last the blow fell. On the 7th August Henry landed at Milford Haven, and on the 22nd the battle of Bosworth was fought and Richard killed.

Henry VII escorted to the city.

From Bosworth field Henry set out for London. He was met at Shoreditch by a deputation from the City, accompanied by the Recorder, and was presented with a gift of 1,000 marks. 967 The standards taken on the field of battle were deposited with much pomp and ceremony in St. Paul's Church, where a *Te Deum* was sung, and for a few days Henry took up his residence in the bishop's palace in St. Paul's Churchyard. 968

The sweating sickness, Sept.-Oct., 1485.

A cloud soon overshadowed the rejoicings which followed Henry's accession. An epidemic hitherto unknown in England, although visitations of it followed at intervals during this and the succeeding reign, made its appearance in the city towards the close of September. The "sweating sickness," as this deadly pestilence was called, carried off two mayors and six aldermen within the space of a week 969 — so sudden and fatal was its attack. Sir Thomas Hille, who was mayor at the time of its first appearance, fell a victim to it on the 23rd September, and was succeeded by William Stocker, appointed on the following day. 970 Within four days Stocker himself was dead. There remained little more than a month before the regular day of election of a mayor (28 Oct.) 971 for the year ensuing, and John Warde was called upon to take office during the interval. 972 He appears to have entertained but little affection for the city, and the civic authorities had some difficulty in getting him to reside in London, 973 where his duties required his presence. When the mayoralty year expired he was not put in nomination for re-election. He probably went back into the country, glad to get away from the pestilential city, and Hugh Brice was elected in his stead. 974 Fortunately for the city, the epidemic departed as suddenly and unexpectedly as it came. By the end of October it had entirely disappeared, and allowed of Henry's coronation taking place on the 30th of that month.

A City loan of £2,000.

Within a fortnight of his arrival in London Henry issued a writ of summons for his first parliament. It was not so much for the purpose of obtaining supplies that he was anxious that parliament should meet at the earliest opportunity; he was desirous of obtaining as soon as possible a parliamentary title to the crown. As for his immediate necessities, he preferred to apply to the City. He asked for a loan of 6,000 marks, or £4,000; but the citizens would not advance more than half that sum. The loan was repaid the following year—"every penie to the good contentation and satisfying of them that disbursed it." 975

Henry's marriage with Elizabeth of York, Jan., 1486.

In January, 1486, Henry married the Princess Elizabeth, daughter of Edward IV, and heiress of the Yorkist family. He had previously taken the precaution of committing to the Tower the Earl of Warwick, son of Clarence, for fear lest he might set up a title to the crown. 976 After his marriage he set out on a progress through the country, and on his return to London, in June, was met by the mayor and citizens at Putney, and escorted by them down the river to Westminster. 977

The insurrection of Lambert Simnel, 1487.

City gifts to the king, June and July, 1487.

A rumour that the Earl of Warwick had escaped from the Tower gave an opportunity for an imposter, Lambert Simnel, to personate the earl. In order to satisfy the Londoners that the rumour of Warwick's escape was a fabrication, Henry caused his prisoner to be paraded through the streets of the city, and exposed to public view at St. Paul's. After Simnel's defeat (16 June, 1487), the Common Council agreed (28 June) to send a deputation, consisting of two aldermen, the recorder, and four commoners, with a suite of 24 men, to meet the king at Kenilworth, and at the same time voted the king a present of £1000. 978 This gift was quickly followed (11 July) by the grant of another loan of £2,000 to be levied on the civic companies as before. 979

The king escorted to London, Oct., 1487.

The City's gift to the queen at her coronation, 25 Nov., 1487.

In October Henry was expected in London, 980 and the Common Council again showed their loyalty by agreeing that the mayor and aldermen should ride forth to meet his highness, clad in cloaks of scarlet, and accompanied by a suite of servants clothed in medley, at the cost of the "Chamber." With them also rode a contingent from the various civic guilds, clothed in violet, and numbering over 400 horsemen. The Mercers, the Grocers, the Drapers, the Fishmongers, and the "Taillours," each sent 30 mounted representatives of their guild; the Goldsmiths sent 24, whilst the rest sent contingents varying from one to twenty. 981 On the occasion of the queen's coronation, which took place the following month (25 Nov.), she was made the recipient of a gift of 1,000 marks by the City. 982

Henry VII and Brittany, 1488-1492.

The king would willingly have remained at peace if he were allowed, from motives of economy if for no other reason. England, however, could not sit still and see Brittany overwhelmed by the French king. Before assistance could be sent to the Duchess Anne, it was imperative that money should be raised. At the close of 1488 the Common Council voted the king a loan of £4,000. The money was ordered to be raised by assessment on the companies, but the practice was not to be drawn into precedent. The king, like a good paymaster as he always was, whatever other defects he may have had, repaid the money in the following year. 983

Parliamentary supplies and City loans.

Early in the following year parliament 984 granted large supplies which enabled Henry to despatch 6,000 Englishmen to Anne's assistance, but which caused much discontent among the "rude and beastlie" people of Yorkshire and Durham. 985 In June, 1491, another loan of £3,000 was raised, this time by assessment on the wards; 986 and in October Henry declared to parliament his intention of invading France in person. A grant of two fifteenths and two tenths was immediately made to assist him in his expedition by parliament; whilst the City contributed a "great benevolence," the fellowship of Drapers contributing more than any other fellowship, and every alderman subscribing, whether he wished it or no, the sum of £200. The amount contributed by the commonalty exceeded £9,000. 987 Thus furnished with supplies, the king crossed over to Calais on the 6th October, 1492. The campaign, however, had scarcely opened before Henry gladly accepted the liberal terms offered him by the French king, and peace was signed at Etaples (3 Nov.).

Perkin Warbeck conspiracy, 1496-1497.

The success which, brief as it was, had attended Simnel's enterprise was sufficient to encourage a hope that a better planned project might end in overturning the throne. A report was accordingly blazed abroad that Richard, Duke of York, brother of King Edward V, was yet alive, not having been murdered in the Tower, as had been supposed; and a man called Perkin Warbeck or Warboys, a native of Tournay, assumed the name of Richard Plantagenet and succeeded in getting a large number of people in Ireland and Scotland to believe that in his person they in fact saw Richard, Duke of York, the rightful heir to the crown. James IV of Scotland not only gave him in marriage the lady Catherine Gordon, daughter of the Earl of Huntley, but led an army into England in hopes that the appearance of the pretended prince might raise an insurrection in the northern counties. Instead, however, of joining the invaders the English prepared to repel them, and James retreated into his own country. This took place in 1496. Parliament granted large supplies to enable the king to meet the danger, but the inhabitants of Cornwall, sick of the constant demands made of them for money, and aware of the large treasure which Henry had already amassed, openly resisted any attempt at further taxation and determined to march on London.

The city put into a state of defence.

The Londoners, who not only abstained from opposing the new demand for money, but volunteered a loan to the king (15 Nov.) of £4,000, 988 lost no time in putting their city into a state of defence. Six aldermen and a number of representatives from the livery companies were deputed to attend to the city's ordnance. 989 The mayor was to be allowed twelve armed men in addition to his usual suite, and the sheriffs forty sergeants and forty valets in order to assist them in keeping the peace within the city. Communication was to be kept up at least once in the day between the mayor and the Lord Chancellor. Houses which had been set up on the city's walls, or within sixteen feet of them, were to be abated. John Stokker, who filled the not unworthy office of Common Hunt, 990 was ordered daily to ride out to learn the king's pleasure and report thereon to the mayor and aldermen. Among those appointed to guard the city's gates and Temple Bar was Alderman Fabyan, the chronicler. 991 The state of anxiety which prevailed in the city at this crisis is illustrated by "Jesus Mercy" at the head of one side of the page of the City's record, on which the above orders are entered, whilst on the other side are the words *vigilie temporis turbacionis.* 992

The rebels defeated at Blackheath, 22 June, 1497.

Perkin Warbeck in Cornwall.

Surrenders to the king's forces and is brought prisoner to London, Oct., 1498.

Is executed at Tyburn, 1499.

By the 22nd June, 1497, all immediate danger had passed, the rebels being on that day utterly defeated at Blackheath. Their leaders were taken and executed; the rest were for the most part made prisoners, but were soon afterwards dismissed without further punishment. The leniency displayed towards them by Henry was ill-repaid by their afterwards flocking to the standard of the *soi-disant* Richard IV, King of England, who availed himself of their mutinous disposition and appeared in their midst at Bodmin. The news of Perkin Warbeck having arrived in Cornwall from Ireland was brought to the mayor and aldermen of the City of London by letter from the king, which was read to the Common Council on Saturday, the 16th

September. 993 The rebels made an unsuccesful attempt to get possession of Exeter, but hearing of the approach of the king's forces, Perkin Warbeck withdrew to Taunton, leaving his followers to take care of themselves. From Taunton he went to "Mynet" (Minehead) accompanied by less than sixty adherents, 994 and by the 12th October the king was able to inform the Mayor that Peter "Warboys" had voluntarily submitted himself and had confessed to his being a native of Tournay. 995 The king had him conveyed to London and paraded through the streets on horseback, in a species of mock triumph, and caused his confession to be printed and scattered over the country that people might see the real character of the man. For a time he appears to have been detained in lax custody about the court, but after he had made an attempt to escape and reach the sea-coast, and been re-captured, he was sent to the Tower. There he got into communication with the unfortunate Earl of Warwick, and entered into a plot for effecting his own and the earl's liberty. A charge was formulated against the earl on the most trivial grounds, of a conspiracy to seize the Tower, and Warbeck was indicted as an accomplice. The former, being found guilty by his peers, was beheaded on Tower Hill, while Perkin and three of his accomplices were hanged at Tyburn. 996

Visit of Henry VIII as a boy to the city, 30 Oct., 1498.

In the meantime Prince Henry, who afterwards succeeded his father on the throne as King Henry VIII, but was at the time a child of seven years, paid a visit to the city (30 Oct., 1498), where he received a hearty welcome and was presented by the Recorder, on behalf of the citizens, with a pair of gilt goblets. In reply to the Recorder, who in presenting this "litell and powre" gift, promised to remember his grace with a better at some future time, the prince made the following short speech:— 997

His speech.

> "Fader Maire, I thank you and your Brethern here present of this greate and kynd remembraunce which I trist in tyme comyng to deserve. And for asmoche as I can not give unto you according thankes, I shall pray the Kynges Grace to thank you, and for my partye I shall not forget yor kyndnesse."

In anticipation of the prince's visit, a proclamation had been made by the civic authorities with the view of purging the city of infectious disease, to the effect that all vagabonds and others affected with the "greate pockes" should vacate the city on pain of imprisonment. 998

Negotiations for a marriage between Prince Arthur and Catherine of Aragon.

Preparations for reception of the princess, Nov., 1499.

The removal of Warwick—"the one judicial murder of Henry's reign"—if not suggested by Spain, was an act which could not be otherwise than grateful to the Spanish king. For five years past negotiations had been proceeding for a marriage between Prince Arthur and Catherine of Aragon. Warwick's death cleared away the last of Henry's serious competitors, and "not a doubtful drop of royal blood" remained in the kingdom to oppose Arthur's claim to the succession. The princess was expected shortly to arrive in England, and a committee composed of aldermen and commoners was appointed (Nov. 1499) to consult with the king's commissioners as to the preparations to be made for her reception. 999 Nearly two years, however, elapsed before she set foot in England. In May, 1500, there were again rumours of her approach, and the Common Council voted a sum of money to be levied on the wards to defray the expenses of her reception. 1000

Death of an infant prince, June, 1500.

The "garnysshyng of the pagents" for the festive occasion 1001 was interrupted by the death of Edmund, the king's infant son. On the 19th June the members of the various craft guilds were ordered to line the streets of Old Bailey and Fleet Street, through which the funeral procession was to pass on its way to Westminster. The mayor and aldermen were to stand, clad in their violet gowns, near Saint Dunstan's Church, and the next morning to go to Westminster by barge to attend the solemn requiem. 1002

The marriage of Prince Arthur with Catherine of Aragon, 14 Nov., 1501.

There was no necessity for hurry in regard to the pageants. More than a twelvemonth was yet to elapse before they were wanted. At length—on the 2nd October, 1003 1501—the princess landed at Plymouth, and five days later the City received notice from the king of her approach to London. The marriage was solemnized at St. Paul's on the 14th November, the princess being presented with silver flagons by the City in honour of the occasion. 1004 Five months later (2 April, 1502) the bride was a widow, Prince Arthur having died at the early age of fifteen.

More rejoicings in the city, March, 1503

In 1503 the streets of the city were again put into mourning, for in February of that year Henry lost his queen. A long account of the manner of "receyvyng of the corps of the most noble princes Quene Elizabeth" is given in the City's Archives. 1005 In the following month the streets presented a very different appearance, the occasion being the solemnization of the league made between Henry and the King of the Romans. Bonfires were ordered to be lighted at nine different places, and at each of them was to be placed a hogshead of wine, with two sergeants and two sheriffs' yeomen to prevent disturbance; but seeing that it was the Lenten season and that the queen had so recently died, there was to be no minstrelsy. The City Chamberlain was instructed to provide a certain quantity of "Ipocras," claret, Rhenish wine and Muscatel, besides comfits and wafers, and two pots of "Succade" and green ginger, to be presented on the City's behalf to the ambassadors of the King of the Romans, lying at "Pasmer Howse"; a similar gift being presented the following day on behalf of the sheriffs. 1006

Charter of Henry VII to the Tailors of London, 6 June 1503.

Henry's chief merit was that he established order, and for this the citizens were grateful. This improvement on the weak government of his immediate predecessors had only been carried out, however, at the cost of extension of royal power, and the City was made to suffer with the rest of the kingdom. In 1503 the civic authorities were deprived by statute of their control over the livery companies, 1007 and in the same year the Tailors of London obtained a charter which gave umbrage to the mayor and aldermen of the City, as ousting them of their jurisdiction. The Tailors maintained their independence, and their wardens are expressly mentioned as refusing to join the Mercers, Grocers, Drapers, Fishmongers, Goldsmiths and other fraternities in a petition to parliament (1512) for placing them formally under the rule of the mayor and aldermen, from which they were frequently breaking away. 1008

Henry's charter to the City, 23 July, 1505.

It was not until 1505 that the City succeeded in getting its charter 1009 from Henry, and then only on payment of the sum of 5,000 marks. The terms of the charter, moreover, were far from satisfactory, and an attempt was made to get them altered and obtain an abatement of the fine, 1010 but to no purpose.

Henry's high-handed policy towards the City, 1506-1509.

Henry continued his high-handed policy towards the City up to the day of his death, and thereby greatly increased his treasure. His chief instruments were Empson and Dudley, who took up their residence in the city, occupying two houses in Walbrook, whence each had a door into a garden of the Earl of Oxford's house in St. Swithin's Lane. 1011 There they used to meet and concert measures for filling the king's purse and their own. In 1506 Henry removed Robert Johnson, a goldsmith, from the shrievalty within three days of his election, and put William Fitz-William in his place. Johnson took the matter so much to heart that he died. 1012 In the same year Thomas Kneseworth, the late mayor, was committed to the Marshalsea, together with the sheriffs who had served under him, and only regained his liberty on payment of a large sum of money. 1013 In 1507 Sir William Capel, Alderman of Walbrook Ward, who had already fallen a victim to Empson and been heavily fined under an obsolete statute, was again attacked and fined £2,000 for supposed negligence during his mayoralty. Rather than submit to such extortion he went to prison, and remained there until the king's death, when he obtained his freedom and was soon afterwards re-elected mayor. 1014 Lawrence Aylmer, another mayor, was also a victim of Henry's tyranny, and was committed to the compter, where he remained for the rest of the reign. 1015

Marriage of the Princess Mary, Dec., 1508.

In the meantime the Archduke Philip happened to fall into Henry's hands (Jan., 1506). Whilst crossing the sea to claim the kingdom of Castile in right of his wife, he was driven by stress of weather into Weymouth. Henry was too shrewd a politician not to make the most of so lucky an event, and detained him in a species of honourable captivity, until Philip had promised him the hand of his sister Margaret with a large dower. This marriage alliance was destined never to be realised. Another scheme, however, was subsequently proposed and met with more success. This was a marriage of Henry's own daughter with Philip's son Charles, Prince of Castile. News of their engagement was conveyed to the mayor and aldermen of the City by a letter from the king himself (25 Dec., 1507), in which he expatiated on the benefits, political and commercial, likely to arise from the match. 1016

This letter was followed by another from the king, dated from Greenwich, the 23rd June following, in which the Corporation was informed that for the assurance of execution of the marriage treaty both parties had given pledges, and that the City of London was, among other cities and towns, included in letters obligatory to that effect, which letters he begged should be sealed without delay with the Common Seal of the City. 1017 And so, after the manner of the times, the boy of eight was married (by proxy) to the girl of twelve, amid great rejoicings in London (17 Dec., 1508). 1018

Henry's taste for the fine arts.

If Henry amassed wealth, it was not from any miserly motive. He well knew the value of the money, and that peace at home was never better secured than by a full treasury. He made, moreover, a princely use of his money, encouraging scholarship, music, and architecture, and dazzled the eyes of foreign ambassadors with the splendour of his receptions. That he had a fine taste in building no one can deny who has once seen the chapel of King's College, Cambridge, or the chapel that bears his name at Westminster.

The King's Chapel and Chantry at Westminster.

Originally intended by Henry as a resting place for the remains of his uncle, Henry VI, the last mentioned edifice was diverted from its purposes and became the chantry as well as the tomb of Henry VII himself. Anxiety for his soul caused him to bind the Abbot of Westminster by heavy penalties to the due observance of his obit. These penalties were set out in six books or deeds, sealed with the Common Seal of the City of London, and formally delivered to the king by a deputation of the mayor and aldermen, who received in return a seventh book to remain in their custody. In 1504—the year that Pope Julius sanctioned the removal of the remains of Henry VI from Windsor to Westminster—the mayor and citizens formally sealed the "books" before the Master of the Rolls at the Guildhall. Two years later certain livery companies undertook to keep the king's obit on the day that the mayor for the time being went to take his oath at the Exchequer. 1019

The king's death, 22 April, 1509.

The king died at his palace of Shene, recently renamed in his honour "Richmond," on the 22nd April, 1020 1509. Just before his death he granted a general pardon and paid the debts of prisoners committed to the compters of London and to Ludgate for debts amounting to forty shillings or less. 1021 His corpse was conveyed from Richmond to St. Paul's on the 9th May, being met on its way at St. George's Bar, in Southwark, by the mayor, aldermen and a suite of 104 commoners, all in black clothing and all on horseback. The streets were lined with other members of the companies bearing torches, the lowest craft occupying the first place. Next after the freemen of the city came the "strangers"—Easterlings, Frenchmen, Spaniards, Venetians, Genoese, Florentines and "Lukeners"—on horseback and on foot, also bearing torches. 1022 These took up their position in Gracechurch Street. Cornhill was occupied by the lower crafts, ordered in such a way that "the most worshipful crafts" stood next unto "Paules." A similar order was preserved the next day, when the corpse was removed from Saint Paul's to Westminster. The lowest crafts were placed nearest to the Cathedral, and the most worshipful next to Temple Bar, where the civic escort terminated. The mayor and aldermen proceeded to Westminster by water, to attend the "masse and offering." The mayor, with his mace in his hand, made his offering next after the Lord Chamberlain; those aldermen who had passed the chair 1023 offered next after the Knights of the Garter, and before all "knights for the body"; whilst the aldermen who had not yet served as mayor made their offering after the knights. 1024

When King Henry VIII was about to make an expedition to France in 1544, the Court of Aldermen gave notice to the Bishop of London that the obit of Henry VII would be kept on Friday, the 16th May, on which day there would be a general procession, and that the observance would be continued until the king departed out of the realm, and then on every Friday and Wednesday until his return. 1025

CHAPTER XIII.

Proceeding against Empson and Dudley and their agents.

One of the first acts of the new king was to grant Letters Patent absolving the City of all trespasses committed before the date of his accession, 1026 and to offer restitution to all who had suffered at the hands of Empson and Dudley or their agents. Empson and Dudley were themselves committed to the Tower and afterwards executed. In the meantime an enquiry was opened in the city as to recent proceedings against Capel and others.

It was found that six men, whose names were John Derby, *alias* Wright, a bowyer, Richard Smyth, a carpenter, William Sympson, a fuller, Henry Stokton, a fishmonger, Thomas Yong, a saddler, and Robert Jakes, a shearman—all of whom had more than once been convicted of perjury, and on that account been struck off inquests—had contrived to get themselves replaced on the panel, and had been the chief movers in the recent actions against the late mayor and other officers of the city. They had, moreover, taken bribes for concealment of offences of forestalling and regrating. Being found guilty, on their own confession, of having brought false charges against many of the aldermen, the Court of Common Council adjudged the whole of the accused to be disfranchised. Three of them, who were found more guilty than the rest, were sentenced to be taken from prison on the next market day, on horseback, without saddles, and with their faces turned towards the horses' tails, to the pillory on Cornhill. There they were to be set "their heddes in the holys" until proclamation of their crime and sentence was read. The lesser offenders were spared the pillory, but were condemned to attend on horseback at Cornhill, whence all the offenders were conducted to the Standard in Fleet Street "by the most high ways," where the proclamation was again read. The culprits were then taken back to prison and made to abjure the city on pain of imprisonment at the pleasure of the mayor and aldermen. 1027 Among the charges brought against Derby was one to the effect that being on a jury he had received the sum of ten shillings and "a quarter of ffisshe for his howsehold," a bribe which a suitor had tendered by the advice and counsel of Thomas Yong, saddler, who was apparently acting as Derby's accomplice. 1028

City gift on occasion of the king's coronation, 24 June, 1509.

On the occasion of the king's coronation, which took place on Midsummer-day soon after his marriage with Catherine of Aragon, his brother's widow, the citizens presented the king and queen with the sum of £1,000 or 1,500 marks. Two-thirds of the gift was given expressly to the king, the remaining one-third being a tribute of respect to the queen. The money was to be raised in the city by way of a fifteenth, but the poor were not to be assessed. 1029 The procession from the Tower to Westminster was equal to, if it did not surpass, any spectacle that had yet been witnessed in the city for its gorgeousness and pomp. The streets were railed and barred from Gracechurch Street to Cheapside at the expense of the livery companies who lined the way, 1030 "beginning with base and meane occupations and so ascending to the worshipful crafts." The Goldsmiths of London were especially conspicuous for their marks of loyalty on that day. Their stalls, which were situate by the Old Change at the west end of Chepe, were occupied by fair maidens dressed in white and holding tapers of white wax, whilst priests in their robes stood by with censers of silver and incensed the king and queen as they passed. 1031

The war with France, 1512-1513.

After three years of indolent and luxurious ease Henry became embroiled in continental troubles. In 1511 a holy league had been formed for the purpose of driving the French out of the Milanese, and Henry's co-operation was desired. A parliament was summoned to meet early in the following year. 1032 After granting supplies 1033 it unanimously agreed that war should be proclaimed against France. The campaign of 1512 ended ingloriously, and the French king threatened to turn the tables on Henry and to invade England. Henry rose to the occasion and at once set about strengthening his navy. On the 30th January, 1513, he addressed a letter to the Corporation of London desiring them to furnish him with 300 men, the same to be at Greenwich by the 15th February at the latest. 1034 Proclamation was thereupon made in the city for all persons who were prepared to join the war to appear at the Guildhall any time before the 10th February, where, if approved, they would be furnished with sufficient harness and weapons, without any charge, and also with sufficient wages at the king's cost. 1035

The city was suffering at the time from great scarcity of wheat, and each alderman was called upon to contribute the sum of £5 towards alleviating the distress which prevailed. A contract was made with certain Hanse merchants to furnish the city with 2,000 quarters of wheat and rye respectively by Midsummer-day, whilst the royal purveyors were forbidden to lay hands on wheat, malt or grain entering the port of London. 1036 Under the circumstances it could have been no great hardship, but rather an advantage to rid the city of 300 mouths. On the 1st February, 1513, the aldermen were instructed to enquire in their respective wards as to the number of men each ward could furnish, and two days later the livery companies were ordered to find the sum of £300 to defray the expense connected with fitting out the men. If more than £300 were needed they were to draw on the Chamber, but any money not expended out of that sum was to be paid into the Chamber. 1037 The companies raised the sum of £405, the Mercers contributing £35, the Grocers, Drapers, Fishmongers and Goldsmiths respectively £30, and the rest sums of smaller amount. 1038 There was some difference of opinion as to the nature of the uniform to be worn by the city's contingent. At length it was settled that the soldiers' coats should be white, with a St. George's cross and sword, together with a rose, at the back and the same before. Their shoes were to be left to the discretion of the muster-masters. 1039

The Battle of Spurs, 16 Aug., 1513.

Henry himself now crossed over to France. The campaign proved more successful than the last, for the French being attacked at Guinegate, were seized with so great a panic that Henry achieved a bloodless victory. From the hasty flight of the French cavalry, the engagement came to be known as the Battle of Spurs. This victory secured the fall of Terouenne and was followed shortly afterwards by the capture of Tournay.

Peace with France, 1514.

Notwithstanding these successes, however, Henry found it necessary to make peace in the following year. His allies had got what they wanted, and the conquest of France was as far off as ever. It remained only to make as good a bargain as he could. The French king consented to the payment of a large sum of money, in return for which he was given Henry's sister Mary in marriage, although she was already affianced, if not married, to Prince Charles of Castile. This was the work of the king's new minister, Wolsey.

The New Learning.

To the apostles of the New Learning—as the revival of letters which commenced in the last reign came to be called—to Erasmus, to Archbishop Warham, to More and to Colet, the war at its outset had been eminently distasteful. With the accession of Henry VIII to the throne they had hoped for better things. War was to be for ever banished and a "new order" was to prevail.

Thomas More.

Of its connection with More and Colet the City is justly proud. At the opening of Henry's reign the future lord chancellor was executing the duties of the comparatively unimportant post of under-sheriff or judge of the Poultry Compter, a post which he continued to hold until 1517.

1040 He had received his education in the city at St. Antony's School in Threadneedle Street, a school which had already achieved a great reputation and afterwards reckoned among its pupils the famous Whitgift. Later in life he shut himself up for four years in the Charterhouse of London, living a life of devotion and prayer, but without taking any vow. 1041

Dean Colet.

The father of John Colet, Dean of St. Paul's, had taken an active part in municipal life. Henry Colet had been alderman first of Farringdon Ward Without and afterwards of the Wards of Castle Baynard and Cornhill, 1042 and as alderman of the last mentioned ward he had died towards the close of 1505. He had served as sheriff in 1477 and as mayor in 1486.

Education in the city.

Up to the time of Henry VI education had been carried on in the city chiefly by means of schools attached to the various city churches and religious houses. By order of Henry VI, and at the instigation of four city ministers, 1043 grammar schools were established in several parishes. The school of St. Antony attached to the hospital of the same name, of which Dr. John Carpenter was at the time master, received an endowment from Henry VI for the maintenance of scholars at Oxford. The school continued to flourish some time after the dissolution of the hospital. There was also a school attached to the hospital of St. Thomas of Acon, as famous in its day as that of St. Antony, but of which little is known until after the suppression of the religious houses by Henry VIII, when it passed into the hands of the Mercers' Company and became known, as it is to this day, as the Mercers' School.

The City of London School.

The Dr. John Carpenter just mentioned must not be confounded with the Town Clerk of that name, the compiler of the famous *Liber Albus* and the founder of the City of London School. There is little known of the foundation of this latter school beyond the statement made by Stow a century and a-half later, that he "gave tenements to the city for the finding and bringing up of four poor men's children with meat, drink, apparel, learning at the schools in the universities, etc., until they be preferred, and then others in their places for ever." 1044 Within the last few years the City Chamberlain's accounts—touching "the lands of Mr. John Carpenter, sometyme commen clarke of this cittie"—have been brought to light, and serve to supplement in a small way Stow's meagre but valuable statement. The rental or amount with which the Chamberlain charged himself for the year 1565 or 1566 is there set down as £41 0s. 4d., and the discharge—embracing a quit rent due to the Dean and Chapter of Westminster, and expenses incurred in overseeing, clothing and feeding four poor children "being founde at scoole and lerning by the bequeste of the sayde Master Carpenter"—amounted to £19 12s. 8d., leaving a balance to the City of £21 7s. 8d. 1045 From so modest a beginning arose the school which, situate on the Thames Embankment, now numbers over 700 scholars.

St. Paul's School.

There was a school attached to St. Paul's long before Colet's day, just as there is one now, independent of the school of Colet's foundation, and devoted mainly to the instruction of the Cathedral choristers. Soon after Colet's appointment to the Deanery in 1505 he experienced no little dissatisfaction with the Cathedral School, where great laxity prevailed, more especially in the religious education of the "children of Paul's," and so, about the year 1509—the year of Henry's accession—having recently come into a considerable estate by the death of his father, he set about acquiring a small property situate at the east end of St. Paul's Church for the purpose of establishing another school which would better realise his own ideal of what a school should be than the existing Cathedral School. Colet's School grew apace. In 1511 he was in negotiation with the Court of Aldermen for the purchase "of a certen grounde of the citie for an entre to be hadde into his new gramer scole." 1046 By January of the next year (1512) he had succeeded in obtaining the assent both of the Court of Aldermen and Common Council to the purchase by him of a "certen grounde in the Olde Chaunge for the inlargyng of his gramer scole in Powly's Churcheyerd" for the sum of £30. 1047 The property was conveyed to him by deed, dated the 27th September, which deed was sealed with the common seal on the 7th October following. 1048 The question as to whom he should entrust the management of his school caused Colet no little anxiety. He eventually decided to confide its revenues and management entirely to the Mercers' Company, and when asked the reason for his so doing replied that "though there was nothing certain in human affairs he yet found the least corruption in them." 1049

Considerable rivalry existed among the various grammar schools of the city, more especially between the boys of Colet's School and the boys of the more ancient foundation of St. Antony, which, for a long time, had the reputation for turning out the best scholars. Public disputations were held in the open air. The St. Paul's boys meeting St. Antony's boys would derisively call them St. Antony's pigs, that saint being generally represented with a pig following him, and challenge them to a disputation; the latter would retaliate by styling their rivals "pigeons of St. Paul's," from the bird which then, as now, frequented St. Paul's Churchyard. From questions of grammar, writes Stow, 1050 they usually fell to blows "with their satchels full of books, many times in great heaps, that they troubled the streets and passengers." After the decay of St. Antony's School the rivalry was taken up, but in a more friendly way, by the later foundation of the Merchant Taylors' School.

Provincial grammar schools founded by citizens of London.

But the citizens of London did not limit their efforts in the cause of education to their own city. Throughout the country there are to be found grammar schools which owe their establishment to the liberal-mindedness and open-handed generosity of the city merchant. 1051 Their existence bears testimony to the kindly feeling which men who had grown rich in London still bore to the provincial town or village which gave them birth and which they had left in early life to seek their fortune in the great metropolis.

To take but a few instances: Sir John Percival, a merchant-tailor, who in 1487 filled the subordinate office of Lord Mayor's carver, performing his duties so well that the mayor, Sir Henry Colet, nominated him one of the sheriffs for the year ensuing by the time honoured custom of drinking to him at a public dinner, founded a school at Macclesfield. Stephen Jenyns, another merchant-tailor, did the same thing at Wolverhampton. Sir Thomas White, another member of the same company, founded two schools in the provinces, one at Reading and another at Bristol, besides the College of St. John at Oxford. Sir William Harper, yet another merchant-tailor, established a school at Bedford.

The Mercers' Company rivalled the Merchant-Taylors' in the number of schools established in the country through the liberality of its members. Sir John Gresham founded one at Holt, in Norfolk; Sir Rowland Hill, an ancestor of the originator of the Penny Postal scheme, another at Drayton, in Shropshire; whilst schools at Horsham, in Sussex, and West Lavington, in Wiltshire, were erected by two other mercers, Richard Collier and William Dauntsey. There exist at the present day at least four schools which owe their foundation to wealthy members of the Grocers' Company, the well known school at Oundle, co. Northampton, upon which the Company have expended on capital account the sum of £35,000, having been founded by Sir William Laxton; another at Sevenoaks, in Kent, by William Sevenoke, a native of the place, who rose from very humble circumstances to the chief magistracy of the city; another at Witney, in Oxfordshire, by Henry Box, and another at Colwall, co. Hereford, by Humphry Walwyn. Sir Andrew Judd, a member of the Skinners' Company, established a school at Tonbridge, whilst Sir Wolstan Dixie, another skinner, performed the same charitable act at Market Bosworth. Lastly, Sir George Monoux and Thomas Russell, both of them members of the Drapers' Company, founded schools at Walthamstow and at Barton-under-Needwood, co. Stafford, respectively.

Birth of the Princess Mary, Feb., 1516.

On the Feast of St. Matthew (21 Sept.), 1515, a messenger arrived in the city from Wolsey desiring the mayor and aldermen to attend that evening at St. Paul's to return thanks to Almighty God for the queen, who was quick with child. The summons was obeyed, 1052 and in the following February (1516) the Princess Mary was born.

The city and Cardinal Wolsey, 1516.

By this time Wolsey had risen to be a great power in the State. In 1514 he had been made Archbishop of York, and in the following year a cardinal. His high position as a prince of the Church, as well as his authority with the king, rendered it desirable for the citizens to keep well with him. On the 6th March, 1516, it was resolved to send a deputation to the cardinal for the purpose of securing his favour. No expense was to be spared in the matter, and all costs and charges were to be paid by the Chamber. 1053 In the following June the cardinal handed to the mayor a list of abuses in the city which required reform. Sedition was rife there; the commons were disobedient, the statute of apparel was ignored, vagabonds and masterless folk resorted there and unlawful games were allowed in houses. The king's council required an answer on these points within a few days, and an answer was accordingly given, but the purport of it is not recorded, although it was read to the Court of Aldermen before being despatched. 1054

In November of the same year (1516) the City was in difficulties with the recently erected Court of Star Chamber, and Wolsey, who practically kept the whole business of government in his own hands, came to the City's assistance with advice. It appears that a subsidy was due on the 21st of this month and the City had not paid its quota. The mayor and aldermen were cited to appear before the cardinal and other lords of the council in the Star Chamber at Westminster. Being asked if they had "sworne for their assayng," to the king's subsidy, the Recorder answered on their behalf that such procedure was contrary to Act of Parliament. The cardinal thereupon advised them to agree to give the king £2,000 in order to be discharged of their oaths "or ells every of theym to be sworn of and upon the true value of their substance within the sum of 100 marks." This took place on Saturday, the 22nd, and the mayor and aldermen were to give an answer to the Star Chamber by the following Wednesday. On Tuesday, the 25th, the Court of Aldermen met to consider what was best to be done under the circumstances. The decision they arrived at was that as the present assessment was less than the last, they would, in consideration of the king's letters, make up the sum then payable so that it should equal the last assessment. 1055

Evil Mayday, 1517.

The seditious "brutes" or riots of which Wolsey had complained as daily occurring in the city were soon to assume a serious form. They were occasioned for the most part by the jealousy with which everybody who was not a freeman of the city was looked upon by the free citizen. The influx of strangers and foreigners has been daily increasing, notwithstanding the limitations and restrictions placed upon their residence and mode of trading, 1056 whilst the tendency of freemen had been to leave the city for the country. 1057

Whilst the civic authorities were doing all they could to prevent the possibility of a disturbance arising on the coming May-day 1058—a day kept as a general holiday in the city—occasion was taken by a minister of the church, whose duty it was to preach the usual Spital sermon on Easter Tuesday (14 April), to incite the freemen to rise up against the foreigner and stranger. 1059 When the 1st May arrived all might have been well, had not a city alderman allowed his zeal to outrun his discretion. It happened that John Mundy, 1060 Alderman of Queenhithe Ward, came across some youngsters playing "at the bucklers" at a time when by a recent order they should have been within doors, and he commanded them to desist. This they showed no disposition to do, and when force was threatened raised the cry for 'prentices and clubs. A large crowd quickly assembled and the alderman had to beat a hasty retreat. The mob, now thoroughly roused, proceeded to set free the prisoners in Newgate and the compters, and to attack the strangers and foreigners quartered at Blanchappleton 1061 and elsewhere. Rioting continued throughout the night, but early the following morning they were met by a large force which the mayor in the meantime had collected, and 300 of them were made prisoners, so that by the time that assistance arrived from the court quiet had been restored. A commission of Oyer and Terminer was opened at the Guildhall to try the offenders. John Lincoln, who had not so long ago been appointed surveyor of goods bought and sold by foreigners, 1062 was charged with being the instigator of the riot, and being found guilty was hanged in Cheapside, whilst twelve others were hanged on gallows in different parts of the city. Others received the king's pardon with halters round their necks in token of the fate they deserved. 1063

The City anxious to regain the king's lost favour.

The civic authorities were not unnaturally anxious to make their peace with the king, and to disclaim any complicity in the late outbreak. The Court of Aldermen met on the 11th May to consider how best to approach his majesty on so delicate a subject. It was decided to send a deputation to the lord cardinal to "feel his mind" as to the number of persons that should appear before the king. The next day eight aldermen and the Recorder were nominated by the court "to go the Kinges grace and to knowe his plesure when the Mayr and Aldremen and diverse of the substancyall commoners of this citie shall sue to beseche his grace to be good and gracious lord un to theym and to accept theym nowe beyng most sorrowful and hevye for thees late attemptates doon ayeynst their wylles." 1064

A deputation attends the king at Greenwich, 11 May, 1517.

Wolsey and other lords to be bought over with gifts.

The king's pardon obtained, 22 May.

The deputation forthwith proceeded, clothed in gowns of black, to Greenwich, whither the king had gone on the 11th May. The Recorder as usual acted as spokesman, and humbly prayed the royal forgiveness for the negligence displayed by the mayor in not keeping the king's peace within the city. The king in reply told them plainly his opinion that the civic authorities had winked at the whole business, and referred them to Cardinal Wolsey, his chancellor, who would declare to them his pleasure. 1065 With this answer the deputation withdrew and reported what had taken place to the mayor, who had wisely kept away. It was clear that above all things the favour of the cardinal had to be obtained. For this purpose a committee was appointed, whose duty it was to "devise what thinges of plesur shalbe geven to my lord Cardynall and to other of the lordes as they shall thynk convenient for their benevolences doon concernyng this last Insurreccioun." 1066 By the 22nd May matters had evidently been accommodated. On that date the king sat at Westminster Hall in great state, surrounded by the lords of his council and attended by the cardinal. The mayor and aldermen and chief commoners of the city, chosen from the leading civic companies, 1067 had arrived by nine o'clock in the morning clad in their best liveries, "according as the cardinal had commanded them." 1068 Wolsey knew the king's weakness for theatrical display. At Henry's command all the prisoners were brought into his presence. They appeared, to the number of 400 men and eleven women, all with ropes round their necks. After the cardinal had administered a rebuke to the civic authorities for their negligence, and had declared that the prisoners had deserved death, a formal pardon was proclaimed by the king, the cardinal exhorting all present to loyalty and obedience. It was some time before the effects of the late outbreak disappeared. Compensation for losses had to be made; 1069 some were bound over to keep the peace; 1070 and counsel were employed to draw up a statement of the points of grievance between the citizens and merchant strangers for submission to the king. 1071 In September there were rumours of another outbreak, but the civic authorities were better prepared than formerly, and effectually stopt any such attempt by putting suspected persons into prison.

Lest any unfavourable report should reach the cardinal, the Recorder and another were ordered to ride in all haste to Sion, where Wolsey was thought to be, and if they failed to find him there, to follow him to Windsor and to report to him the active measures that had been taken to prevent any further insurrection in the city. 1072 "Evil May-day" was long remembered by the citizens, who raised objection to Thomas Semer or Seymer, who had been sheriff at the time, being elected mayor ten years later. 1073 In May, 1547, all householders were straitly charged not to permit their servants any more to go maying, but to keep them within doors. 1074

The epidemic of 1518.

With gibbets all over the city, each bearing a ghastly freight, and the summer approaching, it is scarcely surprising that the city should soon again be visited with an epidemic. "At the city gates," wrote an eye-witness, "one sees nothing but gibbets and the quarters of these wretches"—the wretches who had been hanged for complicity in the late disturbance—"so that it is horrible to pass near them." 1075 The "sweating sickness," which had again made its appearance in 1516, and had never really quitted the city (except for a few weeks in winter), now raged more violently than ever, accompanied by measles and small-pox. The king ordered all inhabitants of infected houses to keep indoors and hang out wisps of straw, and when compelled to walk abroad to carry white rods. 1076 This order, however, was badly received in the city and gave rise to much murmuring and dissatisfaction. 1077 The civic authorities did what they could to mitigate the evil by driving out beggars and vagabonds, and removing slaughter-houses outside the city walls, 1078 as well as by administering relief to the poorer classes by the distribution of tokens or licences to solicit alms. These tokens consisted of round "beedes" of white tin, bearing the City's arms in the centre, to be worn on the right shoulder. 1079 In the midst of so much real suffering, there were not wanting those who took advantage of the charitable feeling which the crisis called forth and were not ashamed to gain a livelihood by simulating illness. Such a one was Miles Rose, who on the 11th March, 1518, openly confessed before the Court of Aldermen that he had frequently dissembled the sickness of the "fallyng evyle" (or epilepsy) in divers parish churches in the city, on which occasions "jemewes" of silver, called cramp rings, would as often as not be placed on his fingers by charitable passers-by, with which he would quickly make off, pocketing at the same time many a twopence which had been bestowed upon him. 1080

Marriage of the infant Princess Mary with the Dauphin, 5 Oct., 1518.

The city could scarcely have recovered its wonted appearance after the ravages of the pestilence before its streets were enlivened with one of those magnificent displays for which London became justly famous, the occasion being an embassy from the French king sent to negotiate a marriage treaty between Henry's daughter Mary, a child but two years of age, and the still younger Dauphin of France. The City Records, strange to say, appear to be altogether silent on this subject, and yet the embassy, for magnificent display, was such as had never been seen within its walls before. We can understand that the embassy was not acceptable to the thrifty middle-class trading burgess, when we read that it was accompanied by a swarm of pedlars and petty hucksters who showed an unbecoming anxiety to do business in hats, caps and other merchandise, which under colour of the embassy had been smuggled into the country duty free. 1081 The foreign retail trader was at the best of times an abomination to the free burgess, and this sharp practice on the part of the Frenchmen, coming so soon after the recent outburst against strangers on Evil May-day, only served to accentuate his animosity—"At this dooing mannie an Englishman grudged, but it availed not." 1082 The ambassadors were lodged at the Merchant Taylors' Hall, which, owing to the ill-timed action of the French pedlars, had the look of a mart. On Sunday, the 3rd October, the king, with a train of 1,000 mounted gentlemen richly dressed, attended by the legates and foreign ambassadors, went in procession to St. Paul's to hear mass; after which the king took his oath—a ceremonial which the French admiral declared to be "too magnificent for description." On the following Tuesday (5 Oct.) the marriage ceremony—so far as it could be carried out between such infants—was celebrated at Greenwich, and a tiny gold ring, in which was a valuable diamond, placed upon Mary's finger. 1083

Preparations for the reception of the legate in the city, July, 1519.

In the following year (July, 1519) the streets witnessed another scene of gaiety. This time it was a visit of the legate, Cardinal Campeggio, for which the civic authorities made great preparations. 1084 In the first place the mayor and aldermen, in their gowns and cloaks of scarlet, were ordered to take up their position at 9 o'clock on the morning of Relic Sunday (*i.e.*, the third Sunday after Midsummer Day) at St. Paul's stairs (*the stayers wtin poulys*). Next to them were to stand the Skinners, then the Mercers and other worshipful crafts in their order, clothed in their last and best livery. In this manner the street was to be lined on either side from the west door of St. Paul's down to Baynard's Castle. Upon the arrival of the lord cardinal and other lords at the Cathedral the mayor and aldermen were to head the procession and seat themselves in the choir to hear *Te Deum* sung. Bonfires or "pryncypall fyres" were to be lighted at St. Magnus corner, Gracechurch, Leadenhall, the conduit on Cornhill, St. Thomas "of Acres," the Standard and little conduit in Cheap, the Standard in Fleet Street, and in Bishopsgate Street; whilst cresset lights and small fires "made after the manner of Midsummer-night" were to add to the gaiety of the scene. Men-at-arms, well harnessed and apparelled, were to keep certain streets, whilst the aldermen and their constables were to keep watch and ward in their best array of harness. The ambassadors, who were to be lodged in Cornhill, were to be escorted home at night by the aldermen with torches, and to await their commands. There was one other, perhaps not unnecessary, direction to be followed, which was to the effect that if by any chance the strangers should be overcome by the hospitality of the city, or, in the words of the record—"yf eny oversyght be wt moche drynke of the strangers"—the citizens were to "lett theym alone and no Englishemen to medyle wt theym."

The legate lands at Deal, 23 July, 1519.

A story told of his passage through the city.

The legate landed at Deal on the 23rd July, and by slow stages was conducted with every mark of respect to London. His passage through the city was associated with an episode of a decidedly comic character if we are to believe the chronicler. A story is told 1085 that the night before Campeggio entered London, Wolsey sent him twelve mules with (empty) coffers, in order to give a semblance of wealth to the legate and his retinue. In Cheapside one of the mules turned restive and upset the chests, out of which tumbled old hose, shoes, bread, meat, and eggs, with "muche vile baggage," at which the street boys cried "See, see my lord legate's treasure!" The story, however, is on good authority deemed more malicious than probable.

The contest for the empire, 1519.

In January, 1519, the Emperor Maximilian died and left the imperial crown to be contested for by the kings of France and Spain. It eventually fell to the latter, and Charles V of Spain was elected Emperor Charles I, the event being celebrated by a solemn mass and *Te Deum* at St. Paul's, followed by a banquet at Castle Baynard. 1086

The emperor's visit to the city, 1522.

Both France and Germany were eager to secure the co-operation of Henry. Charles anticipated the meeting which was to take place between Henry and Francis on the famous Field of the Cloth of Gold by coming over in person to England (May, 1519) and having a private conference with his uncle. The young emperor did not visit the city on this occasion; but in 1522, when war had broken out between him and Francis and he was again in England, he was escorted to the city with great honour and handsomely lodged in the palace of Bridewell. Nearly £1,000 was raised to meet the expenses of his reception and of furnishing a body of 100 bowmen for the king's service. 1087

The king and his guest and ally were met at St. George's Bar in Southwark by John Melborne, 1088 the mayor, accompanied by the high officers of the city, clothed in gowns of "pewke," each with a chain of gold about his neck. 1089 A "proposicioun" or address was made by Sir Thomas More, now under-treasurer of England, who was afterwards presented by the City with the sum of £10 towards a velvet gown, 1090 whilst other speeches made in the course of the procession were composed by Master Lilly, 1091 of Euphues fame, the first high master of Colet's School.

Pestilence and famine, 1519-1522.

Between the first and second visits of the emperor the citizens had witnessed some strange sights and had gone through much suffering and privation. The city had scarcely ever been free from sickness, and famine and pestilence had followed one another in quick succession. In September, 1520, the fellowships or civic companies subscribed over £1,000 for the purchase of wheat 1092 to be stored at the Bridgehouse, where ovens were fitted up. 1093 Mills for grinding corn already existed in the Thames hard by. 1094 The following year the plague raged to such an extent that every house attacked was ordered to be marked with St. Antony's cross, "otherwise called the syne of Tav," 1095 and citizens were forbidden to attend the fair at Windsor for fear of carrying infection to the court. 1096

Again a scarcity of corn was feared, and the Bridge-masters were authorised by the Court of Common Council to purchase provisions, the corporation undertaking to give security for the repayment of all monies advanced by the charitably disposed for the purpose of staving off famine. 1097 Early in 1522 (15 Jan.) died Fitz-James, Bishop of London, carried off with many others by "a great death in London and other places of the realm." 1098

Execution of the Duke of Buckingham, 1521.

The citizens had also in the meanwhile witnessed the arrest and execution of the Duke of Buckingham, son of the duke who figured so prominently before the citizens when the crown was offered to Richard III at Baynard Castle. He was seized one day whilst landing from his barge at the Hay Wharf, on a number of charges all more or less frivolous. His attendants were dismissed to the duke's "Manor of the Rose," in the parish of St. Laurence Pountney 1099—on the site of which recently stood Merchant

Taylors' School—whilst he himself was conducted to the Tower (16 April, 1521). An indictment was laid against him at the Guildhall before Sir John Brugge, lord mayor, and others (8 May). After a trial at Westminster which lasted some days, he was found guilty of high treason, and condemned to be hanged, drawn and quartered, and to suffer such other atrocities as usually accompanied the death of a traitor in those days. The king, however, satisfied with his condemnation, spared him these indignities, and the duke was allowed to meet his death at the block. His corpse was reverently carried from the Tower to the Church of the Austin Friars by six poor members of that Order. 1100

The duke had other friends in the city besides these poor religious men, who thus requited in the only way they could many acts of kindness done to their Order by Buckingham in his life time, and his death gave rise to much disaffection and seditious language for some time afterwards. 1101

City loan of £20,000 to assist the king against France, 1522.

Before the emperor left England he succeeded in committing Henry to an invasion of France. In order to carry out his object the king needed money, and the City was asked to furnish him with the sum of £100,000. 1102 Ten days later (26 May) the City agreed to advance £20,000. The livery companies were to be called upon to surrender their plate, and foreigners as well as citizens were to be made to contribute. 1103

The aldermen to be assessed with the commoners and not to be severed.

The question arose whether the aldermen should be jointly assessed with the commoners or by themselves. The mayor and aldermen were willing to contribute the sum of £3,000, 1104 but this offer the Common Council "nothyng regarded," but sent the common sergeant to talk the matter over with them. After long consultation the mayor and aldermen sent back word that it was more "convenient" that they should be assessed with the commoners and not to be severed. 1105

In the meantime a hasty valuation had been made by the command of Wolsey of the plate of the livery companies, and of the ready money lying in their halls, the whole value of which was estimated to be £4,000. This, together with the sum of £10,000 which the Court of Aldermen purposed raising among the wealthier class of citizens, was all that the cardinal was given to expect from the City. 1106 On the 24th May the deputation, which had ridden with all speed after the cardinal in order to make this report, returned to the city and reported to the Court of Aldermen that his grace was in no wise satisfied with the City's offer, and that he expected the City to furnish the king with at least £30,000, of which £10,000 was to be ready within three days. 1107 The matter was compromised by the City consenting to advance £20,000.

In June the Recorder had an interview with Wolsey respecting the security to be given for repayment of the loan. The cardinal refused to allow that certain abbots, abbesses and priors, who had been named, should enter into bond, and the citizens were obliged to be content with the personal securities of the king and Wolsey himself. Touching the plate of the halls, the cardinal wished only to take it in case of absolute necessity, and then only at a fair price. He desired the owners to bring it to the Tower, "there to be coyned and they [*i.e.*, the government] to pay the seyd money that so shalbe coyned." The result of the Recorder's interview was reported to the Court of Aldermen the 17th June. 1108 A committee had already (2 June) to take an account of the plate brought in and to enter its true weight in a book. 1109

A further loan of 4,000 marks.

Letter of thanks from Wolsey, 3 Sept., 1522.

The recent loan of £20,000 had scarcely been raised 1110 before the citizens found it necessary to make a further advance of 4,000 marks. Their liberality was repaid by a gracious letter from Wolsey himself, in which he promised to see the money repaid in a fortnight, 1111 and to extend to them his favour. What vexed the citizens more than anything was being compelled to make oath before the cardinal's deputy sitting in the Chapter House of St. Paul's as to the amount each was worth in money, plate, jewels, household goods and merchandise,—a system of inquisition recently introduced. 1112

The City makes a stand against further loans. Nov., 1522.

Others follow its example.

As if all this were not enough Wolsey demanded another loan before the end of the year. This was too much even for the patient and open-handed London burgess. The Common Council determined (4 Nov.) to put a stop to these extortionate demands, and resolved that, "As touchyng the Requeste made by my lorde cardynalles grace for appreste or aloone of more money to the kynges grace, they can in no wise agre thereto, but they ar and wilbe well contendid to be examyned upon their othes yf it shall please his grace so to do." 1113 The stand thus made by the citizens against illegal exactions gave courage to others. The king's commissioners were forcibly driven out of Kent, and open rebellion was threatened in other counties. 1114

Appeal to parliament, April, 1523.

There was only one course left open to Henry, and that was to summon a parliament. For nearly eight years no parliament had sat. It was now summoned to meet on the 15th April, 1523, not at Westminster, but at the house of the Blackfriars. 1115 The names of the city's representatives are on record. The aldermen elected one of their body, George Monoux, and with him was associated "according to ancient customs," the city's Recorder, William Shelley; whilst the commons elected John Hewster, a mercer, and William Roche, a draper 1116

A few days after the election a committee of fourteen members was nominated to consider what matters should be laid before parliament as being for the welfare of the city. 1117 Sir Thomas More was chosen Speaker. The enormous sum of £800,000 was demanded. Expecting some hesitation on the part of the Commons, Wolsey himself determined to argue with them, and suddenly made his appearance in state. Finding that his speech was received in grim silence, he turned to More for a reply. The Speaker, falling on his knees, declared his inability to make any answer until he had received the instructions of the House, and intimated that perhaps the silence of the Commons was due to the cardinal's presence. Wolsey accordingly departed discomforted. 1118 His attempt to overawe parliament marks the beginning of his downfall. He still kept well with the city, however, and rendered it several small services.

The City and Wolsey, 1523.

Emboldened by their recent success the citizens determined to make a stand against other exactions, and when in May, 1523, another demand was made for one hundred bowmen, as in the previous year, they sent their charter to the cardinal and begged that the article touching citizens not being liable to foreign service might remain in force. A similar demand was made in the following November, and again the assistance of Wolsey was called in. 1119 The City on the other hand had recently conferred a favour on the cardinal by discharging Robert Amadas, his own goldsmith, from serving as alderman when elected in March of this year. 1120

The king and queen of Denmark in the city.

In June the king and queen of Denmark paid a visit to the city and attended mass at St. Paul's, 1121 when the Court of Aldermen made them a present of two hogsheads of wine, one of white and another of claret, and two "awmes" of Rhenish wine, two fresh salmon, a dozen great pike, four dozen of "torchettes," and eight dozen of "syses." 1122

England invaded by the Scots. 1523.

The joint attack of Henry and the emperor against France in 1523 proved as great a failure as that of 1522. In the midst of the campaign Henry was threatened with danger nearer home. The Scots marched southward, and created such a panic in the city that a solemn procession, in which figured Cuthbert Tunstal, Bishop of London (successor to the unfortunate Fitz-James), the mayor and aldermen, all the king's justices, and all the sergeants-at-law, took place every day for a week. 1123 After a futile attack upon Wark Castle the invaders withdrew and all danger was over. 1124

Monoux refuses to accept the mayoralty a second time, Oct., 1523.

When the Feast of St. Edward (13 Oct.) came round, George Monoux, alderman and draper, who had already (1514-15) once filled the office of mayor of the city, was re-elected; but refusing to accept the call of his fellow-citizens he was fined £1,000. It was thereupon declared by the Court of Aldermen that anyone who in future should be elected mayor, and refused to take up office, should be mulcted in a like sum. 1125 Monoux's fine was remitted the following year, and he was discharged from attendance, although keeping his aldermanry, on account of ill health. In return for this favour he made over to the Corporation his brewhouse situate near the Bridgehouse in Southwark. 1126

The king pledges himself to repay the City loan of £20,000.

Before the close of the year (3 Dec., 1523) the king pledged himself by letters patent to repay the loan of £20,000 which the City had advanced for his defence of the realm and maintenance of the wars against France and Scotland. 1127

Formation of a league against France.

The disappointment experienced by Wolsey in not being selected to fill the Papal chair on the death of Adrian VI induced him to take measures for transferring his master's power from the imperial court to the court of France. In the meantime a league was formed between Henry, the emperor, and Charles, Duke of Bourbon, for the conquest and partition of France. During the formation of this league some correspondence between England and the Continent appears to have been lost in a remarkable manner, to judge from the following proclamation, 1128 made the 10th July, 1524:—

Proclamation for the recovery of lost letters, 10 July, 1524.

> *"My lorde the maire streitly chargith and commaundith on the king or soveraigne lordis behalf that if any maner of person or persons that have founde a hat with certeyn lettres and other billes and writinges therin enclosed which lettres been directed to or said soveraigne lorde from the parties of beyond the see*

let hym or theym bryng the said hat lettres and writinges unto
my said lorde the maire in all the hast possible and they shalbe
well rewarded for their labour and that no maner of person kepe
the said hat lettres and writinges nor noon of them after this
proclamacioun made uppon payn of deth and God save the king."

The king of France made prisoner at Pavia, 24 Feb., 1525.

Rejoicing in the city.

The news of the defeat and capture of the French king at Pavia (24 Feb., 1525) was hailed by Henry with great delight. The crown of France was now, he thought, within his grasp. On Saturday, the 11th March, a triumph was made in the city to celebrate "the takynge of the Frenche kyng in Bataill by Themporer and his alies." 1129 Bonfires were lighted at different places, one being in Saint Paul's Churchyard near the house where lay the foreign ambassadors. The Chamberlain was ordered to provide a hogshead of wine at every fire. The city minstrels filled the air with music, and the parish clerks attended with their singing children, who sat about the bonfires and sang ballads and "other delectable and joyfull songs." On the Sunday following the king and queen and officers of state attended a *Te Deum* at St. Paul's, the legate himself pronouncing the benediction. 1130

The Amicable Loan, 1525.

Henry's first impulse was to take advantage of the French king's misfortune; the cardinal, on the other hand, saw danger in the predominating influence of Charles in Europe, and would gladly have seen his master join hands with Francis against the emperor. He was nevertheless bound to carry out the king's wishes as if they were his own, and money was necessary for the purpose. Instead of resorting to a benevolence—a mode of raising money already declared by parliament to be illegal—he suggested that the people should be asked for what was called an Amicable Loan, on the old feudal ground that the king was about to lead an expedition in person. The citizens were among the first to whom Wolsey made application. Were they of opinion, he asked, that the king should undertake the expedition to France in person? If so, he could not go otherwise than beseemed a prince, and this he could not do without the city's aid. The sum they were asked to subscribe did not, he said, amount to half their substance, which the king might very well have demanded. When it was objected that trade had been bad, Wolsey lost his temper and declared that it was better that some citizens should suffer rather than that the king should be in want, and that if they refused to pay it might "fortune to cost some their heddes." 1131 At length the citizens agreed to grant the king a sixth part of their substance, which Henry graciously acknowledged by letter (25 April), 1132 saying that it was not his wish to overburden them, for he valued their prosperity more than ten such realms as France. The letter was read, by Wolsey's express wish, to the Common Council on the 28th, when it was agreed to ask for a fortnight's grace before sending an answer to so important a missive. 1133 A deputation was forthwith despatched to Hampton Court to solicit the cardinal's mediation, but not being able to obtain an interview they returned, and steps were taken to raise the money required.

When the cardinal was informed later on that the alderman of each ward was holding an enquiry as to the means of the inhabitants he affected to be very angry. "They had no right to examine anyone," he said; "I am your commissioner, I will examine you one by one myself." The mayor (Sir William Bailey) thereupon threw himself at the cardinal's feet beseeching him that since it was by Act of Common Council that the aldermen had sat in their respective wards for the purpose of taking the benevolence—a procedure which he now perceived to be against the law—the Act should by the Common Council be revoked. "Well," said Wolsey "I am content," and he then proceeded to ask how much the mayor and aldermen then present were prepared to give. When the mayor incautiously remarked that if he made any promise there and then it might perhaps cost him his life, Wolsey again became furious. What! the mayor's life threatened for obeying the king's orders! He would see to that.

In the country the loan met with so much opposition that a rebellion was feared. At length, finding it was impossible to collect the money, Wolsey sent (19 May) for the mayor and aldermen and informed them that the king had given up all thoughts of his expedition to France, and that they were pardoned of all that had been demanded of them. 1134

A truce between England and France.

French ambassadors lodged in the city, 1527.

Before many weeks elapsed Wolsey saw with satisfaction a truce made between Henry and the queen regent of France. 1135 Early in 1526 the French king regained his liberty by virtue of a treaty which he at once repudiated, and war between him and the emperor was renewed, but England remained virtually at peace. In the following year (1527) the cardinal himself paid a visit to the French king and superintended the drawing up of articles for a permanent peace. By September all was settled, and Wolsey returned to England. Ambassadors from France shortly afterwards arrived, and were lodged in the Bishop of London's palace in St. Paul's Churchyard. The City made them valuable presents at the instance of the lord cardinal. 1136

Troubles over Wythypol's election as alderman, 1527-1528.

Wythypol again summoned to take office.

Committed to Newgate, 6 Feb., 1528.

Again summoned to take office, 22 May.

The election of Paul Wythypol, 1137 a merchant-tailor, as alderman of the Ward of Farringdon Within, in 1527, again brought Henry and the citizens into variance. The king desired Wythypol's discharge, at least for a time. The Court of Aldermen hesitated to accede to the request and consulted Wolsey. 1138 He recommended them an interview with the king at Greenwich. To Greenwich they accordingly went (24 Feb.) by water, where they arrived in time to give a formal reception to the cardinal, who landed soon afterwards from his barge. After a few words had passed between the cardinal and the municipal officers, the former entered the palace, whilst the latter waited in the king's great chamber till dinner time. When that hour arrived they were bidden to go down to the hall, where the mayor was entertained at the lord steward's mess, and the aldermen received like attention from the comptroller and other officers of state. The city's Counsel who had accompanied the mayor and aldermen were entertained at the table of "master coferer." Dinner over, the company returned to the great chamber, where they were kept waiting till the evening. At length the mayor and aldermen were bidden to the king's presence in his secret chamber. What took place there the writer of the record declares himself unable to say, 1139 and, although the mayor afterwards made a report of the matter to the court, no particulars are recorded in the City's archives. The practical outcome of the interview appears to have been that Wythypol was left unmolested for a whole twelve-month. When that time had elapsed he was again summoned before the Court of Aldermen either to accept office or take the oath prescribed. 1140 Refusing both these propositions he was committed to Newgate. 1141 This took place on the 6th February, 1528. On the 3rd March he appeared in person before the Court of Aldermen and desired a respite from office, or to be allowed to pay a fine. Being asked the amount of fine he was prepared to pay, he offered £40, and at the same time asked to be discharged from office for a period of three years. This offer was declined, and Wythypol was again ordered to take the oath prescribed for his discharge. 1142 Nearly three months were allowed to elapse before any further steps were taken, when, on the 22nd May, the court again ordered Wythypol to appear at its next meeting, and to take up office, or else take the oath, or pay such fine as should be assessed by the mayor, aldermen and common council. 1143 It is certain that he did not take office, so the conclusion must be that he availed himself of one or other of the alternatives open to him. John Brown was elected alderman of Farringdon Within shortly afterwards, but he was discharged by the Common Council, and the aldermanry was subsequently filled by John Hardy being translated to it from Aldersgate Ward. 1144

A great dearth in the city, 1529.

In addition to an epidemic of sickness, 1145 the city was threatened the following year with a famine, notwithstanding the fact that large quantities of grain had been stored up in various parts of the city by order of the municipal authorities. The country had suffered recently by heavy rains, and large tracts of land had been inundated. In anticipation of trouble, a large stock of wheat had been laid in, but when it came to the point of disposing of it, the bakers of the city and the bakers of Stratford-at-Bow declined to take it except at their own price, until compelled by threats and, in some cases, imprisonment. 1146

The legatine court at the Blackfriars, 1529.

For some years past Henry had been meditating a divorce from Catherine of Aragon, his brother's widow, but it was not until 1529 that the assent of the Pope was at last obtained to try the validity of the marriage. The legatine court sat in the city at the house of the Blackfriars, where every arrangement was made to add dignity to the proceedings. At its head sat the two cardinals, Campeggio and Wolsey, on chairs covered with cloth of gold, and on their right sat Henry himself. 1147 The sudden suspension of all proceedings after the court had sat for some weeks, and the revocation of the cause to the Court of Rome, led to Wolsey's downfall. In October the seals were taken from him and given to Sir Thomas More, his furniture and plate were seized, and he himself ordered to remove from London.

The lord mayor's banquet, 28 Oct., 1529.

A few days after Wolsey's disgrace a banquet was held at the Guildhall on the occasion of the swearing in of Ralph Dodmer, the newly-elected mayor. It is the first lord mayor's banquet of which any particulars have come down to us, and they are interesting as recording the names of the chief guests. The mayor's court, the scene of the feast, was boarded and hung with cloth of Arras for the occasion. One table was set apart for peers of the realm, at the head of which sat the new lord chancellor and at the bottom the lords Berkeley and Powis. At either side of the table sat nine peers, among whom were the dukes of Norfolk and Suffolk, the one being the treasurer and the other the marshal of England, Sir Thomas Grey, Marquis of Dorset, the Earl of Oxford, high chamberlain, and the Earl of Shrewsbury, lord steward of England, Tunstal, Bishop of London, Sir Thomas Boleyn, Lord Rochford, whose daughter Anne was shortly to experience the peril of sharing Henry's throne, Lord Audley, and others. At two other tables, placed between the court of orphans and the mayor's court, were entertained a number of knights and other gentlemen, whose names are not recorded. 1148

The fall of Wolsey, 1529-1530.

It was not long before further proceedings were taken against the king's late minister. On the 3rd November (1529), after the lapse of six years, parliament met in the city at the palace of Bridewell. The City was represented by Thomas Seymer, an alderman and ex-mayor, John Baker, the City's Recorder, John Petyte, grocer, and Paul Wythypol, 1149 the merchant-tailor whose election as alderman had recently created no little trouble. Among other members was Thomas Cromwell, 1150 a friend of Wolsey, and destined soon to take his place as the king's chief adviser. A bill for disabling the cardinal from being restored to his former dignities was carried by the Lords and sent down to the Commons (1 Dec.). There it is said to have met with the strenuous opposition of Cromwell. Of this, however, there is some doubt, as it is uncertain whether the bill provoked any discussion, parliament being shortly afterward prorogued (17 Dec.) and the unhappy cardinal left in suspense as to what fate was in store for him. 1151 At Christmas he fell ill, and the king's heart became so far softened towards his old favourite that early in the following year (Feb., 1530) he was restored to the archbishopric of York with all its possessions except York-place (Whitehall) in Westminster, which Henry could not bring himself to surrender. His colleges were seized; the college he had founded at Ipswich was sold; but his college at Oxford, known as Cardinal College, was afterwards re-established under the name of Christ Church. He himself was not allowed to rest long in peace. He was summoned to London on a charge of treason, for which there was little or no foundation, but the troubles of the last two years had rendered him so infirm that he died on the way.

CHAPTER XIV.

The House of Commons and the Clergy, 1529.

Although Wolsey was no more, his works followed him. He it was, and not Henry, who first conceived the idea of church reform, towards which some steps had been taken in Wolsey's lifetime. It was left for Henry to carry out the design of his great minister. When the king laid his hand on the monasteries, he only followed the example set by the cardinal in 1525, when some of the smaller religious houses in Kent, Sussex and Essex were suppressed for his great foundation of Oxford. To assist him in carrying out his design he turned to parliament. Relieved as they now were of the oppression of the great nobles, the Commons were ready to use their newly-acquired independence against the clergy, who exacted extravagant fees and misused the powers of the ecclesiastical courts. Acts were passed regulating the payment of mortuary fees and the fees for probate, whilst another Act restricted the holding of pluralities and the taking of ferms by church-men. 1152 The clergy threatened to appeal to Rome, but were warned that such action would be met with pains and penalties as opposed to the royal prerogative. 1153

Disputes touching tithes payable to city clergy, 1527-1534.

In the city the question of tithes payable to the clergy had been always more or less a vexed question. Before the commencement of the thirteenth century the city clergy had been supported by casual dues in addition to their glebe land. These casual payments were originally personal, but subsequently became regulated by the amount of rent paid by parishioners for their houses. A question arose as to whether the citizens were also liable to pay personal tithes on their gains, and it was eventually decided that they were so liable. 1154

On the 31st August, 1527, a committee, which had been specially appointed to enquire into matters concerning the city's welfare, reported, among other things, upon the tithe question as it then stood in the city. 1155 The "curates," they said, had purchased a Bull of Pope Nicholas, on the 6th August, 1453, and this Bull had been confirmed by Act of Common Council on the 3rd March, 1475. Not only was the amount of the tithe payable fixed by the Bull, but the Bull itself was to be publicly read by the curates four times a year, so that no doubt should exist in the minds of the parishioners. This the curates had failed to do, and had caused their parishioners heavy legal expenses in disputing demands for tithes. One man was known to have spent as much as £100 in his own defence. The committee suggested that the whole question should be referred to the Bishop of London, and that a translation of the Bull should be exhibited in every church. The citizens were the more aggrieved because many parsonages and vicarages were let to ferm. 1156

The curates' book of articles.

The curates made their defence in a book of eighteen articles touching tithes and other oblations, the chief point being that every householder, time out of mind, had been bound to pay to God and the Church one farthing out of every 10s. of rent, a half-penny out of 20s. and so forth, on 100 days of the year; amounting in all to 2s. 1d. for every 10s. rent *per annum*. This manner of payment proving tedious, the curates and their parishioners came to an agreement that 1s. 2d. should be paid on every 6s. 8d. or noble, and this sum the curates had been receiving time out of mind, none reclaiming or denying. But, inasmuch as this payment by occupiers of houses was only ordained for a "dowry" to the parish churches of London which had no glebe lands, the curates demanded that all merchants and artificers, with other occupiers of the city, should pay personal tithes of their "lucre or encrece" according to the common law, and as "well conscyoned" men had been in the habit of paying in times past. 1157 The book of articles was laid before the Court of Common Council on the 16th February, 1528, by Robert Carter and six other priests, on behalf of their entire body. On the following 16th March the Court of Aldermen for themselves agreed to pay tithe at the forthcoming Easter according to the Bull of Pope Nicholas, and not after the rate of 1s. 2d. on the noble, 1158 whilst four days later the Common Council decided that, for the sake of convenience, bills should be posted in every parish church within the city showing the number of offering days (viz., eighty-two) and the amount to be offered by inhabitants of the city. 1159

So matters continued until, early in 1534, it was agreed to submit the whole question to the lord chancellor and other members of the council, who made their award a few days before Easter. 1160 It decreed that at the forthcoming festival every subject should pay to the parson or curate of his parish after the rate of 2s. 9d. in the pound, and 16 pence half-penny in the half-pound, and that every man's wife, servant, child and apprentice receiving the Holy Sacrament should pay two pence. These payments were to continue to be paid "without grudge or murmur" until such time as the council should arrive at a final settlement. 1161

Elsing Spital and Holy Trinity Priory surrendered to the king, 1530-1531.

In the meanwhile the city had been made to feel the heavy hand of the king and of his new minister, Thomas Cromwell. In May, 1530, Elsing Spital, a house established by William Elsing, a charitable mercer, for the relief of the blind, but which had subsequently grown into a priory of Augustinian canons of wealth and position, was confiscated by the Crown. What became of the blind inmates is not known. In the following year (1531) the Priory of Holy Trinity, Aldgate, shared the same fate. The priory had existed since the time of Henry I and the "good queen" Matilda, 1162 and its prior enjoyed the singular distinction of being *ex officio* an alderman of the city. The canons were now removed to another place and the building and site bestowed by Henry upon his chancellor, Sir Thomas Audley. 1163

The Great Beam reconveyed to the City after the lapse of ten years, 1531.

Between 1531 and 1534 the City enjoyed some respite from attack. It even recovered some of its lost privileges. In 1521 Henry had deprived the City of its right to the Great Beam, and of the issues and profits derived from it, and had caused a conveyance of it to be made to Sir William Sidney. In 1531 the beam was re-conveyed to the City. 1164 The Grocers' Company were scarcely less interested in the beam than the City, for to them was deputed the choice of weighers, who were afterwards admitted and sworn before the Court of Aldermen. Both the City and the company used their best endeavours to recover their lost rights, the former going so far as to sanction the distribution of the sum of £23 6s. 8d. between the king's sergeant, the king's attorney, and one "Lumnore," 1165 a servant of "my lady Anne," 1166 with the view of gaining their object the easier. 1167 A compromise was subsequently effected by which Sir William Sidney continued to hold the beam at an annual rent payable to the City, 1168 until, in 1531, he consented to a surrender, and it became again vested in the Corporation.

Feeling in the city at Henry's marriage with Anne Boleyn, 1533.

Finding it hopeless to obtain the Pope's sanction to his divorce from Catherine, Henry at last lost all patience, and on the 25th January, 1533, was privately married to Anne Boleyn. The match was unpopular with the citizens, who took occasion of a sermon preached on Easter-day to show their dissatisfaction. According to Chapuys, the Spanish ambassador, who sent an account of the affair to the emperor, the greater part of the congregation got up and left the church when prayers were desired for the queen. When Henry heard of the insult thus offered to his new bride he was furious, and forthwith sent word to the mayor to see that no such manifestation should occur again. Thereupon, continues Chapuys, the mayor summoned the guilds to assemble in their various halls and commanded them to cease murmuring against the king's marriage on pain of incurring the royal displeasure, and to order their own journeymen and servants, "and, a still more difficult task, their own wives," to refrain from speaking disparagingly about the queen. 1169

The queen's passage from the Tower to Westminster, 31 May, 1533.

It was perhaps on this account that the civic authorities excelled themselves in giving the queen a suitable reception as she passed from the Tower to Westminster on the 31st May. The Court of Aldermen directed (14 May) the wardens of the Haberdashers to prepare their barge as well as the "bachelers" barge for the occasion. Three pageants were to be set up, one in Leadenhall and the others at the Standard and the little Conduit in Cheapside. The Standard was to run with wine. A deputation was appointed to wait upon the king's council to learn its wishes, and enquiry was to be made of the Duke of Norfolk whether the clergy should take part in the day's proceedings, and whether the merchants of the Steelyard or other strangers should be allowed to erect pageants. 1170

The City's gift of 1,000 marks.

The Court of Common Council had on the previous day (13 May) voted a gift of 1,000 marks to be presented to the queen at her coronation, and a further sum to be expended in the city "for the honor of the same." 1171 Catherine of Aragon and Anne Boleyn were the only queens of king Henry VIII who were crowned, and on both occasions the citizens of London performed the customary services. 1172

The Act of Succession, 1534.

In September (1533) Anne gave birth to a daughter, who afterwards ascended the throne as Queen Elizabeth. In the following spring (1534) parliament passed an Act of Succession, which not only declared Elizabeth (and not Mary, the king's daughter by Catherine of Aragon) heir to the crown, but required all subjects to take an oath acknowledging the succession. Commissioners were appointed to tender the oath to the citizens, 1173 and by the 20th April the "most part of the city was sworn to the "king and his legitimate issue by the queen's grace now had and hereafter to come." 1174 A fortnight later deeds under the common seals of the livery companies "concernyng the suretye state and succession" of the king were delivered to Henry in person at Greenwich by a deputation of aldermen. 1175

Proceedings against those objecting to subscribe to the Act of Succession.

The oath, nevertheless, met with much opposition, more especially among the clergy and the religious orders. Elizabeth Barton, known as the "holy maid of Kent," and some of her followers, among them being Henry Gold, rector of the church of St. Mary Aldermary, were executed at Tyburn for daring to speak against the king's marriage. 1176 The friars proved extremely obstinate, and Henry sent commissioners to seek out and suppress all those friaries that refused to submit.

The monks of the Charterhouse, 1534-1535.

The inmates of the London Charterhouse, who might well have been left to enjoy their quiet seclusion from the world, were startled by a visit from the king's commissioners calling upon them to take the oath. The manner of their reception by John Houghton, the prior, and his brethren and subsequent proceedings are graphically described by Maurice Chauncy, 1177 one of the inmates, who was more compliant than his brethren to the king's wishes, and thereby saved his life. The prior and Humphrey Middlemore, the procurator of the convent, were committed to the Tower for counselling opposition to the commissioners. There they were visited by the Archbishop of York and the Bishop of London, who persuaded them at last that the question of the succession was not a cause in which to sacrifice their lives for conscience sake. The result was that after a while Houghton and his companion declared their willingness to submit. On the 29th May the commissioners received oaths of fealty from Prior Houghton and five other monks, and on the 6th June Bishop Lee and Sir Thomas Kitson, one of the sheriffs, received similar oaths from a number of priests, professed monks and lay brethren or *conversi* belonging to the house. 1178 The oaths of obedience to the Act were given under reservation "so far as the law of God permitted," and for a time the monks were left in comparative quiet, some few of them, of whom Cromwell entertained the most hope of submission, being sent, by his direction, to the convent of Sion. 1179

The Act of Supremacy, 1534.

Execution of Houghton and others, 1535.

The exhortations of the "father confessor" were not without some measure of success, several of the Carthusians being induced to alter their opinions as to the king's demands. The seal of doom, however, was fixed on the order by the passing of the Act which called upon its members to renounce the Pope and acknowledge the royal supremacy. 1180 Fisher and More denied the king's title of Supreme Head of the Church, and were committed to the Tower. At this crisis there came to London two priors of Carthusian houses established, one in Nottinghamshire and the other in Lincolnshire. They came to talk over the state of affairs with Houghton. An interview with Cromwell, recently appointed vicar-general or king's vicegerent in matters ecclesiastical, was resolved on. The king might possibly be prevailed upon to make some abatement in his demands. Cromwell, however, no sooner discovered the object of their visit than he committed them to the Tower as rebels and would-be traitors. As they still refused to acknowledge the king's supremacy in the Church, in spite of all efforts of persuasion, they were brought to trial, together with Father Reynolds of Sion, on a charge of treason. A verdict of guilty was, after some hesitation on the part of the jury, found against them, and they were executed at Tyburn (4 May, 1535), glorying in the cause for which they were held worthy to suffer death. Houghton's arm was suspended over the gateway of the London Charterhouse, in the fond hope that the rest of the brethren might be awed into submission. This atrocious act of barbarism had, however, precisely the opposite effect to that desired. The monks were more resolute than ever not to submit, and not even a personal visit of Henry himself could turn them from their purpose. 1181 Three of them were thereupon committed to prison, where they were compelled to stand in an upright position for thirteen days, chained from their necks to their arms and with their legs fettered. 1182 They were afterwards brought to trial on a charge of treason, convicted and executed (19 June).

The fate of the remaining monks is soon told. In May, 1537, the royal commissioners once more attended at the Charterhouse, when they found the majority of its inmates prepared to take the oath prescribed. Ten of them, however, still refused, and were committed to Newgate and there left to be "dispatched by the hand of God," in other words to meet a painful and lingering death from fever and starvation. The following month the remnant of the community made their submission, and the London Charterhouse, as a monastic institution, ceased to exist.

Execution of Fisher and More, 1535.

Fisher and More were now brought from the Tower, where they had lain six months and more, and convicted on a similar charge of treason. Their sentence was commuted to death by beheading. Fisher was the first to suffer (19 June, 1535). His head was set up on London Bridge and his body buried in the churchyard of All Hallows, Barking. More suffered a few weeks later (6 July). His head, too, was placed on London Bridge, but his body was buried in the Tower, whither the remains of Fisher were afterwards carried. On the 15th December the Court of Aldermen publicly condemned a sermon preached by Fisher "in derogation and diminution of the royal estate of the king's majesty." 1183

The Pilgrimage of Grace, 1536.

When, in the following year (1536), the smaller monasteries—those of less than £200 a year—were dissolved by Act of Parliament, and the inhabitants of Lincolnshire and Yorkshire, taking fright lest the king and Cromwell should proceed to despoil the parish churches, set out on the Pilgrimage of Grace, Henry sought the City's aid. On the 10th October a letter from the king was read before the Court of Aldermen, desiring them to dispatch forthwith to his manor of Ampthill, where the nobles were about to wait upon his majesty, a contingent of at least 250 armed men, 200 of which were to be well horsed, and 100 to be archers. 1184 The mayor, Sir John Allen, 1185 lost no time in issuing his precept to the livery companies for each of them to furnish a certain number of bowmen and billmen, well horsed and arrayed in jackets of white bearing the City's arms. They were to muster in Moorfields within twenty-four hours. The Mercers were called upon to furnish the largest quota, viz., twenty men; the Grocers, Drapers, Tailors and Cloth-workers respectively, sixteen men, and the rest of the companies contingents varying from twelve to two. 1186 The Court of Aldermen at the same time took the precaution of depriving all priests and curates, as well as all friars dwelling within the city, of every offensive weapon, so that they should be left with nothing but their "meate knyves." 1187 The king sent a letter of thanks for the city's contingent. 1188

Later on, when Allen had been succeeded in the mayoralty by Sir Ralph Warren, 1189 it was resolved that each member of the court should provide at his own cost and charges twenty able men fully equipped in case of any emergency that might arise, whilst the companies were again called upon to hold men in readiness. 1190

Henry's marriage with Jane Seymour, May, 1536.

Henry in the meantime had got rid of his second wife on the specious ground of her having misconducted herself with more than one member of the court, the real cause being her miscarriage 1191 of a male child, to the king's bitter disappointment. Henry had made up his mind to change his wives until he could find one who would give him a male heir and thus place the succession to the crown beyond all possibility of doubt. The very next day following Anne Boleyn's execution he married Jane Seymour. The marriage necessitated the calling together of a new parliament, when a fresh Act was passed settling the succession on Jane's children and declaring both Mary and Elizabeth illegitimate. Nevertheless, as soon as Mary made formal submission to her father, the king's attitude towards her, from being cold and cruel, changed at once to one of courtesy if not of affection. He was thought to entertain the idea of declaring her heir-apparent. Indeed, on Sunday, the 20th August, she was actually proclaimed as such in one of the London churches—no doubt by some mistake. 1192

Convocation at St. Paul's, 9 June-20 July, 1536.

Whilst parliament was sitting at Westminster convocation was gathered at St. Paul's in the city, and continued to sit there until the 20th July, presided over by Cromwell as the king's vicar-general. The meeting was remarkable for its formal decree that Henry, as supreme head of the Church, might and ought to disregard all citations by the Pope, as well as for the promulgation of the ten articles intended to promote uniformity of belief and worship. 1193

Preparation for the new queen's coronation.

She dies in childbed, 24 Oct., 1537.

In September, 1536, the Court of Common Council agreed to vote the same sum of money for the coronation of the "right excellent pryncesse lady Jane, quene of Englonde," as had been granted at the coronation of "dame Anne, late queene of Englonde." 1194 The money, however, was not required, for the new queen was never crowned. Just one week after the birth of a prince (12 Oct., 1537), afterwards King Edward VI, there was a solemn procession of priests from every city church, with the Bishop of London, the choir of St. Paul's, the mayor, aldermen and crafts in their liveries, for the preservation of the infant prince and for the health of the queen, who lay in a precarious state. 1195 A few days later (24 Oct.) she was dead. The citizens caused her obit to be celebrated in St. Paul's with truly regal pomp. 1196

Anne of Cleves arrives at Dover, 27 Dec., 1539.

Her passage through the city, 4 Feb,. 1540.

Two years later the citizens were preparing to set out to Greenwich in their barge (the mayor, aldermen, and those who had served the office of sheriff, in liveries of black velvet with chains of gold on their necks, accompanied by their servants in coats of russet) to welcome Anne of Cleves, who landed at Dover the 27th December, 1539. 1197 On the 3rd February, 1540, the Court of Aldermen was informed that the king and queen would be leaving Greenwich on the morrow for Westminster, and that it was the king's wish that the commons of London should be in their best apparel, in their barges, to wait upon his highness, meeting at St. Dunstan's in the East at 7 o'clock in the morning and arriving at Greenwich by 8 o'clock. 1198

Cromwell's work of demolition in the city, 1537-1538.

The insurrection which had taken place in the country under the name of the Pilgrimage of Grace was seized by the king as an excuse for suppressing many of the larger monasteries and confiscating their property. He had no such excuse for carrying out his destructive policy in the city. Nevertheless, under the immediate supervision of Cromwell, the work of suppression went on, and before the end of 1538 was well nigh complete. The surrender of the houses of the Black Friars, the Grey Friars and the White Friars followed in quick succession, "and so all the other immediatlie." 1199 Cromwell by this time had removed from his house near Fenchurch to another near the Austin Friars in Throgmorton Street. He had recently asked for a pipe of water to be laid on to his new house, and this the Common Council had "lovingly" granted. 1200 In his private concerns he showed as little regard for the rights of others as in the affairs of State. He did not scruple to remove bodily a small house, the property of Stow's father, in order to enlarge his own garden, giving neither warning beforehand nor explanation afterwards, and "no man durst go to argue the matter." 1201

The hospital of St. Thomas of Acon, which had ministered to the wants of the poorer citizens for nearly 400 years, disappeared, 1202 and was soon followed by the priory and hospital of St. Bartholomew, an institution of even greater antiquity, the hospital of St. Thomas, in Southwark, the priory and hospital of St. Mary without Bishopsgate, known as St. Mary of Bethlem, or "Bedlam," and the Abbey of Graces or New Abbey (sometimes called the Eastminster to distinguish it from the other minster in the west of London) which had been founded by Edward III, near Tower Hill.

The division of the spoil.

A portion of the spoil was, as we have already seen, distributed among court favourites. The site of the house and gardens of the Augustinian Friars in Broad Street Ward was occupied, soon after their suppression (12 Nov., 1538), by the mansion-house of that politic courtier the celebrated Marquis of Winchester, who managed to maintain himself in high station in spite of the changes which took place under the several reigns of Henry VIII, Edward VI, Mary, and Elizabeth, "by being a willow and not an oak." The building known at the present day as Winchester House, in Broad Street, stands near the site of the old mansion-house and garden of William Paulet, first Marquis of Winchester. The Friars' church he allowed to stand; and in June, 1550, the nave was granted, by virtue of a charter permitting alien non-conforming churches to exist in this country, to the Dutch and Walloon churches. 1203 The first marquis dying in 1571, he was succeeded by his son, who sold the monuments and lead from the roof of the remaining portion of the church and turned the place into a stable. 1204 The fourth marquis was reduced to parting with his house, built on the site of the old priory, in order to pay his debts, and appears to have found a purchaser in a wealthy London merchant and alderman of the city, John Swinnerton or Swynarton. 1205

The mayor's effort to save the destruction of the steeple of the Austin Friars Church.

The steeple of the church, which was of so great beauty that the citizens desired its preservation, 1206 was sold by the marquis to Henry Robinson, who forthwith set to work to pull it down on the ground that it was in such a state of decay as to be a danger to the passer-by. Swinnerton, who happened to be mayor at the time, ordered him to stay the work of demolition; he, however, not only hurried on the more, but obstructed the officers sent to put a stop to the work, for which he was committed to Newgate to stay there until he gave security for restoring what he had already pulled down. The thought suggests itself that the fact of Swinnerton having purchased adjacent property may have made him the more zealous in preventing the demolition of the steeple than perhaps he might otherwise have been. However that may be, he lost no time in informing the lords of the council of the state of affairs and asking their advice (16 Feb., 1612). The reply came three days later, and was to the effect that as the City had had the option of purchasing the steeple at even a less price than Robinson had paid for it, and might have come to some arrangement with the marquis to keep it in repair, it could not prevent Robinson, who purchased it as a speculation, making the best he could of his bargain; so that, unless the City consented to accept Robinson's offer to part with his property on payment of his purchase-money and disbursements within a fortnight, down the steeple must come. 1207

The priory of St. Helen without Bishopsgate.

The priory of St. Helen without Bishopsgate was one of the last to be surrendered. In 1542 the nuns' chapel, which at one time was partitioned off from the rest of the church, was made over to Sir Richard Williams, a nephew of Thomas Cromwell, and ancestor of the Protector. The nuns' refectory or hall passed into the hands of the Leathersellers' Company and formed the company's hall until the close of the last century. The conduct of the inmates of the priory had not always been what it should be. 1208 The last prioress, in anticipation of the coming storm, leased a large portion of the conventual property to members of her own family, and at the time of the suppression was herself allowed a gratuity of £30 and a pension.

Friendly relations between the Corporation and religious houses in the city.

The relations existing between the civic authorities and the religious houses in the city were often of a most friendly and cordial character. When, in 1520, the Friars of the Holy Cross wanted assistance for the maintenance and building of their church, they applied to the Corporation as being their "secund founders." 1209 For assistance thus given the friars bound themselves to pray for their benefactors. When, in 1512, the master of St. Bartholomew's hospital obtained a lease for ninety-nine years from the City of a parcel of land on which his gatehouse or porch stood, it was on condition of payment of a certain rent and of his keeping a yearly obit in his church for the souls of the mayor, aldermen and commons of the city; and when the master of the hospital, two years later, attempted to back out of the terms of his lease and asked to be discharged from keeping the obit on the ground that he thought that the payment of the specified rent was sufficient for the premises, the Court of Aldermen unanimously decided that no part of the agreement should be minished or remitted. 1210 When the house of the Sisters Minoresses or Poor Clares, situate in Aldgate, suffered from fire, the Corporation rendered them pecuniary aid to the extent of 300 marks. 1211

It was, however, to the Franciscans or Grey Friars that the citizens of London, individually as well as in their corporate capacity, were more especially attached. Soon after their arrival in England in 1223, they became indebted to the benevolence and generosity of citizens, their first benefactor having been John Ewen, citizen and mercer, who made them a gift of some land and houses in the parish of St. Nicholas by the Shambles. Upon this they erected their original building. Their first chapel, which became the chapel of their church, was built at the cost of William Joyner, who was mayor in 1239; the nave was added by Henry Waleys, who was frequently mayor during the reign of Edward I; the chapterhouse by Walter le Poter, elected sheriff in 1272; the dormitory by Gregory de Rokesley, who was mayor from 1274 to 1281, and again in 1284-5, and whose bones eventually found a resting place in their church; the refectory by another citizen, Bartholomew de Castro; and lastly—coming to later times—a library was added to their house by the bounty of Richard Whitington, as already narrated. It became the custom for the mayor and aldermen, as patron and founders, to pay a yearly visit to their house and church on St. Francis's day (4 Oct.). The custom dates from 1508. In 1522 the visit was for the first time followed by a dinner. 1212

Royal injunction for keeping Parish Registers, 29 Sept., 1538.

In one respect at least, if in no other, Cromwell's action in suppressing religious houses resulted in a benefit to the city of London as well as to the country at large, and this was in the institution of parish registers, not only for baptisms, but also for marriages. It had been his intention to establish them in 1536 to remedy the inconvenience to the public arising from the suppression of the smaller monasteries, and it is evident that some instructions were given at this time, inasmuch as the registers of two city parishes—viz., St. James Garlickhithe and St. Mary Bothaw—commence in

November of this year, 1213 although the royal injunction commanding that registers should systematically be kept up, under penalty of fines, was not published by Cromwell, as vicar-general, until the 29th September, 1538. The delay is to be accounted for by the great discontent which the rumour of his project excited in the country. It was reported that some new tax on the services of the Church was contemplated, and the first in the list of popular grievances circulated by the rebels in the Pilgrimage of Grace was the payment of tribute to the king for the sacrament of baptism. In course of time, as matters became quieter and the government began to feel its own strength, Cromwell resumed a project never altogether abandoned, and caused the injunction to be issued, an action for which posterity must ever be deeply grateful.

Great increase of London poor, consequent on the suppression of religious houses.

On the other hand, the sudden closing of these institutions caused the streets to be thronged with the sick and poor, and the small parish churches to be so crowded with those who had been accustomed to frequent the larger and more commodious churches of the friars that there was scarce room left for the parishioners themselves. The city authorities saw at once that something would have to be done if they wished to keep their streets clear of beggars and of invalids, and not invite the spread of sickness by allowing infected persons to wander at large. As a means of affording temporary relief, collections for the poor were made every Sunday at Paul's Cross, after the sermon, and the proceeds were distributed weekly among the most necessitous, 1214 but more comprehensive steps were required to be taken.

Sir Richard Gresham's letter to the king for conveyance to the City of certain hospitals.

Sir Richard Gresham, 1215 who was mayor at the time (1537-8), took upon himself to address a letter 1216 to the king setting forth that there were three hospitals in the city, viz., St. Mary's Spital, St. Bartholomew's and St. Thomas's, besides the New Abbey on Tower Hill—institutions primarily founded "onely for the releffe, comforte and helpyng of pore and impotent people not beyng able to helpe theymselffes; and not to the mayntenannce of Chanons, Preests, and Monks to lyve in pleasure, nothyng regardyng the miserable people liyng in every strete, offendyng every clene person passyng by the way with theyre fylthy and nasty savours"—and asking that the mayor and aldermen of the city for the time being might have the order and disposition of the hospitals mentioned, and of all the lands, tenements and revenues appertaining to the same. If his grace would but grant this request the mayor promised that a great number of the indigent sick would be relieved, whilst "sturdy beggars" not willing to work would be punished.

Two petitions from the City, Mar., 1539.

The City offers to purchase certain dissolved houses, 1 Aug., 1540.

In March, 1539, the City presented two petitions to the king, one desiring that the late dissolved houses might be made over to them, together with their rents and revenues, in order that relief might be provided for the sick and needy, and the other asking that Henry would be pleased to convey to them the churches of the late four orders of friars, together with their lands and tenements, so that the mayor and citizens might take order for the due performance of divine service therein to the glory of God and the honour of the king. 1217 These petitions having been either refused or ignored, the Court of Common Council, on the 1st August, 1540, authorised the mayor and aldermen to make diligent suit to the king for the purchase of the houses, churches, and cloisters of the dissolved friars, and to make an offer of 1,000 marks for them "yf thei can be gotten no better chepe." 1218 Henry upbraided the City for being "pynche pence" or stingy in their offer, 1219 but as no better offer was made the matter was allowed to stand over, and nothing was done for four years.

The City in difficulties with king and parliament, 1541-1542.

Henry meanwhile took the opportunity afforded him by a full treasury, which rendered him independent of the favour of the citizens, of robbing them of their right of measuring linen-cloth and other commodities, and conferring the same by letters patent on John Godsalve, one of the clerks of the signet. The City's right was incontestable, and had been admitted by the king's chancellor, as well as by the Chancellor of the Court of Fruits and Tenths (a court recently established), and the mayor and aldermen represented the facts of the case to the king himself by letter, dated the 21st July, 1541. 1220 Another "variance" occurred about this time between the City and the Crown touching the office and duties of the City's waterbailiff. 1221

Again, in the spring of 1542, an incident occurred which caused the relations between parliament and the City to be somewhat strained. The sheriffs of that year—Rowland Hill, 1222 an ancestor of the founder of the Penny Post, and Henry Suckley—had thought fit to obstruct the sergeant-at-mace in the execution of his duty, whilst attempting to remove a prisoner, who was a member of parliament, from one of the compters. The arrest of a member of parliament has always been a hazardous operation, and the sheriffs after a time thought better of it and gave up their prisoner. The

Speaker, nevertheless, summoned them to appear at the Bar of the House and finally committed them to the Tower. They were released after two or three days, however, at the humble suit of the mayor. 1223

Precautions against the spread of pestilence, 1543.

In the following year (1543) the plague returned, and extra-precautions had to be taken against the spread of the disease, now that the houses of the friars were no longer open to receive patients and to alleviate distress. Besides the usual order that infected houses should be marked with a cross, the mayor caused proclamation to be made that persons of independent means should undergo quarantine for one month after recovery from sickness, whilst others whom necessity compelled to walk abroad for their livelihood were to carry in their hands white rods, two feet in length, for the space of forty days after convalescence. Straw and rushes in an infected house were to be removed to the fields before they were burnt, and infected clothing was to be carried away to be aired and not to be hung out of window. The hard-heartedness engendered by these visitations is evidenced by the necessity of the mayor having to enjoin that thenceforth no householder within the city or liberties should put any person stricken with the plague out of his house into the street, without making provision for his being kept in some other house. All dogs other than hounds, spaniels or mastiffs kept for the purpose of guarding the house were forthwith to be removed out of the city or killed, whilst watch-dogs were to be confined to the house. 1224 In October the mayor was ordered to resume the weekly bills of mortality, which of late had been neglected, in order that the king might be kept informed as to the increase or decrease of the sickness. 1225 The Michaelmas Law Sittings had to be postponed until the 15th November, and were removed to St. Albans. 1226

Preparation for renewal of war with France, 1544.

Whilst the city was being wasted by disease the king was preparing for war with France. 1227 A joint expedition by Henry and Charles was to be undertaken in the following year (1544). A commission was issued early in the year for raising money in the city, and the lord chancellor himself, accompanied by officers of State, came into the city to read it. Finding that the lord mayor's name appeared third on the commission instead of being placed at its head, the chancellor ordered the mistake to be at once rectified by the town clerk and a new commission to be drawn up, whilst the rest of the lords agreed that at their several sessions on the business of this subsidy the lord mayor should occupy the seat of honour. 1228 By the end of April the chancellor (Audley) had died. His successor, Lord Wriothesley, had not long been appointed before the Court of Aldermen sent a deputation to desire his lordship's favour and friendship in the city's affairs, and agreed to make him a present of a couple of silver-gilt pots to the value of £20 or thereabouts. 1229 On the 24th May the Common Council agreed to provide a contingent of 500 or 600 men at the discretion of the mayor and aldermen, the men being raised from the livery companies. 1230

The re-establishment of St. Bartholomew's hospital, 23 June, 1544.

Just as the king was about to set sail for the continent, he issued letters patent (23 June, 1544) re-establishing the hospital of St. Bartholomew on a new foundation, with the avowed object of providing "comfort to prisoners, shelter to the poor, visitation to the sick, food to the hungry, drink to the thirsty, clothes to the naked, and sepulture to the dead." 1231

The campaign in France of 1544.

Henry crossed over to France, leaving the new queen, Catherine Parr, widow of Lord Latimer, whom he had recently married, regent of the realm. After a long siege, lasting from July until September, he succeeded in taking Boulogne. On Thursday, the 25th September, an order was received by the Court of Aldermen from the lord chancellor, on behalf of the queen regent, to get in readiness another contingent of 500 men well harnessed and weaponed, 100 of whom were to be archers and the rest billmen. The last mentioned were to be provided with "blak bylles or morys pykes." The whole force was to be ready for shipment to Boulogne by the following Saturday. No time was to be lost. The wardens of the city companies were immediately summoned, and each company was ordered to provide the same number of men as on the last occasion. Each soldier was to be provided with a coat of grey frieze, with half sleeves, and a pair of new boots or else "sterte upps." The Corporation for its part appointed five captains, to each of whom was given the sum of £10 towards his apparel and charges, whilst £5 was allowed to each petty captain. These sums were paid out of the "goods" of the mayor and commonalty. 1232

Scarcely had the city recovered from this drain upon its population before it was again called upon to fill up the ranks of the army in France. On Saturday, the 25th October, the Court of Aldermen was ordered to raise another force of 500 men by the following Monday. It was no easy matter to comply with so sudden a demand. The city companies were called upon to contribute as before, any deficiency in the number of men raised by them being made up by men raised by the mayor and aldermen themselves in a somewhat novel fashion. The Court of Aldermen had agreed that each of their number should on the Saturday night make the round of his ward and select "fifty, forty, twenty, or ten" tall and comely men, who should be warned in the king's name to appear the next morning before seven o'clock at the Guildhall. On Sunday morning the mayor and aldermen came to the Guildhall, and took the names of those whom they had selected over night. Two hundred men were eventually set apart to make up the deficiency of those to be provided by the companies. By six o'clock in the evening the whole contingent of 500 men was thus raised, and at nine o'clock on Monday morning they mustered at Leadenhall, whence they were conducted by the sheriffs and city chamberlain to the Tower Hill and handed over to Sir Thomas Arundel, who complimented the civic authorities on the appearance of the men, and promised to commend their diligence to the king. 1233 This same Monday morning (27 Oct.) the mayor received instructions to see that such carpenters and other artificers as had been "prested" for the king's service at Boulogne by the king's master-carpenter kept their day and presented themselves at the time and place appointed on pain of death. 1234 Search was ordered to be made in the following month for mariners lurking in the city, and if any were discovered they were to be forthwith despatched to the ships awaiting them. 1235

City gift to the king on his return from France.

By this time the king had ceased to take a personal part in the campaign and had returned home, the mayor and aldermen giving him a hearty welcome, and making him a suitable present in token of their joy for his return and his success in effecting the surrender of Boulogne. 1236

Opposition to a benevolence in the city, 1545.

At the opening of the next year (1545) Henry demanded another benevolence after the rate of two shillings in the pound. The lord chancellor and others of the king's council sat at Baynard's Castle to collect the benevolence of the city, "callinge all the citizens of the same before them, begininge first with the mayor and aldermen." 1237 Richard Rede, alderman of the ward of Farringdon Without, resisted this demand as unconstitutional, and was promptly despatched to the king in Scotland, where he was shortly afterwards made a prisoner of war. Another alderman, Sir William Roche, of Bassishaw ward, was unfortunate enough to offend the council and was committed to the Fleet. 1238

William Laxton, mayor, knighted, 8 Feb., 1545.

On the 8th February William Laxton, the mayor, was presented to the king at Westminster, when Henry took occasion to thank him and his brother aldermen for the benevolence they had given him. He informed them of the success that had recently attended the English forces under the Earl of Hertford and the lord admiral, Sir John Dudley, whom he had left as deputy of Boulogne, and dismissed them to their homes after conferring upon the mayor the honour of knighthood. 1239

A call for volunteers for the French war. April, 1545.

In the following April volunteers were called for, and those in the city willing to follow the fortunes of war as "adventurers" were asked to repair to the sign of the "Gunne," at Billingsgate, where they would receive directions from John of Caleys, captain of all such adventurers, for their passage to France. 1240 The sessions of the law courts were adjourned in order to give lawyers and suitors an opportunity of showing their patriotism by taking up arms. 1241 The city companies furnished 100 men appareled "with whyte cotes of penystone whytes 1242 or karsies," with a red cross of St. George before and behind, each being provided with a white cap to wear under his "sallett or scull." 1243

The last subsidy to be forthwith paid up.

There yet remained a portion of the last subsidy to be collected, for which purpose the lord chancellor once more paid a visit to the city (12 June) and sat in the Guildhall. Every alderman was straitly charged to call before him every person in his ward who was worth £40 and upwards. The king's affairs were pressing, and this last payment must be immediately forthcoming. 1244

A force of 2,000 soldiers demanded of the City, June, 1545.

A week later (19 June) letters from the king were read to the Court of Aldermen touching the levying of more forces and firing of beacons—a French squadron had appeared off the south coast. It was resolved to adjourn consideration of the message until the following Monday, when the lord chancellor and other lords of the council would again be coming into the city for the subsidy, and their advice could be asked. The outcome of these letters was that the City had to raise a force of 2,000 able men. To do this an assessment of a fifteenth was ordered to be levied on the wards, but in the meantime the money so to be raised was to be advanced by the aldermen. 1245 Not only were the aldermen on this, as on other occasions, mulcted in their pocket, but they were also called upon to personally share with the lord mayor himself and the sheriffs in the extra watch which in the "besye tyme of the warres" was ordered to be kept in the city. 1246 In the meantime a man was despatched by the Court of Aldermen to St. James' Fair to buy five wey of cheese for the city's soldiers who were already at Guildford. The cheese was to be sent by water as far as Kingston, whence it would be conveyed by "the good industrye and help of Master Judde, alderman," to its destination. The bakers of Stratford contracted to send two cart-loads of bread. It was further agreed on the same day that Christopher Fowlke should forthwith go to Guildford, and further if need be, "to guyde the seyd vytayle and to utter the same to the souldyers by thassistence of the sworde berer and the under chamberleyn. And to recyve money for the same." 1247 A flag and a drum were likewise to be despatched forthwith. The citizen soldiers were required to assist in driving out the French, who had effected a landing in the Isle of Wight; but before they arrived the enemy had disappeared. 1248

Boulogne threatened.

The French king now prepared to lay siege to Boulogne, and the citizens were again called upon to furnish soldiers. One thousand men were required, and this number was only raised by enlisting men who had failed to pass previous musters. However, there was no time to pick and choose. 1249

Act for confiscating chantries, &c., 1545.

By this time Henry's resources were fast giving out. A parliament was summoned to meet in November, and again resort was had to confiscation for the purpose of supplying the king with money. An Act was passed which placed 2,000 chantries and chapels and over 100 hospitals at Henry's disposal. 1250

Peace with France proclaimed, 13 June, 1546.

All parties were, however, tired of the war, and in the following June (1546) a peace was concluded. Henry was allowed to retain Boulogne as security for a debt, and the French admiral soon afterwards paid a visit to the city, where he was heartily welcomed and hospitably entertained. 1251

Uniformity of religion enforced, 1546.

Recantation of the rector of St. Mary Aldermary.

Freed from the embarrassment of foreign wars, Henry now had leisure to turn his attention to home affairs, and more particularly to the establishment of that uniformity which he so much desired, and which he endeavoured to bring about by getting rid of all those who differed in opinion from himself. Those who openly declared their disbelief in any one of the "Six Articles," and more particularly in the first article, which established the doctrine of the real presence, ran the risk of death by the gallows, the block or the stake. A city rector, Dr. Crome, of the church of St. Mary Aldermary, got into disgrace for speaking lightly of the benefits to be derived from private masses, and, although his argument tended to minimise the effect of the recent confiscation of so many chantries, he was called upon to make a public recantation at Paul's Cross. 1252

Trial and execution of Anne Ascue.

Others were not so compliant. Among these was Anne Ascue or Ascough, a daughter of Sir William Ascough, of Kelsey, in Lincolnshire, and sometimes known as Anne Kyme, from the name of her husband, with whom she had ceased to live. In June, 1545, she and some others, among whom was another woman, Joan, wife of John Sauterie, of London, had been arraigned at the Guildhall "for speaking against the sacrament of the altar"; but, no evidence being adduced against her, she was on that occasion acquitted and discharged. 1253 Scarcely a year elapsed before she was again in custody. On the 18th June, 1546, she was tried at the Guildhall and condemned to be burned alive as a heretic at Smithfield, where the city chamberlain had orders to erect a "substantial stage," whence the king's council and the civic authorities might witness the scene. 1254

Improved water supply of the city, 1545-1546.

The insanitary condition of the city, occasioned for the most part by an insufficient supply of water, was not improved by the influx of disbanded and invalided soldiers, followed by a swarm of vagabonds and idlers, which took place at the conclusion of peace with France. To the soldiers licences were granted to solicit alms for longer or shorter periods, whilst the vagabonds were ordered to quit the city. 1255 The water question had been taken in hand by the Common Council towards the close of the preceding year (1545), when Sir Martin Bowes entered upon his mayoralty, and a tax of two fifteenths was imposed upon the inhabitants of the city for the purpose of conveying fresh water from certain "lively sprynges" recently discovered at Hackney. 1256 Bowes himself was very energetic in the matter, and before he went out of office he had the satisfaction of seeing a plentiful supply of water brought into the heart of the city from the suburban manor of Finsbury. 1257

St. Bartholomew's Hospital, &c., vested in the City, 13 Jan., 1547.

Henry's reign was now fast drawing to a close. In April, 1546, he had bestowed an endowment of 500 marks a year on the city poor-houses on condition the citizens themselves found a similar sum. 1258 In January, 1547—a few days only before he died—he showed still further care for the city poor by vesting in the Corporation, not only St. Bartholomew's Hospital, thenceforth to be known as the House of the Poor in West Smithfield, but also the house and church of the dissolved monastery of the Grey Friars and the house and hospital of Bethlehem. 1259

A committee appointed to investigate the recently acquired property, 6 May, 1547.

The Corporation lost no time in getting their newly acquired property into working order. On the 6th May the late king's conveyance was read before the Court of Aldermen, and thereupon a committee, of which Sir Martin Bowes was a prominent member, was deputed to make an abstract of the yearly revenues and charges of the house of the Grey Friars and hospital of little Saint Bartholomew, and to report thereon to the court with as much speed as possible. 1260 From a purely monetary point of view the City had made a bad bargain, and had saddled itself with an annual expenditure out of the Corporation revenues to an extent little thought of at the time. 1261

The king's death, 28 Jan., 1547.

On the 28th January, 1547, Henry died "at hys most pryncely howse at Westminster, comenly called Yorkeplace or Whytehall"—the palace which Cardinal Wolsey built for himself, and which Henry appropriated, extending its grounds and preserves in cynical contempt of public convenience and utter disregard of the chartered rights of the citizens of London. 1262 There his corpse remained until the 14th February, when it was removed at 8 o'clock in the morning to Sion House, near Richmond, and thence conveyed to Windsor on the following day.

Edward VI proclaimed king in the city, 31 Jan., 1547.

In the meantime the mayor, Henry Huberthorne, or Hoberthorne, 1263 had been sent for (31 Jan.) to attend the king's council at Westminster, where he received orders to return to the city and cause himself and his brother aldermen to be arrayed in their scarlet robes, in order to accompany the heralds whilst they proclaimed the new king in various parts of the city. This being done, the mayor took steps for securing the peace of the city, and the citizens voted Edward a benevolence of a fifteenth and a half. 1264

Distribution of gowns of black livery.

Edward on his part presented the mayor and aldermen with 104 gowns of black livery, according to the precedent followed at the decease of Henry VII. These gowns were distributed among the mayor and aldermen, the high officers and certain clerks in the service of the Corporation. Ten aldermen accompanied the remains of the late king on their way to Windsor, riding forth in black coats with the rest of the mourners, the harness and bridles of their horses being covered with black cloth. Two of the aldermen, Sir William Laxton and Sir Martin Bowes, had each four servants in their suite, whilst the rest of the aldermen had three, all in black coats. 1265

CHAPTER XV.

Accession and coronation of Edward VI, 1547.

Provision had been made for the succession to the crown on Henry's death by an Act of Parliament passed in 1544, and the princesses Mary and Elizabeth were thereby re-instated in their rights of inheritance as if no question of their legitimacy had ever been raised. As Edward, who was next in succession to the crown, was but a boy, Henry had taken pains to select a council of regency in which no one party should predominate. This council was soon set aside, and Hertford, the king's uncle, got himself appointed Protector of the realm and took the title of Duke of Somerset. At the time of his father's death Edward was residing at Hertford Castle. He was soon afterwards carried thence by his uncle to London and lodged in the Tower, where the mayor, Henry Hoberthorne, went to pay his respects and received the honour of knighthood. 1266

On the 19th the young king passed through the city to Westminster, the mayor riding before him bareheaded with the mace of crystal 1267 in his hand. The streets were lined with members of the livery companies. The conduits, the standard and cross in Chepe, the Ludgate and the Temple Bar had been freshly painted and trimmed with goodly hangings of Arras and cloth of gold for the occasion. At three of the conduits, namely, the conduit in Cornhill, the great conduit in Chepe, and the conduit in Fleet Street, wine was made by artificial means to flow as if from the "festrons" of the conduits themselves. At the little conduit in Chepe were stationed the aldermen of the city, in their scarlet gowns, and the Recorder, who, in the name of the whole city, presented his majesty with 1,000 marks in "hole new sufferaynes" of gold in a purse of purple cloth of gold, which his majesty deigned to accept with his own hand. The next day Edward was crowned. The lord mayor, according to custom, attended with his crystal mace as the king passed from his palace to church, and thence, after mass, to Westminster Hall, and received for his services the customary gold cup, which on this occasion weighed twenty ounces, with its cover and a "leyer" (or laver) silver-gilt weighing six ounces. 1268

Opposition in the city to the sacrament of the mass, 1547-1548.

The work of reformation was now about to be taken seriously in hand. Something, it is true, had been done in this direction under Henry, but in *dilettante* fashion. The ceremony connected with the boy-bishop, which even Colet had thought worthy to be perpetuated in his school, 1269 had been abolished by order of the mayor in 1538. 1270 The ruthless destruction of the shrine of St. Thomas at Canterbury, and the erasure of his name from service-books, had been followed in the city by an order (1539) for a new common seal on which the arms of the city were substituted for the original effigy of the saint. 1271 Henry himself only coquetted with Protestantism; his chief object, if not the only one, was to get rid of the papal supremacy; but among the bourgeois class of the city there was an earnest desire to see an improvement made in the doctrine and discipline of the Church. 1272

Whilst the statute of the Six Articles was still unrepealed, the sacrament of the mass frequently provoked open hostility in the city. Thus, in August, 1538, Robert Reynold, a stationer, was declared upon the oath of five independent witnesses to have been heard to say "that the masse was nawght, and the memento was Bawdrye, and after the consecracioun of the masse yt was idolatrye." He was further charged with having said that it were better for him to confess and be houseled by a temporal rather than a spiritual man. 1273 Again, in February, 1543, Hugh Eton, a hosier of London, was convicted of disguising himself "in fonde fassyon," and of irreverently walking up and down in St. Bride's Church before the sacrament, disturbing the priests at mass and creating a tumult. By way of punishment for his offence he was set in the cage in Fleet Street, "disguised" as he was, with a paper on his head setting forth his offence. He there remained until four o'clock in the afternoon, when he was removed to the compter and condemned to stay there a prisoner until he found sureties for good behaviour. 1274

After the repeal of the statute by Edward's first parliament, the opposition to the "sacrament of the altar," as the mass was called, became greater than ever. 1275 A boy was ordered to be whipt naked in the church of St. Mary Woolnoth for throwing his cap at the host at the time of elevation. 1276 In February, 1548, information was given to the Court of Aldermen of preachers having used "certain words" touching the mass in the churches of St. Dunstan in the east and St. Martin Orgar. 1277 On the 5th May, 1548, the mayor and aldermen resolved to appear the next day before the Lord Protector Somerset and the council, and explain the nature of the misdemeanours of certain preachers, concerning which the mayor had already had some communication with the Archbishop of Canterbury. 1278

In the following month (5 June) the Court of Aldermen investigated a charge made against a city curate that, about a month before, after reciting the common prayers at the choir door at high mass, he had prayed among other things that Almighty God might send the king's council grace and bring them out of the erroneous opinions that they were then in. The informer went on to say that Sir Clement Smith and the Recorder, who were present, laughed at the prayer. But inasmuch as the informer had not been present himself, and that what he had laid before the court was mere hearsay evidence, little attention was paid to it. 1279

Act for abolition of chantries, 1547.

The abolition of chantries initiated by Henry VIII was carried out to a fuller extent by his successor. The statute (1 Edward VI, cap 14) by which this was effected not only deprived a large number of priests of a means of livelihood, but laid them open to insult from those they met in the street. They complained that they could not walk abroad nor attend the court at Westminster without being reviled and having their tippets and caps violently pulled. 1280

Redemption of charges for superstitious uses by the city and companies, 1550.

The same statute—by declaring all chantries, obits, lights and lamps to be objects of superstitious use, and all goods, chattels, jewels, plate, ornaments and other moveables hitherto devoted to their maintenance to be thenceforth escheated to the Crown—dealt a heavy blow to the Corporation of the City of London, as well as to the civic companies and other bodies who owned property subject to certain payments under one or other of these heads. Three years after the passing of the Act the Corporation and the companies redeemed certain charges of this character on their respective properties to the amount of £939 2s. 5-1/2d. by payment to the Crown of no less a sum than £18,744 11s. 2d. 1281

The redemption of these and other charges of a similar character, whilst very convenient to the Crown, saving the trouble and expense of collecting small sums of money, worked a hardship upon the Corporation and the companies. In order to raise funds for redeeming the charges they were obliged to sell property. This property was often held under conditions of reverter and remainders over, unless what was now declared to be illegal was religiously carried out. It was manifestly unfair that they should be made to forfeit property because the conditions under which it was held could no longer be legally complied with. A petition therefore was presented to the king in order to obviate this difficulty, and to enable them to part with the necessary property and at the same time to give a clear title. 1282

Order for demolition of images, pictures, &c., Aug., 1547.

In the meantime (Aug., 1547) an order had gone forth for the demolition of all images and removal of pictures and stained glass from churches. The instructions sent to the lord mayor were very precise. "Stories made in glasse wyndows" relative to Thomas Becket were to be altered at as little expense as possible. Images and pictures to which no offerings and no prayers were made might remain for "garnisshement" of the churches; and if any such had been taken down the mayor was at liberty to set them up again, unless they had been taken down by order of the king's commissioners or the parson of the church. If there existed in any church a "storye in glasse" of the Bishop of Rome, otherwise the Pope, the mayor might paint out the papal tiara and alter the "storye." 1283 These instructions, contained in a letter from the king's council, were duly considered at a Court of Aldermen held on the 22nd September, with the result that every alderman was ordered, in the most secret, discreet and quiet manner he could devise, to visit each parish church in his ward, and to take with him the parson or curate and two or three honest parishioners, churchwardens or others who had had anything to do with the removal of the images that had already been taken down, and, having shut the church door for the sake of privacy, to take a note in writing of what images had formerly been in the several churches, what images had offerings and were prayed to, and what not; who had removed those taken down, and what had been done with them. A report was to be made on these points by every alderman at the next court, so that the lords of the council might be informed thereon and their will ascertained before any further steps were taken. 1284

The havoc worked by the king's commissioners in the city and throughout the country by the reckless destruction of works of art was terrible. The churches were stripped of every ornament, their walls whitewashed, and only relieved by the tables of the commandments. Early in September the commissioners visited St. Paul's and pulled down all the images. In November the rood was taken down with its images of the Virgin and St. John. The great cross of the rood fell down accidentally and killed one of the workmen, a circumstance which many ascribed to the special intervention of the Almighty. From St. Paul's the commissioners proceeded to the church of St. Bride, and so from parish church to parish church. 1285

In the following year (1548) the chapel of St. Paul's charnel house was pulled down and the bones removed into the country and reburied. From a sanitary point of view their removal is to be commended. There is no such excuse, however, for the destruction of the cloister in Pardon churchyard (April, 1549), with its famous picture of the Dance of Death, painted at the expense of John Carpenter, the town clerk of the city, of whom mention has already been made. The fact was that the Protector Somerset required material for building his new palace in the Strand, 1286 to enlarge which he had already pulled down Strand Church, dedicated to Saint Mary and the Holy Innocents. 1287 The destruction of the cloister necessitated a new order of procession on the next Lord Mayor's Day (24 Oct.), when Sir Rowland Hill paid the customary visit to St. Paul's, made a circuit of the interior of the cathedral, and said a *De profundis* at the bishop's tomb. 1288

The citizens and the Grey Friars Church, 1547.

Nor can the civic authorities themselves be altogether acquitted of vandalism. They destroyed the churches of St. Nicholas Shambles and St. Ewin, and sold the plate and windows, but the proceeds were distributed among the poor. 1289 They went further than this. They removed the fine tombs and altars, as well as the choir stalls, from the church of the Grey Friars, where mingled the ashes of some of the noblest and best in the land. There was some excuse, however, for these acts. The house and church of the Grey Friars had been granted to the City at the close of the last reign on the express condition that the churches of St. Nicholas and St. Ewin should be abolished, and that the church of the Grey Friars should be established as a parish church in their place under the name of Christ Church. It was probably in order to render the old monastic church more convenient as a parish church that they removed much of what to the antiquary of to-day would have seemed of priceless value, and at the same time reduced the dimensions of the choir. 1290

The "communion" substituted for the mass, 1548.

At Easter, 1548, a new communion service in English took the place of the mass. 1291 At the election of the mayor on the following Michaelmas-day, on which occasion a mass had always been celebrated at the Guildhall Chapel since the time of Whitington, an endeavour appears to have been made by the Court of Aldermen to effect a compromise between mass and communion, for whilst it ordered that a mass of the Holy Ghost should be solemnly sung in English in the Guildhall Chapel (which had been confiscated by Henry VIII) 1292 as theretofore, it further ordered that the holy communion should be administered to two or three of the priests there at the same mass. 1293 Orders were issued by the king's council that candles should no longer be carried about on Candlemas-day, ashes on Ash Wednesday, palms on Palm Sunday. These practices were now considered superstitious, as also was the "sensyng" which hitherto had taken place in St. Paul's at Whitsuntide, but which the Court of Aldermen now decreed to be abolished, and the preaching of sermons substituted in its place. 1294

The "tuning of the pulpits."

The people were at this time extremely distracted by the various and contradictory opinions of their preachers; and as they were totally incapable of judging of the force of arguments adduced on one side or the other, but conceived that everything spoken from the pulpit was of equal authority, great confusion and perplexity of mind ensued. In order to "tune the pulpits" and to effect uniformity of doctrine and service, the Lord Protector resorted to proclamations, which, although no longer having the authority of statutes as in the reign of Henry VIII, practically answered the same purpose. Preaching was thus restricted to those who had previously obtained a licence from the king, his visitors, the archbishop of Canterbury, or the bishop of the diocese. 1295 The same want of uniformity which appeared in the preachers appeared also in their congregations; some "kepte holy day and manny kepte none, but dyd worke opynly, and in some churches servys and some none, soche was the devysyon." 1296

The insurrections of 1549.

In the meantime great discontent had been caused by the Protector's measures. The rich nobleman and country gentleman said nothing, for their assent had been purchased by gifts of church property, but the tenants and bourgeois class suffered from increased rents, from enclosures and evictions. Church lands had always been underlet; the monks were easy landlords. Not so the new proprietors of the confiscated abbey lands, they were determined to make the most out of their newly-acquired property. 1297 Insurrection broke out in various parts of the country. Not only were enclosures thrown open and fences removed, but a cry was raised for the restoration of the old religion. Information of what was taking place was sent to Sir Henry Amcotes, the mayor, and steps were at once taken (2 July, 1549) for putting the city into a state of defence and for the preservation of the king's peace. A "false draw-brydge" was ordered (*inter alia*) to be made for London Bridge "in case nede should requyer by reason "of the sterrynge of the people (which God defende!) to caste downe thother." 1298 The city gates were constantly watched and the walls mounted with artillery. 1299

Cranmer at St. Paul's, 21 July, 1549.

In the midst of these preparations there was a lull. On the 21st day of July, being the 6th Sunday after Trinity, came Archbishop Cranmer to St. Paul's. He wore no vestment save a cope over an alb, and bore neither mitre nor cross, but only a staff. He conducted the whole of the service as set out in the "king's book" recently published, which differed but slightly from the church service in use at the present day, and he administered the "Communion" to himself, the dean and others, according to Act of Parliament. The mayor and most of the aldermen occupied seats in the choir.

Cranmer's object in coming to the city on that day was to exhort the citizens to obey the king as the supreme head of the realm, and to pray the Almighty to avert the trouble with which, for their sins, they were threatened. 1300

The king passes through the city, 23 July.

Two days later (23 July) the king himself left Greenwich and rode through the city to Westminster, accompanied by the Lord Protector and other nobles. The mayor and aldermen rode out to Southwark, the former in a gown of crimson velvet, the latter in gowns of scarlet, to meet the royal party, and conducted it as far as Charing Cross, where the aldermen took their leave, the king saluting them and "putting of his capp to everie of them." The mayor rode on to Westminster, where the king and the Protector graciously bade him farewell. 1301

Ket's rebellion in Norfolk. 1549.

The aspect of affairs began to look black indeed. By the end of the month Exeter was being besieged by the rebels, and on the 8th August the French ambassador, taking advantage of the general distraction, bade the Lord Protector open defiance at Whitehall. 1302 At midnight instructions were sent to the mayor to seize all Frenchmen in the city who were not denizens, together with their property. By this time, however, Exeter had been relieved and the insurrection in the west had been put down. The western insurgents had demanded the restoration of the mass and the abolition of the English liturgy. Contemporaneously with this religious movement another agitation was being made in the eastern counties, and more especially in Norfolk, which had for its object the destruction of enclosures. With the eastern rebels, who placed themselves under the leadership of Robert Ket, a tanner of Wymondham, the Protector himself sympathized at heart, and the council had to exercise no little pressure before he could be induced to send an efficient force to put them down. At length the rebels were met and defeated by a force under the command of the Earl of Warwick, the son of the extortionate Dudley who was associated with Empson in oppressing the city towards the close of the reign of Henry VII. Ket galloped off the field, leaving his followers to be ridden down and killed by the earl's horsemen. He was shortly afterwards captured in a barn, and eventually brought up to London, together with his brother William, and committed to the Tower. Being arraigned and convicted of treason, they were handed over to the high sheriff of Norfolk and Suffolk. Robert was hanged in chains on the top of Norwich Castle, whilst his brother William suffered a similar fate on the top of Wymondham Steeple. 1303

The fall of Somerset, 1549.

Somerset's fall was now imminent. The citizens hated him, not for his favouring the reformers, but for the injury he had caused to trade and for his having bebased the coinage still further than it had been debased by Henry VIII. His colleagues in the council, who had been pampered with gifts of church lands, were angry with him for the favour he had shown towards those who raised the outcry against enclosures, and they began to show their independence.

Letter from lords of the council to the City accusing the Protector, 6 Oct.

On the afternoon of Sunday, the 6th October, 1549, a letter was sent to the mayor subscribed by Lord St. John, the president of the council, the earls of Warwick, Southampton and Arundel, and other members of the council, containing a long indictment of the Protector's policy and conduct. He was proud, covetous and ambitious. He had embezzled the pay of the soldiers, with which he was building sumptuous houses in four or five different places. Whilst sowing discord among the nobles, he flattered the commons to the intent that, having got rid of the former, he might with the aid of the latter achieve his scarcely veiled design of supplanting the king himself. They had hoped, the letter continues, to have persuaded the duke by fair means to take order for the security of the king's person and the commonwealth; but no sooner was the matter broached to the duke than he showed himself determined to appeal to the arbitrament of the sword. Such being the case, they on their part were no less resolved, with God's help, to deliver the king and the realm from impending ruin, or perish in the attempt. They concluded by asking the civic authorities to see that good watch and ward were kept in the city and that no *matériel* of war was supplied to the duke or his followers. Any letters or proclamations coming from the Protector were to be disregarded. 1304

Letter from Somerset to the mayor, 6 Oct., 1549.

Determined not to be forestalled by his enemies; the duke himself wrote the same day (6 Oct.) to the mayor desiring the City to furnish him forthwith with 1,000 trusty men fully armed for the protection of the king's person. The men were to be forwarded to him at Hampton by the following Monday mid-day at the latest, and in the meantime the citizens were to take steps to protect the king and his uncle, the duke, against conspiracy. 1305

Conference between the lords and the City at Ely Place, 6 Oct., 1549.

Before these letters had been despatched the mayor and aldermen had been summoned by the Earl of Warwick, who now took the lead against Somerset, to meet him and other lords of the council at his house in Ely Place, Holborn. A meeting had accordingly taken place that Sunday morning, when the state of affairs was discussed. After the meeting separated

Warwick came to the city and took up his residence in the house of Sir John York, one of the sheriffs, situate in Walbrook. Sir John Markham, lieutenant of the Tower, was removed, and Sir Leonard Chamberlain appointed in his place, whilst the Court of Aldermen took extraordinary precautions for safe-guarding the city. 1306

Removal of the king to Windsor.

As soon as Somerset was made aware of the Tower being in the possession of his rivals he removed from Hampton Court to Windsor, carrying the young king with him, and despatched a letter to Lord Russell to hurry thither with such force as he could muster. 1307

The City joins the lords against Somerset, 7 Oct., 1549.

On Monday (7 Oct.) the lords of the council sat at Mercers' Hall—they felt safer in London—and thence despatched a dutiful letter to the king, and another (explaining their conduct) to Cranmer. 1308 The Common Council met at seven o'clock that morning, having been warned on Sunday night. 1309 The object of their meeting so early in the day was that no time might be lost before taking into consideration the letters that had been received from Somerset and from the lords. After due deliberation the citizens agreed to throw in their lot with the lords and to assist them "to the uttermost of their wills and powers" in the maintenance and defence of the king's person. 1310

The lords attend a Common Council, 8 Oct., 1549.

On Tuesday (8 Oct.) the Common Council again assembled in the Guildhall to meet the lords by appointment. Rumour had been spread to the effect that it was the intention of the lords to cause a reestablishment of the old religion. 1311 This the lords assured the meeting was far from their minds. They intended no alteration of matters as established by the laws and statutes. All they wanted was to cause them to be maintained as formerly, before they had been "disformed" by the Lord Protector, and for this they prayed the assistance of the citizens. Thereupon the mayor, aldermen and common council, thanking God for the good intentions of their lordships, "promised their ayde and helpe to the uttermost of their lieves and goodes." 1312

A meeting at Sheriff York's house, 9 Oct.

The City agrees to furnish a contingent of soldiers to aid the lords.

On Wednesday (9 Oct.) the lords met at the house of Sheriff York, where they had dined the previous day. 1313 They had heard that Somerset had seized all the armour, weapons and munitions of war he could lay his hands upon, both at Hampton Court and Windsor, and with them had armed his adherents. They again sent letters to the king, the archbishop and others, and declared Somerset to be unworthy to continue any longer in the position of Protector. 1314 The Common Council, which met the same day—"for divers urgent causes moved and declared by the mouth of the recorder and of the lord mayor and aldermen on the king's behalf"—agreed to furnish with all speed 500 men, or if necessary 1,000 men, well harnessed and weaponed, to proceed to Windsor Castle for the delivery and preservation of his majesty. It was subsequently arranged that 100 of the contingent should be horsemen. 1315 By the afternoon of Friday (11 Oct.) the men and horsemen were ready. They mustered in Moorfields, whence they marched through Moorgate, Coleman Street, Cheapside, and out by Newgate to Smithfield, with the Sword-bearer riding before them as captain. At Smithfield they broke off, and were discharged from further service for the time. 1316 There is no evidence to show that the force was ever called upon to proceed to Windsor.

The effect of the City's adhesion to the lords.

Somerset brought to the Tower, 14 Oct.

The adhesion of the City to the lords had in the meanwhile added strength to their cause, many who had at first held back now declaring themselves against Somerset. In this manner they were joined by Lord Chancellor Rich, the Earl of Shrewsbury, Chief Justice Montague and others, whose signatures appear to a proclamation issued on the 8th October setting forth "the verye trowth of the Duke of Somersettes evell government and false and detestable procedynges." 1317 By the end of the week (12 Oct.) the lords felt themselves strong enough to proceed in person to Windsor, where on their knees they explained their conduct to the king, who received them graciously and gave them hearty thanks. The following day (Sunday) was spent in removing some of Somerset's followers; and on Monday (14th) Somerset himself was brought prisoner to London, "riding through Oldborne in at Newgate and so to the Tower of London, accompanied with diuers lordes and gentlemen with 300 horse, the lord maior, Sir Ralph Warren, Sir John Gresham, Mr. Recorder, Sir William Locke and both the shiriffes and other knights, sitting on their horses agaynst Soper-lane, with all the officers with halbards, and from Oldborne bridge to the Tower certaine aldermen or their deputies on horsebacke in every streete, with a number of housholders standing with bils as hee passed." 1318

At the sudden fall of one who for a short time had been all powerful—a little more than a week had served to deprive him of the protectorate and render him a prisoner in the Tower—did it cross the mind of any of the onlookers that he it was who carried away from the Guildhall Library some cartloads of books which were never returned?

Bonner deprived of bishopric of London, 1 Oct., 1549.

There were some who looked upon Somerset's fall as an act of God's vengeance for his having caused Bonner to be deprived of his bishopric of London. On the 1st September last Bonner had preached at Paul's Cross against the king's supremacy. Information of the matter was given to the council, and Bonner was called upon to answer for his conduct before Cranmer and the rest of the commissioners. The informers on this occasion were William Latymer, the parson of the church of St. Laurence Pountney, and John Hooper, a zealous Protestant, who afterwards became Bishop of Gloucester. Whilst under examination before the commissioners Bonner was confined in the Marshalsea. Hooper in the meantime was put up by Cranmer to preach at Paul's Cross, and he took the opportunity thus afforded him of inveighing strongly against Bonner's conduct. Bonner failed to satisfy the commissioners, and on the 1st October was deprived of office and committed to prison during the king's pleasure. "But marke what followeth," writes the chronicler of the Grey Friars, within a week "was proclaymyd the protector a traytor." 1319

The king entertained by Sheriff York, Oct., 1549.

On the 17th October Edward came from Hampton Court to Southwark Place, a mansion formerly belonging to Charles Brandon, Duke of Suffolk, when it was known as Suffolk House. It was now used in part as a mint, and was occupied by Sheriff York in his capacity as master of the king's mint. After dinner the king knighted York in recognition of his hospitality and his past services, an honour personal to York and not extended to his colleague in the shrievalty, Richard Turke. From Southwark Edward set forth to ride through the city to Westminster, accompanied by a long cavalcade of nobles and gentlemen, "the lord mayor bearinge the scepter before his maiestie and rydinge with garter kinge of armes." 1320

Somerset released on parole, 6 Feb., 1550.

Somerset's confinement in the Tower was not of long duration. On the 6th February, 1550, the lieutenant of the Tower received orders to bring his prisoner "with out greate garde or busyness" to Sheriff York's house in Walbrook, where the council was sitting; and on the duke entering into a recognisance to remain privately either at Shene or Sion, and not to travel more than four miles from either place, nor attempt to gain an interview with the young king, he was allowed to depart. 1321

Warwick and the reformers, 1550.

With Warwick, who became the ruling spirit of the council after the fall of Somerset and the abolition of the protectorate, religion was a matter of supreme indifference, and for a time it was uncertain whether he would favour the followers of the old religion or the advanced reformers. He chose to extend his patronage to the latter. The day after Somerset's release from the Tower, Bonner was again brought from the Marshalsea, where he had been roughly used, 1322 and the cause of his deprivation reconsidered by the lords of the council sitting in the Star Chamber, the result being that the previous sentence by Cranmer was confirmed and Bonner again relegated to prison. Bishops were now appointed directly by the king, who in the following April caused Nicholas Ridley, bishop of Rochester, to be transferred to London in Bonner's place; and the see of Westminster, 1323 which had been created in 1540, was united to London. In July Hooper was nominated to the see of Gloucester; but some time elapsed before this rigid reformer could be induced to overcome his prejudice to episcopal vestments (which he denounced as the livery of Anti-Christ) and consent to be consecrated in them. 1324 As soon as the ceremony was over he cast them off.

The City and the borough of Southwark, 1550.

For some time past the City had experienced difficulty in exercising its franchise in the borough of Southwark. That borough consisted of three manors, known respectively as the Guildable Manor, the King's Manor and the Great Liberty Manor. 1325 The first of these—and only the first—had been granted to the City by Edward III soon after his accession. The civic authorities had complained of felons making good their escape from the city to Southwark, where they could not be attacked by the officers of the city; and the king, in answer to the City's request, had made over to them the town or vill of Southwark. 1326 This grant was afterwards confirmed and amplified by a charter granted by Edward IV in 1462, whereby the citizens were allowed to hold a yearly fair in the borough on three successive days in the month of September, together with a court of pie-powder, and with all liberties and customs to such fair appertaining. 1327 In course of time the City claimed the right of holding a market, as well as the yearly fair, twice a week in Southwark. This claim now led to difficulties with the king's bailiff, Sir John Gate. A draft agreement had been drawn up during Somerset's protectorate in the hopes of arranging matters, 1328 but apparently without success.

Charter to the City, 23 April, 1550.

At length the city agreed (29 March, 1550) to make an offer of 500 marks for the purchase of the rights of the Crown in Southwark, 1329 and eventually a compromise was effected. For the sum of £647 2s. 1d. the king conveyed by charter 1330 to the City of London divers messuages in Southwark, with the exception of "Southwark Place" and the gardens belonging to it, formerly the Duke of Suffolk's mansion, and for a further sum of 500 marks he surrendered all the royal liberties and franchises which he or his heirs might have in the borough or town of Southwark. It was expressly provided that this charter was not to be prejudicial to Sir John Gate or to his property and interests. The ancient rent of £10 per annum was still to be paid, and the citizens were to be allowed to hold four markets every week in addition to a fair and court of pie-powder enjoyed since the time of Edward IV. On the 9th May the lord mayor took formal possession of the borough of Southwark by riding through the precinct, after which the Common Cryer made proclamation with sound of trumpet for all vagabonds to leave the city and borough and the suburbs and liberties of the same. 1331

The ward of Bridge Without.

It was originally intended, no doubt, that the borough should be incorporated for all municipal purposes with the city, and that the inhabitants of the borough should be placed on the same footing as the citizens. This, however, was never carried out. Notwithstanding the fact that among the ordinances drawn up (31 July) for the government of the borough, 1332 there was one which prescribed the same customary procedure in the election of an alderman for the new ward of Bridge Without as prevailed in the city; 1333 the inhabitants of the borough have never taken any part in the election of an alderman. The first alderman, Sir John Aylyff, a barber-surgeon, was "nominated, elected and chosen" by the Court of Aldermen, 1334 and was admitted and sworn before the same body on the 28th May, 1850—that is to say, some weeks before the ordinances just mentioned were drawn up.

The alderman of the ward continued to be nominated and elected by the Court of Aldermen until 1711, when, by virtue of an Act of Common Council, the ward was to be offered to the several aldermen who had served as mayor, in order of seniority. If no alderman could be found willing to be translated from his own ward to that of Bridge Without, the Court of Common Council was empowered by another Act passed in 1725 to proceed to the election of an alderman.

The ward of Bridge Without has never sent representatives to the Common Council, inasmuch as its inhabitants refused to "take up their freedom" and bear the burdens of citizenship, and there existed no means for forcing the freedom upon them. In 1835, however, a petition was presented to the Common Council by certain inhabitants of Southwark asking that they might for the future exercise the right of electing not only an alderman, but common council-men for the ward, and that the ordinances of 1550 might be carried out according to their original intention. The petition was referred to the Committee for General Purposes, who reported to the Common Council 1335 to the effect that, considering that the borough of Southwark had never formed part of the City of London, the charter of Edward VI notwithstanding, and that the holding of wardmotes in the borough would materially interfere with the duties of an ancient officer known as a seneschal or steward of Southwark, the petition could not be complied with, except by application to the legislature, and that such a course would neither be expedient or advisable. Another petition to the same effect has quite recently been presented to the Court of Aldermen; but it was equally unsuccessful. 1336

Growing unpopularity of Warwick, 1550-1551.

Warwick had not long taken the place of Somerset before he found himself compelled to make peace with France (29 March, 1550). This he accomplished only by consenting to surrender Boulogne. The declaration of peace was celebrated with bonfires in the city, although the conditions under which the peace was effected were generally unacceptable to the nation and brought discredit upon the earl. 1337 One result of the conclusion of the war was again to flood the streets of the city with men who openly declared that they neither could nor would work, and that unless the king provided them with a livelihood they would combine to plunder the city, and once clear with their booty they cared not if 10,000 men were after them. It was in vain that proclamation was made for all disbanded soldiers to leave the city. They refused to go, and oftentimes came into conflict with the city constables. At length the mayor and aldermen addressed a letter on the subject to the lords of the council (25 Sept.). 1338

The debasement of the currency, 1551.

In the following year the state of the city was rendered worse by a proposal of Warwick to debase the currency yet more. As soon as the proposal got wind up went the price of provisions, in spite of every effort made by the lords of the council to keep it down. They sent for the mayor (Sir Andrew Judd) to attend them at Greenwich on Sunday, the 10th May, and soundly rated him—or, as the chronicler puts it, "gave him some sore words"—for allowing such things to take place. On Thursday, the 28th, the mayor summoned a Common Council, when the Recorder repeated to them the king's orders that the price of wares was not to be raised. The livery companies were to see to it, and there were to be no more murmurings. 1339

Warwick himself excited the anger of the city burgesses by riding through the streets to see if the king's orders against the enhancement of the price of victuals were being carried out. Coming one day to a butcher's in Eastcheap, he asked the price of a sheep. Being told that it was 13 shillings, he replied that it was too much and passed on. When another butcher asked 16 shillings he was told to go and be hanged. The earl's conduct so roused the indignation of the butchers of the city—a class of men scarcely less powerful than their brethren the fishmongers—that they made no secret that the price of meat would be raised still more if the debasement of the currency was carried out as proposed. 1340 Yet, in spite of all remonstrances and threats, a proclamation went forth that after the 17th August the shilling should be current for six pence sterling and no more, the groat for two pence, the penny for a halfpenny, and the halfpenny for a farthing. 1341 The price of every commodity rose 50 per cent. as a matter of course, and nothing that Warwick could do could prevent it. Seeing at last the hopelessness of attempting to overcome economic laws by a mere *ipse dixit*, he caused a "contrary proclamasyon" to be issued, and "sette alle at lyberty agayne, and every viteler to selle as they wolde and had done before." 1342

Warwick's increasing unpopularity raised a hope in the breast of Somerset of recovering his lost power. Some rash words he had allowed to escape were carried to the young king, who took the part of Warwick against his own uncle, and showed his appreciation of the earl's services by creating him Duke of Northumberland (11 Oct.). A few days later Somerset was seized and again committed to the Tower. 1343 The new duke vaunted himself more than ever, and as a fresh coinage was on the eve of being issued, he caused it to be struck with a ragged staff, the badge of his house, on its face. 1344 Some of the duke's servants thought to ruffle it as well as their master, and offered an insult to one of the sheriffs, attempting to snatch at his chain of office as he accompanied the mayor to service at St. Paul's on All Saints' Day, and otherwise creating no little disturbance in St. Paul's Churchyard. The mayor waited until service was over, and then took them into custody. 1345

Trial and execution of Somerset, 22 Jan., 1552.

At the time of Somerset's second arrest the Common Council and the wardens of the several livery companies were summoned to meet at the Guildhall to hear why the duke had been sent for the second time to the Tower, and to receive instructions for safe-guarding the city. They were informed by the Recorder that it had been the duke's intention to seize the Tower and the Isle of Wight, and to "have destroyed the city of London and the substantiall men of the same." 1346 This was, of course, an exaggeration, although there is little doubt that the duke was preparing to get himself named again Protector by the next parliament. On the 1st December he was brought from the Tower by water to Westminster, the mayor and aldermen having received strict orders to keep the city well guarded. 1347 He was arraigned of treason and felony, but his judges, among whom sat his enemy Northumberland himself, acquitted him of the former charge, and those in the hall, thinking he had been altogether acquitted, raised a shout of joy that could be heard as far as Charing Cross and Long Acre. When they discovered that he had been found guilty of felony and condemned to be executed they were grievously disappointed. As he landed at the Crane in the Vintry on his way back to the Tower that evening, and passed through Candlewick (Cannon) Street, the people, we are told, cried "'God save him' all the way as he went, thinkinge that he had clerely bene quitt, but they were deceyved, but hoopinge he should have the kinge's pardon." 1348 According to another chronicler there were mingled cries of joy and sorrow as he passed through London, some crying for joy that he was acquitted, whilst others (who were better informed of the actual state of the case) lamented his conviction. 1349 His execution took place on Tower Hill in January of the next year (1552).

The City and the Royal Hospitals, 1547-1553.

In the meanwhile the civic authorities had been energetically engaged in making regulations for the hospital of the poor in West Smithfield, better known as St. Bartholomew's Hospital, which they had recently acquired, and in grappling with the poverty and sickness with which they were surrounded. Instead of trusting to the charity of those attending the parish churches on Sunday for raising money for the poor, the Common Council, in September, 1547, resorted to the less precarious method of levying on every inhabitant of the city one half of a fifteenth for the maintenance of the poor of the hospital. 1350 The voluntary system, however, was not wholly abolished. In the following April (1548) a brotherhood for the relief of the poor had been established, to which the mayor (Sir John Gresham) and most of the aldermen belonged, each agreeing to subscribe a yearly sum varying from half a mark to a mark. 1351 In September governors were appointed of St. Bartholomew's Hospital—four aldermen and eight commoners 1352— and in the following December the Common Council passed an Act for the payment of 500 marks a year to the hospital, the sum being levied on the livery companies. 1353

St. Thomas's Hospital.

In 1551 the City succeeded in obtaining another hospital. This was the hospital in Southwark originally dedicated to Thomas Becket, but whose patron saint was, after the Reformation, changed to St. Thomas the Apostle. Negotiations were opened in February with the lord chancellor for the purchase of this hospital. 1354 They proceeded so favourably that by the 12th August the hospital and church and part of their endowment were conveyed to the City by deed, whilst the rest of the endowment was transferred by another deed on the following day. 1355 The purchase-money amounted to nearly £2,500.

Christ's Hospital.

Having thus cared for the sick and the poor, the civic authorities next turned their attention to the conversion of a portion of the ground and buildings of the dissolved monastery of the Grey Friars into a hospital for the reception and education of fatherless and helpless children. In 1552 Sir Richard Dobbs 1356 was mayor. He took an active part in the charitable work that was then being carried on in the city, and his conduct so won the heart of Ridley that the bishop wrote from prison shortly before his death commending him in the highest possible terms:—"O Dobbs, Dobbs, alderman and knight, thou in thy year did'st win my heart for evermore, for that honourable act, that most blessed work of God, of the erection and setting up of Christ's Holy Hospitals, and truly religious houses which by thee and through thee were begun." In July the work of adapting the old buildings, rather than erecting new, was commenced, and in a few months the premises were sufficiently forward to admit of the reception of nearly 400 children. The charity was aided by the king's bestowal of the linen vestures used in the city prior to the Reformation, and at that time seized by the commissioners. 1357 Just as the close of the reign of Henry VIII had witnessed the reopening of the church of the Grey Friars under the name of Christchurch, and the celebration of the mass once more within its walls, so now the close of his son's short reign witnessed the restoration of their house and buildings, and their conversion, in the cause of education and charity, into Christ's Hospital.

Bridewell Hospital.

There was yet another class of inhabitant to be provided for, namely, those who either could not or would not work. On behalf of these a deputation 1358 was appointed by the City to present a petition to the king that he would be pleased to grant the disused palace of Bridewell to the municipality for the purpose of turning it into a workhouse. The deputation was introduced by Ridley, who himself wrote in May of this year (1552) to secretary Cecil on the same subject. 1359 The efforts of the bishop and the deputation were rewarded with success. In the following spring (1553) the king not only consented to convey the palace to the municipal body, but further gave 700 marks and all the beds and bedding of his palace of the Savoy for the maintenance of the workhouse. 1360 The City having thus become possessed of the several hospitals of St. Bartholomew, St. Thomas, Christ's and Bridewell, the king, a few days before his death, granted the mayor, aldermen and commonalty a charter of incorporation as governors of these Royal Hospitals in the city. 1361

CHAPTER XVI.

Northumberland's conspiracy, 1553.

The death of Edward VI took place on the 6th July, 1553, although it was not generally known until two days afterwards. By his father's will the Princess Mary became heiress to the throne. Northumberland was aware of this. He was equally aware that if Mary succeeded to her brother's crown matters might go hard with him. He therefore persuaded Edward to follow the precedent set by his father and re-settle the succession to the crown by will. He succeeded moreover in getting the late king to name as his successor the Lady Jane Grey, grand-daughter of Mary Duchess of Suffolk, the younger sister of Henry VIII, and he took the further precaution of marrying her to his own son, Lord Guildford Dudley. It was in vain that the judges and law officers of the Crown pointed out that the Act of Parliament which authorised Henry to dispose of the crown by will, in the case of his children dying without heirs, did not apply to Edward. Councillors and judges, and even Cranmer himself, were forced to signify their assent by subscribing to the will, which was dated (21 June) a fortnight only before Edward's death.

Northumberland well knew the advantage to be got by securing the co-operation of the city in prosecuting his scheme, so he persuaded the mayor (Sir George Barnes), a number of aldermen (including Sir John Gresham, Sir Andrew Judd, Thomas Offley and Sir Richard Dobbs), and several of the leading merchants of the city to append their signatures to the will. 1362 The king had been already dead two days before Northumberland sent for them to Greenwich and acquainted them of the fact, exhorting them at the same time to sign the document. 1363

Lady Jane Grey proclaimed queen, 10 July, 1553.

On the 10th July the Lady Jane was brought from Richmond and lodged in the Tower, and that same evening was proclaimed queen at the Cross in Chepe. The mayor took no part in the ceremony, and only one of the sheriffs (William Gerard or Garrard) attended the heralds. If Northumberland thought that the citizens would favour Lady Jane merely because she was a Protestant he was mistaken. The proclamation was received with undisguised coldness, and "few or none said God save her." 1364 Nor was it better received by the country at large. The eastern counties rose and in a few days Mary was at the head of 30,000 men. No time was to be lost, and Northumberland at once set out from London to meet her. As he passed through the city he noticed that none wished him "God speed."

Queen Mary proclaimed, 19 July.

No sooner was his back turned than the lords of the council, seeing how matters were going, and eager to throw off the yoke which the duke had placed on their necks, determined upon proclaiming Mary queen. It was necessary, however, that the City should first be informed of their intention, and that, too, without creating too much attention. One of their number therefore took the opportunity of the mayor riding abroad on Wednesday, the 19th July, to accost him privately and bid him and the sheriffs, and such of the aldermen as he could get together at short notice, to meet the lords of the council within an hour at the Earl of Pembroke's place at Castle Baynard. The mayor hurried back, sent for the Recorder and some of the aldermen, and with them proceeded to the place appointed, where they found the council assembled. They were informed of the intention of the lords, and the mayor was bidden to accompany them to Cheapside for the purpose of proclaiming Queen Mary. Their object soon got wind; a crowd followed them to Cheapside, and when the proclamation was made there was such a throwing up of caps and such cries of "God save Queen Mary" that nothing else could be heard. The civic authorities, as well as the lords of the council, thereupon proceeded to St. Paul's to hear a *Te Deum*; after which the lords withdrew from the city, leaving orders, however, for Queen Mary to be proclaimed in other parts of the city according to custom. The next day (20 July) they returned and dined with the mayor, sitting in council, after dinner, until four o'clock in the afternoon, whilst the church bells rang all day long. 1365

Northumberland sent to the Tower, 25 July.

As soon as Northumberland heard of the turn affairs had taken, he caused Mary to be proclaimed at Cambridge, where he happened to be quartered, "castinge up his capp after as if he had bene joyfull of it." His simulated enthusiasm, however, availed him nothing, and orders were issued for his arrest. Special precautions were taken to avoid disturbance on the day (25 July) that he passed through the city on his way to the Tower, every householder in the several wards through which he and his fellow prisoners were to pass being instructed to hold himself in readiness within doors with a clean halberd, and a bill or "pollox" for such service as the alderman might appoint. 1366 No disturbance took place, the populace contenting itself with cursing the duke and calling him traitor, and making him take off his hat as he passed through Bishopsgate and continue his journey bareheaded. 1367

Queen Mary enters the city. 3 Aug.

On the evening of the 3rd August Queen Mary made her first entry into the city, accompanied by her sister Elizabeth. She had come from Newhall, in Essex, where a few days before she had been presented with the sum of £500 in gold by a deputation of the Court of Aldermen accompanied by the Recorder. 1368 On the 2nd August it was decided that the lord mayor and his brethren should ride out the next afternoon to meet her majesty at the Bars without Aldgate, and taking their places appointed by the herald-of-arms, should accompany the royal procession. 1369 The reception which the new queen met with in the city must have been gratifying. The mayor, on approaching her, handed to her the civic sword, which was given to the Earl of Arundel to carry before her. The mayor himself bore the mace. By express permission of the Court of Aldermen a number of Florentine and other merchant strangers were allowed to attend on horseback, and to erect a pageant at Leadenhall. 1370 The whole length of the streets through which the queen had to pass on her way to the Tower had been lavishly decorated, and was lined with members of the various civic companies in their livery gowns. Nothing was omitted that could please the eye or ear. 1371

A touching scene took place as Mary was about to enter the Tower. The widow of the Duke of Somerset, to whose policy as protector Mary had offered a steady opposition, met the queen at the Tower gate, and in company with the Duke of Norfolk, Stephen Gardiner and others, who had been confined in the Tower in the late reign, knelt down and saluted her. Mary, in a charitable mood, kissed each of them, claimed them as her own prisoners, and shortly afterwards granted them their liberty. 1372

Mary releases the bishops and restores the mass.

A week later (10 Aug.) the remains of the late king were carried from Whitehall to Westminster and laid in Henry the Seventh's Chapel, the service being conducted wholly in English, the communion taking the place of the mass, and the priests being vested in a surplice only, in accordance with the provisions of the Book of Common Prayer. For a short time after Mary's accession it was thought that she would be content if the Church were restored to the position it was in at the time when Henry VIII died. It was not long before the new queen shewed this opinion to be erroneous. The Prayer Book of King Edward VI was set aside, the high altars that had been removed were restored, and mass was restored. Ridley was sent to the Tower and Bonner brought out from the Marshalsea and reinstated in the bishophric of London. Gardiner, who had been deprived of his see of

Winchester and kept prisoner in the Tower, not only recovered his freedom and his see, but was made the queen's chancellor. On the other hand, Cranmer and "Mr. Latimer" were sent to the Tower.

Disturbances in the city.

The change that was being wrought caused some little disturbance in the city. When Doctor Bourne, who had been put up by the queen to preach at Paul's Cross one Sunday in August, began to pray for the dead, and to refer to Bonner's late imprisonment, one of his hearers threw a knife at him whilst others called the preacher a liar. The queen was so angry at this that she sent for the mayor and aldermen and told them plainly that she would deprive the city of its liberties if they could not better preserve peace and good order within its walls. 1373

A few days later she issued a proclamation in which, whilst making no secret of her wish that everyone would conform to the religion "which all men knew she had of long tyme observed, and ment, God willing, to contynue the same," she deprecated men calling each other heretic or papist, but willed that everyone should follow the religion he thought best until further orders were taken. 1374 The mayor in the meantime had also issued his precept against any sermon or lecture being read other than the Divine Service appointed until the queen's further pleasure should be made known. 1375

Lest any disturbance should arise on the following Sunday (20 Aug.), when Bishop Gardiner's chaplain was to preach at Paul's Cross, the queen sent the captain of the guard with 200 men, who surrounded the pulpit, halberd in hand. The mayor, too, had ordered the livery companies to be present "to herken yf any leude or sedicious persons made any rumors" — a precaution which much pleased the queen. 1376

Election of Thomas White mayor, 29 Sept., 1553.

When Michaelmas-day (the day on which the election of the new mayor for the ensuing year was to take place) came round, the choice of the citizens fell upon Sir Thomas White. 1377 In accordance with the new order of things, the election was preceded by the celebration of mass in the Guildhall Chapel as of old.

The queen's coronation, 1 Oct.

The day after the election of the new mayor the queen passed through the city from the Tower to Whitehall for her coronation. The streets presented their usual gay appearance on this occasion, and the queen was made the recipient of the "accustomed" gift of 1,000 marks on behalf of the city. 1378 On the day of the coronation (1 Oct.) the daily service at St. Paul's had to be suspended because all the priests not under censure for Protestantism or for having married were summoned to assist at Westminster. 1379

Mary's first parliament, Oct.-Nov., 1553.

When Mary appeared before her first parliament 1380 she found her subjects in many points opposed to her. They were willing to restore the worship and practice of the Church as they existed before the death of Henry VIII, but they showed a determination neither to submit to Rome nor to restore to the Church the property of which it had been deprived. They knew, moreover, of her anxious wish to marry Philip, son of the emperor Charles V, and yet did not hesitate to present to her a petition against a foreign marriage. It was a bold step for parliament to take in those days, and showed that it was determined to win back its ancient rights and no longer to be the tool of the crown. Mary was not one likely to yield in a matter on which she had once set her heart. Rather than take its advice she dissolved parliament. The result was an insurrection.

Trial at the Guildhall of Lady Jane Grey, Cranmer and others, Nov., 1553.

In the meanwhile the aged Cranmer and the youthful Lady Jane Grey — she "that wolde a been qwene" — her husband and two of her husband's brothers had been brought to trial at the Guildhall (13 Nov). The axe was borne before them on their way from the Tower, as if in anticipation of the verdict. The Lady Jane is described as clad in a black gown, with velvet cap and black hood, having a black velvet book hanging at her girdle, whilst she carried another in her hand. 1381 Each of the accused pleaded guilty, and sentence of death was passed; its execution was, however, delayed owing to the outbreak known as Wyatt's Rebellion.

Outbreak of Wyatt's Rebellion. Jan., 1554.

The ostensible cause of the rebellion was the queen's determination at all hazards to marry Philip, whose ambassadors arrived at the opening of the new year (1554). The civic authorities had been warned to treat them handsomely, a warning which was scarcely necessary, for the citizens have never allowed political differences to interfere with their hospitality; and accordingly one of the ambassadors was lodged at Durham Place, near Charing Cross, another at the Duke of Suffolk's house hard by, whilst a third shared apartments with the chancellor "Nigro" (Philip Negri) in Sir Richard Sackville's house at the conduit in Fleet Street. To each and all of the guests the City sent presents of wax, torches, flour and every kind of meat, game and poultry. 1382 Formal announcement of the intended match was made by the chancellor on the 14th January, but it was received with every sign of discontent and misgiving, "yea and therat allmost eche man was abashed, loking daylie for worse mattiers to growe shortly after." 1383 The following day (15 Jan.)—the day on which the rebellion under Wyatt broke out in Kent, to be followed by risings in Devonshire and Norfolk—the mayor and aldermen were summoned to court and ordered to bring with them forty of the chief commoners of the city, when the lord chancellor informed them of the queen's intention, and exhorted them as obedient subjects to accept her grace's pleasure and to remain content and quiet. He warned them, at the same time, to see that the queen's wishes respecting religious services in the city were strictly carried out, on pain of incurring her high indignation. 1384

The city put into a state of defence.

Steps were taken for putting the city into a proper state of defence. The civic companies were ordered to set watches as on similar critical occasions, and no gunpowder, weapons or other munitions of war were allowed to be sent out of the city. Chains were set up at the bridge-foot and at the corner of New Fish Street. The borough of Southwark was called upon to provide eighty tall and able men, well harnessed and weaponed, for the safeguard of the queen's person and of the city, 1385 whilst the livery companies at a few hours' notice furnished a force of 500 men to be speedily despatched by water to Gravesend. 1386

The queen's speech at the Guildhall, 1 Feb., 1554.

Whatever faults Queen Mary had, she was by no means deficient in courage. On the same day (1 Feb.) that Wyatt appeared with his forces at Southwark, she came to the Guildhall 1387 and there addressed a spirited harangue to the assembled citizens. 1388 She plainly told them that her proposed marriage was but a Spanish cloak to cover the real purpose of the rebellion, which was aimed against her religion. She was their queen, and they had sworn allegiance to her; they surely would not allow her to fall into the hands of so vile a traitor as Wyatt was. As for her marriage, it had been arranged with the full knowledge of the lords of the council, as one of expediency for the realm. Passion had no part in the matter. She had hitherto, she thanked God, lived a virgin, and doubted not she could, if necessary, live so still. At the close of her speech, which, we are told, was delivered in a loud voice so that all might hear, she bade the citizens to pluck up heart and not to fear the rebels any more than she did. She then quitted the hall and went up into the aldermen's council chamber and there refreshed herself, after which she rode through Bucklersbury to the Vintry, where she took barge to Westminster.

In the meantime the Spanish ambassadors had taken fright at Wyatt's approach and had "sped themselves awaie by water, and that with all hast." 1389 Many inhabitants of the city had also deserted their fellow burgesses at this critical time, and their names were submitted to the Court of Aldermen for subsequent enquiry. 1390 They were, according to Foxe, afraid of being entrapped by the queen and perhaps put to death.

A force of 1,000 men raised in the city.

In response to the queen's speech the citizens at once set to work to raise a force of 1,000 men for the defence of the city, the mayor and aldermen each in his own ward taking a muster. So busy was everyone on Candlemas-day (2 Feb.) that the civic authorities omitted to attend the afternoon service at St. Paul's, and the mayor's serving-men waited upon him at dinner ready harnessed. 1391 Even the lawyers at Westminster "pleaded in harness." 1392

Wyatt and his followers before Ludgate.

Wyatt made prisoner and lodged in the Tower.

The defensive precautions taken by the mayor and aldermen were sufficient to prevent Wyatt making good his entry into the city by Southwark and London Bridge. Foiled in this direction he sought to approach the city from another side, but had to march as far as Kingston before he could cross the Thames. Many of his followers in the meantime deserted him. 1393 Nevertheless he continued to make his way, with but little opposition, to Ludgate, which, contrary to his expectation, he found shut in his face. He had been recognised by a tailor of Watling Street, who seeing the force approaching cried, "I know that theys be Wyettes ancienttes," and forthwith closed the gate. 1394 That Wyatt had supporters in the city may be gathered from the half-hearted opposition that he met with in Southwark, as well as from the fact that many of the soldiers raised in the city and neighbourhood deserted to Wyatt at the outset of the rebellion. 1395 Wyatt himself exhibited no little disappointment at finding Ludgate closed against him instead of the aid which he evidently had expected. "I have kept touch" said he, as he turned his back on the city. 1396 He had scarcely reached Temple Bar before he was overcome by a superior force and yielded himself a prisoner. After a short stay at Whitehall he was removed to the Tower.

Execution of Lady Jane Grey, Wyatt and others.

The failure of the revolt was fatal to Lady Jane Grey, and she was beheaded within the Tower (12 Feb.) almost at the same time that her husband was being executed outside on Tower Hill. By the strange irony of fortune, it fell to the lot of Thomas Offley to perform the duties of sheriff at Dudley's execution, although he had himself been one of the supporters of the Lady Jane in her claim to the crown. For the next few days the city presented a sad spectacle; whichever way one turned there was to be seen a gibbet with its wretched burden, whilst the city's gates bristled with human heads. 1397 Wyatt himself was one of the last to suffer, being brought to the block on Tower Hill on the 11th April. His head and a portion of his body, after being exposed on gallows, were taken away by his friends for decent burial. 1398

Measures for preserving the peace.

On the 17th February proclamation was made for all strangers to leave the realm, on the ground that they sowed the seeds of their "malycyouse doctryne and lewde conversacioun" among the queen's good subjects; 1399 and this had been followed in the city by precepts to each alderman to call before him all the householders of his ward, both rich and poor, on Wednesday the 7th March, at six o'clock in the morning, and strictly charge them that they, their wives, their children and servants behave themselves in all things and more especially in matters of religion, following the example of the queen herself. All offenders were to be reported forthwith. 1400

The lord mayor before the Star Chamber.

A report having got abroad in the city that the lords of the council had endeavoured to extract a confession from Wyatt implicating the Princess Elizabeth in the late rebellion, the mayor was ordered by Bishop Gardiner to bring up the originator of the rumour before the Star Chamber. When Sir Thomas White appeared with the culprit, one Richard Cut by name, a servant to a grocer in the city, he was soundly rated by Gardiner for not having himself punished the offender, and when he replied that the party was there present for the Star Chamber to deal with according to its pleasure, was again rebuked:—"My lord, take heed to your charge, the Citie of London is a whirlepoole and a sinke of evill rumors, there they be bred, and from thence spred into all parts of the realme." 1401 Cut paid the penalty for his love of gossip by being made to stand two days in the pillory and by the loss of his ears. 1402

Demand of money from the city, 1554.

The suppression of the revolt left Mary at liberty to carry out her matrimonial design. But before accomplishing this she was determined to place such a garrison in or near London as should prevent similar outbreaks in future. For this purpose she applied to the citizens for a sum of 6,000 marks. Thus called upon to supply a rod for their own backs, the citizens demurred. They at first proposed to offer the sum of 1,000 marks, or at the most £1,000; they afterwards agreed to contribute double the first mentioned sum, 1403 and this was accepted. The money was raised by contributions from the different livery companies, the Merchant Taylors, the Mercers, the Grocers, the Drapers, the Fishmongers, the Goldsmiths, and the Haberdashers being called upon to subscribe the sum of £100 respectively, whilst the rest of the companies paid sums varying from £80 to forty shillings. 1404 No sooner had the citizens satisfied the queen in this respect than they were called upon to send 200 soldiers to Gillingham, in Kent, there to be embarked for foreign service under the Lord Admiral. The City again demurred, and asked to be excused the necessity of forwarding the men beyond Billingsgate or the Tower Wharf and also of providing them with accoutrements. It was to no purpose, both men and accoutrements had to be found. 1405 On the 10th April the chamberlain received orders to see that the city's artillery was in readiness and to increase the store of gunpowder. 1406 Wyatt was to be executed the next day, and these orders were probably given in anticipation of a disturbance.

Trial at the Guildhall of Nicholas Throckmorton, 17 April.

That Wyatt still had friends in the city is shown by the bold attitude taken up by the jury in the trial (17 April) of one of his accomplices, Nicholas Throckmorton, against whom they brought in a verdict of not guilty. 1407 For this they were bound over to appear before the Star Chamber. Four of the twelve made submission; the rest, among whom were Thomas Whetstone, a haberdasher, and Emanuel Lucar, a merchant tailor, were committed some to the Tower and the rest to the Fleet, where they remained for six months. In the meantime the Court of Aldermen wrote (19 July) to the council in their favour, but with little success. 1408 A month later (19 August) a deputation waited on the Court of Aldermen for advice as to what future steps had best be taken for obtaining the release of their brethren in the Fleet, when they were told that the wives of the prisoners or the prisoners' friends should first make suit to the council for their release, after which the court would see what they could do. 1409 At length the prisoners were summoned once more (26 Oct.) before the Star Chamber, when they one and all declared that they had only acted in accordance with their conscience, whilst Lucar, more outspoken than the rest, asserted that "they had done in the matter like honest men and true and faithful subjects." Such plain speaking ill suited the judges, who thereupon condemned the offenders to a fine of 1,000 marks apiece and imprisonment until further order. Eventually five out of the eight were discharged (12 December) on payment of a fine of £220, and ten days later the rest regained their liberty on payment of £60 apiece. 1410

The queen's marriage, July, 1554.

A parliament which met in April (1554) 1411 gave its consent to Mary's marriage with Philip, but refused to re-enact the old statutes for the persecution of heretics. On the 19th July Philip landed at Southampton, and on the 21st Mary herself notified the event to the citizens of London, 1412 who for some time past had been making preparations for giving both queen and king a fitting reception, and who immediately on receipt of the news of Philip's landing caused bonfires to be lighted in the streets. 1413

The passage of the king and queen through the city, 19 Aug.

Mary rode down to Winchester to meet Philip, 1414 and on the 25th became his wife. It was not until the 17th August that the royal pair approached the city. On that day they came by water from Richmond to Southwark, the king in one barge, the queen in another. After taking refreshment at the Bishop of Winchester's palace, and killing a buck or two in the bishop's park, they retired to rest. 1415 Special orders were given to the aldermen to keep a good and substantial double watch in the city from nine o'clock in the evening (17 Aug.) until five o'clock the next morning, such watch to continue until further notice. 1416 The authorities differ widely as to the precise day on which the royal party passed through the city. The city's own records point to the afternoon of Sunday the 19th August as the day. On the morning of that day the Court of Aldermen sat, and a letter from the queen commending them for their forwardness in "making shewes of honour and gladnes" for the occasion was read to the wardens of all the companies for them to communicate to the members. The wardens were further enjoined to give strict orders to the members of their several companies to honestly use and entreat the Spaniards in all things, both at their coming in with the king and queen and ever afterwards. The same morning a speech which the Recorder had prepared for the occasion in English was handed over to the master of St. Paul's School to be turned into Latin. None too much time was allowed the worthy pedagogue for the purpose, for he was to give it back that same afternoon so that the Recorder might "make and pronounce yt to the kinges majesty at his comynge in." 1417

A curious incident is related in connection with the royal procession through the city. The conduit in Gracious Church Street, which had been newly painted and gilded, bore representations of the "nine worthies," and among them Henry the Eighth and Edward the Sixth. Instead of carrying a sword or mace like the rest, Henry had been portrayed with a sceptre in one hand and a book bearing the inscription *Verbum Dei* in the other. This catching the eye of Bishop Gardiner as he passed in the royal train, he was very wroth and sent for the painter, asked him by whose orders he had so depicted the king, called him "traitor" and threatened him with the Fleet prison. The poor painter, who for the first time had been made to realise the change that was taking place, pleaded that what he had done had been done in all innocence, and hastened to rectify his mistake by removing the bible from the picture and substituting in its place a pair of gloves. 1418

The reconciliation with Rome, 1554.

In November (1554) a new parliament 1419 was called, which proved more ready than the last to comply with the queen's wishes. It re-enacted the statutes for burning heretics and agreed to a reconciliation of the Church of England with the See of Rome, but it refused to sanction the surrender of Church lands. Bonner had already taken steps to purge his diocese of heresy by issuing a series of articles (14 Sept.) to which every inhabitant, clerical and lay, was expected to conform. 1420 That there was room for improvement in matters touching religion and public decorum there is no doubt, otherwise there would have been no need of proclamations such as those against the arrest of persons whilst conducting service in church, 1421 against wrangling over passages of scripture in common taverns and victualling houses, 1422 or against carrying of baskets of provisions and leading mules, horses or other beasts through St. Paul's. 1423

The mayor and aldermen endeavoured to set a good example by constant attendance at the services and by joining in processions at St. Paul's as in former days. 1424 The law forbidding the eating of meat in Lent, except by special licence, was vigorously enforced. 1425 Ale-houses and taverns were closed on Sundays and holy days, and interludes were forbidden. 1426

Opposition to the reestablishment of the old religion.

Nevertheless the attempt to restore the old worship within the city was often met with scornful mockery, sometimes attended with violence. A dead cat, for instance, was one day found hanging in Cheapside, its head shorn in imitation of a priest's tonsure, and its body clothed in a mock ecclesiastical vestment, with cross before and behind, whilst a piece of white paper to represent a singing-cake was placed between its forefeet, which had been tied together. Bonner was very angry at this travesty of religion, and caused the effigy to be publicly displayed at Paul's Cross during sermon time. A reward of twenty marks was offered for the discovery of this atrocious act, but with what success we do not know. 1427

On another occasion, when the Holy Sacrament was being carried in solemn procession through Smithfield on Corpus Christi-day (24 May), an attempt was made to knock the holy elements out of the hands of the priest. The offender was taken to Newgate, where he feigned to be mad. 1428 Again, on the following Easter-day a priest was fiercely attacked by a man with a wood-knife whilst administering the sacrament in the church of St. Margaret, Westminster. The culprit was seized, and after trial and conviction paid the penalty of his crime by being burned at the stake. 1429 A pudding was once offered to a priest whilst walking in a religious procession, 1430 the offender being afterwards whipt at the "Post of

Reformation," which had been set up in Cheapside in 1553. 1431 But all this defiance shown to Mary's attempt to restore the old worship only led her to exercise more drastic methods for accomplishing her purpose.

The Marian persecution, 1555.

By the opening of 1555 her own strong personal will had overcome the conciliatory policy of her husband, who was content to restrain his fanaticism within the limits of expediency, and the Marian persecution commenced. On the 25th January a proclamation was issued in the name of the king and queen, and bearing the signature of William Blackwell, the town clerk of the city, enjoining the lighting of bonfires that afternoon in various places in token of great joy and gladness for the abolition of sundry great sins, errors and heresies which lately had arisen within the realm of England, and for the quiet renovation and restitution of the true Catholic faith of Christ and his holy religion. 1432 This proclamation was but a prelude to other fires lighted for a very different purpose, which the mind even at this day cannot contemplate without a shudder. The first victim of the flames for conscience sake was John Rogers, once vicar of St. Sepulchre's church and prebendary of St. Paul's. He was burnt in Smithfield "for gret herysy" in February of this year, in which month Hooper, who had been deprived of his bishopric of Gloucester, suffered the same fate in his own cathedral city. 1433 In the following May another city vicar, John Cardmaker, otherwise known as John Taylor of St. Bride's, who had been a reader at St. Paul's and had publicly lectured against the real presence, was burnt in Smithfield with John Warne, an "upholder" of Walbrook. 1434

Few weeks passed without the fire claiming some human victim either in London or the provinces. On the 9th February Thomas Tomkins, a godly and charitable weaver of Shoreditch, and William Hunter, a young London apprentice, were with four others condemned to the stake. The two named met their fate in Smithfield, one on the 16th March and the other on the 26th. The rest were removed into Essex and there consigned to the flames, three of them in March and one in the following June. 1435

In October Bishops Latimer and Ridley were burnt at Oxford. "Be of good comfort, Master Ridley, and play the man" — cried Latimer encouragingly to his fellow sufferer—"we shall this day light such a candle, by God's grace, in England as I trust shall never be put out." In March of the following year (1556) Cranmer, after some display of weakness, suffered the same fate, on the same spot, and with no less fortitude. And thus for two years more the fires were kept alive in London and in the country; the Lollard's tower at St. Paul's serving as a prison for heretics, 1436 and proving more often than not but a step to Smithfield.

Renewed opposition to strangers in the city.

Throughout Mary's reign the strife between the citizens and merchant strangers was renewed. She had herself added to the evil by her marriage with Philip, causing the city to be flooded with Spaniards, who took up their abode in the halls of the civic companies. 1437 A rumour got abroad early in September, 1554, that 12,000 Spaniards were coming over "to fethe the crown," 1438 and this accounts for precepts being sent to the several aldermen of the city on the 27th September enjoining them to make a return of the number of foreigners that had come to reside in their ward during the past nine or ten days, and whence they came. 1439 The favour shown by the Crown to the merchants of the Steelyard was especially annoying to the freemen of the city. 1440 It was to little purpose that the mayor and aldermen issued orders from time to time against giving work to foreigners and prohibiting all such from opening shops within the city. 1441 The struggle between citizen and stranger still went on. In 1557 the corporation made an effort to induce the king and queen to revoke the favours shown to the merchants of the Steelyard in prejudice of the liberties of the city, 1442 and eventually the privileges were revoked on the ground that the merchants of the Hanse had not kept faith with the Crown. 1443 In the same year the exclusiveness entertained by the citizens towards foreigners made itself felt more particularly against that class of foreigner which kept open school in the city for teaching writing. Certain scriveners, freemen of the city, made a complaint before the Court of Aldermen against foreigners keeping writing-school within the city and its liberties. 1444 The chamberlain's conduct of shutting in the shop windows of foreigners teaching children to write was approved by the mayor and aldermen, 1445 whilst freemen were allowed to keep open school provided they entered into a bond not to engross deeds. 1446 Occasionally foreigners were successful in obtaining licences from the civic authorities for teaching writing, but it was only on condition they kept their lower windows closed. 1447

Philip leaves England, 4 Sept., 1555.

The queen obtains a City loan of £6,000, Aug., 1556.

War declared against France, 7 June, 1557.

In the meantime the disposition of the queen towards heretics became more relentless in proportion as her temper became more soured from ill-health, by disappointment in not having off-spring, and by the increasing neglect of her by her husband. Tired of her importunate love and jealousy, Philip took the first opportunity of quitting her side and crossed over to the continent (4 Sept., 1555) on a visit to the Emperor Charles. The abdication of the latter towards the close of 1556 made Philip master of the richest and most extensive dominions in Europe, and his greatest wish at the time was to engage England in the war which was kindled between Spain and France. In this he received the support of Mary, who had in August (1556) succeeded in obtaining a loan from the city of £6,000. 1448 The seizure of the castle of Scarborough by Thomas Stafford, 1449 second son of Lord Stafford, in which he was reported to have received encouragement from the King of France, was made a *casus belli*, and Henry was proclaimed an open enemy (7 June, 1557). 1450 French subjects were allowed forty days to quit the country, and letters of marque were issued by proclamation on the 9th June. 1451 On the 5th July Philip once more left England for Flanders, 1452 having succeeded in the object for which he had come, viz., the declaration of war against France.

A City contingent joins the expedition to France.

The citizens of London at once began to take stock of their munitions of war. On the 22nd June the Chamberlain was instructed to prepare with all convenient speed four dozen good *splentes* and as many good *sallettes* or *sculles* for the city's use, and to cause a bowyer to "peruse" the city's bows and to put them in such good order that they might be serviceable when required. 1453 In the following month a large force crossed over to France under the leadership of Lords Pembroke, Montagu and Clinton. To this force the City of London contributed a contingent of 500 men, the best (according to Machyn 1454) that had ever been sent. They mustered at the Leadenhall on the 16th July in the presence of Sir Thomas Offley, 1455 the mayor, the sheriffs and Sir Richard Lee, and were conveyed thence by water to Gravesend and Rochester under the charge of ten officers, whose names are duly recorded. 1456

The City called upon to furnish another contingent of 1,000 men, 31 July.

On the last day of July the queen informed the civic authorities by letter of the departure of her "deerest lord and husband" to pursue the enemy in France, and desired them to get in readiness 1,000 men, a portion of whom were to be horsemen, well horsed and armed, and the rest to be archers, pikes and billmen. The force was to be ready by the 16th August at the latest, after which date it was to be prepared to set out at a day's notice. The letter contained a schedule of names of individuals to whom the queen had made special application, and these were not to be called upon by the municipal officers to make any contribution, neither were the tenants of those noblemen and gentlemen already on active service in France. 1457

The citizens make demur, but in vain.

The Court of Aldermen was taken aback at such a demand coming so soon after the setting out of the previous force, and on the 4th August it instructed the Recorder and one of the sheriffs to repair to the queen's council "for the good and suer understandyng of her majesty's pleasure" in the matter. The deputation was further instructed to remind the lords of the council not only of the ancient liberties and franchises of the city on the point, but also of the city's lack of power to furnish a number of men exceeding any it had ever been called upon to furnish before. 1458 It was all to no purpose; the men had to be provided; and the matter having been fully explained to the wardens of the several livery companies, they succeeded in raising the force required. 1459

The French king defeated at St. Quentin, 27 Aug., 1557.

The defeat of the French king at St. Quentin was celebrated in the city by a solemn procession to St. Paul's, in which figured the mayor and aldermen in their scarlet gowns. 1460 The joy of the citizens was shortlived. Philip's caution did not allow him to avail himself of the opportunity thus offered him of marching on the French capital, and before the end of the year matters had taken a different turn.

The loss of Calais, 7 Jan., 1558.

A city force despatched, 24 Jan., 1558.

In December a Spaniard named Ferdinando Lygons was commissioned to raise 300 mounted archers in the city of London and county of Middlesex. 1461 At the opening of the new year (2 Jan., 1558) the queen wrote to the corporation desiring to be at once furnished with 500 men out of the 1,000 men the city had been ordered to keep in readiness since July. As the matter was urgent they were not to wait to supply the men with coats. 1462 The force was required for the defence of Calais, which was now in a critical position. On the 9th January another letter was sent by Mary marked, *Hast, Hast Post, Hast, For lief, For lief, For lief, For lief!* demanding the full contingent of 1,000 men. 1463 Calais had fallen two days before, 1464 and Mary was determined not to rest until the town had been recovered. Diligent search was at once instituted throughout the city for all persons, strangers as well as freemen, capable of wearing harness; 1465 and the livery companies and fellowships were called upon to provide double the number of men they had furnished in July last. 1466 On the 13th the queen wrote to say that a violent storm, which had occurred on the night of the 10th January, had so crippled the fleet that her forces could not be conveyed across the channel; the civic authorities were therefore to withhold sending their force to the sea-coast until further orders, but to keep the same in readiness to start at an hour's notice. 1467 On the 19th January the citizens were informed by letter that Philip's forces were on their way to Flanders, under the Duke of Savoy, and that the channel was being kept open by a fleet under Don Luis Carvaial. One half of the force of 1,000 men, furnished with armour and weapons and coats of white welted with green and red crosses, was to be despatched to Dover by the end of the month, thence to sail for Dunkirk for service under the Earl of Rutland. The City was to take especial care that the contingent should be chosen from the handsomest and best picked men, and superior to those last sent. 1468 The force mustered at the Leadenhall, the 24th January, for inspection by the mayor, and at five o'clock in the evening were delivered over to the captains for shipment. 1469 Three days later the lords of the council instructed the mayor to make a return of the number of foreigners residing still within the city, and to make proclamation on the next market day that it should be lawful thenceforth for anyone to seize the persons of Frenchmen who had not avoided the city pursuant to a previous order, and to confiscate their goods and chattels to his own proper use. 1470

A city loan of £20,000, March, 1558.

Mary succeeded in March in raising a loan in the city of £20,000 (she had asked for 100,000 marks or £75,000 1471) on the security of the crown lands. The loan bore interest at the rate of twelve per cent., and a special dispensation was granted to avoid the penalties of the Usury Act. 1472 The money was raised by assessment on the livery companies. On the 16th March the Court of Aldermen summoned the wardens of the twelve principal companies to attend at the Guildhall at eight o'clock the next morning, in order that they might learn how much the lords of the council had "**tottyd**" against each of them towards the loan. The smaller companies were to attend in the afternoon of the same day in order to be informed of the sums the Court of Aldermen deemed fit that each should contribute to assist their wealthier brethren. The total amount subscribed by the greater companies was £16,983 6s. 8d., of which the Mercers contributed £3,275. The lesser companies subscribed £1,310, in sums varying from £30 to £500. 1473

Death of Mary, 17 Nov., 1558.

It is probable that Mary wanted this loan to enable her to prosecute the war. The country was not disposed, however, to assist her in this direction. The people were afraid of rendering Philip too powerful. Disappointed both in her public and domestic life, she fell a victim to dropsy and died on the 17th November—"wondering why all that she had done, as she believed on God's behalf, had been followed by failure on every side—by the desertion of her husband, and the hatred of her subjects." The loss of Calais so much affected her that she declared that the name of the town would be found impressed upon her heart after death. On the occasion of her funeral the City put in its customary claim for black livery cloth, but more than one application had to be made before the cloth was forthcoming. 1474

CHAPTER XVII.

The ascension of Elizabeth, 17 Nov., 1558.

The accession of Elizabeth, after the gloomy reign of her sister, was welcomed by none more joyfully than by the citizens of London, who continued to commemorate the day with bonfires and general rejoicing long after the queen had been laid in her grave. 1475 When news was brought of her sister's death Elizabeth was at Hatfield. Within a week she removed to London and took up her abode at the Charterhouse. The sheriffs went out to meet her as far as the boundary of the county of Middlesex, the limit of their jurisdiction, dressed in coats of velvet, with their chains about their necks and white rods in their hands. Having first kissed their rods, they handed them to the queen, who immediately returned them, and the sheriffs thereupon joined the gentlemen of the cavalcade and rode before her majesty until they met Sir Thomas Leigh, 1476 the mayor, and his brethren the aldermen. The sheriffs then fell back and took their places among the aldermen. 1477 From the Charterhouse she removed after a stay of a few days to the Tower, amid the blare of trumpets, the singing of children and the firing of ordnance.

The queen's coronation, 15 Jan., 1559.

The Court of Common Council (21 Nov.) agreed to levy two fifteenths on the inhabitants of the city for the customary present to be given the new queen on her passing through the city to her coronation, which was to take place on the 15th January following, as well as for defraying the costs of pageants on the occasion. 1478 Committees were appointed to see that the several conduits, the Standard and Cross in Cheap, and other parts of the city were seemly trimmed and decked with pageants, fine paintings and rich cloth of Arras, silver and gold, as at the coronation of Queen Mary, and better still if it conveniently could be done. 1479 Among those appointed to devise pageants for the occasion and to act as masters of the ceremony was Richard Grafton, the printer. 1480 Eight commoners were appointed by the Court of Aldermen (17 Dec.) to attend upon the chief butler of England at the cupboard at the coronation banquet. 1481

A strike among the painters.

A curious instance of a strike among painters is recorded at this time. The painters of the city, we are told, utterly refused to fresh paint and trim the great conduit in Cheap for the coronation for the sum of twenty marks. This being the case, the surveyors of the city were instructed to cause the same to be covered with cloth of Arras having escutcheons of the queen's Arms finely made and set therein, and the wardens of the Painters' Company were called upon to render assistance with advice and men for reasonable remuneration. 1482

Elizabeth's policy of moderation, 1558.

The main object which Elizabeth kept before her eyes, from first to last, was the preservation of peace—peace within the Church and without. Her natural inclination was towards the more ornate ritual of the Roman Church, but the necessity she was under of gaining the support of the Protestants, whom even the fires of Smithfield had failed to suppress, inspired restraint. All her actions were marked with caution and deliberation. From the day of her accession religious persecution in its worst form ceased. Non-conformity was no longer punished by death. Preachers who took advantage of the lull which followed the Marian persecution and resumed disputatious sermons, as they did more especially in the city, were silenced by royal proclamation, 1483 which ordered them to confine themselves to reading the gospel and epistle for the day, and the Ten Commandments, in the vulgar tongue, without adding any comment. They were further ordered to make use of no public prayer, rite or ceremony other than that already accepted until parliament should ordain otherwise.

The Act of Uniformity and Supremacy, 1558.

Parliament met in January, 1559, and at once acknowledged the queen's legitimacy and her title to the crown, an acknowledgment which she had failed to obtain from the Pope. An Act of Uniformity was passed forbidding the use of any form of public prayer other than that set out in the last Prayer Book of Edward VI, amended in those particulars which savoured of ultra-Protestantism. The same parliament also passed an Act of Supremacy, which dropt the title of supreme head of the Church with reference to the queen, but still upheld the ancient jurisdiction of the Crown over all ecclesiastics. Having accomplished this much, parliament was dissolved (8 May).

The restoration of the Prayer Book and abolition of the Mass, 1559.

On the following Whitsunday (14 May) Divine Service was conducted in the city in English according to the Book of Common Prayer. 1484 Commissioners were appointed in July "to ride about the realm for the establishing of true religion," four being nominated for the city, whose duty it was to call before them divers persons of every parish and make them swear to observe "certain injunctions newly set out in print." 1485 The election of a new mayor at Michaelmas was followed by the celebration of a "communion" in the Guildhall Chapel." 1486

Ultra-Protestant reformers in the city, 1559.

The success of Elizabeth's policy was unfortunately marred by the excess of zeal displayed by the reformers. More especially was this the case in the city of London. Had the inhabitants bent their energy towards putting down the disgraceful trafficking that went on within the very walls of their cathedral church, shutting up gambling houses, and stopping interludes and plays which made a jest of religion, instead of leaving such abuses to be corrected by royal proclamation, 1487 their conduct would have met with universal approbation. Instead of this they again set to work pulling down roods, smashing up ancient tombs and committing to the flames vestments and service books—the work of years of artistic labour 1488— until the wanton destruction was restricted, if not altogether stopped, by the queen's orders. 1489

The claims of Mary Stuart, 1559-1560.

In the meantime the state of affairs with France and Scotland demanded Elizabeth's attention. The marriage of Mary Stuart with the Dauphin of France had taken place in April, 1558, and the sudden death of Henry II of France by an accident at a tournament had soon afterwards raised her and her husband to the throne. Mary now assumed the arms and style of Queen of England, and the life-long quarrel between her and Elizabeth was about to commence. By the end of the year (1559) Mary had collected a sufficient force at her back to render her mistress of Scotland. In the following January a French fleet was ready to set sail. Nevertheless Elizabeth refused to take any active measures to meet the enemy and to prevent them effecting a landing. On the 6th she caused proclamation to be made for French subjects to be allowed perfect freedom as in time of peace, but English vessels were to be held in readiness "untill yt maye appeare to what ende the greate preparaciouns of Fraunce do entende." 1490 Long after the appearance of a French fleet off the coast of Scotland, and when it had been driven to take refuge in Leith harbour, Elizabeth still declared her intention of keeping, if possible, on friendly terms with France if only the "insolent titles and claims" of Francis and Mary might cease and Scotland left in peace. 1491 With the aid of soldiers and seamen provided by the City 1492 the French were forced to surrender, and, by a treaty signed at Edinburgh, agreed to leave Scotland and to acknowledge Elizabeth's right to the English crown.

The French war, 1562-1564.

In 1561 Mary, who had declined to recognise the treaty of Edinburgh from the first, returned to Scotland, in spite of Elizabeth's prohibition, and soon succeeded in drawing over many Protestants to her side. In the following year an opportunity offered itself to Elizabeth for striking a blow at her rival—not in Scotland, but in France. A civil war had broken out between the French Protestants—or Huguenots, as they were called—and their Catholic fellow-subjects, and Elizabeth promised (Sept., 1562) to assist the leaders of the Huguenots on condition that Havre—or Newhaven, as the place was then known—was surrendered to her as security for the fulfilment of a promise to surrender Calais. The queen (23 July, 1562) applied by letter to the City of London for a force of 600 men to be held in readiness to march at a moment's notice. She had determined, the letter said, to put the sea coast into a "fencible arraye of warre." 1493 The men were ordered to muster at the Leadenhall on the 18th September. 1494 The aim and object of the expedition was set out in a "boke" or proclamation. 1495

Soldiers for the defence of Havre. 1563.

In 1563 a peace was patched up, and the Catholics and Huguenots united in demanding from Elizabeth the restoration of Havre. The queen refused to surrender the town, and again called upon the City of London to furnish her with 1,000 men for the purpose of enabling her to secure Havre, and to compel the French to surrender Calais as promised. 1496 The Court of Aldermen hesitated to raise so large a force, and sent a deputation of three of their court to wait upon the lords of the Privy Council the same afternoon, with a view to having the number reduced to 500 on the ground that the City had supplied so many soldiers during the past year. 1497 The deputation having reported to the court the next day (3 July) that the Privy Council would make no abatement in the number of soldiers to be furnished, it was agreed to renew the application. 1498 Again the City's request was refused, and the full number of 1,000 men was apportioned among the livery companies. 1499 The citizens, jealous as they always were of the stranger within their gates, availed themselves of a too literal interpretation of a royal proclamation and seized all the Frenchmen they could find in the city with all their belongings. They even went so far as to attack the house of the French ambassador, and would probably have gone yet further lengths had they not been stopt by peremptory orders from the queen. 1500

On the 8th July the City was informed by letter from the queen that the French had already commenced the siege of Havre, and was asked to have 400 out of the 1,000 men ready to set sail with Lord Clinton by the 16th. 1501 This letter was immediately followed by another from Lord Clinton summoning every inhabitant of the city "usinge the exercise of eny kynde of water crafte" before the lord high admiral or his deputy at Deptford on a certain day. 1502 The Common Hunt, the city's water-bailiffs, two sergeants-at-mace and two sheriff's officers were appointed by the Court of Aldermen to "conduct" the city's contingent to the fleet lying in the Thames. 1503

The loss of Havre, July, 1563.

Before the end of July Havre was lost. 1504 The garrison had been attacked by a plague, which for more than a twelvemonth had been rampant in London, 1505 and the Earl of Warwick, the commander of the town, found himself compelled to accept such terms as he could obtain. The garrison was allowed to leave with all munitions of war. Whilst proclaiming to her subjects the surrender of the town—not through any cowardice on the part of the garrison, but owing to a "plage of infectuous mortall sickness" inflicted by the Almighty—Elizabeth pleaded for tender care and charity to be shown to the soldiers on their return, due precaution being taken by the principal officers of every city, town and parish against the spread of infection. 1506

Peace between England and France signed, 13 April, 1564.

The approaching end of the war with France is foreshadowed by an order of the Court of Aldermen (25 Nov., 1563) touching the re-delivery to the various civic companies of the "harness" which they severally provided for the war, and which had been forwarded from Portsmouth and was lying in the Guildhall Chapel. 1507 Peace was signed on the 13th April, 1564, and on the 31st July a proclamation was issued for disbanding the navy. 1508 Throughout the war Elizabeth had been careful to keep on good terms with Spain, and English vessels found molesting Spanish ships under pretext of searching for French goods were ordered to be arrested. 1509 An interruption of commerce with Flanders had been threatened, owing to the Duchess of Parma having forbidden the importation of English woollen cloth into the Low Countries for fear of infection from the plague, but Elizabeth retaliated by closing English ports to all Flemish vessels, and matters were accommodated. 1510

The restoration of St. Paul's Cathedral, 1561-1565.

The period of peace and tranquillity which ensued enabled the citizens to bestow more attention on their own affairs. Their cathedral stood in urgent need of repairs. Its steeple had been struck by lightning in 1561, and 3,000 marks had already been expended on its restoration. 1511 An application to the City from the lord treasurer in 1565 for a sum of £300 towards roofing one of the aisles of the cathedral came as a surprise to the Court of Aldermen, who caused enquiries to be made as to the receipt and delivery of contributions already made, and returned for answer that the City of London had long ago delivered "all such mony as the sayd cyty dyd at eny tyme grant or agree to geve or paye towards the sayd work." His lordship was desired "no further to charge or burden the sayd cytye wth the payment of any more mony towards the sayd work." 1512 Nevertheless the City was called upon for a further contribution two years later (June, 1567), when negotiations were entered into between the City, the Bishop of London and the Dean and Chapter of Saint Paul's, which ended in the Corporation agreeing to find forty foders of lead for roofing the south aisle of the cathedral, and lending a sum of £150 to the bishop and the dean and chapter, on condition the latter granted a further lease to the City of the manor of Finsbury for a term of 200 years beyond the term yet unexpired. 1513 Whilst repairs were being carried out in the cathedral itself, something was also being done outside the building to render the accommodation for hearing the sermons preached at Paul's Cross more convenient for the mayor and aldermen and municipal officers. A gutter which conducted rainwater upon the heads of the lord mayor's suite at sermon time was removed; the bench on which the civic officials sat was enlarged for their better convenience, and places erected for the accommodation of aldermen's wives. 1514

Sir Thomas Gresham and the City Burse. 1565-1566.

The rapid increase of commerce under the fostering care of Elizabeth rendered the erection of a Burse or Exchange for the accommodation of merchants "to treate of their feate of merchandyzes" a pressing necessity. The matter had been mooted thirty years before, but little had been done beyond ascertaining the opinion of merchants as to the most convenient site. 1515 The project, however, took root in the mind of Sir Richard Gresham, an alderman of the city, whose business had occasionally carried him to Antwerp, where he became familiar with the Burse that had been recently set up there, and in 1537 (the year that he was elected mayor) he forwarded to Thomas Cromwell, then lord privy seal, a design for a similar Burse to be erected in London. Finding little or no attention paid to his communication he again (25 July, 1538) wrote to Cromwell suggesting the erection of a Burse in Lombard Street—the site favoured by city merchants—at a cost of £2,000. If the lord privy seal would but bring pressure to bear upon Sir George Monoux, a brother alderman but a man of "noe gentyll nature," to part with certain property at cost price, he (Gresham) would undertake to raise £1,000 towards the building before he went out of office, and he would himself carry Cromwell's letter to Monoux and "handle him" as best he could. 1516 This application had the desired effect. On the 13th August Henry VIII addressed a letter to Monoux desiring him to dispose of certain tenements about Lombard Street which were required for the commonweal of merchants of the city, and to come to terms with Gresham as to the amount to be paid for them. Both parties having referred the matter to Sir Richard Rich, Chancellor of the Court of Augmentations of the Crown, as arbitrator, the City agreed to pay a yearly sum of twenty marks for the houses that were required. Monoux refusing to accept this sum, another letter was despatched to him from the king urging him not to stand in the way of a project so useful to merchants and tending so much to the "beautifitye" of the city. To this second appeal Monoux gave way, and received the cordial thanks of Henry by letter dated the 25th November. 1517 Nothing more was done in the matter until it was taken up many years later by Sir Thomas Gresham, son of Sir Richard. 1518 Acting, as he did for a long succession of years, as Queen Elizabeth's agent in Flanders, Sir Thomas spent much of his time in Antwerp. 1519 When he was not there himself he employed a factor in the person of Richard Clough to conduct his affairs. In 1561 this Richard Clough, in a letter addressed to his principal from Antwerp (31 Dec.), 1520 expressed much astonishment at the City of London being so far behind continental towns:—"Consideryng what a sittey London ys, and that in so many yeres they have nott founde the menes to make a bourse! but must walke in the raine, when ytt raineth, more lyker pedlers then marchants; and in thys countrie, and all other, there is no kynde of pepell that have occasion to meete, butt they have a plase meete for that pourpose." Indeed, Clough got quite excited over the thought that London, of all cities in the world, possessed no decent accommodation for merchants transacting their everyday business, and declared his readiness to build "so fere a bourse in London as the grett bourse is in Andwarpe" and that "withhoutt molestyng of any man more than he shulld be well dysposyd to geve."

It was not long before Gresham made up his mind that London should have a Burse, and in May, 1563, the Court of Aldermen deputed Lionel Duckett, who was also a mercer, to sound Gresham as to "his benevolence towards the makyng of a burse." 1521 But however desirous Gresham might be to prosecute the work, he was prevented from doing so by stress of business. Commercial difficulties arose between England and the Low Countries owing to the proclamation of the Duchess of Parma. Up to the year 1564 Gresham was forced to make Antwerp his place of abode, and could only occasionally visit London; since that time, however, his business allowed him to look upon London as his permanent residence, and he only crossed over to Antwerp when special circumstances rendered it necessary. An additional reason for the delay in carrying out Gresham's project may perhaps be found in the fact that, during his absence on the queen's business in 1563, Elizabeth had, with her usual parsimony, cut down Gresham's allowance of twenty shillings a day for "his diets." Gresham complained bitterly of this abridgment of his income in a letter to Secretary Cecil, and also in another letter couched in more guarded terms to the queen herself. 1522 In both letters he set out the sum total of the money (£830,000) which he had negotiated for the queen, and referred to his having broken a leg in her majesty's service and to his declining years. Whatever may have been the cause of the delay, it was not until the 4th January, 1565, that a definite offer was made by Gresham to erect a "comely burse" at his own cost and charge, provided the City would furnish a suitable site. This offer was accepted. 1523

Difficulties of obtaining a site.

Difficulties at once presented themselves in finding a site. It was originally proposed to obtain from the Merchant Taylors' Company a plot of land between Lombard Street and Cornhill, but the company refused to part with the property and a new site had to be chosen. 1524 No sooner was this done, and a place selected to the north of Cornhill, than a difficulty arose between the City and the Dean and Chapter of Canterbury as to the terms of purchase. 1525 This having been successfully overcome and the site purchased, the next step was to invite subscriptions, not only from members of the livery companies, but from merchant adventurers beyond the sea. 1526 Such a liberal response was made to this invitation 1527 that on the 7th June, 1566, Sir Thomas Gresham was able to lay the first stone of the new building, a deed of trust between the City and Gresham having previously (14 May) been executed. 1528

Strong foreign element in connection with the building of the first Burse.

It is curious to note the strong foreign element in connection with the building of Gresham's Burse. The architect as well as the design of the building came from abroad. The clerk of the works (Henryk) 1529 and most of the workmen were foreigners, Gresham having obtained special permission from the Court of Aldermen for their employment. 1530 Most of the material for structural as well as ornamental purposes (saving 100,000 bricks provided by the City) 1531 came from abroad, and to this day the Royal Exchange is paved with small blocks of Turkish hone-stones believed to have been imported in Gresham's day, and to have been relaid after the several fires of 1666 and 1838. It was the employment of these strangers which probably gave rise to an order of the Court of Aldermen (19 June, 1567) that an officer should be appointed to attend at the Burse daily "for a competent season," to see that no "misorder" be done to any of the artificers or other workmen there employed, and to commit to ward any that he should find so-doing. 1532

The Burse opened by Q. Elizabeth, 23 Jan., 1571.

By the 22nd December, 1568, the Burse was so far complete as to allow of merchants holding their meetings within its walls, but it was not until the 23rd January, 1571, that the queen herself visited it in state and caused it thenceforth to be called the Royal Exchange. Her statue which graced the building bore testimony to the care and interest she always displayed in fostering commercial enterprise.

Wanton damage done to the new Burse.

On the door of a staircase leading up to a "pawne" or covered walk on the south side of the building there had been set up the arms and crest of Gresham himself, which some evilly disposed person took it into his head to deface. A proclamation made by the mayor (16 Feb., 1569) for the apprehension of the culprit does not appear from the city's records to have proved successful. 1533 Some years later (21 March, 1577) the mayor had occasion to issue another proclamation for the discovery of persons who had defaced and pulled away "certen peces of timber fixed to thendes and comers of the seates" 1534 in the Royal Exchange, with what result we know not.

Insurance business carried on at the Royal Exchange.

In 1574 the Court of Aldermen appointed a committee to confer with Gresham touching the "assurance" of the Royal Exchange. 1535 The connection between the new Burse and insurance is remarkable. The principle of insurance policies had been introduced into the city by the Lombards as early as the thirteenth century, 1536 and a Lombard Street policy became a familiar term. 1537 When the Lombard Street merchants quitted their old premises for the more commodious Exchange they carried thither their insurance business with them, and a part of the new building was devoted exclusively to this branch of commerce. A grant of letters patent which Elizabeth made to Richard Candler for the making of policies and registering of assurances within the city was objected to by the Court of Aldermen, as being contrary to the liberties of the City, and a deputation was appointed to wait upon the lords of the Privy Council to have it revoked. 1538 This was early in 1575. A year later we find Candler making answer to a bill of fees drawn up by certain aldermen and citizens of London, respecting his office. 1539

In order to put an end to the frequent disputes which arose in the Royal Exchange among merchants on matters of insurance, the Court of Aldermen appointed two of their number to consider the difficulty and to report thereon. They made their report to the court on the 29th January, 1577. 1540 They had, in accordance with the oft-repeated desire expressed to previous lord mayors by the lords of the Privy Council, consulted with their brethren the aldermen, as well as with merchants of the city, both Englishmen and foreigners, and had drawn up orders agreeable to those that had hitherto been used in Lombard Street, to which all countries had been accustomed to submit. The orders, however, not yet being completed, the Court of Aldermen decided upon appointing arbitrators from year to year to deal with all matters of insurance, and so relieve the lords of the Privy Council of the trouble which they had hitherto experienced on that score at a time when they had weightier matters to attend to. The arbitrators were to receive one penny in the pound amongst them in all cases, whether the claim were for whole losses, part, 1541 or averages. Their decision was to bind both assurer and assured, and they were to sit twice a week (Monday and Thursday) "in the offyce howse of assurances" in the Royal Exchange. They were to be attended by the "register of assurances," whose business it was to summon witnesses. A poor-box was to be provided, to which the party assured, on judgment, should contribute twelve pence.

Music and football at the Exchange.

On Sundays and holy days the Exchange was enlivened during a portion of the year with the music of the city waits, who were ordered by the Court of Aldermen (April, 1572) to play on their instruments as they had hitherto been accustomed at the Royal Exchange, from seven o'clock till eight o'clock in the evening up to the Feast of Pentecost, after which they were to commence playing at eight p.m., and "to hold on" till nine p.m. up to Michaelmas. 1542 There is another circumstance connected with the same building that deserves a passing notice, which is that football used to be played within its walls, a game forbidden in 1576 to be played any longer either there or in any of the city's wards. 1543

Gresham College and Lectures.

The citizens of London are indebted to Sir Thomas Gresham for something more than their Royal Exchange. By will dated 5th July, 1575, proved and enrolled in the Court of Husting, 1544 Gresham disposed of the reversion of the Royal Exchange and of his mansion-house in the parish of St. Helen, Bishopsgate, after the decease of his wife, to the mayor and corporation of the city and to the wardens and commonalty of the Mercers' Company in equal moieties in trust (*inter alia*) for the maintenance of seven lectures on the several subjects of Divinity, Astronomy, Music, Geometry, Law, Physic and Rhetoric. In 1596 these two corporate bodies came into possession of the property, and in the following year drew up ordinances for the regulation of the various lectures. According to the terms of Gresham's will the lectures were delivered at Gresham House. When Gresham House, which escaped the Fire of London, became dilapidated, the City and the

Company on more than one occasion petitioned Parliament for leave to pull it down and to erect another building on its site. The proposal, however, was not entertained, but in the year 1767 an Act was passed vesting Gresham House in the Crown for the purpose of an Excise Office, and providing for the payment by the Crown to the City and Company of a perpetual annuity of £500 per annum. For some time the lectures ceased to be delivered for lack of accommodation. When they were next delivered it was at the City of London School, where they continued until Gresham College was erected in Basinghall Street. 1545

The Act of Uniformity strictly enforced, 1565.

In the meantime Protestantism had been gaining ground in England as well as on the continent. Many who in the evil days of the Marian persecution had sought refuge in Switzerland and Germany had returned to England as soon as they were assured of safety under Elizabeth, and had introduced into the country the religious tenets of Calvin they had learnt abroad. Elizabeth found herself confronted not only by Catholics but by Puritans. As she felt herself seated more strongly on the throne she determined to enforce more strictly than hitherto the Act of Uniformity. In 1565 the London clergy were ordered to wear the surplice and to conform in other particulars. Between thirty and forty of them—and those the most intelligent and active of them—refused and resigned their cures. Their congregations supported them, and thus a large body of good Protestants were driven into opposition. But there all action against them ceased. It was otherwise with the Protestants on the continent, where a determination arrived at in the same year that Elizabeth enforced the Act of Uniformity, to suppress heresy, led to the most horrible persecution, and drove many of the inhabitants to seek refuge in England.

Gresham's hospitality to Cardinal Chastillon, 1568.

Of the hundreds of foreigners who sought this country, driven from France or Spain by religious persecution, 1546 none was more hospitably received than the brother of the great Coligny, the Cardinal Chastillon. The Bishop of London having excused himself entertaining the cardinal at Fulham, his eminence was lodged and hospitably treated for a whole week by Gresham. During his visit he paid a visit, Huguenot as he was, to the French Church established in the city, where his co-religionists were allowed to worship without fear of molestation. He further paid his host the compliment of visiting the Exchange, then approaching completion. At the end of the week he removed to Sion House, where accommodation had been found for him. 1547

The city crowded with refugees from the continent.

The influx of refugees from the continent was far from being an unmixed blessing. Whilst some settled peacefully down and taught the London artizan the art of silk-weaving, others betook themselves to the river's side, where they defied the civic authorities. 1548 A fresh return was ordered to be made of their number. 1549 It became necessary to forbid aliens remaining in the city more than a day and a night; they might reside in other places if they liked, but not in the city of London. 1550 Mortality increased so much that a committee hud to be appointed (March, 1569) "to peruse about the cytie where apte and convenient places maye be had and founde for the buryall of the deade in tyme of plage and other tymes of gret deathe," and to report thereon to the Court of Aldermen. 1551 An acre of ground, more or less, near Bethlem Hospital was subsequently prepared as a cemetery by the civic authorities, 1552 whilst a friend of the mayor agreed under certain conditions to enclose it with a wall, erect a pulpit and make other improvements at his own cost. 1553

The Prince of Orange receives substantial assistance from the citizens.

In the course of time the persecuted Netherlanders took heart of grace, encouraged by the gallant conduct of the Prince of Orange, their leader, no less than by the active assistance and sympathy of their brethren in England, who were continually passing to and fro with munitions of war, in spite of proclamations to the contrary. 1554 "Whilst Elizabeth dribbled out her secret aid to the Prince of Orange the London traders sent him half-a-million from their own purses, a sum equal to a year's revenue of the Crown." 1555

The decline of Antwerp London's opportunity.

The queen applies to the merchant adventurers for a loan.

The decline of Antwerp which followed Alva's administration marks the foundation of London's supremacy in the world of commerce. Hitherto the queen had been accustomed through Gresham, her factor, to raise what money she required by loans from merchants abroad. Merchant strangers were well content to lend her money at ten or twelve per cent., seeing that the City of London was as often as not called upon to give bonds for repayment by way of collateral security. 1556 When that door was closed to her she turned to her own subjects, the Company of Merchant Adventurers, to whom she had shown considerable favour. Her first application to this company for a loan was, to her great surprise, refused. The matter was afterwards accommodated through the intervention of Sir Thomas Gresham; and as the confidence of the city merchants increased, loans were afterwards frequently negotiated between them and the Crown, much to the convenience of one party and to the advantage of the other. 1557

The first public lottery, 1567-1569.

As another means of raising money Elizabeth had resort to a lottery—the first public lottery ever held in London, although the game called "The Lott" was not unknown in the city in the reign of Henry VIII. 1558 The lottery was advertised in 1567 as being a very rich lottery general, without any blanks, containing a number of good prizes of ready-money, plate and divers sorts of merchandise, the same having been valued by expert and skilful men. The lottery was, as we should say at the present day, "under the immediate patronage" of the queen herself, and the proceeds, after deducting expenses, were to be devoted to the repair of harbours and other public works conducive to strengthening the realm. Besides the prizes, of which a long list is set out in the city's records, there were to be three "welcomes" or bonuses given to the first three winners of lots. The first person to whom a lot should happen to fall was to have for "welcome" a piece of silver-gilt plate of the value of £50, and the second and third fortunate drawers were to have respectively, in addition to their prizes, a piece of gilt plate of the value of £20. The prizes, the chief of which amounted to £5,000 sterling, although the winner was to receive only £3,000 in cash, the rest being taken out in plate and tapestry, 1559 were exhibited in Cheapside at the sign of the Queen's Arms, the house of Antony Derick, goldsmith to Elizabeth and engraver to the Mint in this and the preceding reign. 1560 The mayor and aldermen agreed to put into the lottery thirty "billes or lottes" at the least under one posy, viz.:—*God preserve the Cytye of London quod M and A.* Any profit that might arise from the lots was to be equally divided between them. 1561

The livery companies of the city were also invited to subscribe to the lottery as well as the Company of Merchant Adventurers. 1562 On the 4th August the livery of the Merchant Taylors' Company were summoned to their hall to declare the amount each individual was ready to venture—"all under our posy in the name of this Common Hall," the posy subsequently determined upon being the following:—

"One byrde in hande is worthe two in the woode,
Yff wee have the greate lott it will do us good." 1563

The "reading" of the lottery was postponed till the 10th January, 1569. 1564 It took place at the west door of St. Paul's, commencing on the 11th day of that month, and continued day and night until the 6th May following. 1565 It was reported at the time that Elizabeth withdrew a large sum of the prize-money for her own use previous to the drawing of the lots, and this report, whether well founded or not, created no little disgust among the subscribers. 1566

English merchants in Antwerp arrested by order of Alva, 1568.

Elizabeth retaliates by seizing treasure on board Spanish vessels.

Before the close of 1568 Alva had severed the last links connecting England with the Low Countries by suddenly seizing and imprisoning all English merchants found at Antwerp on the ground that certain Spanish treasure-ships had been detained in England. Such conduct on his part was characterized by Elizabeth as "verie straunge and hertofore in no tyme used betwixt the Crowne of England and the House of Burgondye wt owt some manner of former conferrence proceedyng and intelligence had of the myndes and intentions of the prynces themselves on both sides," and she forthwith issued a proclamation for the seizure of Spanish vessels and merchants found in English ports by way of reprisal. 1567 She was careful to show that any former detention of Spanish vessels served as a mere pretence for Alva's conduct. Certain Spanish vessels of small tonnage, called "zabras," had, it was true, entered English harbours in the west country, and the bullion and merchandise had been discharged on English soil; but all this had been done in order to prevent the ships and cargo falling into the hands of the French ships which threatened them. Some of the treasure had been even "borrowed"; but this was not contrary to the honorable usage of princes in their own dominions. The Spanish ambassador had called upon her majesty to ask that the vessels and cargo might be given up, "pretending the monye to appertaine to the king his maister," which her majesty had declared her willingness to assent to as soon as she should have had communication from the west country. The ambassador, who was asked to return in four or five days to receive the ships and treasure, had failed to appear, and her surprise was great to find that orders had been given for the arrest of her subjects at Antwerp on the very day (29 Oct.) that the Spanish ambassador was with her majesty. Such was the account of the matter as given in the queen's proclamation to the citizens of London. But there are other and contradictory accounts. Whoever may have been the rightful owner of the treasure, which in all probability was on its way to Flanders for payment of Alva's soldiers, 1568 the opportunity of dealing a blow to Spain and at the same time of replenishing the Exchequer at home afforded by the presence of the ships in English waters was thought too good to be lost.

Order to seize Flemish merchants and their goods in London, Jan., 1569.

On the 5th January the mayor received orders from Sir Nicholas Bacon to seize all Flemings' goods to the queen's use, inasmuch as it was quite possible that what had taken place in Flanders had been done without the King of Spain's commission. The following day the mayor informed the council that he had arrested the bodies and goods of certain merchant strangers in the city. 1569 Throughout the greater part of the month frequent letters passed between the city, the merchant adventurers, the merchants of the staple and the lords of the council concerning Alva's proceedings and measures to be taken by way of reprisal. The citizens showed themselves very anxious to devise measures of retaliation and to avail themselves to the utmost of the opportunity afforded them of avenging themselves of their foreign rivals, as the following memorial signed by the mayor and nine of the principal merchants of the city proves:— 1570

"First, we doe thinck it very needfull and necessary that wth all possible speed the bodies, shipps and goodes of all the subiects of the said king be had under arrest, and their bodies to be sequestred from their houses, comptinghouses, books, warehouses and goods; and they themselves to be committed unto severall and sure custodie and keeping. And that alsoe comission may be granted to sage persons to enquire and trie out all coulorable transports and contracts don since the XXth of December last by any of the subiects of the said king or by any other nation. And that a proclamation be made by the queene's mates aucthorite forthwth for the avoiding of collorable bargaines, transports and contracts hereafter to be made."

Thomas Rowe 1571 (he had not yet received the honour of knighthood), who was mayor at the time, happened to be a connection by marriage of Sir Thomas Gresham, having married Mary, the eldest daughter of Sir John Gresham, of Titsey, Sir Thomas's uncle. It was owing to this connection that the mayor received information of Alva's arbitrary proceedings before the news reached the ears of Secretary Cecil; for Gresham's factor at Antwerp, Richard Clough, had lost no time in despatching a special messenger to his master, who, immediately after hearing the news, broke in upon the mayor's slumbers at twelve o'clock on the night of the 3rd January in order to communicate the same to him. The next morning the mayor wrote to Sir William Cecil informing him of what had occurred and how under the circumstances he (the mayor) had taken upon himself to stay the despatch of letters abroad for a while. 1572

Alva's envoy demands restitution.

Towards the end of January, 1569, the Duke of Alva sent over an agent, Monsieur D'Assoleville, to demand the restitution of the treasure. The mayor deputed John Gresham and another to escort the envoy from Gravesend to London, where he was lodged at Crosby Place, at that time the mansion house of William Bond, alderman of Candlewick Street Ward. 1573 At first he demanded an audience with the queen herself, but was fain to be content with a reference to her council. 1574 The treasure in the meantime had been removed to London for greater security. 1575 Negotiations proving fruitless the agent returned to Antwerp, "having succeeded in obtaining from Elizabeth nothing beyond the assurance that she was ready to surrender the treasure when his master promised indemnity to all her subjects in the Low Countries, and agreed solemnly to ratify the ancient treaty of alliance between the Crown of England and the House of Burgundy." 1576

Gresham suggests minting the Spanish treasure, 14 Aug., 1569.

That such a large amount of treasure should be lying idle did not commend itself to the mind of so astute a financier as Sir Thomas Gresham. He accordingly suggested to Sir William Cecil by letter (14 Aug., 1569) that the queen should cause it to be minted into her own coin, and thereby make a profit of £3,000 or £4,000. As for repayment, her majesty could effect it by way of exchange, to her great profit, or give bonds for a year or more to the merchants who owned the money, and who, in Gresham's opinion, would willingly accede to such proposal. 1577 Bold as this suggestion was, it appears, nevertheless, to have been carried into execution. 1578

The City Courts closed to Spanish suitors, 11 July, 1570.

The hardships already experienced by Spanish merchants from stoppage of commercial intercourse with England must have been materially increased the following year by an order of the Court of Aldermen (11 July, 1570) to the effect that all matters and suits brought by merchant strangers, subjects of the King of Spain, in any of the Queen's Majesty's Courts within the city of London for the recovery of a debt should be stayed, and no manner of arrest or attachment allowed until further notice, unless the stranger suing were a denizen or a member of the Church. 1579

Failure of efforts to effect a mutual restoration of goods seized.

Spanish goods ordered to be sold.

The respective claims of England and Spain referred to arbitration.

By proclamation made the last day of June, 1570, English merchants who had suffered loss by Alva's proceedings were desired to make a return of such loss to the officers of one or other of the cities or towns of London, Southampton, Bristol, Chester, Newcastle, Hull or Ipswich, as they should find it most convenient, 1580 and on the 20th July following every Englishman into whose hands any goods belonging to Spanish subjects might have come was ordered to make a certificate under his hand and seal into the Court of the Admiralty, in the city of London, for her majesty to take further order thereon as should be thought meet. 1581 Negotiations, which had been renewed for mutual restitution, again broke down, for when the terms on which restitution was to be effected were to be reduced to writing, or, in the language of the record, "*put into mundum*," 1582 the Spanish commissioners were found to have no authority to arrange matters, whilst at the same time they wished to introduce clauses and conditions which Elizabeth could in no wise accept. Seeing that she was being played with, and knowing that much of the goods of English merchants seized in Spain and the Netherlands had already been sold, the queen determined to put up for sale the Spanish merchandise which for three years had been in English hands. Proclamation to this effect was made the 14th January, 1572. 1583 The queen showed every desire to treat the Spanish merchants with consideration. The sale was entrusted to Spanish subjects, who, upon their oath, were to make sale of all the ships, goods, wares and merchandise arrested, to the utmost advantage they could; and Spanish owners were allowed, either by themselves, their factor or attorney, freely to enter the realm within thirty days after the date of the proclamation to attend the sale, provided they made no attempt against her majesty or the peace of the country and departed immediately the sale was over. This proclamation, coupled with the hopelessness of Alva's case and the manifestation of discontent displayed by his own ruined merchants, led to articles being drawn up (25 Mar.) between Elizabeth and the King of Spain for an adjustment of their respective claims. Sir Thomas Gresham had previously (4 Feb.) been directed by letter from Lord Burghley and Sir Walter Mildmay to deliver up certain bonds of the Governor and Company of Merchant Adventurers to be cancelled now that the whole matter was to be referred to arbitration. 1584

Insurrection of the Earls of Northumberland and Westmoreland, 1569.

To add to the queen's difficulties, Mary, who had been deposed from the throne of Scotland and had sought shelter in England, was importuning her for assistance for the recovery of her lost crown. Whilst Elizabeth hesitated either to replace her rival in power or to set her at liberty, the Earls of Northumberland and Westmoreland endeavoured to carry out a scheme for marrying Mary to the Duke of Norfolk and forcing Elizabeth to acknowledge her as successor to the crown of England. The Duke of Norfolk obeyed the queen's summons to attend the court, and was committed to the Tower (Oct., 1569). 1585 The earls refused to obey the summons, and rose in insurrection. On the 24th November they were proclaimed traitors. 1586 Troops were sent against them, but they cowardly left their supporters to their own fate and fled to Scotland. The rebellion, fruitless as it proved to be, caused no little excitement in the city.

Measures taken for safe-guarding the city.

The same day that the earls were proclaimed traitors the Mayor of London issued his precept to the several aldermen, enjoining them to take steps for safe-guarding the city and taking into custody all rogues, masterless men and vagabonds. 1587 On the following day another precept was issued to the several livery companies for providing a certain number of soldiers, "well and sufficientlie furnyshed wth a jerkyn and a paire of gally sloppes of broad clothe, collor watchet, one calyver wth flaske and tuchebox, a moryan, a sworde and a dagger." 1588 The soldiers were to be ready to serve her majesty at an hour's warning. The Chamberlain received orders to amend the several gates of the city and the portcullises belonging to them, as well as to repair the city's guns and put them in readiness, and lay in a stock of powder and shot to serve as occasion should require. 1589 By the 12th December all fear of immediate danger had passed away, and the livery companies were ordered to receive back the armour and weapons supplied to the soldiers and to keep them in their hall. The men were to be dismissed to their several industries, but still to hold themselves in readiness for service at an hour's warning if occasion should require them. A week later the soldiers were dismissed to their houses, those who had no house being allowed sixpence a day until called upon for active service. 1590

Papal Bull of excommunication against Elizabeth, 1570.

Although the rising in the north had failed, the Catholics were not without hope. They were encouraged by the issue of a Papal Bull excommunicating Elizabeth and absolving her subjects from their allegiance. This Bull was affixed to the door of the Bishop of London's palace by a man named John Felton. The queen was alarmed. She believed that the long-threatened union against her of the Catholic powers had at length been effected. Felton was seized and tried at the Guildhall. He was found guilty, and paid the penalty of his rashness by being hanged, drawn and quartered. 1591 His exemplary punishment failed, however, to put a stop to Catholic intrigues against Elizabeth.

Rejoicing in the city after the battle of Lepanto, 7 Oct., 1571.

The defeat of the Turkish fleet at Lepanto by Don John of Austria (7 Oct., 1571) was commemorated two days later in London by a thanksgiving service at St. Paul's, 1592 which was attended by the mayor, Sir William Allen, 1593 the aldermen and members of the companies in their liveries. In the evening of the same day bonfires were lighted in the streets of the city by precept of the mayor. 1594 The immediate effect of the victory was the release of a large number of captives (variously estimated at 12,000 and 14,000) 1595 from Turkish slavery, for whose redemption the citizens were constantly being called upon to subscribe. 1596

Peace and commercial prosperity, 1572.

Whilst the Low Countries were winning their way to freedom from the Spanish yoke, and France was suffering the horrors of Saint Bartholomew's day (24 Aug., 1572), England remained tranquil, and the city merchant had little cause to complain, except, it might be, on account of the number of strangers who rivalled him in his business. 1597 For the better preservation of peace members of the French and the Dutch churches were ordered (28 Sept.) not to leave their houses after 9 o'clock at night. 1598

The shifting policy of Elizabeth towards Spain and France, 1572-1574.

So long as the Spanish king turned a deaf ear to the exhortations of the Pope, and refused to make a descent upon England, Elizabeth was able to cope with Catholicism at home by peaceful measures. But the time was approaching when she could no longer refuse to give practical assistance to her struggling co-religionists on the continent. The Netherlands had for some time past been preparing for open revolt against the barbarous government of Alva. In 1572 a party seized Brill, and thus laid the foundation of the Dutch Republic. It wanted but the active adhesion of Elizabeth to enable the French to drive the Spaniards out of the country, but this the queen was as yet unwilling to give. Two years later (1574) she offered her services to effect an understanding between Spain and the Netherlands, but her mediation proved futile. Both in 1572 and 1574 there are signs of military preparations having taken place in the city. In the first mentioned year Elizabeth held a review of the city troops in Greenwich Park. 1599 In 1574 the city was called upon to furnish 400 soldiers for the queen's service, and steps were taken to allot to the livery companies their quota of men or money in view of future calls. 1600 A store of gunpowder was also laid up. 1601

Piracy rampant, 1575-1576.

If one thing more than another was calculated to precipitate a rupture between England and Spain it was the action of English seamen, who roved the seas and indirectly rendered assistance to the Netherlanders by plundering Spanish vessels, in spite of all proclamations to the contrary. 1602 The Londoner was not behind-hand in this predatory warfare.

A loan of £30,000, June, 1575.

A city Chamberlain dismissed from office.

In June, 1575, the queen borrowed a sum of £30,000 from the citizens on security. 1603 The money was subscribed by the wealthier class of citizens, and a moiety of the loan was repaid in little more than a twelvemonth. 1604 Whatever may have been her faults, Elizabeth honestly paid her debts, and when she discovered in 1577 that money which she had repaid to certain officials had not reached the hands of the original creditor, she forthwith issued a proclamation commanding all such creditors to send in their claims in writing to the chief officer of her majesty's household. 1605 It is difficult to dissociate altogether this proclamation from the removal of George Heton from the office of Chamberlain of the City three months afterwards. 1606

The city called upon to furnish soldiers, 1578.

In February, 1578, the City was called upon to provide 2,000 arquebusiers. Refusal was useless, although an attempt was made to get the number reduced to 500. The mayor had scarcely issued his precept to the aldermen to raise the men before he received another order for 2,000 to be trained as directed in handling and using their weapons and kept in readiness for future service. 1607 One hundred and fifty men were ordered (12 June) to be ready at an hour's notice for foreign service. 1608 Strangers and foreigners were not exempt. 1609 Some of the city companies were slow in paying their quota of expenses of fitting out the men, and pressure had to be brought to bear on them by the Court of Aldermen. 1610

Count Casimir at Gresham House, Jan., 1579.

Death of Sir Thomas Gresham, 21 Nov., 1579.

Count Casimir presented by the city with a gift of 500 marks.

In the following year Casimir, Count Palatine of the Rhine, paid a visit to England to answer a charge brought against him by the English envoy in Holland, of having used forces against the Netherlanders which had been despatched from these shores for their support. On the evening of Thursday, the 22nd January, 1579, the Count landed at the Tower, where he was received by a party of noblemen and others, among whom we may conjecture was the Mayor of London and representatives of the city. 1611 Thence he was conducted by the light of cressets to Gresham's house, in Bishopsgate Street, where he was received with music and lodged and feasted by the worthy owner for three days. The honour thus shown to Gresham is only one more proof of the esteem and respect in which he was universally held by all parties, and, "in truth," as his biographer justly remarks, 1612 "his great experience, his long and familiar intercourse with men of all grades and professions, from princes and nobles—with whom ... he was on as intimate a footing as the impassable barrier of rank will permit—to the lowliest of his own dependants, the knowledge of men and manners which he must have derived from foreign travel, and his acquaintance with all the languages of civilised Europe, must have rendered him, towards the close of his life especially, as favourable a specimen as could have been selected of the English gentleman of that day." Casimir's reception was one of the last acts of public service performed by Gresham, for before the close of the year he had died (21 Nov.). On Sunday (25 Jan.) the Count was conducted to Westminster for an interview with the queen, after which lodgings were assigned to him in Somerset House. The court of Common Council had already (23 Jan.) voted "Duke Cassimerus" a gratification "in moneye or anye other thinge" to the value of 500 marks. 1613 His visit was one round of feasting, hunting and sight-seeing; one day dining with the lord mayor, another with the merchants of the Steelyard; one day hunting at Hampton Court, and another day witnessing athletic sports at Westminster. That the Count succeeded in clearing his character may be surmised from the fact of his receiving the Order of the Garter before his departure. 1614

The plague in the city, 1580-1583.

In the following year the plague, which had been very virulent towards the end of 1577, and from which the city was seldom entirely free, appeared at Rye (June, 1580). A twelvemonth later it was raging in London, but as the weather grew colder its virulence abated, allowing of the resumption of the lord mayor's feast. The respite was short. In the spring of 1582 it was again rife in the city, increasing in fatality during the hot season and continuing until the winter of 1583. 1615 Business was often at a standstill, the law courts had to be removed to the country, and the sittings of the London Husting suspended. 1616

St. Paul's Churchyard, which served as the burial ground to no less than twenty-three city parishes, became overcrowded and greatly added to the insanitary condition of the city by its shallow graves. The mayor informed the lords of the council of this state of affairs by letter (15 May, 1582), in which he says that scarcely any grave was then made without exposing corpses, and that the heat of the crowds standing over the shallow graves caused noxious exhalations. It was currently reported at the time that the gravediggers were the cause of the shallow graves "as being desirous to have the infection spred that they might gaine by burieng." 1617

CHAPTER XVIII.

Preparations for war.

The time was fast approaching when the queen would find herself unable any longer to maintain her frequent cry to the council board, "No war, my lords, no war!" and she began to concert measures to frustrate any attempt that might be made to attack her crown and realm by the subtle device of the Pope's emissaries or the more open hostility of Philip.

Troubles in Ireland, 1579-1583.

There were two ways in which the Pope and Spain could attack England, the one by making a descent upon the coast, the other by undermining the loyalty of the queen's subjects by the aid of missionaries. A descent upon the English coast was, for the present at least, out of the question, but it was possible to wound England by fostering insurrection in Ireland. Accordingly, in 1579, a large force landed at Limerick under the authority of the Pope. It was, however, overpowered and destroyed by Lord Grey, the lord deputy. 1618

Then followed the rebellion under the Earl of Desmond, who six years before had regained his liberty on a promise to use his influence to destroy the Catholic religion in Ireland. 1619 Throughout the Desmond rebellion the Londoners were constantly being called upon to furnish men and munition of war. The trouble was protracted by the landing of a force of 800 men from Spain, with the connivance, if not with the authority, of Philip. When the rebellion was suppressed distress drove many Irish to England, and the city became their chief refuge. 1620 A special day was appointed for apprehending "all suche rogishe and begging Ireishe people as well men weomen as children" as should be found wandering abroad in the city, 1621 and steps were taken subsequently to convey all Irish beggars to Bristol with the view of sending them back to their native land. 1622

The Jesuits in the city, 1580-1581.

Whilst appealing to force to accomplish their object in Ireland, the Catholics resorted to intrigue to gain the same object in England and Scotland. For some years past there had been a steady flow from the continent of seminary priests, who worked silently and secretly making converts to the old religion. Every precaution was taken to prevent their inculcating their dangerous opinions into the minds of the inhabitants of the city and drawing them off from their allegiance to the queen and to the established Church. The aldermen were instructed to make return of those in their ward who refused to attend church. This was in 1568. 1623 In 1574 all strangers who had crept into the city under colour of religion and were found to be of no church were ordered to leave. 1624 In the following year (9 June, 1575) every stranger was called upon to subscribe the Articles of religion before he was allowed to take up his residence within the city, and those who refused to subscribe or to attend church were to give bond for their appearance before her Majesty's Commissioners for Ecclesiastical Causes to answer such matters as should be objected against them. 1625 The aldermen were instructed to make diligent search in their several wards for such as held conventicles under colour of religion and inter-meddled with matters of State and civil governance. 1626 In 1580 a regular Jesuit mission, under two priests, Campion and Parsons, was despatched to England as part of an organised Catholic scheme. Campion had at one time been a fellow of St. John's College, Oxford. Their first step was to remove a difficulty under which devout Catholics had laboured ever since the issue of the Bull of excommunication against Elizabeth in 1571. That Bull had reduced them to the necessity of choosing between disobedience to the Church and treason to the queen. The new missionaries helped them out of the dilemma by explaining that the censures of the Church only applied to heretics; Catholics might feign allegiance and the Church would say nothing.

The Recusancy Laws, 1581.

Under these circumstances it can scarcely be wondered at that the government proceeded to strong measures—A proclamation was issued requiring English parents to remove their children from foreign seminaries, and declaring that to harbour Jesuit priests was to harbour rebels; 1627 whilst parliament imposed fines upon all who refused to attend the service of the established Church, in addition to the penalties imposed in 1571 upon those who claimed to absolve subjects from their allegiance and to receive them into the Church of Rome. In the city a strict watch was again ordered to be kept on all those who failed to attend regularly their parish church. 1628 It was further proposed to appoint special preachers to counteract the baneful influence of the Jesuit priest, and the Bishop of London was ordered to make a list of the best preachers and to appoint them districts. 1629

Special preachers appointed for the city, 1581-1582.

These instructions Bishop Aylmer forwarded to the lord mayor with a request for a contribution to enable him and his associates, the dean of St.

Paul's and the dean of Windsor, to carry them into effect. The mayor replied (6 Sept., 1581) that, as for himself, his office was already so burdensome, both in work and expense, that it would go hard with him if he was called upon to pay more than any other parishioner in a Church matter. Both he and his brethren the aldermen were no less desirous than others to promote the knowledge of true religion and to inculcate obedience to the queen by lectures in the city, but the commons would have to be consulted first. He enclosed a list of lectures already established in the several parishes, and drew attention to the great yearly charge incurred by the companies and private persons in the city in maintaining students at the universities to serve the Church in the office of preaching and reading. 1630 This expense, the mayor said, warranted the City and the Companies asking to be no further burdened. The writer concluded by intimating that, however willing the corporation might be to assist in the good work, its ability to do so had been much diminished by the indiscreet demeanour of the bishop's own chaplain, Mr. Dyos, who had recently defamed the citizens in a public sermon at Paul's Cross, "as favorers of userers, of the familye of love and puritanes," saying "that if the appointing of preachers were committed to us we wold appointe preachers such as should defend usirie, the familie of love and puritanisme as they call it." The City was liable to make mistakes, just as the bishop himself had made a mistake in appointing so indiscreet a person for his chaplain, but in other respects they had no cause to reproach themselves in the matter of appointments. In conclusion they desired his lordship to take order for the reparation of their good fame.

Hitherto the City had received no direct communications from the Privy Council on the subject, but three days after the date of the lord mayor's letter to the Bishop of London the lords of the council made a direct appeal to the mayor and aldermen suggesting that a collection should be made among the clergy and other inhabitants of the city in order to "oppose the supersticion of popery wch by the coming over of divers Jesuits and seminarie preistes hath ben of late much increased." 1631 Little appears to have been done in the matter by the civic authorities until the beginning of the next year, when the first step was taken by the appointment of a committee (25 Jan., 1582). 1632

Arrest and execution of Campion.

Campion meanwhile had been arrested and subjected to cruel torture. He was eventually executed. Parsons, his companion, escaped to the continent, where he continued to carry on an intrigue against the life of Elizabeth in conjunction with Allen, who some years before had established the famous seminary at Donay for the purpose of keeping up a supply of Jesuit priests for England.

Breach with Spain, Jan., 1584.

In 1583—soon after Edward Osborne 1633 had been elected to the mayoralty—a conspiracy, which had long been on foot, for the assassination of Elizabeth and the invasion of England by a French army was discovered. Matters began to look serious, and it behoved the queen to dismiss the Spanish ambassador from England (Jan., 1584) and to see to her forces. Lord Burghley drew up "a memoryall of dyvers thynges nesessary to be thought of and to be put in execution for this sommer for ye strength of ye realme to serve for martiall defence ageynst ether rebellion or invasion," 1634 containing suggestions for holding musters and training soldiers. The navy was got ready for sea.

Muster of 4,000 men in Greenwich Park, 1584.

In April (1584) the City received orders to muster 4,000 men and to revive the military shows on the eve of the Feasts of St. John the Baptist and St. Peter the Apostle as accustomed to be held in the days of Henry VIII. These displays had gradually fallen into desuetude; it was now the queen's policy to renew them. 1635 The citizens showed themselves equal to the emergency, and "mustered and skirmished" daily at Mile End and St. George's Field, so that in little more than a month they were in a fit state of discipline and training to appear in Greenwich Park before the queen herself, who thanked them graciously for their energy and pains, and declared that she had no subjects more ready to suppress disloyalty and to defend her person. 1636

Assassination of Prince of Orange, 10 July, 1584.

In July news arrived of the assassination of the Prince of Orange (10 July). Englishmen well knew that those who plotted against his life were plotting also against the life of their queen, and with wonderful unanimity— Catholics and Protestants alike—they joined in a "Bond of Association" for the defence of her majesty's person. The terms of the association were afterwards embodied in a bill and submitted to parliament, specially summoned for the purpose. 1637

Dutch envoys to Elizabeth, June, 1585.

Staggered by the sudden loss of their beloved leader, the Netherlanders despatched envoys the following year (1585) to England offering to acknowledge Elizabeth as their sovereign. Upon their arrival in London the envoys were lodged and hospitably entertained—although not at the City's expense—in Clothworkers' Hall, 1638 and on the 29th June were received in audience by the queen at Greenwich. After much hesitation, as was her wont, she at last consented to take the Netherlands under her protection and to despatch troops to their assistance, but only on condition that the States gave security for expenses to be incurred. 1639

Recruits for service in the Low Countries, July, 1585.

On the 9th July the mayor, Sir Thomas Pullison, 1640 issued his precept to the aldermen for each to make a survey in his ward of all such persons as were suitable and willing for service in the Low Countries, where it was intended they should have good allowance. 1641

The fall of Antwerp and despatch of Leicester to the Low Countries, 1585.

Every effort was made to save Antwerp, but it was too late. By chaffering and bargaining with the envoys Elizabeth had lost her opportunity and Antwerp fell (19 Aug.). She could be resolute at times, but it wanted much to rouse her into activity. The news of Antwerp's fall administered to her the necessary incitement to deal "roundly and resolutely" with her new allies. Fresh forces were despatched to Flanders under the Earl of Leicester, making in all some 10,000 men that had already been sent thither, nearly one-fourth of which had been furnished by the city of London. 1642 The queen grumbled at having to send so many—"I have sent a fine heap of folk thither, in all ... not under 10,000 soldiers of the English nation," said she to the envoys in October 1643—and she kept the earl so short of money that he had to mortgage his estate. 1644 The City did what it could and made him a present of £500 in "newe angells," but the City itself was in pecuniary difficulties and was compelled to borrow or "take up" money to defend its title to its own lands, 1645 which had been in constant jeopardy ever since the appointment of the royal commission to search for "concealed lands" in 1567. 1646

The city flooded with strangers from France and Flanders.

The direct effect of the fall of Antwerp upon the city of London was to flood its streets more than ever with strangers, and on the 30th October, 1585, the mayor was once more called upon by the lords of the Privy Council to make a return of the number of strangers within the city, and more especially of the number of French and Flemish strangers that had arrived "sithens the beginninge of the presente trobles moved by the house of Guise in Fraunce and the rendringe of the towne of Andwerpe." 1647 In April and May of the following year (1586) the year of the disastrous battle at Zutphen and of the death of the *Chevalier sans peur et sans reproche*, Sir Philip Sidney—another call was made in the city for volunteers for service in the Low Countries, 1648 and the civic companies were ordered to lay in a stock of gunpowder to be ready "uppon eny ymminent occacioun." 1649

Discovery of the Babington plot, Aug., 1586.

Whilst operations, more or less active, were being carried on in the Netherlands against Spain, a new Catholic conspiracy against the life of Elizabeth, with Anthony Babington at its head, was discovered by Walsingham. The delight of the citizens at the queen's escape drew forth from her a letter which she desired to be read before the Common Council, and in which she testified her appreciation of their loyalty. The letter was introduced to the council by some prefatory remarks made by James Dalton, a member of the court, in which he expatiated upon the beauties of the reformed Church as contrasted with the Roman religion. 1650 The discovery of the plot led to stringent measures being taken against suspected persons in the city, and returns were ordered to be made setting forth for each ward: (1) the names of the ablest men for service, (2) the names of those past service, (3) the names of all who were suspected as to religion, and (4) the names of all strangers born. 1651

Execution of Mary Stuart, 8 Feb., 1587.

The discovery had also another effect: it brought the head of Mary Stuart to the block. A commission of peers sitting at Fotheringhay found that the conspiracy had been "with the privitie of the said Marie pretending tytle to the crowne of the realme of England," and it only remained for Elizabeth to sign the warrant for her execution to remove for ever a dangerous rival. This, however, the queen long hesitated to do, and when at length prevailed upon she caused public proclamation to be made of the reasons which induced her to take the extreme course. 1652

A threatened famine in the city, Nov., 1586

To add to the general gloom, England was threatened before the close of the year (1586) with a famine, caused partly by the inclemency of the seasons and partly by a "corner" in wheat, which some enterprising engrossers had managed to bring about. 1653 In November the mayor caused the city companies to lay in 6,000 or 7,000 quarters of wheat and rye for the relief of those who had already suffered from the extreme dearth, and to raise a sum of £2,500 over and above such sums as they had hitherto disbursed for the provision of corn and grain, 1654 and the Court of Aldermen (3 Jan., 1587) agreed to erect a new garner at the Bridgehouse. 1655

Philip's preparations for invasion, 1587.

After the execution of Mary Stuart, Philip of Spain laid claim to the crown of England. For years past he was known to have been preparing a fleet for an invasion of the country. Preparations were now almost complete, and in 1587 expectation was that the fleet might be seen any day bearing down upon the English coast. The inhabitants of villages and towns on the south coast forsook their homes in terror of the invasion and sought shelter inland. 1656 The evil hour was put off by the prompt action of Drake, who, with four ships of the royal navy and twenty-four others supplied by the City and private individuals, 1657 appeared suddenly off the Spanish coast, and running into Cadiz and Lisbon, destroyed tons of shipping under the very nose of the Spanish lord high admiral, and threw into the sea the vast military stores that had been accumulated there. Having thus accomplished the object for which he set sail—that of "singeing the king of Spain's beard"—he returned, and the sailing of the Armada was put off for a year.

Preparations in England, 1587-1588.

Preparations were in the meanwhile pushed on in the city to meet the attack whenever it should be made. Ten thousand men were levied and equipped in a short space of time. 1658 Any inhabitant of the city assessed in the subsidy-book at £50 in goods, and who, being under fifty years of age, was called upon to serve, and refused, was forthwith committed to Newgate. 1659 If any fault was to be found with the city's force it was the inefficiency of its officers, whom the municipal authorities always claimed to appoint. The Earl of Leicester, who was in command of the camp which had been formed at Tilbury, held but a poor opinion of Londoners as a fighting force. 1660 "For your Londoners," wrote the earl to Walsingham, 1661 I see their service will be little, except they have their own captains, and having them, I look for none at all by them when we shall meet the enemy." He declares that he knows what burghers be well enough, even though they be "as brave and well trained" as the Londoners; they would be useless without good leaders, 1662 and on this he had always insisted. He warns Walsingham against yielding to the wishes of "townsmen" at such a critical juncture, for they would look for the like concession at other times. The Londoners were not peculiar in their desire to have their own officers, according to the earl's own showing, for the letter continues:—"You and my lords all know the imperfection at this time, how few leaders you have, and the gentlemen of the counties here are likewise very loth to have any placed with them to command under them, but well pleased to have some expert man with them to give them advice." Two years later a code of regulations for the "trayninge of capytaynes" was forwarded by the government to the city, and there put into execution. 1663

The City fits out sixteen ships and four pinnaces.

In addition to the land force the City agreed (3 April, 1588) to furnish and fully equip for war sixteen of the largest and best merchant ships that could be found in the Thames, and four pinnaces to attend on them.

1664 A committee was nominated to sit at Clothworkers' Hall and take the necessary steps for fitting out the vessels, the cost of which was to be met by an assessment on citizen and stranger alike. 1665 Nothing was said at the time about victualling the fleet, but we learn from a later entry in the City's Journal that they were victualled for three months. On the 16th July the City agreed to supply victuals for "those twentie shipps lately sett forth" for one month longer, and on the 10th August the Common Council again passed a similar resolution. 1666

The fate of the Armada, July, 1588.

At last the blow fell. On Friday, the 19th (o.s.) July, the Armada was sighted off the Lizard. A strong wind from the south-west was blowing at the time, and it was thought advisable to let the fleet pass and to follow it up with the English vessels then lying in Plymouth harbour. On the following day the two fleets hove in sight of each other. According to the report made to Walsingham by Richard Tomson—a Londoner serving on board the *Margaret and John*, one of the ships furnished by the City—the Spanish fleet numbered at that time 136 sail, ninety of which were large vessels, whilst the English fleet numbered no more than sixty-seven. 1667

Notwithstanding the great superiority of the enemy's fleet in numbers and tonnage, the English admiral, Lord Howard, opened fire the next morning, but took care not to come to close quarters. "We had some small fight with them that Sunday afternoon," reported Hawkins to Walsingham. 1668 The admiral had other reasons for preserving caution. His ships were but ill-furnished with provisions and with ammunition, and even thus early he had to beg the Secretary of State to send him "for God's sake some powder and shot." 1669 The same deficiency of ammunition was experienced the whole time that the two fleets were opposed to each other, and but for this the enemy would not have got off so cheaply as it did. Scarcely a day passed without some cannonading taking place, but never a general engagement. The English trusted to their superior seamanship and to the greater activity of their own light vessels compared with the heavier and more unwieldly Spanish galleons. Again and again they poured broadside after broadside into the enemy, but always making good their retreat before the Spanish vessels could turn in pursuit. On Tuesday (23 July), wrote Hawkins, they had "a sharp and long fight" off Portland, on Thursday "a hot fraye." And thus the Armada made its way up channel, pestered with the swarm of English vessels that would never leave it at peace. On the Saturday following (27 July) it finally dropped anchor in Calais roads, with the intention of awaiting there the arrival of Alexander Farnese with his promised aid before making a direct descent upon the English coast. Farnese did not arrive for the reason that he was blockaded by the Dutch fleet; but the English received an accession of strength by the arrival of Lord Henry Seymour with a squadron of sixteen ships, which hitherto had been lying off Folkestone. 1670

At this juncture the lord mayor (Sir George Bond), having received information of the critical state of affairs and that a general engagement was imminent, issued his precept to the aldermen to summon the pastors and ministers of each ward, and bid them call their parishioners to church by toll of bell or otherwise, both in the morning and afternoon of this eventful Saturday, in order that humble and hearty prayers might be offered to Almighty God "by preaching and otherwise," as the necessity of the times required. 1671 Three days before (24 July) he had given orders for a strict watch and ward to be kept in the city, and for a goodly supply of leather buckets in case of fire. 1672

Richard Tomson and the London ship *Margaret and John*.

After more than one consultation together, the English commanders determined to resort to stratagem. They sent for a number of useless hulks from Dover, and having filled them with every kind of combustible, sent them all aflame on Sunday night into the thick of the enemy. The result was a panic; cables were cut and frantic attempts made to escape what seemed imminent and wholesale destruction. The ships fell foul of each other; some were wrecked and others burnt. When Monday morning dawned only eighty-six vessels out of 124 that had anchored off Calais thirty-six hours before could be found, and these for the most part were seen driving towards the coast of Flanders. The English fleet at once prepared to follow in pursuit, but attention was for a time drawn off to the action of the flagship of the squadron of galeasses, a huge vessel which had become disabled by loss of rudder, and the crew of which were endeavouring by the aid of oars to bring into Calais harbour. The Lord Admiral Howard at once bore down upon her in the *Ark*, but the water proved too shallow. The London ship *Margaret and John* followed suit and, although of less tonnage than the *Ark*, got aground. Richard Tomson sent home a graphic account of the exploit that followed. 1673 Both ships sent out long boats to capture the rich prize as she lay stuck fast upon the harbour bar. Tomson himself formed one of the little band of volunteers. The boats were soon alongside the galeass, its huge sides towering high above them. There then ensued "a pretty skirmish for half-an-hour," wrote Tomson, "but they seemed safely ensconced in their ships, while we in our open pinnaces and far under them had nothing to shroud and cover us." Fortune at last favoured the attackers. The Spanish commander fell dead on his deck with a bullet through his head. A panic seized the sailors, most of whom jumped overboard and tried by swimming and wading to reach the shore. Some succeeded, but many were drowned; whilst those who remained on board signified their readiness to capitulate by hoisting a couple of "handkerchers" on rapiers. The English lost no time in clambering up the sides of the monster, and at once commenced plundering the vessel and releasing the galley slaves. They were only waiting for the tide to take their prize in tow and carry her off when they were warned by the governor of Calais against making any such attempt. They were free to plunder the vessel if they liked, but make prize of the vessel itself they must not, and this order the governor showed himself ready and able to enforce by opening fire from the fort. Tomson and his fellow volunteers were heartily disgusted at having after all to surrender their prize, "the verye glory and staye of the Spanish armye, a thing of very great value and strength."

The naval engagement off Gravelines 29 July, 1588.

This exploit being ended and the long boats having returned to their respective ships, the lord admiral started in pursuit of the Spaniards. Seeing them coming up the Spanish commander immediately prepared for action. An engagement—described by Hawkins as "a long and great fight"—took place off Gravelines and lasted six hours. The English pursued the same tactics as before, and with like success. Without losing a single ship of their own they succeeded in riddling the best Spanish ships through and through, and at last the Armada was forced to bear away towards the open sea. The English followed and made a pretence of keeping up the attack, but by this time nearly all their ammunition as well as food had given out.

The Armada driven northward.

From Tuesday (30 July) until the following Friday (2 Aug.) the pursuit was, nevertheless, maintained by Howard, Drake and Frobisher. On Sunday (4 Aug.) the strong south-wester which had prevailed rose to a gale, and the English fleet made its way home with difficulty. It was otherwise with the Armada. Crippled and forlorn, without pilots and without competent commander, the great fleet was driven northward past the Hebrides and eventually returned home in a decimated condition by the west coast of Ireland.

Preparations in the city for receiving sick and wounded, 29 July.

In the meantime the civic authorities took order for receiving the sick and wounded and administering to their comfort. Two aldermen—Sir Thomas Pullison and Sir Wolstan Dixie—were deputed (29 July) by their brethren to ride abroad among the innholders, brewers, bakers and butchers of the city to see that they did not enhance the price of provisions and that they well entertained all soldiers who arrived in the city. 1674 The City agreed, moreover, to re-victual the ships it had furnished and to provide them with munition and other requisites. A fresh tax was imposed for the purpose of "marine and land affairs." 1675

Reports as to the fate of the Armada, July-Aug., 1588.

It was a long time before any certain news arrived in the city of the ultimate fate of the Armada. There had been rumours abroad that the English fleet had been victorious—with so many Londoners serving in the fleet, it would have been strange indeed if their friends at home had been kept in absolute ignorance of what was taking place in the channel—and bonfires had been lighted, but these rumours were often incorrect and sometimes lead to mischief. The mayor therefore issued his precept to the aldermen on the 30th July—the day after the engagement off Gravelines—bidding them see that the inhabitants of their several wards refrained from crediting any news that might be reported of the vessels at sea but what they received from the mayor himself. The precaution was necessary "for the avoyding of some dislike that may come thereof." 1676 On the 1st August, so critical were the times, the mayor issued a precept by the queen's orders forbidding householders to quit the city, that they might the better be ready for the queen's service if required. 1677 On the 4th the citizens were informed that if they had any friend or servant detained as prisoner in the Spanish dominion, or bound to the galleys, whom they wished to set free, they might have Spanish prisoners allotted to them to assist towards ransom. 1678

The queen attends a public thanksgiving service at St. Paul's, 24 Nov., 1588.

The first public notification of the complete destruction of the Armada was made in a thanksgiving sermon preached by the Dean of St. Paul's on Tuesday, the 20th August, at Paul's Cross, in the presence of the mayor and aldermen and the livery companies in their best gowns. 1679 In November the queen resolved to attend a public thanksgiving service at St. Paul's in person, Monday, the 18th, being the day that was originally fixed. Great preparations were made for the occasion. The livery companies were ordered to take up their appointed stations at eight o'clock in the morning and to follow in the train of the royal procession until the "preaching place" was reached. Places were to be kept by a detachment of the "yeomanry" of each company sent on at six o'clock for that purpose. The "governors of the hospital" of each company were also to attend, staff in hand, and repair to the "skaffold" for them appointed. After dinner the companies were to return immediately to their stations and to wait there until her majesty returned to Somerset House. 1680 The day was afterwards changed from Monday, the 18th, to Sunday, the 24th, when the queen came in great state to St. Paul's. After prayers she took her seat in a closet built out of the north wall of the church and facing Paul's Cross, where she heard a sermon preached by the Bishop of Salisbury. That being over she was entertained at dinner in the bishop's palace, and afterwards returned to Somerset House. 1681

Monuments in city churches to Frobisher, Hawkins and Martin Bond.

Whilst the City is justly proud of its own share in the defence of the kingdom at this great crisis in the nation's history, it has not neglected to give honour where honour was most due. Of the great naval commanders the "sea dogs" of that age—the faces of at least two of them were familiar to the citizens. Both Frobisher and Hawkins owned property in the city, and in all probability resided there, like their fellow seaman and explorer, Sir Humphrey Gilbert, who was living in Red Cross Street, in the parish of St. Giles, Cripplegate, in 1583, the year that he met his death at sea. 1682 The same parish claims Frobisher, whose remains (excepting his entrails, which were interred at Plymouth, where he died) lie buried in St. Giles's Church, and to whom a mural monument was erected by the vestry in 1888, just three centuries after the defeat of the Armada, to which he had contributed so much. If Hawkins himself did not reside in the city, his widow had a mansion house in Mincing Lane. 1683 He, too, had probably lived there, for although he died and was buried at sea, a monument was erected to his memory and that of Katherine, his first wife, in the church of St. Dunstan-in-the-East. 1684 There is one other—a citizen of London and son of an alderman—whose name has been handed down as having taken an active part in the defence of the kingdom at this time, not at sea, but on land. A monument in the recently restored church of St. Helen, Bishopsgate, tells us that Martin Bond, son of Alderman William Bond, "was captaine in ye yeare 1588 at ye campe at Tilbury, and after remained chief captaine of ye trained bands of this citty until his death." The monument represents him as sitting in a tent guarded by two sentinels, with a page holding a horse.

Disorganized state of the camp at Tilbury.

It was well that the Spaniards suffered defeat at sea, for had they been able to effect a landing they would have made short work with the half-trained and dissatisfied soldiers in the camp at Tilbury, and London would have been at their mercy. Even the presence of Elizabeth herself, riding on horseback through the camp, as she did on the 8th August, was but poor compensation to the soldiers for the want of victuals and wages. Many sold their armour and weapons to pay themselves as soon as the camp broke up. Citizens of London were warned by royal proclamation (20 Aug.) 1685 against purchasing armour and weapons offered by soldiers, who were declared to "have most falsly and slanderously given out that they weare compelled to make sale of them for that they receaved noe pay, which is most untruely reported." Any armour or weapons bought before publication of the proclamation was to be delivered up to the mayor with particulars as to the way the purchase had been effected and compensation would be allowed.

City loans of £30,000 and £20,000, Sept.-Dec., 1588.

Notwithstanding the extreme parsimony with which Elizabeth had fitted out both army and navy, the cost of preparations to meet the attack of Spain had been great, and she was obliged to borrow money. In September (1588) the City advanced her the sum of £30,000, receiving her bond for repayment in the following March; and in the following December she borrowed a further sum of £20,000 to be repaid by the following April. Both sums were raised among the livery companies. 1686

Expedition to Spain under Norris and Drake, April-July, 1589.

In March of the following year (1589) parliament granted a liberal supply, but the grant was accompanied by a request that Elizabeth would no longer await the assaults of Spain, but carry the war into the enemy's country. This the queen declared her inability to undertake on the score of poverty. She promised, however, to give what assistance she could to any of her subjects who relished such enterprise. Norris and Drake were at hand, ready and willing to undertake the work on these terms. Already (in January) the City had been called upon to furnish them with 400 strong and able men. 1687 At the end of March 1,000 more were required, and each alderman was instructed to search in his ward for all able and masterless men and all other persons fit for service that were householders and not charged with families, and to bring them to the Leadenhall. 1688 With these and other forces the expedition set sail, but beyond storming Vigo and committing some damage at Corunna, it accomplished nothing and returned in July.

Disbanded soldiers and sailors in the city.

Again the city was threatened with danger and disease from the presence of disbanded soldiers and sailors, who were apt to carry their freebooting habits wherever they went, more especially when starvation stared them in the face. Sir Martin Calthorp did what he could to relieve them, paying out of his own pocket no less a sum than £100. His conduct was applauded by the lords of the council, who authorised him to raise a further sum towards assisting the soldiers to their homes in the country by allowing them a half-penny a mile. 1689

Soldiers ordered to return to their own homes.

A royal proclamation was subsequently (20 Aug.) issued promising payment of any money due to mariners who would make a written application to the Admiralty. Soldiers were to return to the country where they had been pressed and apply to the justices or other officers who pressed them, and who would make a certificate to the lieutenant of the county, when the soldiers would receive "reasonable contentment." 1690 This, however, failed entirely to remedy the evil. 1691 Four days before this proclamation precept had been issued to the aldermen for a good and substantial double watch to be kept throughout the night of the 16th August until noon of the next day. There had been a report abroad of a large meeting of soldiers and sailors to take place as early as five o'clock on the morning of the 17th in the neighbourhood of Tower Hill. 1692

Elizabeth and Henry IV of France, 1589-1591.

The revolution which followed the assassination of the French king by Jaques Clements about this time (Aug., 1589) brought fresh anxiety to Elizabeth, who felt bound to support the Protestant Henry of Navarre with all the means at her command, as an indirect way of carrying on the war against Spain. Four thousand men were to be despatched for his assistance, 1,000 of whom the City was called upon to supply. As they were to be picked men the lords of the council ordered double the number, or 2,000 men, to be got ready, in order that expert officers might review them and select the number required. 1693 The demand was enforced by a letter from the queen herself, in which she drew attention to the necessity of assisting one whose preservation was of so much importance to England. 1694 The city's gates were at once closed by the mayor's orders to prevent the exodus of "lusty, strong, able and young men" to avoid service. 1695 Although Henry IV was materially assisted by the arrival of English troops, their operations were chiefly confined to Normandy.

The City and the Earl of Essex, 1591.

A further contingent of 400 men was shortly afterwards (22 June) demanded by the queen, 300 of which were to be got ready at once. More care than usual was to be bestowed on their selection, as they were to be employed under the Earl of Essex, 1696 with whom the City happened at this time to be out of favour. What was the precise cause of the City's disgrace does not appear; we only know that the civic authorities were anxious to recover the good will of one so near the person of the sovereign, and to this end made him a "small present," thanking him for his past services, for the general defence of the realm, and of all Christian estates professing the Gospel and true religion of Almighty God, and assuring him that they were not so much presenting him with money, in sending him a gratuity, as with "the hart of the citie." They begged that if some private offence had been given to his lordship he would "wrappe it up" in this public testimony of their hearty good wills. 1697

The City agrees to fit out six ships and a pinnace, 16 June, 1591.

In the meantime the Common Council had, at the queen's request, agreed (16 June) to fit out six ships of war and one pinnace at a cost of £7,400, to be levied on the companies. This sum was afterwards raised to £8,000. 1698 Towards the close of the year (9 Nov.) the lord mayor and sheriffs were called upon to levy 200 able men to be "pioners." They were to be chosen out of the city of London and the county of Middlesex, and to be despatched to Dieppe for service under the Earl of Essex "a service vearie necessarie and we hope not of any long continuaunce," 1699 wrote the queen. In addition to men, the queen wanted money; and the Common Council agreed (18 Sept.) to lend her £20,000 for three months, afterwards renewed for six months. 1700

Search to be made for Spanish emissaries in disguise.

In the meantime Spanish emissaries, disguised as soldiers, mariners, merchants, gentlemen with comely apparel, and even as "gallantes," decked out in colours and feathers, had been doing the work of Philip silently but surely. Some had resorted to the Universities; some to the Inns of Court; whilst others had insinuated themselves into private families; but wherever they took up their abode, and in whatsoever capacity, their one aim and object had been to seduce the queen's subjects from their allegiance. So successful had been their efforts that Philip meditated another attack on England in 1592. At length commissioners were appointed in all parts of the country to search for these "venemous vipers." Householders were at the same time directed to enquire into the antecedents of those who lodged with them, and to mark if they attended Divine Service or not. A register or calendar of particulars respecting them was to be kept, to be shown on demand. 1701 Here is a description of one whose arrest was desired in 1596:— "A yonge man of meane and slender stature aged about xxvjtie wth a high collored face, red nose, a warte over his left eye, havinge two greate teeth before standinge out very apparant, he nameth himselffe Edward Harrison borne in Westmerland, apparelled in a crane collored fustian dublet, rounde hose, after the frenche facion, an olde paire of yollowe knit neather stockes, he escaped wthout either cloake, girdle, garters or shoes." 1702

Privateering expeditions against Spain, 1591-1592.

Whilst all exportation of munitions of war, corn and other victual into Spain or Portugal was strictly forbidden, 1703 the merchants of London, as well as noblemen and wealthy country gentlemen, were encouraged to deal blows at the enemy by fitting out privateers for scouring the Spanish Main. 1704 Many a rich prize was thus brought home, the spoil being divided by specially appointed commissioners, 1705 whose duty it was, among other things, to see that the Crown was not defrauded of the custom due upon the goods thus captured." 1706 The "fleet of the city of London" was very successful in this kind of work, and a sum of £6,000 fell to its lot as prize-money in 1591. This sum was ventured again in an expedition undertaken by Raleigh in the following year, 1707 with the result that the City netted no less a sum than £12,000, its share of the spoil of a rich "carraque" that Raleigh had captured. 1708

Proposal to build a pest-house for the city, 1592.

This lucky windfall befell the citizens at a time when money was sorely needed for building a pest-house or hospital for sufferers from the plague, which again visited the city at the close of 1592. 1709 The cost of such a building was estimated at £6,000. Various schemes were proposed for raising the money. At one time (July, 1593) it was resolved that the several livery companies which had taken shares in Raleigh's venture should contribute twelvepence in the pound of their clear gain towards the object. 1710 Later on (May, 1594) the companies were called upon to contribute one-third of their clear gain. Even this proved insufficient, and had to be supplemented by a "benevolence" in each ward. 1711 Another year went by, and the hospital was still unfinished. 1712

The hysterical Anne Burnell.

The strain which the continuation of the war and the threatened renewal of a Spanish invasion imposed upon the inhabitants of London at large was a great one, and appears to have affected the mind of a weak and hysterical woman, Anne Burnell. She gave out that she was a daughter of the king of Spain, and that the arms of England and Spain were to be seen, like *stigmata*, upon her back, as was vouched for by her servant Alice Digges. After medical examination, which proved her statement to be "false and proceedinge of some lewde and imposterouse pretence," she and her maid were ordered to be whipt, — "ther backes only beeinge layd bare," — at the cart's tail through the city on a market day, "with a note in writinge uppon the hinder part of there heades shewinge the cawse of there saide punishmente." 1713

Six ships, two pinnaces and 350 men provided by the City against Spain, July, 1594.

On the 16th July, 1594, the queen informed the citizens by letter of the king of Spain having made preparations to get possession of the harbour of Brest, and her determination to oppose him. She had given orders for certain companies of soldiers to be levied in divers counties, and she called upon the citizens to furnish her with a contingent of 450 men. They were to be well trained and supplied with armour and weapons; their "coate and conduct monye" would be found for them. 1714 The Court of Common Council met on the following day and agreed to provide the number of soldiers required. 1715 It had already (15 July) agreed to furnish six ships and two pinnaces for her majesty's service, 1716 which William Garraway and other owners of ships contracted to find for the sum of £5,000. 1717

Sir John Spencer and his daughter.

On Michaelmas-day (1594) John Spencer—"Rich Spencer" as he was called, from his extraordinary wealth—was elected mayor for the ensuing year. 1718 His daughter, much against her father's will, married Lord Compton. To thwart the matrimonial designs of a nobleman was in those days a perilous task, and Alderman Spencer was committed to the Fleet "for a contempt" in endeavouring to conceal his daughter. "Our Sir John Spencer, of London"—writes John Chamberlain 1719 to Dudley Carleton (15 March, 1599)—"was the last weeke committed to the Fleet for a contempt and hiding away his daughter, who, they say, is contracted to the Lord Compton; but now he is out again, and by all meanes seekes to hinder the match, alledging a precontract to Sir Arthur Henningham's sonne. But upon his beating and misusing her she was sequestred to one Barkers, a proctor, and from thence to Sir Henry Billingsleyes, 1720 where she yet remaines till the matter be tried. If the obstinate and self-willed fellow shold persist in his doggednes (as he protests he will) and geve her nothing, the poore lord shold have a warme catch."

A few weeks after Spencer's confinement in the Fleet we find him at variance with his brother aldermen for digging a pit on his estate near "Canbury," or Canonbury, and thereby drawing off water which should have gone to supply the poor of St. Bartholomew's Hospital to his own mansion. A request was sent to him by the mayor and Court of Aldermen to cease the conveyance of water until further order had been taken therein. 1721 Two years later his "doggednes" once more got him into trouble, and he was committed to Wood Street Compter for refusing to pay certain small sums of money due from him towards furnishing soldiers and armour. 1722 He died the 30th March, 1609, leaving behind him £80,000.

His daughter, who inherited her father's money, was possessed also of some of her father's spirit, and Lord Compton appears to have got "a warme catch" indeed to judge from a letter she addressed to him soon after her father's death. After reminding her "sweete life" of the care she had ever taken of his estate and of her excellent behaviour, she begs him to allow her £1,600 per annum, to be paid quarterly, besides £600 a year for charitable works. She will have three horses for her own saddle "that none shall dare to lend or borrow; none lend but I, none borrow but you." She will have so many gentlemen and so many gentlewomen to wait upon her at home, whilst riding, hunting, hawking or travelling. When on the road she will have laundresses "sent away with the carriages to see all safe," and chambermaids sent before with the grooms that the chambers may be ready, sweet and clean. Seeing that her requests are so reasonable she expects her husband to find her children in apparel and schooling, and all her servants in wages. She concludes by declaring her will to have her houses handsomely furnished, not omitting "silver warming pans," warns her husband against lending money to the lord chamberlain, and prays him to increase her allowance and double her attendance on his becoming an earl. 1723

The capture of Cadiz, July, 1596.

Spencer was succeeded in the mayoralty by Sir Stephen Slaney, and the latter's year of office proved a busy one. Spain was meditating another descent on England "with a greate navy of shippes by sea and huge powers of men by lande," and the City was expected to furnish sixteen ships and 10,000 men for land service. The naval demand was extravagant, and after some remonstrance was reduced to one for twelve ships and two pinnaces, with a complement of 1,200 men. 1724 The City made an attempt to get a reduction made also in the land force, but with what success is not clear. This was in December, 1595. The money was found by imposing a tax of 2s. 8d. in the pound for goods and 4s. in the pound for lands on every inhabitant of the city, 1725 and by advances made by the livery companies. 1726 On the 8th January (1596) the queen addressed a very gracious letter of thanks to the City for the promptitude displayed in furnishing the ships. 1727 Instead of waiting for Spain to attack, Elizabeth carried the war into the enemy's country, and Cadiz was captured six months later by Essex and Howard. This exploit, in which the city of London took its share, has been described 1728 as the most brilliant that had ever been achieved by English arms between Agincourt and Blenheim, and it was celebrated in London with bonfires and general rejoicing. 1729 As soon as the Common Council heard of the arrival of the fleet from its successful voyage it despatched commissioners to see after the City's share of prize money. 1730

Calais falls into the hands of Spain, April, 1596.

In the meantime (April, 1596) the queen's tortuous and parsimonious policy had led to Calais falling into the hands of Spain. She had called upon the Londoners to furnish 1,000 soldiers to assist in raising the siege, but it is a question whether they ever got beyond Dover. 1731 Roused for the time to a more energetic line of action, she determined to prevent, if possible, the sister town of Boulogne falling into the hands of Spain, and she called upon the city of London to supply 405 men towards the force to be despatched in the autumn for its defence. 1732

Reinforcements for the Netherlands, July, 1596.

The necessity of recruiting the garrison of the cautionary town of Flushing, from which troops had recently been withdrawn for service on the high seas, compelled the queen to apply again to the City (July, 1596) for a contingent of 200 men. 1733

A demand for ten ships to be furnished by the City, Dec., 1596.

This constant drain on the resources of the city at length called forth a remonstrance. The city was being threatened with famine at the close of the year (1596), when another demand arrived for ten ships to be fitted out for the public service. The matter was referred to a committee, and a reply was drawn up, which was practically a refusal to obey the commands of the council. 1734

The City's reply.

It set forth the utter inability of the citizens, however willing they might be, to supply more ships. They had already expended on sea service alone, and irrespective of their disbursements in 1588, no less a sum than 100,000 marks within the last few years; so that the lords of the council would see that the citizens had not been wanting in good will and affection towards] that service. The same good will still remained, but there was lacking the like ability, owing partly to former charges by sea and land, but more especially to the great scarcity of victual which had continued in the city for the past three years, and had compelled many who had formerly been well off to reduce their expenditure, whilst others had been obliged to relinquish their trades and break up their households. As a proof of the poverty existing in the city their lordships were reminded that when wheat was offered at a very moderate rate many were too poor to purchase any. The wealthier sort would therefore have to be called upon to subscribe towards the maintenance of the poorer class, and so be rendered less able to contribute to other demands. The letter proceeded to draw their lordships' attention to what after all was the reason which weighed most with the citizens for refusing to contribute any more to the naval service. "Besides theis defectes" wrote the mayor and corporation "we may not conceale the great discontentment and utter discouragement of the common people wthin this citie touchinge their adventure in the late viage to the towne at *Cales* [Cadiz] wch albeit it was perfourmed wth soe great honor and happy successe as that the enemye was greatly weakned, the army enritched and such store of treasure and other comodities (besides that wch was thear embeazelled) brought safe home as was sufficient to defraye the charges of the whole voyage, yet forasmuch as neither their principall nor any parte thereof was restored unto them contrarie to the meaninge of the contract set downe in writinge under the signatures of two noble persons in her highnes name, they are made hereby utterly unfitt and indisposed for the like service to be done hereafter." 1735 The Cadiz adventure—they went on to say—had cost the City £1,900, a great part of which sum was still not collected, whilst the City's Chamber was already in debt to the extent of £14,000 and utterly unable to afford relief. The writers, in conclusion, expressed themselves ready to contribute towards the defence of the whole realm in like proportion as others of her majesty's subjects, and with this arrangement they felt sure her majesty would be well content.

What was the effect of this reply does not appear; but in one respect the queen was more than a match for the citizens. They had pleaded scarcity of provisions and poverty as an excuse for not carrying out her recent orders. Very good; let the livery companies, whose duty it was to find men and money when required, practise a little self-restraint in the coming summer (1597). Let them, she said, forbear giving feasts in their halls and elsewhere, and bestow half the money thus saved on the poor; and the order of the Court of Aldermen went forth accordingly. 1736

Affairs in Ireland, 1594-1599.

For some years past it had always been feared lest Spain should again endeavour to strike at England through Ireland. A rising in Ulster under Hugh O'Neill, known in England as the Earl of Tyrone, in 1594 was followed by an appeal to Spain for help in 1595. Philip acceded to the request and another Armada was got ready; but the fleet had scarcely put to sea before it suffered a similar fate to the Armada of 1588 and was shattered by a storm (Dec., 1596). The Tyrone rebellion necessitated further calls on the City for men and money. In May, 1597, it was asked to furnish 500 men, such as Sir Samuel Bagnall might approve of. 1737 In the following year—when Bagnall met with a crushing defeat on the Blackwater—it was called upon to supply a further contingent of 300 men and to lend the queen a sum of £20,000. 1738 In 1599 Elizabeth sent her favourite Essex to conquer Ireland in good earnest, to prevent the country falling into the hands of Spain. She at the same time called upon the City for more soldiers, and borrowed another sum of £60,000 on mortgage. 1739

A scare in London, July-Aug., 1598.

In the meantime a report again got abroad that a Spanish fleet was assembling at Brest for a descent on England. On the 25th July, 1598, the lords of the council wrote to the mayor calling upon him to see that some twelve or sixteen vessels were provided with ordnance and powder for the defence of the Thames, and the court of Common Council at once took the necessary steps for fitting out the ships as well as for mustering a force of 3,000 men, afterwards raised to 6,000. 1740 The city's forces and the charge of the river were confided to the Earl of Cumberland. Sir Thomas Gerrard had at first been appointed colonel of the Londoners, "but for an old grudge since the last parliament they wold none of him." 1741 It was proposed to throw a bridge of boats across the Thames near Gravesend, after the fashion of Parma's famous bridge erected across the Scheldt in 1585, and the court of Common Council (4 Aug.) gave orders for collecting "hoyes, barges, lighters, boardes, cordes" and other material necessary for the purpose. 1742 This project was, however, abandoned in favour of sinking hulks in the channel of the river if occasion should arise. Watch was ordered to be strictly kept in the city night and day, lanterns to be hung out at night and the streets blocked with chains. 1743 It had been rumoured that the Spanish fleet had been descried off the Isle of Wight, and although the rumour proved false it caused no little alarm in the city and gave rise to these precautions. 1744 After a few days the supposed danger passed away. The fleet, which had been rapidly got together, and included twelve ships and thirty hoys furnished by the city for the defence of the river, put to sea nevertheless, whilst the land forces were gradually disbanded. 1745

The abortive insurrection of the Earl of Essex, Feb., 1601.

The administration of Essex in Ireland was a signal failure, and he made matters worse by quitting his post without leave and forcing his presence upon the queen. He had hoped to recover her good grace by his unexpected appearance. Elizabeth was not to be thus cajoled. She ordered him into custody, deprived him of his offices, and, what was of more importance to him, refused to renew his patent of a monopoly of sweet wines. Although the earl soon regained his liberty he could not forget his disgrace, and his overweening vanity drove him to concert measures against the government. In 1601 he rode at the head of a few followers into the city, expecting the citizens to rise in his favour. The mayor had, however, been forewarned, and

1,000 men were held in readiness in each ward fully armed for the safeguard of the city. 1746 The earl and his band proceeded to the house of Thomas Smith, in Fenchurch Street, one of the sheriffs, who had represented himself, or been represented by others, as able and willing to further the earl's cause. That the sheriff was thought by his fellow citizens to have been implicated in Essex's mad attempt is seen from the fact that within a week he was deprived, not only of his sheriffwick, but also of his aldermanry, 1747 but to what extent he had compromised himself it is difficult to determine. Finding the citizens averse to a rising and his passage stopped by pikemen under the command of Sir John Gilbert and Sir Robert Cross, who respectively had charge of Ludgate and Newgate, 1748 and who refused to surrender them except to the sheriff in person as the queen's representative, the earl and his company hastened to the riverside and returned to Essex House by water. He was subsequently arrested and committed to the Tower, together with two of his accomplices, the Earls of Rutland and Southampton. Another of his followers, the Earl of Bedford, was committed for a while to the custody of Leonard Holiday, a city alderman. 1749 The queen, who had shown no more agitation at the news of the attempt to raise the city than "of a fray in Fleet Street," 1750 took an early opportunity of thanking the citizens and her subjects generally for the loyalty they had displayed. 1751

A sum of £200 was distributed by the civic authorities among the officers engaged in the city's defence, but the two knights at Ludgate and Newgate refused to accept any gratuity. 1752 For a week or more strict guard was kept at the city's gates, whilst bodies of troops fully armed were kept in readiness at the Royal Exchange and Saint Paul's Churchyard in case of disturbance. 1753 Essex was brought to trial on a charge of treason, convicted and executed (25 Feb.). Sheriff Smith was made to undergo a severe cross-examination, but appears to have got off with his life. 1754

Mountjoy's conquest of Ireland, 1600-1603.

Lord Mountjoy, who had succeeded Essex in Ireland, set to work systematically to bring the country into complete submission. The conquest was not effected without considerable aid from the city of London. From 1600 to 1602 the citizens were being constantly called upon to supply fresh forces for Ireland. 1755 A Spanish force which at length came to Tyrone's assistance in 1601, and established itself at Kinsale, was compelled to surrender. The work of the sword was supplemented by famine; until at last Tyrone himself was carried in triumph to Dublin, and the conquest of Ireland was complete.

The parliament of 1601.

Mountjoy's work could not be carried on without money, and Elizabeth had been compelled in 1601 to summon a parliament to obtain supplies. Hitherto the Puritans, who began in the early part of the reign to gain a hold in the House of Commons, and had gradually increased in strength, had been content, in the presence of a common danger, to refrain from offering any systematic opposition to Elizabeth's government. But now that the defeat of the Armada, the death of Philip II and the firm establishment of Henry IV on the throne of France had removed all danger from abroad, they began to change front. As soon as the House met the Commons chose Croke (or Crooke), the City's Recorder, their Speaker, an honour which the City acknowledged by ordering (3 Nov.) a gift of forty marks to be made to him. 1756 When the question of supplies came before the House they were readily granted, but a bill was introduced to abolish patents of monopolies, which the queen had been in the habit of lavishly bestowing upon her favourites by virtue of her prerogative, and by which the price of nearly every commodity had been grievously enhanced. It was in vain that the minority in the House found fault with the Speaker for allowing the queen's prerogative to be called in question. The majority had the nation at its back; and finding this to be the case Elizabeth, who knew when to give way, yielded with grace. When a deputation of the Commons waited upon her and expressed the gratitude of the House at her concession, she replied in words full of kindness and dignity, thanking the Commons for having pointed out her error, and calling God to witness that she had never cherished anything but what tended to her people's good, "Though you have had," she assured them, "and may have, many princes more mighty and wise sitting in this seat, yet you never had, or ever shall have, any that will be more careful and loving."

The last days of Elizabeth, 1601-1603.

These were the last words addressed by the queen to her people, and their truth was borne out by her conduct throughout her long reign. Under her the country had become united and prosperous. By the citizens of London she was especially beloved, for they always found in her a supporter of trade and commerce. If the Hanseatic towns behaved unfairly to the merchant adventurers Elizabeth promptly retaliated upon the merchants of the Steelyard. She had threatened to close the Steelyard altogether in 1578, when English merchants were ordered to quit Hamburg, and twenty years later (1598), when fresh difficulties had arisen, the threat was carried out. 1757

The queen rarely left London to make one of her many gorgeous progresses from country house to country house or returned home without some notice being sent to the city to allow of its inhabitants taking "the comfort of behoulding her royall persone." 1758 Her love of personal admiration and of handsome men continued to the last. As late as November, 1602, she commanded the mayor and aldermen and a number of the "best and most grave" citizens to attend her from Chelsea to Westminster, and the mayor, knowing her weakness, ordered the livery companies to choose the "most grave and comlie" members to join the procession. 1759 In the early morning of the 24th March, 1603, she died at Richmond, to the sincere regret of the citizens no less than of the nation at large.

Footnotes

1. Strype remarks of Thames water that it "did sooner become fine and clear than the New River water, and was ever a clearer water."—Strype, Stow's Survey, ed. 1720, bk. i, p. 25. Another writer speaks of "that most delicate and serviceable ryver of Thames."—Howes's Chron., p. 938.

2. During Edgar's reign (958-975), the foreign trade of the City had increased to such a degree, and notably with a body of German merchants from the Eastern shores of the Baltic, called "Easterlings" (subsequently known as the Hanse Merchants of the Steel-yard), that his son and successor Ethelred drew up a code of laws for the purpose of regulating it.

3. "Et ipsa (*i.e.* Lundonia) multorum emporium populorum terrâ marique venientium."—Hist. Eccl., lib. ii, cap. iii.

4. Stubbs, Const. Hist., i, 409.

5. See ordinances made by the Earl (32 Eliz.).—Hunter's Hallamshire (1819), p. 119.

6. Luttrell, Diary, i, p. 314.

7. "At Suetonius mira constantia medios inter hostes Londinium perrexit, cognomento quidem coloniæ non insigne, sed copia negotiatorum et commeatuum maxime celebre."—Tacitus, Ann., xiv, 33.

8. For the direction of the various routes, see Elton's Origins of Engl. Hist., p. 344 note.

9. Stubbs, Const. Hist., i., 60.

10. The church of St. Peter-upon-Cornhill claims a Roman origin, but its claim is unsubstantiated by any proof.

11. This appeal took the following form:—"The groans of the Britons to Aetius, for the third time Consul [*i.e.* A.D. 446]. The savages drive us to the sea, and the sea casts us back upon the savages; so arise two kinds of

death, and we are either drowned or slaughtered." —Elton, Origins of Engl. Hist., p. 360.

12. "Postea vero explorata insulæ fertilitate et indigenarum inertia, rupto fœdere, in ipsos, a quibus fuerant invitati arma verterunt." — Newburgh, Hist. Rerum Anglic. (Rolls Series No. 82). Procœmium. p. 13.

13. Anglo-Sax. Chron., ii, 12.

14. "In qua videlicet gente tune temporis Sabertus, nepos Ethelberti ex sorore Ricula, regnabat quamvis sub potestate positus ejusdem Ethelberti, qui omnibus, ut supra dictum est, usque ad terminum Humbræ fluminis, Anglorum gentibus imperabat." —Bede, Lib. ii, c. iii.

15. "Quorum [i.e., Orientalium Saxonum] metropolis Lundonia civitas est." —Bede, Lib. ii, c. iii. So, again, another writer describes London at the time it was devastated by the Danes in 851 as "Sita in aquilonari ripa Tamesis fluminis in confinio East-Sæxum et Middel-Sæxum, sed tamen ad East-Sæxum illa civitas cum veritate pertinet." —Flor. Wigorn., (ed. by Thorpe, for Engl. Hist. Soc.), i, 72.

16. Kemble. Saxons in England, ii, 556.

17. "Mellitum vero Lundonienses episcopum recipere noluerunt, idolatris magis pontificibus servire gaudentes. Bede, Lib. ii, cap. vi.— Cf. Flor. Wigorn., i, 13.

18. "Ecclesiam ... beati Petri quæ sita est in loco terribili qui ab incolis Thorneye nunenpatur ... quæ olim ... beati Æthelberti hortatu ... a Sabertho prædivite quodam sub-regulo Lundoniæ, nepote videlicet ipsius regis, constructa est." —Kemble, Cod. Dipl., 555.

19. Roger de Hoveden (Rolls Series No. 51), i, 8, 16, 18.

20. Norton, Commentaries on the City of London, 3rd ed., p. 53, &c.

21. Thorpe, 114. The Troy weight was kept in the Husting of London and known as the Husting-weight.—Strype, Stow's Survey (1720), Bk. v., 369.

22. Anglo-Sax. Chron., ii, 55.

23. "And in the same year [i.e. 851] came three hundred and fifty ships to the mouth of the Thames, and landed, and took Canterbury and London by storm." —Id. ii, 56.

24. Anglo-Sax. Chron., ii, 64, 65.

25. The Anglo-Saxon Chronicle—the existence of which in its present form has been attributed to Alfred's encouragement of literature—seems to convey this meaning, although it is not quite clear on the point. Henry of Huntingdon (Rolls Series No. 44, pp. 148-149) ascribes the recovery of London by Alfred to the year 886. The late Professor Freeman (Norman Conquest, i., 56) does the same, and compares the status of London at the time with that of a German free city, which it more nearly resembled, than an integral portion of a kingdom.

26. Freeman, Norman Conquest, i, 279.

27. Anglo-Sax. Chron., ii., 67. Cf. "Lundoniam civitatem honorifice restauravit et habitabilem fecit quam etiam. Ætheredo Merciorum comitti servandam commendavit."—Flor. Wigorn., i, 101.

28. Stubbs, Const. Hist., i, 405.

29. Anglo-Sax. Chron., ii, 71.

30. According to Henry of Huntingdon (Rolls Series No. 74. p. 150) Alfred diverted the waters of the Lea that his enemy's ships were stranded.

31. -Id., ii. 71. Cf. "Quarum navium Lundonienses quasdam Lundoniam vehunt, quasdam vero penitus confringunt."—Flor. Wigorn., i, 115.

32. Judicia Civitatis Lundoniæ, Thorpe, 97, 103.

33. This is the earliest mention of a guildhall in London; and the ale-making which took place at the meeting of the officers of the frith-guild, accounts in all probability for Giraldus Cambrensis (Vita Galfridi, Rolls Series No. 21 iii., c. 8.) having described the Guildhall of London as "Aula publica quæ a potorum conventu nomen accepit."

34. "Notwithstanding the butt-filling and feasting, this appears to have been a purely religious and social guild, and, although it may have subsequently become a power in the city, so far, it is only of importance as the first evidence of combination among the inhabitants of London for anything like corporate action."—Loftie, Hist. of London, i, 68.

35. Laws of Athelstan.—Thorpe, 93.

36. Judicia Civitatis Lundoniæ.—Thorpe, 100.

37. Gross, The Gild Merchant, i, 178-179.

38. Wilkins, Leges Anglo-Sax., p. 59.

39. "And if a merchant thrived so that he fared thrice over the wide sea by his own means [cœæøte, craft] then was he thenceforth of thane-right worthy." (Thorpe, 81.) The word cœæøte is similarly translated in Wilkins's Leges Anglo-Saxonicæ; (ed. 1721, p. 71.) *per facultates suas*; but there seems no reason why it should not be taken to mean literally a craft or vessel. The passage occurs in a list of "People's Rank" which "formerly" prevailed, and is probably of Athelstan's time, even if it did not form part of the Judicia Civitatis Lundoniæ.—Wilkins, *op. cit.* p. 70 note.

40. Anglo-Sax. Chron., ii, 105.

41. Anglo-Sax. Chron., ii, p. 114.

42. *-Id.* ii, p. 115.

43. *-Id.* ii. pp. 117, 118. Annal. Monast., Waverley (Rolls Series No. 36), ii, p. 173.

44. The towns of Leicester, Lincoln, Nottingham, Stamford, and Derby, which for many years were occupied by the Danes, were so called.

45. Anglo-Sax. Chron., ii, pp. 118, 119.

46. *-Id.* ii, p. 119. Henry of Huntingdon (Rolls Series No 74), p. 180.

47. Anglo-Sax. Chron., ii, p. 120.

48. *-Id.* ii, p. 120. *Cf.* "Ad hæc principes se non amplius Danicum regem admissuros in Angliam unanimiter spoponderunt."—Flor. Wigorn., i, p. 169.

49. The Heimskringla or Chronicle of the kings of Norway, translated from the Icelandic of Snorro Sturleson, ii. pp. 8-11.

50. Anglo-Sax. Chron., ii, 120.

51. Anglo-Sax. Chron., ii, 121.

52. *-Id.* ii., 122.

53. Malmesbury, Gesta Regum (Rolls Series, No. 90), i, 215.

54. Freeman, Norman Conquest, i, 308.

55. Thorpe, Ancient Laws and Institutes, 127, 128.

56. In course of time the natives of Denmark acquired the privilege of sojourning all the year round in London—a privilege accorded to few, if any other, foreigners. They enjoyed moreover the benefits of the 'the law of the city of London' (*la lei de la citie de Loundres*) in other words, the right of resorting to fair or market in any place throughout England.—Liber Cust. pt. i, p. 63.

57. Freeman, Norman Conquest, i, 418.

58. Anglo-Sax. Chron., ii, 122.

59. "At oppidanis magnanimiter pugnantibus repulsa."—Malmesbury, i, 216.

60. Anglo-Sax. Chron., ii, 123.

61. -*Id.* ii, 121, 123. Henry of Huntingdon relates that Eadric caused a panic on the field of battle by crying out that Edmund had been killed. "Flet Engle, flet Engle, ded is Edmund."

62. Freeman, Norman Conquest, i, 437.

63. Freeman, Norman Conquest, i, 538.

64. "The 'lithsmen' (ship-owners) of London, who with others raised Harold to the throne, were doubtless such 'burg-thegns.'"—Gross, The Gild Merchant, i, 186. *Cf.* Lingard, i, 318. Norton Commentaries, pp. 23-24.

65. Green, Conquest of England, p. 462. Loftie, Hist. of London, i, 73. "The Londoners who attended must have gone by way of the river in their 'liths.'"—Historic Towns, London (Loftie), p. 197.

66. Anglo-Sax. Chron., ii, 129.

67. At the death of Harold, Harthacnut was invited to accept the crown by an embassy from England, of which the Bishop of London was a member. He accepted the offer and crossed over from the continent with a fleet of sixty ships, manned by Danish soldiers, and his first act was to demand eight marks for each rower; an imposition that was borne with difficulty. Anglo-Sax. Chron. ii, 132.

68. Anglo-Sax Chron., ii, 132.

69. Freeman, Norman Conquest, 2nd ed., ii. 5. But according to Kemble (Saxons in England, ii, 259 note), Edward's election took place at a hastily convened meeting at Gillingham.

70. "London, que caput est regni et legum. semper curia domini regis."—Laws of Edward Confessor, Thorpe, p. 197 note.

71. For a list of gemóts held in London from A.D. 790, see Kemble's Saxons in England, ii, 241-261.

72. Malmesbury, i, 242-244. Freeman, ii, 148-332.

73. Freeman, ii, 324.

74. Sed omnis civitas duci obviam et auxilio processit et præsidio acclamantque illi omnes una voce prospere in adventu suo. "Life of Edward Conf." (Rolls Series No. 3.), p. 406.

75. "Interim quosdam per internuntios, quosdam per se cives Lundonienses, quos variis pollicitationibus prius illexerat, convenit, et ut omnes fere quæ volebat omnino vellent, effecit."—Flor. Wigorn., i., 209.

76. Anglo-Sax. Chron., ii, 165-167.

77. "Aldredus autem Eboracensis archiepiscopus et iidem Comites cum civibus Lundoniensibus et butsecarlis, clitonem Eadgarum, Eadmundi Ferrei Lateris nepotem, in regem levare volueren, et cum eo se pugnam inituros promisere; sed dum ad pugnam descendere multi se paravere, comites suum auxilium ab eis retraxere, et cum suo exercitu domum redierunt."—Flor. Wigorn., i, 228.

78. Such is the description of William's march, as given by Malmesbury (ii, 307). Another chronicler describes his march as one of slaughter and devastation.—Flor. Wigorn., i, 228.

79. The bishop was certainly Norman, and so probably was the port-reeve.

80. Anglo-Sax. Chron. ii, 168-169.

81. This charter is preserved in the Town Clerk's Office at the Guildhall. A fac-simile of it and of another charter of William, granting

lands to Deorman, forms a frontispiece to this volume. The late Professor Freeman (Norman Conquest, second edition, revised 1876, iv, 29) wrote of this venerable parchment as bearing William's mark—"the cross traced by the Conqueror's own hand"—but this appears to be a mistake. The same authority, writing of the transcript of the charter made by the late Mr. Riley and printed by him in his edition of the *Liber Custumarum* (Rolls Series, pt. ii, p. 504), remarks that, "one or two words here look a little suspicious"; and justly so, for the transcript is far from being literally accurate.

82.   -Cf. "*Ego volo quod vos sitis omni lege illa digni qua fuistis Edwardi diebus Regis.*" These words appear in the xivth century Latin version of William's Charter, preserved at the Guildhall.

83.   Liber Albus (Rolls Series i, 26).

84.   Opinions differ as to the derivation of the term port. Some, like Kemble, refer it to the Lat. *portus*, in the sense of an enclosed place for sale or purchase, a market. ("Portus est conclusus locus, quo importantur merces et inde exportantur. Est et statio conclusa et munita."—Thorpe, i, 158). Others, like Dr. Stubbs (Const. Hist., i, 404 n.), connect it with Lat. *porta*, not in its restricted signification of a gate, but as implying a market place, markets being often held at a city's gates. The Latin terms *porta* and *portus* were in fact so closely allied, that they both alike signified a market place or a gate. Thus, in the will of Edmund Harengeye, enrolled in the Court of Husting, London, we find the following: "Ac eciam lego et volo quod illa tenementa cum magno portu vocato le Brodegate ... vendantur per executores meos."— Hust. Roll, 114 (76).

85.   Norton, Commentaries on the City of London, 3rd ed., pp. 258-259.

86.   "London and her election of Stephen," a paper read before the Archæol. Inst. in 1866, by the late Mr. Green (p. 267).

87.   Freeman, Norman Conquest, v, p. 55.

88.   There appears to be no doubt that the charter preserved at the Guildhall had a seal, but not a fragment remains.

89.   "Et dicunt quod prefatus dominus conquestor ante fundacionem ecclesie predicte et confeccionem carte sue de qua superius fit mencio auctoritate parliament sui et per duas cartes suas quas dicti maior et Cives hic proferunt scilicet per unam earam dimissit tunc civibus London' totam dictam civitatem et vice-comitatum London' cum omnibus appendiciis

rebus et consuetudinibus eis qualitercumque pertinentibus.... Et per alteram concessit et auctoritate supradicta confirmavit eisdem civibus et successoribus suis quod haberent predicta ac omnes alias libertates et liberas consuetudines suas illesas quas habuerunt tempore dicti Sancti Regis Edwardi progenitoris sui."—Letter Book K, fo. 120 b.

90.   "Tantaque pax suis regnavit temporibus, quod puella virguncula auro onusta, indempnis et intacta Angliam potuit peragrare."—Mat. Paris, Hist. Angl. (Rolls Series No. 44), i, 29.

91.   Anglo-Sax. Chron., ii, p. 187. Flor. Wigorn., ii, p. 19.

92.   Anglo-Sax. Chron., ii, p. 187. Flor. Wigorn., ii, p. 19.

93.   Stow's Survey (Thoms's ed.), p. 121.

94.   Malmesbury. ii, 375.

95.   Anglo-Sax. Chron., ii, 189.

96.   -*Id.*, ii, 202.

97.   "Those of the council who were nigh at hand."—Anglo-Sax. Chron., ii, 204.

98.   Mat. Paris, Hist. Angl. (Rolls Series No. 44) i, 176.

99.   See Round's Geoffrey de Mandeville (p. 366), where the writer conjectures the date of the charter to have been between 1130 and 1135, and brings evidence in favour of it having been purchased by the payment of a large sum of money.

100.   Set out under fifteen heads in the City's *Liber Albus*. (Rolls Series) i, 128-129.

101.   Stubbs, Const. Hist., i, 404, 405. Round, Geoffrey de Mandeville. p. 356.

102.   The sum of 100 marks of silver recorded (Pipe Roll, 31 Hen. I) as having been paid for the shrievalty in 1130, appears to have been more of the nature of a fine than a *firma*.

103.   "Whereas from time immemorial there have been and of right ought to be two sheriffs of this city, which said two sheriffs during all the

time aforesaid have constituted and of right ought to constitute one sheriff of the county of Middlesex...."—Preamble to Act of Common Council, 7th April, 1748, re Nomination and election of Sheriffs. Journal 59, fo. 130b.

104.   Round, Geoffrey de Mandeville, p. 357. Mr. Round's statements (*op. cit.*, Appendix P), that "this one *firma* ... represents one *corpus comitatus*, namely Middlesex, inclusive of London," and that "from this conclusion there is no escape," are more capable of refutation than he is willing to allow.

· 105.   "It is probable that whilst the Sheriff in his character of Sheriff was competent to direct the customary business of the Court, it was in that of *justitia* that he transacted business under the King's writ."—Stubbs, Const. History, i, 389, note.

106.   "Post hoc prædictus Justitiarius ... accessit ad Gildhalle Londoniarum, et ibi tenuit placita de die in diem ... et incontinenti ... ilia terminavit nullo juris ordine observato contra leges civitatis et etiam contra leges et consuetudines cujuslibet liberi hominis de regno Anglie. Quod vero cives semper calumpniaverunt, dicentes quod nullus debet placitare in civitate de transgressionibus ibidem factis nisi vicecomites Londoniarium."—Lib. de Ant. (Camd. Soc.), p. 40.

107.   Round. Geoffrey de Mandeville. pp. 107-113, 373, and Appendix K.

108.   Mat. Paris (Hist. Angl. i, 251), ascribes the incessant turmoil of the latter part of the reign to the vengeance of the deity for this breach of faith.

109.   "Id quoque sui esse juris, suique specialiter privilegii, ut si rex ipsorum quoquo moclo obiret, alius suo provisu in regno substituendus e vestigio succederet."—Gesta Stephani (Rolls Series No. 82), iii, 5-6.

110.   "With the solemn independent election of a king, the great part which London was to play in England's history had definitely begun."—Green, London and her Election of Stephen.

111.   Gesta Stephani (Rolls Series No. 82). iii. 17.

112.   Round, Geoffrey de Mandeville, p. 18.

113.   "Eodem anno in Pentecoste resedit rex Londoniæ in Turri, episcopo tantum modo Sagiensi præsente: ceteri vel fastidierunt vel timuerunt venire. Aliquanto post, mediante legato, colloquium indictum est inter

imperatricem et regem. si forte Deo inspirante pax reformari posset."—
Malmesbury, Hist. Nov. (Rolls Series No. 90.), ii, 564.

114. "Juravit et affidavit imperatrix episcopo quod omnia majora
negotia in Anglia præcipueque donationes episcopatuum et abbatiarum
ejus nutum spectarent, si eam ipse cum sancta ecclesia in dominam reciperet
et perpetuam ei fidelitatem teneret.... Nec dubitavit episcopus imperatricem
in dominam Angliæ recipere, et ei cum quibusdam suis affidare, quod,
quamdiu ipsa pactem non infringeret ipse quoque fidem ei custodiret."—
Id., ii, 573.

115. "Ventilata est hesterno die causa secreto coram majori parte
cleri Angliæ ad cujus jus potissimum spectat principem eligere, simulque
ordinare."—*Id.*, ii, 576.

116. "Missos se a communione quam vocant Londoniarum."—
Malmesbury, (Hist. Nov.), ii, 576. Exception may be taken to
translating *communio* as 'commune'; but even if the municipal organization
represented by the French term *commune* did not at this period exist in the
City of London in all its fulness, the "communal idea" appears to have been
there.—Stubbs, Const. Hist., i. 407.

117. "Omnes barones qui in eorum coramunionem jamdudum recepti
fuerant."—Malmesbury, *Ibid.*

118. "Proficiscitur inde cum exultatione magna et gaudio, et in
monasterio Sancti Albani cum processionali suscipitur honore et jubilo.
Adeunt eam ibi cives multi ex Lundonia, tractatur ibi sermo multimodus de
reddenda civitate."—Contin. Flor. Wigorn. (Thorpe), ii, 131.

119. "Erecta est autem in superbiam intolerabilem, quia suis incerta
belli prosperavissent."—Hen. of Huntingdon (Rolls Series No. 74), p. 275.

120. "Infinitæ copiæ pecuniam, non simplici cum mansuetudine sed
cum ore imperioso ab eis exegit."—Gesta Stephani (Rolls Series No. 82), iii,
75.

121. "Interpellata est a civibus, ut leges eis regis Edwardi observari
liceret, quia optimæ erant, non patris sui Henrici quia graves erant. Verum
illa non bono usa consilio, præ nimia austeritate non acquievit eis, unde et
motus magnus factus in urbe; et facta conjuratione adversus eam quam cum
honore susceperunt. cum dedecore apprehendere statuerunt."—Contin.
Flor. Wigorn. (Thorpe), ii, 132.

122. Malmesbury (Hist. Nov.), ii, 577-578. "Sed tandem a Londoniensibus expulsa est in die Sancti Johannis Baptiste proximo sequenti"—Lib. de Ant. (Camd. Soc), p. 197.

123. "Anno prædicto [*i.e.* 7 Stephen, A.D. 1141], statim in illa estate, obsessa est Turris Lundoniarum a Londoniensibus, quam Willielmus [*sic*] de Magnaville tenebat et firmaverat."—Lib. de Ant. (Camd. Soc.), p. 197. From this it would appear that the father still held the office of constable. A charter of the empress, however, which Mr. Horace Round prints in his book on Geoffrey de Mandeville (pp. 88, *seq.*) points to the son as being constable at the time.

124. Round, Geoffrey de Mandeville, pp. 88-95.

125. It is not to be supposed that the earl consented to assist the queen without meeting with some return for his services, more especially as the queen was prepared to go all lengths to obtain her husband's liberty. See Round's Geoffrey de Mandeville, p. 119.

126. "Gaufrido de Mandevilla, qui jam iterum auxilio eorum cesserat, antea enim post captionem regis imperatrici fidelitatem juraverat, et Londoniensibus maxime annitentibus, nihilque omnino quod possent prætermittentibus quo imperatricem contristarent."—Malmesbury (Hist. Nov.), ii, 580.

127. "Magnæ ex Lundoniis copiæ."—Newburgh, Hist. Rerum. Angl. (Rolls Series No. 82.), i, 42. "Cumque invictâ Londoniensium catervâ."— Gesta Stephani (Rolls Series No. 82), iii, 80. The Londoners sacked Winchester mercilessly. "Londonienses, cum maxima militum regalium parte, modis horrendis Wintoniensem civitatem expilavere."—Gesta Stephani, iii, 84.

128. The precedent thus set by Stephen, of submitting to the ceremony of a second coronation after a period of captivity, was afterwards followed by Richard I, on his return from captivity abroad.

129. This is the date assigned to the charter by Mr. Horace Round, (Geoffrey de Mandeville, pp. 138-144). *Cf.* Appendix to 31st Report of Deputy Keeper of the Public Records, p. 3.

130. The date assigned by Mr. Round to this charter is between Christmas, 1141, and the end of June, 1142.

131.   "Et convenciono eidem Gaufredo Comiti Essex quod dominus meus Comes Andegavie vel ego vel filii nostri nullam pacem aut concordiam cum Burgensibus Lund[oniæ] faciemus, nisi concessu et assensu præ-dicti Comitis Gaufredi quia inimici eius sunt mortales."—Round's Geoffrey de Mandeville, p. 168.

132.   Newburgh, Hist. Rerum Angl. (Rolls Series No. 82), i. 48. Henry of Huntingdon (Rolls Series No. 74), p. 278.

133.   Sometimes called the Treaty of Wallingford.

134.   The general joy is depicted in glowing colours by Henry of Huntingdon, (p. 289.) *Cf.* Anglo-Sax. Chron., ii., 235.

135.   Fitz-Stephen's Stephanides, Stow's Survey (Thoms's ed.), p. 208.

136.   Freeman, Norman Conquest, v., 325.

137.   A cartulary of the Mercers' Company contains a copy of a grant from Thomas Fitz-Theobald to the hospital of St. Thomas of Acon of "all that land, with the appurtenances, which was formerly of Gilbert Becket, father of the Blessed Thomas the Martyr, Archbishop of Canterbury, where the said Blessed Thomas the Martyr was born (*duxit originem*), to build a church (*basilicam*) in honour of Almighty God and the Blessed Virgin Mary, and of the same most glorious martyr."—Watney, Account of the Hospital of St. Thomas of Acon (privately printed 1892), pp. 9, 237.

138.   Liber Albus (Rolls Series), i, pp. 26, 27.

139.   This charter (with fragment of seal) is preserved at the Guildhall. It bears no date, but appears to have been granted between 1154 and 1161.

140.   Contin. Flor. Wigorn., ii, 138.

141.   "De filiis et parentibus nobilium civitatis" and again "filii et nepotes quorundam nobilium civium Londoniarum."—Benedict of Peterborough (Rolls Series No. 49), ii, 155.

142.   By a strange anomaly, a man who underwent ordeal by water was only adjudged innocent if he sank to the bottom and was drowned. Hence the old man's caution!

143.   Roger de Hoveden (Rolls Series No. 51), iii, 28. According to Richard of Devizes (Rolls Series No. 82, iii, 387), Longchamp obtained the chancellorship by bribery.

144.   Benedict (Rolls Series No. 49). ii, 106.

145.   *-Id.* ii, 143.

146.   *-Id.* ii, 158.

147.   Preface to Roger de Hoveden, iii, p. lxxvii. Girald. Cambr. Vita Galfridi (Rolls Series No. 21). iv, 397.

148.   Richard of Devizes, iii, 414. Benedict, ii, 213.

149.   Ralph de Diceto (Rolls Series No. 68), ii, 99. Girald. Cambr. (Vita Galfridi). iv, 397-398. Roger de Hoveden, iii. 140.

150.   Richard of Devizes. (Rolls Series No. 82), iii. 415. Benedict, 213. Girald. Cambr. (Vita Galfridi), iv, 405.

151.   "Johannes comes frater regis et archiepiscopus Rothomagensis, et omnes episcopi, comites et barones regni qui aderant, concesserunt civibus Lundoniarum communam suam, et juraverunt quod ipsi eam et dignitates civitatis Lundoniarum custodirent illibatas, quandiu regi placuerit. Et cives Lundoniarum et epispcopi et comites et barones juraverunt fidelitates regi Ricardo, et Johanni comiti de Meretone fratri ejus salva fidelitate, et quod illum in dominum suum et regem reciperent, si rex sine prole decesserit." — Benedict of Peterborough (Rolls Series No. 49), ii, 214. *Cf.* Roger de Hovedene (Rolls Series No. 51), iii, 141; Walter de Coventry (Rolls Series No. 58), ii, 5-6.

152.   *-Supra* p. 49.

153.   "In crastino vero convocatis in unum civibus, communione, vel ut Latine minus vulgariter magis loquamur, communa seu communia eis concessa et communiter jurata." — Vita Galfridi, iv, 405.

154.   Const. Hist., i, 407.

155.   Referring to the year 1191, he writes, "we have the date of the foundation of the commune." — *Id.*, i, 629.

156.   "Concessa est ipsa die et instituta communia Londoniensium, in quam universi regni magnates et ipsi etiam ipsius provinciæ episcopi

jurare coguntur. Nunc primum in indulta sibi conjuratione regno regem deesse cognovit Londonia quam nec rex ipse Ricardus, nec prædecessor et pater ejus Henricus, pro mille millibus marcarum argenti fieri permisisset. Quanta quippe mala ex conjuratione proveniant ex ipsa poterit diffinitione perpendi, quæ talis est—communia tumor plebis, timor regni, tepor sacerdotii."—Chron. Stephen, Hen. II, Ric. I (Rolls Series No. 82), iii, 416.

157. "It is impossible to avoid a suspicion," writes Bishop Stubbs, "that the disappearance of the port-reeve and other changes in the municipal government, signify a civic revolution, the history of which is lost."—Const. Hist., i, 406n.

158. Merewether and Stephens, Hist. of Boroughs (1835), i, 384. No authority, however, is given for this statement.

159. The entire MS. was published in Latin by the Camden Society in 1846; and a translation of the original portion of the work was afterwards made by the late Mr. H. T. Riley, under the title "Chronicles of the Mayors and Sheriffs of London, A.D. 1188 to A.D. 1274."

160. "The correct date of the accession of Richard has never been ascertained. No records appear to be extant to fix the commencement of the reign of any king before the accession of John."—Nicholas, Chronology of Hist., p. 285.

161. Fos. 45, 63 and 63b.

162. Or simply Thedmar.

163. It is thus that Riley reads the word which to me appears to be capable of being read "Grennigge."

164. Calendar of Wills. Court of Husting, London, part. I., p. 22. From another Will, that of Margery, relict of Walter de Wynton, and one of Fitz-Thedmar's sisters—she is described as daughter of "Thedmar, the Teutonic"—it appears that other sisters of Fitz-Thedmar married into the well-known city families of Eswy and Gisors.—Id., part i, p. 31.

165. "Ibi etiam dispositium est, penes quem pecunia collata debeat residere: scilicet sub custodia Huberti Walteri Cantuariensis electi, et domini Ricardi Lundoniensis episcopi, et Willelmi comitis de Arundel et Hamelini comitis de Warenna et majoris Lundoniarum."—Roger de Hoveden (Rolls Series No. 51), iii, 212.

166.   Preserved at the Guildhall.

167.   Ralph de Diceto (Rolls Series No. 68), ii, p. 114.

168.   "Denique ad ingressum principis ita ornata est facies amplissimæ civitatis ut Alemanni nobiles qui cum ipso venerant et redemptione regia exinanitam bonis Angliam credebant opum magnitudine obstupescerent." — William of Newburgh (Rolls Series No. 82), i, p. 406.

169.   "Cives vero Lundonienses servierunt de pincernaria, et cives Wintonienses de coquina." — Roger de Hoveden (Rolls Series No. 51), iii, 12.

170.   Brit. Mus., Harl. MS. 3,504, fo. 248.

171.   "Si invenissem emptorem Londoniam vendidissem." — Richard of Devizes (Rolls Series No. 82), iii, 388.

172.   "Frequentius enim solito . . imponebantur eis auxilia non modica et divites, propriis parcentes marsupiis volebant ut pauperes solverent universa." — Roger de Hoveden (Rolls Series No. 51), iv. 5. "Ad omne edictum regium divites, propriis fortunis parcentes, pauperibus per potentiam omne onus imponerent." — Newburgh, (Rolls Series No. 82), ii. 466.

173.   Newburgh, ii., 466.

174.   Mat. Paris, ii, 57. A similar character is given him by Roger de Hoveden. Dr. S. R. Gardiner describes him as an alderman of the city, and as advocating the cause of the poor artisan against the exactions of the wealthier traders. — Students' History of England, i, 169.

175.   "Pauperum et veritatis ac pietatis adversarii." — Mat. Paris, ii. 57.

176.   Newburgh, ii, 470.

177.   "And for the time," adds Dr. Gardiner, "the rich tradesmen had their way against the poorer artisans." — Students' History of England, i, 170.

178.   Chronicles of Mayors and Sheriffs, p. 2.

179.   Freeman, Norman Conquest, v, 709.

180.   Mat. Paris, ii, 143. Roger of Wendover (Rolls Series No. 84), ii, 83-87.

181. -*Id.* ii, 146.

182. -*Id.* ii, 153.

183. Ann. of Bermondsey (Rolls Series No. 36), in, 453.

184. Mat. Paris, ii, 154-156.

185. As to the services and franchises of Fitz-Walter, both in time of peace and war, see Lib. Cust., (Rolls Series), part i, pp. 147-151.

186. Introd. to Lib. Cust, p. lxxvii.

187. The sword of St. Paul, emblematic possibly of his martyrdom, still remains in the City's coat of arms. It has often been mistaken for the dagger with which Sir William Walworth is said to have killed Wat Tyler.

188. The story is told in Mr. Riley's Introduction to the Liber Custamarum (p. lxxix), on the authority of the Chronicle of Dunmow.

189. He is said to have made a similar attempt upon the wife of Eustace de Vesci, a leading baron. — (Blackstone, Introd. to Magna Carta, pp. 289, 290).

190. Mat. Paris, ii, 156. A different complexion, however, is put on this event by another chronicler. According to Walter de Coventry (Rolls Series, No. 58, ii, 220) the barons made their way into the City by stealth, scaling the walls at a time when most of the inhabitants were engaged in divine service, and having once gained a footing opened all the City gates one after another.

191. By charter, date 8th May, 1215, preserved at the Guildhall.

192. Mat. Paris, ii, 159, 161, 164, 186.

193. Roger of Wendover (Rolls Series No. 84), ii, 117.

194. Stubbs, Select Charters, p. 298.

195. "Moram autem faciebant barones in civitate Londoniæ per annum et amplius cum civibus confœderati, permittentes se nullam pacem facturos cum rege nisi assensu utriusque partis." — Annals of Waverley (Rolls Series No. 36), ii, 283.

196. Mat. Paris, ii, 161, 165.

197. Contin. Flor. Wigorn. ii, 167, 171. Chron. of Mayors and Sheriffs, p. 3.

198. Mat. Paris, ii, p. 179.

199. Confession of the Vicomte de Melun.—Mat. Paris, ii, 187.

200. Mat. Paris, ii, 200.

201. Chron. of Mayors and Sheriffs, p. 4.

202. Strype, Stow's Survey, 1720, Bk. i, p. 62. They had settled in Holborn soon after their arrival in 1220.

203. Mat. Paris, ii, 385.

204. -Id., ii, 218, 220.

205. Liber de Ant. fol. 38. According to this authority (fol. 38b), the peace was ratified 23rd September, at Merton.

206. Mat. Paris, ii, 222.

207. Often spoken of as the Treaty of Lambeth (Rymer's Fœdera, i, 148.)

208. The sum mentioned by Matthew Paris (ii. 224) is £5,000 sterling, but according to a marginal note in the Liber de Ant. (fol. 39) it would appear to have been only £1,000, which, according to the compiler of that record, Louis repaid the Londoners as soon as he arrived home, out of pure generosity (*mera liberalitate sua*). On the other hand, Matthew Paris (ii, 292) under the year 1227, narrates that Henry extorted from the citizens of London 5,000 marks of silver, on the ground that that was the sum paid by the Londoners to Louis on his departure, to the king's prejudice.

209. Walter of Coventry. (Rolls Series No. 58), ii, 239.

210. Mat. Paris, ii, 251, 252.

211. Roger of Wendover, (Rolls Series No. 84), ii, 265, 267.

212. Probably Saint Giles in the Fields, a hospital founded by Matilda, wife of Henry I.

213. "Cives autem Londonienses, qui eundem H[ubertum] propter suspendium Constantini oderant, lætati sunt de tribulalionibus suis, et ilico

conquesti sunt de eo, quod concivem suum injuste suspendit, et absque judicio."—Mat. Paris, ii, 345.

214. *-Id.*, ii, 346, 347. Chron. of Mayors and Sheriffs, pp. 6, 7.

215. "Dicebabur enim ... quod alienigenæ qui plus regni perturbationem desiderabant quam pacem, præfatum comitem Cestriæ ad domini sui regis infestationem et regni inquietationem inducere conarentur."—Walter of Coventry, ii, 251.

216. Mat. Paris, ii, 382, 384, iii, 90.

217. Freeman, Norman Conquest, v, 469, 470. "Et quia communitas nostra sigillum non habet, præsentes literas signo communitatis civitatis Londoniarum vestræ sanctitati mittimus consignatas."—Mat. Paris, iii, 17.

218. Chron. of Mayors and Sheriffs, pp. 7, 8.

219. French Chronicle (Camden Soc., No. 28), ed. by Aungier (Riley's translation), pp. 241-244.

220. Chron. of Mayors and Sheriffs, p. 11.

221. *-Id.*, pp. 13, 14, 16.

222. Chron. of Mayors and Sheriffs, pp. 16, 17, 61. Mat. Paris, iii., 62, 80-81.

223. Mat. Paris, ii, 323.

224. "Quia dominus rex obligabatur de debitis non minimis erga mercatores de vino, de cera, de pannis ultramarinis, a civibus pecuniam multam extorsit et Judæis, nec tamen inde mercatores plenam pacationem receperunt."—Mat. Paris, ii, 496.

225. "Cives tanien videntes aliud sibi non expedire, omnia benigne remiserunt."—Mat. Paris, iii, 72.

226. *-Id.*, iii, 43.

227. Ann. of Worcester (Rolls Series No. 36), iv., 407.

228. "Unde, ne exorta contentione lætitia nuptialis nubilarètur, salvo cujuslibet jure, multa ad horam perpessa sunt, quæ in tempore opportuno fuerant determinanda."—Mat. Paris, Hist. Angl., ed. 1684, P. 355. *Cf.* City

Records, Liber Ordinationum, fo. 193 b. Brit. Mus. Cotton MS. Vespasian, C. xiv. fos. 113-114.

229.   Chron. of Mayors and Sheriffs, pp. 9, 20, 45, 53.

230.   -*Id.*, p. 21.

231.   An early instance of this parliament being so designated is found in the *Liber de Antiquis* of the City's Records (fol. 75b.) where the words *insane parliamentum* occur.

232.   This agreement between the king and barons is termed a "Charter" by Fitz-Thedmar, who says it bore the seals of the king and of many barons.—Chron. of Mayors and Sheriffs, p. 41.

233.   Chron. of Mayors and Sheriffs, p. 43.

234.   -*Id.*, pp. 33-39.

235.   -*Id.*, pp. 45, 46.

236.   Chron. of Mayors and Sheriffs, p. 47.

237.   -*Id.*, p. 52.

238.   The Bull was confirmed by Alexander's successor Pope Urban IV. and the later Bull was read at Paul's Cross, by the king's orders in the following year (1262), *Id.*, p. 53.

239.   Chron. of Mayors and Sheriffs, p. 56.

240.   -*Id.*, p. 57.

241.   -*Id.*, p. 58.

242.   Chron. of Mayors and Sheriffs, p. 59. "A similar uprising of the middle class of citizens was taking place about this period in other towns. They are spoken of by chroniclers of the same stamp as Fitz-Thedmar as ribald men who proclaimed themselves 'bachelors,' and banded themselves together to the prejudice of the chief men of the towns (*majores urbium et burgorum*)"—Chron. of Thomas Wykes (Rolls Series No. 36), iv, 138.

243.   Chron. of Mayors and Sheriffs, pp. 59-60.

244.   -*Id.*, p. 60.

245. Ann. of Dunstaple (Rolls Series No. 36). iii. 222-223. Chron. of Thos. Wykes (*Ibid*) iv, 136. Rishanger (Rolls Series No. 28, ii, 18), places this event after the Mise of Amiens (23rd Jan., 1264).

246. Annales Londonienses.—Chron. Edward I and II (Rolls Series No. 76) i, 60.

247. Chron. of Mayors and Sheriffs, p. 62.

248. -*Id.*, pp. 64, 65.

249. Ann. of Dunstaple. iii, 230, 231.

250. The number of Londoners who accompanied Leicester to Lewes is not given. Thomas Wykes mentions it to have been very large, for the reason that the number of fools is said to be infinite! "Quo comperto comes Leycestriæ glorians in virtute sua, congregata baronum multitudine copiosa, Londoniensium innumerabili agmine circumcinctus, quia legitur stultorum infinitus est numerus."—(Rolls Series No. 36), iv, 148.

251. Chron. of Mayors and Sheriffs, p. 66; Ann. of Dunstaple, iii, 232; Thos. Wykes, iv, 149, 150; Rishanger (Rolls Series No. 28), 27.

252. Chron. of Mayors and Sheriffs, p. 67.

253. -*Id.*, p. 74.

254. Fitz-Thedmar gives the number of representatives of each city and borough as four: "De qualitet civitate et burgo iiii homines."—Chron. of Mayors and Sheriffs, p. 75.

255. Chron. of Mayors and Sheriffs, p. 77. This anecdote is inserted in the margin of Fitz-Thedmar's chronicle, the writer expressing his horror at the "wondrous and unheard of" conduct of "this most wretched mayor."

256. The story is told by Thos. Wykes. (Rolls Series No. 36), iv, 163.

257. Lib. de. Ant. fo. 94b.

258. Chron. of Mayors and Sheriffs, p. 119. Circumstantially as the chronicler relates the story, he appears only to have inserted it as an afterthought. Mr. Loftie (Hist, of London, i, 151), suggests that possibly the news of Fitz-Thomas' death might have been the occasion of its insertion.

259. Aungier, Fr. Chron. (Riley's Transl.), p. 235.

260. "His lordship the king had summoned to Wyndleshores all the earls, barons, [and] knights, as many as he could, with horses and arms, intending to lay siege to the City of London [and] calling the citizens his foes."—Chron. of Mayors and Sheriffs, p. 81.

261. Chron. of Mayors and Sheriffs, p. 82.

262. At one time the parish of All Hallows Barking is spoken of as being in the County of Middlesex, at another as being within the City—Hust. Roll. 274, (10), (12).

263. In narrating this, Fitz-Thedmar again discloses his aristocratic proclivities by remarking, "Such base exclamations did the fools of the vulgar classes give utterance to" on this occasion, viz., the election of William Fitz-Richard as Sheriff of Middlesex and Warden of London.—Chron. of Mayors and Sheriffs, pp. 90, 91.

264. Chron. of Mayors and Sheriffs, pp. 83, 85.

265. "Regina etiam rogavit pro Londoniensibus de quibus rex plures recepit ad pacem suam."—Ann. of Winchester (Rolls Series, No. 36), ii, 103.

266. Chron. of Mayors and Sheriffs, pp. 146, 147.

267. Ann. of Dunstaple. (Rolls Series, No. 36), iii, 245.

268. Chron. of Mayors and Sheriffs, p. 95. The citizens appear to have been divided, as indeed they often were, on the question of admitting the Earl.

269. Chron. of Mayors and Sheriffs, pp. 95, 97.

270. Chron. of Mayors and Sheriffs, p. 96.

271. -Id., pp. 97, 100.

272. Dated "Est Ratford," 16th June, 1267. Chron. of Mayors and Sheriffs, pp. 98-100.

273. Dated 26th March, 1268. The original is preserved at the Guildhall (Box No. 3). A copy of it, inserted in the Lib. de Ant. (fo. 108b), has the following heading:—"Carta domini regis quam fecit civibus Lond', *sub spe*

inveniendi ab eo meliorem gratiam," the words in italics being added by a later hand.

274.   Chron. of Mayors and Sheriffs, p. 113. Ann. of Waverley (Rolls Series No. 36), ii, 375.

275.   Chron. of Mayors and Sheriffs, p. 129.

276.   Lib. de Ant., fo. 120.

277.   Chron. of Mayors and Sheriffs, pp. 129-130.

278.   Chron. of Mayors and Sheriffs, p. 153.

279.   Chron. of Mayors and Sheriffs, pp. 154, 159.

280.   Chron. of Mayors and Sheriffs, p. 164.

281.   The series of Husting Rolls for Pleas of Land, preserved at the Guildhall, commence in the mayoralty of Hervy's successor.

282.   Chron. of Mayors and Sheriffs, pp. 205-208.

283.   What Fitz-Thedmar means when he says (Chron. of Mayors and Sheriffs, p. 171), that "only one part of the seal of the Commonalty of London" was appended to Hervy's so-called "charter" is hard to determine. The common seal of the city was at this period in the custody of the mayor for the time being. Under Edward II, it was for the first time entrusted to two aldermen and two commoners for safe keeping.—City Records, Letter Book D, fo. 145b. *Cf.* Ordinances of Edward II, A.D. 1319.

284.   Chron. of Mayors and Sheriffs, pp. 169-171.

285.   Chron. of Mayors and Sheriffs, pp. 173-5.

286.   "Et quod nullus alienigena in libertatem civitatis prædictæ admittatur nisi in Hustengo ... et si non sint de certo mestero, tune in libertatem civitatis ejusdem non admittentur sine assensu communitatis civitatis illius."—Lib. Custumarum (Rolls Series), pt. 1, pp. 269-270.

287.   "The establishment of the corporate character of the city under a mayor marks the victory of the communal principle over the more ancient shire organisation, which seems to have displaced early in the century the

complicated system of guild and franchise. It also marks the triumph of the mercantile over the aristocratic element."—Stubbs, Const. Hist., i, 630, 631.

288. "The guilds continued to elect until 1384, when the right of election was again transferred to the wards." City Records, Letter Book H, fos. 46b, 173.

289. Chron. Edward I and II. (Rolls Series No. 76), i, 84. Chron. of T. Wykes (Rolls Series No. 36) iv, p. 259.

290. Dated from "Caples in the land of Labour" (*Caples in terra laboris*) or Capua, 19th January, 1273. This letter was publicly read in the Guildhall on the 25th March following.—Chron. of Mayors and Sheriffs, p. 163.

291. Chron. of Mayors and Sheriffs, p. 161.

292. -*Id.*, p. 172.

293. -.*Id*, pp. 132, 140-2.

294. Chron. of Mayors and Sheriffs, pp. 143-4.

295. -*Id.*, pp. 145, 146.

296. Chron. of Mayors and Sheriffs, pp. 147, 148.

297. Chron. of Mayors and Sheriffs, pp. 149, 150.

298. -*Id.*, p. 165.

299. -A.D. 1279. "Eodem anno escambia et novæ monetæ extiterunt levata apud turrim Londoniensem; et Gregorius de Roqesle major monetæ per totam Angliam."—Chron. Edw. I and II. (Rolls Series No. 76. i. 88).— Aungier Fr. Chron. (Transl.) p. 239.

300. The name of John Horn with the addition. "Flemyng" occurs in the 14th cent.—Hust. Roll. 64 (67), 81 (74).

301. For one month after the Feast of St. Botolph the Abbot [17 June], the Court of Husting in London was closed, owing to the absence of citizens attending the fair. The right of appointing their own officers to settle disputes arising at the fair was granted to the citizens of London at the close of the Barons' War.—Chron. of Mayors and Sheriffs, p. 176.

302.   Peace was signed before the end of July.—Rymer's Fœdera, (ed. 1816), vol. i. pt. 2, p. 513.

303.   A series of MS. books extending from a.d. 1275 to 1688, deriving their title from the letters of the alphabet with which they are distinguished, A, B, C, &c, AA, BB, CC, &c. We are further aided by chronicles of the reigns of Edward I and II, edited by Bishop Stubbs for the Master of the Rolls. A portion of these chronicles the editor has fitly called "Annales Londonienses." There is even reason for believing them to have been written by Andrew Horn, citizen and fishmonger, as well as eminent jurist of his day. He died soon after the accession of Edward III. and by his will, dated 9th Oct., 1328, (Cal. of Wills, Court of Husting, i, 344) bequeathed to the city many valuable legal and other treatises, only one of which (known to this day as "Liber Horn,") is preserved among the archives of the Corporation.

304.   Chron. of Mayors and Sheriffs, p. 239.

305.   Stubbs, Select Charters, p. 447.

306.   Chron. Edward I and II, (Rolls Series). Introd. vol. i, p. xxxiii.

307.   -Id., i, 92.

308.   Contin. Flor. Wigorn., ii, 229. 230. Tho. Wykes (Ann. Monast. Rolls Series No. 36), iv, 294. Ann. of Worcester (Ibid), iv, 486. Walter de Heminburgh (Eng. Hist. Soc.), ii, 13.

309.   They were, in the language of Stow, "hanged by the purse." (Survey, Thoms' ed., p. 96). Cf. "He was hanged by the nek and nought by the purs." (Chaucer, Cook's Tale. l. 885). The story is recorded in Aungier's French Chron. (Riley's translation), p. 240; and in Chron. Edward I and II (Rolls Series i, 92-93).

310.   Stubbs, Select Charters, pp. 472-474.

311.   Letter Book C, fo. 52. Riley's Memorials, p. 21.

312.   Rolls Series, i, 51-60. Cf. Lib. Ordinationum, fos. 154b, seq.

313.   The circumstances of Rokesley's visit to the justices at the Tower are set out in the city's "Liber Albus" (i, 16), from a MS. of Andrew Horn, no longer preserved at the Guildhall. The story also appears in Chron. Edward I and II (Rolls Series No. 76), i, 94.

314.   In 1293 the king appointed Elias Russell and Henry le Bole his "improvers" (*appropriatores*) in the city:—Chron. Edward I and II, (Rolls Series No. 76, i, 102). Their duties were practically identical with those of sheriffs, and Bishop Stubbs places a marginal note over against the appointment,—"Sheriffs appointed by the king." Walter Hervy is recorded as having removed certain stones near Bucklersbury when he was "improver" of the city (Letter Book A, fo. 84. Riley's Memorials, p. 25). This was probably done in 1268, when the city was in the king's hand, and Hervy and William de Durham were appointed bailiffs "without election by the citizens."—Chron. Mayors and Sheriffs, pp. 112, 113.

315.   Letter Book A, fo. 132b.

316.   -*Id.*, fo. 110.

317.   Chron. Edward I and II, i, 98.

318.   Letter Book A, fo. 95. Riley's Memorials, p. 26.

319.   "From the very day of his accession, Edward was financially in the hands of the Lombard bankers; hence arose, no doubt, the difficulty which he had in managing the City of London; hence came also the financial mischief which followed the banishment of the Jews; and hence an accumulation of popular discontent, which showed itself in the king's lifetime by opposition to his mercantile policy, and, after his death, supplied one of the most efficient means for the overthrow of his son."—Chron. Edward I and II. Introd. vol. i, pp. c, ci.

320.   Writ to the Sheriff of Middlesex, dated 2nd Jan., 1293. Letter Book B, fo. 25. Contin. Flor. Wigorn., ii, 266.

321.   Ann. of Dunstaple (Rolls Series No. 36), iii, 390. The chronicler acquits the king of complicity in this sacrilege.

322.   Contin. Flor. Wigorn., ii, 274.

323.   Letter Book C. fo. 20.

324.   -*Id.*, fos. 21b, 22. (Riley's Memorials, pp. 31-33). Liber Custum., i, 72-76.

325.   Chron. of Walter de Hemingburgh (Eng. Hist. Soc.), ii. 108, 109.

326.   Letter Book C, fo. 22b.

327.   By the bull *Clericis Laicos*, Boniface VIII had recently forbidden the clergy to pay taxes to any layman.—Chron. of Walter de Hemingburgh (Eng. Hist. Soc.), ii, 113-116.

328.   Stubbs, Const. Hist., ii, 130, 131, 134.

329.   Chron. of Walter de Hemingburgh, ii, 121.

330.   -*Id.*, ii, 126, 127.

331.   -*Id.*, ii, 149, 151.

332.   Letter Book B, fo. xxxvii (101b).

333.   Preserved among the City Archives (Box 26). *Cf.* Letter Book C, fo. xxiv, b.

334.   Letter Book B, fo. 93.

335.   Letter Book C, fo. 24. (Riley's Memorials, 37).

336.   Strictly speaking, a talliage could only be charged on the king's demesnes, and these did not include the City of London.

337.   Chron. Edward I and II (Rolls Series), i, 132.

338.   Aungier, Fr. Chron. (Riley's Transl.), 247. Chron. Edward I and II (Rolls Series), i, 139.

339.   Chron. Edward I and II (Rolls Series), i, 146. Hemingburgh ii, 248.

340.   Aungier, Fr. Chron. (Riley's Transl.), 247 n.

341.   "Tunc visa est Londonia quasi nova Jerusalem monilibus ornata."—Chron. Edward I and II (Rolls Series No. 76), i, 152.

342.   "Ad quam coronationem major, aldermanni et cives Londoniarum induti samiteis et sericeis vestimentis et ex armis Angliæ et Franciæ depictis, coram rege et regina Karolantes, et servi civium ad illud festum, ut moris est, de cupa servientes, omnibus intuentibus inauditum proviserunt gaudium."—*Id. ibid.*

343.   Letter Book C, fo. 93 (Riley's Memorials, p. 64).

344.   Letter Book D, fo. 96 (Memorials, pp. 69-71).

345.   Letter Book C, fo. 97 b (Memorials, p. 69).

346.   Letter Book D, fo. 104 (Memorials, pp. 72-74).

347.   Chron. of Mayors and Sheriffs, pp. 224-225.

348.   Letter Book D, fo. 147b.

349.   *-Id.*, fo. 125b.

350.   "Eodem anno (*i.e.* 1302), die Lunæ ivto Kalendas Februarii, restitutus est Richerus de Refham in honore aldermanniæ Londoniarum, et factus est aldermannus de Warda de Basseishawe." — Chron. Edward I and II, i, 104.

351.   Among those who were called to account was a woman remarkable for her name — "Sarra la Bredmongesterre." A selection of the cases enquired into is printed in Riley's Memorials, pp. 86-89.

352.   "Sed quia idem Richerus fuerat austerus et celer ad justitiam faciendam nulli parcendo, et quia fecit imprisonare Willelmum de Hakford, mercer, ideo dictus W, et sui complices insurrexerunt in ipsum et ideo depositus fuit ab officio majoris et postea aldermanniæ suæ." — Chron. Edw. I and II, i, 175-176.

353.   Letter Book D, fo. 142.

354.   *-Id.*, fos. 142b-143b (Memorials pp. 93-98.)

355.   *-Id.*, fos. 142b, 143b, 145b.

356.   Chron. Edward I and II. i, 203.

357.   Lib. de Antiq., fo. 43b. Aungier's Fr. Chron. (Riley's Transl.), p. 250.

358.   Letter Book C, fo. 45.

359.   Letter Book C, fo. 92b (Memorials p. 63).

360.   The city chose as its representatives, Nicholas de Farendone, John de Wengrave, and Robert de Kelleseye. Letter Book D. fos. 149b, 151, 151b.

361.   *-Id.*, fos. 151b, 152 (Memorials pp. 102-104.)

362. -*Id.*, fo. 168 (Memorials, pp. 105-106).

363. Letter Book D, fos. 164, 164b.

364. Letter Book E, fo. 18. (Memorials, pp. 108-110).

365. Letter Book D, fo. 165.

366. Chron. Edward I and II, ii, 55, 56.

367. Letter Book E, fo. 84. (Memorials, pp. 128-129).

368. Chron. Edward I and II, i, 285.

369. Aungier's French Chron. (Riley's translation), p. 252.

370. Lib. Cust. (Rolls Series) i, 269.

371.   Dated York, 8th June, 1319. These letters patent are preserved at the Guildhall (Box No. 4). Ten days later [18th June] Edward granted an ample inspeximus charter to the city, the original of which does not appear among the archives. *See* Lib. Cust. i, pp. 255-273.

372. Aungier, Fr. Chron. (Riley's translation), p. 253.

373. In this year [1318-19] the new charter was confirmed by the king, and cost £1,000. *Id.*, p. 252.

374. Chron. Edward I and II, Introd., vol. ii, p. lxxxiv.

375. Lib. Cust. (Rolls Series) i, 285-432.

376. Rolls Series i, 51-60. Copies of the Ordinances are also to be found in the Liber Horn (fos. 209, *seq.*) and Liber Ordinationum (fos. 154b *seq.*) of the city's archives.

377. Lib. Cust. i, 289, 308.

378. Lib. Cust., i, 296.

379. -*Id.*, i, 308-322.

380. -*Id.*, i, 322-324.

381. -*Id.*, i, 324-325.

382. -*Id.*, i, 347-362.

383. "Et fuit illo die post horam vesperarum antequam Justiciarii et duodenæ perfiniebant; sed neminem eodem die indictaverunt."—Lib. Cust., i, 366.

384. Lib. Cust., i, 371-374.

385. -*Id.*, i, 378. Chron. Edward I and II, i, 291. Aungier, Fr. Chron., p. 253.

386. "Qui cum quasi leones parati ad prædam ante Pascham extitissent, nunc, versa vice, quasi agni vicissim facti sunt."—Lib. Cust., i, 383-384.

387. Chron. Edward I and II. i, 216, 272.

388. Lib. Cust., i, 408, 409.

389. -*Id.*, i, 425.

390. Chron. Edward I and II, i, 291. The precise date of his election is not known. Bishop Stubbs, in his introduction to the Chronicle cited (i, p. lxxxii), states it to have taken place in January. This can hardly have been the case, inasmuch as the city had not been taken into the king's hands before the middle of February—forty-one days after the commencement of the Iter. See Lib. Cust. i, p. 378.

391. Letter Book E, fos. 119b-120 (Memorials, pp. 142-144).

392. Chron. Edward I and II, i, 293, 296.

393. -*Id.*, i, 297.

394. Dated, Boxle, 25 October. Patent Roll 15, Edward II, Part 1, m. ii.

395. Chron. Edward I and II, i, p. 298. Re-elected "by the commons at the king's wish."—Aungier Fr. Chron. (Riley's transl.), p. 254.

396. Chron. Edward I and II, i, pp. 298-299.

397. Aungier, Fr. Chron., pp. 254, 255.

398. The charter, dated Aldermaston, 12th December, 15 Edward II [A.D. 1321], with seal (imperfect) attached, is preserved at the Guildhall (Box No. 4.)

399.   Chron. Edward I and II, i, 301.—Aungier. Fr. Chron. (Riley's transl.). p. 255.

400.   "Car c'est le plus perilleux peuple [sc. the English] qui soit au monde et plus outrageux et orgueilleux et de tous ceux d' Angleterre les Londriens sont chefs ... ils sont fors durs et hardis et haux en courage; tant plus voyent de sang respandu et plus sont cruels et moins ebahis."— Froissart's Hist. (ed. Lyon, 1559), pp. 333-334.

401.   Macaulay, Hist., cap. iii.

402.   Aungier. Fr. Chron. (Riley's transl.), pp. 257, 264.

403.   Chron. Edward I and II. i, 303.

404.   -Id., i. 305. Aungier. Fr. Chron. (Riley's transl.), p. 257.

405.   By the king's writ, dated Ravensdale, 29 Nov., Letter Book E. fo. 148. According to the French Chronicle (Aungier, p. 258) Chigwell recovered the mayoralty on the feast of St. Nicholas [6 Dec.]. On the 7th Dec. he was admitted and sworn into office.

406.   Chron. Edward I and II, i, 301, 305, 318 n.

407.   "Propter insidiantes domini regis et aliorum malorum hominum." —Id., i, 306.

408.   -Id., i, 307.

409.   Aungier, Fr. Chron., p. 259.

410.   Chron. Edward I and II, i, 308. Easter is given as the date of her departure by the Fr. Chron. (p. 259), Easter Day falling on the 15th April in that year.

411.   Aungier, Fr. Chron. (Riley's transl.), p. 260.

412.   See her proclamation issued at Wallingford, 15th Oct. Rymer's Fœdera, vol. ii, part 1, pp. 645, 646.

413.   Chron. Edward I and II, i, 314, 315.

414.   Dated Baldock, 6 Oct., 1326. City's Records, Pleas and Memoranda, Roll A I, membr. x (12).

415. Aungier. Fr. Chron. (Riley's translation), pp. 262, 263.

416. Chron. Edward I and II, i, 315, 316. Aungier, Fr. Chron., p. 263.

417. Chron. Edward I and II, ii, 310. Murimuth, Chron. (Eng. Hist. Soc.), p. 48.

418. Chron. Edward I and II, i, 321, ii, 310. Aungier, Fr. Chron. (Riley's translation), p. 264. Murimuth (Eng. Hist. Soc.), pp. 48, 49.

419. The proclamation is headed, *Proclamacio prima post decessum episcopi Exoniensis et ipsius decollacionem.*—City's Records, Pleas and Memoranda, Roll A 1, membr. 2 dors.

420. Aungier, Fr. Chron., p. 265.

421. Chron. Edward I and II, i, 318.

422. Chron. Edward I and II, i, 323. Pleas and Memoranda, Roll A 1, memb. 2.

423. Dated 28 February, 1326-7. Chron. Edward I and II, i, 325-326.

424. Dated 6 March, 1326-7. Preserved at the Guildhall (Box No. 5).

425. In *re* Islington Market Bill, 3 Clk, 513. See also Stat. 5 and 6, William IV, cap. cxi, ss. 46 *et seq.*

426. -*Vide sup.*, p. 104.

427. According to the common law of the land, no market could be erected so as to be a "nuisance" to another market within a less distance than six miles and a half and a third of another half.—Bracton "De Legibus Angliæ" (Rolls Series No. 70), iii, 584.

428. Dated 4 March, 1326-7.

429. Chron. Edward I and II, i, 325.

430. The king's letters asking for assistance were dated from Nottingham, 29 April and 2 May.—City's Records, Pleas and Mem., Roll A 1, membr. iv dors, and ix.

431. The names of the troopers are set out in full, under the several wards, in Pleas and Memoranda, Roll A I, memb. ix. The compiler of the

"Annales Paulini" (Chron. Edward I and II, i. 333), gives the number of the City contingent as 100 men, adding feelingly "sed proh pudor! nil boni ibi facientes sine honore revertuntur."

432. Dated Topclyf, 10 July.—Pleas and Mem., Roll A 1, membr. ii (4).

433. -*Id.*, Roll A 1, membr. iii.

434. Writ dated Lincoln, 23 September.—*Id.*, Roll A 1, membr. v (7) dors.

435. -*Id.*, Roll A 1. memb. iii.—In July, 1323, the Exchequer had been transferred from York to Westminster, "and great treasure therewith."—Aungier's Fr. Chron. (Riley's transl.), p. 258.

436. Pleas and Mem., Roll A 1. membr. iii, and v (7).

437. Pleas and Memoranda, Roll A 1. membr. xxii.

438. -*Id.*, Roll A 1. membr. xxii, dors.—According to the Chronicle of Lanercost (Bannatyne Club, p. 261), it was the *Londoners* who refused to give up the stone.

439. Rymer's Fœdera (1830), Vol. iii, pt. ii, p. 716. Stanley's Memorials of Westminster Abbey (2nd ed.), pp. 60-64.

440. Rymer's Fœdera (1821) Vol. ii, pt. ii, pp. 734, 740. Pleas and Mem., Roll A 1, membr. xx dors. Chron. Edward I and II, i. 339-340.

441. The city was represented by Stephen de Abyndon and Robert de Kelseye. The writ was dated Clipston, 28 August, and the return made the 10th October.—Pleas and Mem., Roll A 1. membr. xxiii-xxiv.

442. Letter dated 27 September.—Pleas and Mem., Roll A 1, membr. xxiii (27) dors.

443. -*Id.*, Roll A 1, membr. xxiv (28) dors.

444. "Quod dictus Hamo fuit pessimus vermis qui venit in civitate jam xx annis elapsis et amplius, et quod nunquam foret bona pax in civitate dum viveret et quod bonum esset valde si capud ejus a corpore truncatur."—Pleas and Mem., Roll A 1, membr. xxiii dors.

445. Pleas and Mem., Roll A 1, membr. 29.

446. *-Id.*, Roll A 1, membr. 29 dors.

447. *-Id., ibid.*—Notwithstanding this disavowal, it is said that no less than 600 Londoners assisted the Lancastrian cause.—Chron. Edward I and II. Introd. Vol. i, p. cxx.

448. Chron. Edward I and II, i, 343.—Letter Book E, fo. 179b. (Memorials, pp. 170-171).

449. Pleas and Mem., Roll A 1, membr. 31.

450. See letter from the mayor, &c., to the king informing him that his wishes had been carried out.—*Id.*, Roll A 1. membr. xxviii (32).

451. At Christmas, both the primate and the city despatched letters to Edward, who was then at Worcester, to that effect.—*Id.*, Roll A 1. memb. xxviii (32).

452. Chron. Edward I and II. i, 343-344.

453. Pleas and Mem., Roll A 1. membr. xxviii (32).

454. Chron. Edward I and II. i, 242-243.

455. *-Id.*, i, 245, 346.

456. *-Id.*, i. 246-247.

457. The will is enrolled in the records of the Court of Husting, Roll 61 (17). His devise to St. Paul's was challenged by John de Pulteney, and execution stayed.

458. According to the compiler of the "Annales Paulini" (Chron. Edward I and II, i, 352), Mortimer was taken "in camera Isabelle reginæ."

459. She died in 1357. and was buried in the church of the Grey Friars, in the city.

460. "The last days of Queen Isabella."—Archæol., vol. xxxv, p. 464.

461. On her first arrival in London she was conducted by a cavalcade of citizens to the Bishop of Ely's house in Holborn, and after her marriage, was made the recipient of a present of gold and silver and a great store of all kinds of provisions. Her coronation, which took place two years later (Feb.,

1330), was also made the occasion for a further display of their loyalty and affection.—Chron. Edward I and II, i, 338, 339, 349.

462. Green, Hist. of the English People, i, 410. Imposts on wool, writes Bishop Stubbs, became of such importance at this period that "the merchants again seemed likely to furnish the realm with a new estate."—Const. Hist., ii. 379.

463. -Supra, pp. 112-115.

464. "Eodem anno (i.e., 1326) post Pascha dominus rex habuit consilium apud Westmonasterium; et ordinatum fuit ibi quod mercatores emerent lanas. corias et plumbum, in certis locis Angliæ, Walliæ et Hyberniæ, et illa loca vocantur Stapel."—Chron. Edward I and II, i, 312. Cf. Pleas and Mem., Roll A 1, membr. 15.

465. Dated 23 April, 1327. Pleas and Mem., Roll A 1, membr. i (3) dors.

466. Dated Nottingham, 30 April (1327). Rymer's Fœdera. Vol. ii, pt. ii. p. 705.

467. Writ to the collector of dues in the port of London and other places on both sides of the Thames as far as Gravesend. Dated Overton, 2 July, 1 Edward III (a.d. 1327). Pleas and Mem., Roll A 1, membr. 7 dors (cedula).

468. -Id., Roll A 1, membr. 7 dors.

469. Letters patent, dated Lincoln, 23 Sept., 1 Edward III (a.d. 1327). Id., Roll A 1, membr. 7 dors.

470. Writ to sheriffs to see the restrictions carried out, dated York, 1 March, 2 Edward III (a.d. 1327-8). Id., Roll A 1, membr. 24 dors.

471. Dated from Coventry. Id., Roll A 1, membr. 18 dors.

472. Return to writ, dated 12 January, 1 Edward III (A.D. 1327-8).— Pleas and Mem., Roll A 1, membr. 20.

473. Letter from the Mayor, &c., of York, to the City of London, dated 29 January, and reply.—Pleas and Mem., Roll A 1, membr. xix (23).

474. Id. ibid.

475. *Id.,* Roll A 1, membr. xvii (20) dors. The letter was sent in reply to one from the City's representatives, Grantham and Priour, asking for instructions.

476. Pleas and Mem., Roll A 1, membr. xix (23) dors.

477. He had been an intimate favourite of Edward II. and had been removed, with others, from that king's service in 1311. Notwithstanding this, he appears as the king's Chamberlain in 1316. Ten years later, when the city was in the hands of an infuriated mob, and the king confined at Kenilworth, John de Charleton took the Earl of Arundel prisoner and caused him to be beheaded. In 1329 the citizens received peremptory orders from Edward III, not to harbour him in the city.—Chron. Edward I & II. i, 247.

478. Pleas and Mem., Roll A 1, membr. 24.

479. Pleas and Mem., Roll A 1, membr. 24.

480. Letter Book E, fo. 183. (Memorials, p. 169.)

481. "In 1333 they were again established in England, but merchants ignored them, and in the following year they were abolished. From 1344 onwards they are frequently discussed in parliament and assemblies of the merchants; and by the statute of 1353 the system was consolidated."— Stubbs, Const. Hist., ii, 412.

482. Letter Book G. fos. 35b, 76.

483. Rymer's Fœdera (1821), vol. ii, pt. ii. p. 765.

484. Chron. Edward I and II, i, 247, 249.

485. Chron. Edward I and II. i, 249, 251.

486. Rymer's Fœdera (1821), vol. ii, pt. ii, p. 815.

487. Rex Franciæ subtiliavit viis et modis quibus potuit qualiter deturbaret regem Angliæ et repatriare faceret ne tantum destrueret et debellaret regnum Scotiæ.—Knighton (Rolls Series No. 76), i, 476.

488. -*Id.,* i, 461.

489. Letter Book E, fos. 1-4—(Memorials, pp. 187-190).

490. John de Grantham was allowed 60 shillings for a horse which he lost whilst going to this parliament on the city's business. (Letter Book F, fo. 9b.) It is, however, not clear that Grantham attended the parliament as a city member.

491. Chron. Edward I and II, ii. 122.

492. Letter patent, dated 12 August.—Pleas and Mem., Roll A 1, membr. 35.

493. -*Id. ibid.*

494. Letter patent, dated Westm., 24 March.—Letter Book F., fo. 6.

495. -*Id.*, fo. 6b.

496. Chron. Edward I and II, i, 366.

497. The king's letter, dated Stamford, 1 June, 1337.—Letter Book F, fo. 6b.

498. Letter Book F, fos. 4-5.

499. Charter dated Westminster, 26 March, 1337, preserved at the Guildhall (Box No. 5). The king made frequent attempts to annul this charter.—Letter Book F, fo. 197; Letter Book G, fos. 11b, 41b.

500. -*Id.*, fo. 9.

501. -*Id.*, fo. 9b. (Memorials, p. 197).

502. -*Id.*, fo. 10b.

503. Stubbs, Const. Hist., ii, 380.

504. Letter Book F, fo. 42.

505. Pleas and Mem., Roll A 3, membr. 3 and 3 dors.

506. Stubbs, Const. Hist., ii, 380-381.

507. Letter Book F, fos. 3, 3b.

508. -*Id.*, fo. 14b. *Id.*, fo. 18b.

509. Pleas and Mem., Roll A 5, membr. 3 dors.

510. -*Id.*, membr. 5 dors.

511. -*Id.*, membr. 6. On the 23 October, the Duke of Cornwall, whom the king had nominated regent during his absence abroad, wrote to the Mayor, &c., of London, bidding him put the city into a posture of defence.—Letter Book F, fo. 19.

512. -*Skumarii*: a scummar, a rover. Skeats' Glossary to the Bruce (Early Eng. Text Soc. *s. v.*)

513. Letter Book F, fos. 22b-23.

514. Pleas and Mem., Roll A 3, membr. 1.

515. Letter Book F, fly leaf. (Memorials, p. 204.)

516. Letter Book F, fly-leaf. The passage was printed by the late Mr. Riley, although somewhat inaccurately, in his Memorials (p. 205). The original MS. runs thus: "Item in Camera Gildaule sunt sex Instrumenta de Laton vocata Gonnes cum quinque teleres ad eadem. Item pelete de plumbo pro eidem Instrumentis que ponderant iiijc li et dj. Item xxxij li de pulvere pro dictis instrumentis."

517. The late Mr. Riley misread "roleres" for "teleres" (the writing is not very legible), and therefore thought the passage referred to heavy ordnance.

518. Richard Hastinges bequeaths by will in 1558 his bows and arrows, with "tyllers" &c.—Calendar of Wills, Court of Hust., London, ii, 670.

519. Congregacio Maioris Aldermannorum et unius hominis cujuslibet warde civitatis pro negociis communitatem tangentibus die veneris proxima post festum Sancte Katerine Virginis (25 Nov.) anno xiijc contra adventum domini regis et regine de partibus transmarinis.—Pleas and Mem., Roll A 3, membr. 10.

520. Letter Book F, fo. 30b.

521. Letter Book F, fo. 32b. (Memorials, pp. 208-210.)

522. Pleas and Mem., Roll A 3, membr. 12 dors.

523. Letter Book F, fo. 34b.

524. Letter Book F, fo. 39.

525. Pleas and Mem., Roll A 3, membr. 20-21. Letter Book F, fo. 37b.

526. A cedula inserted between membranes 19 and 20 of Pleas and Mem., Roll A 3.

527. Aungier, Fr. Chron. (Riley's transl.), 277.

528. Murimuth, Contin. Chron. (Rolls Series No. 93), p. 116. Avesbury (*Ibid*), p. 323.

529. Aungier's Fr. Chron. (Riley's transl.), pp. 283-285. Murimuth, p. 117.

530. Pleas and Mem., Roll A 3, membr. 22.

531. Letter Book F, fos. 45b-49. Murimuth, pp. 118, 119.

532. Murimuth, p. 119.

533. Letter Book F, fo. 49.

534. Dated 26 May, 1341. This charter, which was granted with the assent of parliament, is preserved at the Guildhall (Box No. 5.)

535. Pleas and Mem., Roll A 3, membr. 25 dors.

536. -*Id.*, Roll A 5. membr. 17.

537. Stubbs, Const. Hist., ii, 392 note. Aungier's Fr. Chron. (Riley's transl.), 290.

538. Murimuth, 155.

539. Letter Book F, fos. 81-84b.

540. Commission, dated Windsor, 20th March, 1345. *Id.* fo. 98b.

541. -*Id.* fos. 99, 109, 110.

542. Letter Book F, fo. 111.

543. -*Id.*, fo. 116b.

544. Murimuth (Rolls Series, No. 93, p. 198) states that the number of vessels great and small amounted to 750; whilst in another Chronicle the same writer says that they numbered more than 1,500 (Chron. ed. for Eng. Hist. Soc., p. 164.)

545. Letter Book F. fo. 119. Murimuth (Rolls Series), p. 198.

546. Murimuth (Rolls Series), pp. 205-211.

547. Letter Book F, fo. 120b.

548. -*Id.*, fos. 121-125b.

549. Letter Book F, fos. 127, 127b, 130.

550. -*Id.*, fos. 132b-133b.

551. -*Id.*, fos. 139, 140.

552. -*Id.*, fo. 140 b.

553. Hist. Angl. (Rolls Series No. 28), i, 272. *Cf.* Chron. Angliæ (Rolls Series No. 64). p. 26.

554. It was the first of the three pestilences (the others occurring in 1361 and 1369) which served occasionally as land marks in history for dating conveyances and other records.—See Bond's Handy-book for verifying dates, p. 311.

555. Stow extravagantly conjectures that no less than 50,000 perished within a year, all of whom were buried in Walter Manny's cemetery, near the Charterhouse. Another chronicler states that 200 were buried there alone between February and April, 1349.—Avesbury (Rolls Series No. 93), p. 407.

556. Whilst the king forbade the encouragement of beggars by gifts of charity, the municipal authorities fixed the price of labour.—Letter Book F. fos. 163, 168, 169, 181. At the close of the year (1349) a statute—known as the Statute of Labourers—was passed, fixing the scale of wages at the rate prevalent before the Black Death, and ordering punishment to be inflicted on those who demanded more.

557. Letter Book F, fo. 168.

558. -*Id.*, fo. 191b.

559. By writ, dated 1 July. Letter Book F, fo. 185b.

560. Letter Book F, fos. 187b, 188b.

561. Avesbury (Rolls Series No. 93), p. 412.

562. Letter Book F, fos. 174, 176.

563. Rot. Parl., ii, 155.

564. Letter Book G, fo. 47.—Their cost, amounting to nearly £500, was assessed on the wards.

565. Letter Book G, fo. 53b. (Memorials, pp. 285-289).

566. Walshingham (Rolls Series No. 28), i, 283. Chron. Angliæ (Rolls Series No. 64), p. 37.

567. Letter Book G, fos. 65-67.

568. Letter Book G, fo. 60.

569. Relief on this point was afforded by the king in February, 1359, by the issue of a writ to the effect that the names of his purveyors should be handed to the Mayor and Sheriffs of London, and that the purveyors shall not seize any victuals until they had shown and read their commission.—Letter Book G, fo. 74.

570. Walshingham, i, 288.

571. Letter Book G, fo. 133.

572. Stow's Survey (Thom's ed. 1876), pp. 41, 90.—If we include David, King of Denmark (as some do), the number of kings entertained on this occasion was five, and to this day the toast of "Prosperity to the Vintners' Company" is drunk at their banquets with five cheers in memory of the visit of the five crowned heads.—See a pamphlet entitled *The Vintners' Company with Five*, by B. Standring, Master of the Company in 1887.

573. Letter Book G, fo. 133.—The list of subscribers, as printed in Herbert's Introduction to his History of the Twelve Great Livery Companies (p. 32), is very inaccurately transcribed.

574. -*Id.*, fo. 158.

575. -*Id.*, fos. 225b, 226b, 235b, 236b.

576. -*Id.*, fo. 228b.

577.   Letter Book G, fo. 247b.—The money was advanced on the security of Exchequer bills. The names of the contributors and the several sums contributed, covering three folios of the Letter Book, have been for some reason erased.

578. -*Id.*, fos. 263, 270.

579. Fasciculi Zizaniorum (Rolls Series No. 5), introd., p. xxviii.

580. Letter Book G, fos. 274b-275.

581. -*Id.*, fo. 268.

582. Letter Book G, fos. 268b, 270.

583.   The number of parishes is elsewhere given as 110.—*Id.*, fo. 275. A list of London benefices, under date 31 Edward I [1302-3], is given in the City's Liber Custumarum (i, 228-230), the number being 116.

584. Ralph de Diceto (Rolls Series No. 68), pref. vol. i, p. lvi.

585. Chron. Edward I and II, introd., vol. i., p. xli.

586. Letter Book G, fo. 271. (Memorials, pp. 350-352).

587. -*Id.*, fo. 289b.

588. Walsingham, i, 315.

589. Letter Book G, fos. 297, 298, 304b, 306b, 307.

590. Letter Book G, fo. 312b. Letter Book H, fos. 17-19b.

591.   The parliament was originally summoned for the 12th February, but did not meet before the 28 April. The city members were John Pyel and William Walworth, Aldermen, William Essex and Adam Carlile, commoners.—Letter Book H. fos. 28. 29.

592. Chron. Angliæ (Rolls Series No. 64), 78, 79.

593. Walsingham i, 321. Higden's Polychron (Rolls Series No. 41), viii, 385. Chron. Angliæ (Rolls Series No. 64), pp. 94, 392.

594. Letter Book H, fo. 45b.

595. See the king's letter, dated "Haddele" Castle, 29 July, 1376.— Letter Book H, fo. 44.

596. The names of the representatives of the guilds forming the first Common Council of the kind are placed on record.—Letter Book H, fos. 46b, 47.

597. -Id., fo. 44b.

598. Letter Book H, fo. 46.

599. -Id., fos. 47, 161; Journal 11, fo. 89.

600. Charter, dated 26 May, 15 Edward III, *Supra* p. 188.

601. Letter Book H, fo. 173.—The names of those elected by the wards to the Common Council two years later (9 Ric. II), are inserted on a cedula between membranes, 15 and 16, of Pleas and Memoranda, Roll A 27.

602. Walsingham, i, 327. Chron. Angliæ, pp. 142, 143. Modern writers, however, have discovered some good qualities in this lady.—See Notes and Queries, 7th Series, vol. vii, pp. 449, *et seq.*

603. Chron. Angliæ, p. 130.

604. See Hust., Rolls, 95, (130) (13O); 97, (9); 98, (73) (74) (82); 109, (6) (7) (8); also Will of William Burton—Calendar of Wills, Court of Hust., London, ii, 301.

605. Letter Book H, fo. 77b.

606. -Id., fo. 47b.

607. Pat. Roll, 3 Ric. II, part 1.

608. "Ut de cetero non major, antiquo more, sed capitaneus Londoniis haberetur, et quod Marescallus Angliæ in illa civitate, sicut alibi, reos arestare valeret; cum multis petitionibus quæ; manifeste obviabant urbis libertatibus et imminebant civium detrimento."—Chron. Angliæ, p. 120.

609. Chron. Angliæ, pp. 123-125, 397; Walsingham, i, 325.

610. Chron. Angliæ, pp. 125, 398.

611. -*Id.*, pp. 127, 128.

612. Chron. Angliæ, p. 129.

613. Letter Book H, fos. 58, 59.

614. Chron. Angliæ, p. 134.

615. Chron. Angliæ, p. 129.

616. -*Id.*, pp. 136-137, 142-143.

617. Chron. Angliæ, pp. 146-149. The chronicler expresses the utmost joy and astonishment at the sudden change in the duke's manner. It was (he says) nothing less than a miracle that one who had so recently demanded a present of precious stones and 100 tuns of wine, as the price of his favour, should now appear so complacent.

618. -*Id.*, pp. 150, 151.

619.   "Londonienses præcipue obloquebantur, dicentes jam perpaucorum proceruin corda fore cum Rege, eos solos sibi fideles esse; quorum Rex licet ironice, vocabatur a nonnullis proceribus, eo quod ipsi multum juvissent eum in coronatione sua."—Walsingham i, 370; *Cf.* Chron. Angliæ, p. 200.

620. Chron. Angliæ, p. 153.

621. Lib. Cust. ii, 467, 468. It appears from the City Records, that the king's butler in ordinary could claim the office of Coroner of the city.—See Letter Book H, fos. 68, 77b.

622. The Isle of Wight had been surprised and taken, Rye had been captured, Hastings had been destroyed by fire, and Winchelsea would have fallen into the hands of the enemy but for the bold defence made by the Abbot of Battle.—Walsingham i, 340-342; Chron. Angliæ, pp. 151, 166, 167.

623. Letter Book H, fos. 76-77, 83.

624.   Et deputati sunt ad hujus pecuniæ custodiam duo cives Londonienses, scilicet Willelmus Walworthe et Johannes Philipot.—Chron.

Angliæ, p. 171. Eight other citizens, viz., Adam Lovekyn, William Tonge, Thomas Welford, Robert Lucas, John Hadley, John Northampton, John Organ, and John Sely, were appointed collectors of the two fifteenths.— Letter Book H, fo. 90.

625. Dated 4 Dec, 1377. Preserved at the Guildhall (Box No. 9).

626. Letter Book H, fo. 82.

627. Chron. Angliæ, p. 194: Walsingham i, 367. It was stated before parliament, in 1378, that Walworth and Philipot had laid out every penny of the subsidy.—Stubbs, Const. Hist., ii, 445 note.

628. Chron. Angliæ, pp. 199, 200. Philipot again showed his patriotism in 1380, by providing money and arms for an expedition sent to assist the Duke of Brittany.—Id., p. 266. He died in the summer of 1384.—Walsingham, ii, 115.

629. Letter Book H, fo. 95.

630. "Et idcirco locum illum elegerant præmeditato facinori; ne Londonienses, si Londoniis fuisset Parliamentum prædictum, sua auctoritate vel potentia eorum conatus ullatenus impedirent."—Walsingham, i, 380.

631. Letter Book H, fo. 101b. (Memorials, p. 427).

632. Letter Book H, fos. 109b, 110.

633. -Id., fos. 107, 108, 109.

634. -Id., fos. 111b, 113.

635. Letter Book H, fos. 128, 132.

636. The story of the insurrection under Wat Tyler, and of his death at the hands of Walworth, as told in Letter Book H, fo. 133b (Memorials, pp. 449-451), varies in some particulars from that given by Walsingham (i, 454-465), and in the Chronicon Angliæ (pp. 285-297).

637. Letter Book H, fo. 134.

638. -Id., fo. 134b.

639. Pleas and Mem., Roll A 24, membr. 9.

640. Walsingham, i, 467-484; ii, 23.

641. Walsingham, ii, 13.

642. -*Id.*, ii, 9, 10.

643. Letter Book H, fos. 149b, 150.

644. "Homo duri cordis et astutus, elatus propter divitias et superbus, qui nec inferioribus adquiescere, nec superiorum allegationibus sive monitis flecti valeret quin quod inceperat proprio ingenio torvo proposito ad quemcunque finem perducere niteretur."—Walsingham, ii, 65.

645. Letter Book H, fo. 144. (Memorials, p. 463).

646. Letter Book H, fo. 146b.

647. -*Id.*, fos. 153-154.

648. Walsingham, ii, 71. From the City's Records it appears that early in 1383, William Baret was alderman of Philipot's ward (Cornhill); but in the following year, when Brembre succeeded to his mayoralty, and the so-called "king's party" was again in the ascendant, Philipot again appears as alderman of his old ward, continuing in office until his death (12 Sept., 1384), when he was succeeded by John Rote.—Letter Book H, fos. 163, 174.

649. Letter Book H, fo. 155b.

650. Letter Book H, fo. 154.

651. Letter Book H, fo. 168. Three years later, "the folk of the Mercerye of London" complained to parliament that Brembre and his "upberers" had on this occasion obtained his election by force—"through debate and strenger partye."—(Rot., Parl. iii, 225). There is no evidence of this in the City's Records, although there appears to have been a disturbance at his re-election in 1384. It may be to this that the Mercers' petition refers. It is noteworthy that at the time of his election in 1383, Brembre was not an alderman, although in the previous year, and again in the year following his election, he is recorded as Alderman of Bread Street Ward.—Letter Book H, fos. 140, 163, 174.

652. Breve quod piscenarii libertatis civitatis Londoniæ exerceant artem suam ut consueverunt. Dated 27 Nov., 1383.—Letter Book H, fo. 172.

653. *-Id.*, fos. 154-154b, 176-177.

654. Dated 26 Nov., 7 Ric. II. Preserved at the Guildhall (Box No. 9).

655. Pleas and Mem., Roll A 27, membr. 3 dors.

656. Letter Book H, fos. 166, 167.

657. Pleas and Mem., Roll A 27, membr. 3.

658. Writ dated 9 February; Letter Box H, fo. 173b.

659. *-Id.*, fos. 173b, 174b.

660. *-Id.*, fo. 174.

661. Letter Book H, fo. 179.

662. Letter Book H, fo. 179b; Walsingham, ii, 116.

663. Hidgen, Polychron. (Rolls Series No. 41), ix, 45 *seq.*

664. "Hæc autem omnia sibi fieri procurarunt æmuli piscarii, ut dicebabur, quia per illos stetit quod ars et curia eorum erant destructæ." — Higden, ix, 49.

665. Letter Book H, fo. 92. (Memorials, pp. 415-417).

666. Letter Book H, fo. 182. The names of those specially summoned are set out in Pleas and Mem., Roll A 27, membr. 15.

667. Pleas and Mem., Roll A 27, membr. 4, 5 and 6.

668. Higden, ix, 50, 51.

669. Letter Book H, fo. 182.

670. Letter Book H, fo. 198b.

671. Pleas and Mem., Roll A 27, membr. 26.

672. Letters patent of pardon received the king's sign manual on the 3 June, 1386 (Letter Book H, fo. 216), but the prisoners were not released before April in the following year. — See Higden, Polychron. ix, 93.

673. Letter Book H, fo. 214. (Memorials, p. 494).

674. Rot. Parl. iii, 227, cited by Riley in his "Memorials," p. 494, note.

675. Letter Book H, fo. 176b.

676. This letter, which was dated the 27 April, was delivered to Lord Zouche at his house by John Reche, Common Pleader, and Ralph Strode and John Harwell, Sergeants-at-Arms.—Letter Book H, fo. 215b.

677. "Super quo dominus Rex respondit quod licet in sua potestate fuerat cum ipsis, Johanne, Johanne et Ricardo agere graciose bene tamen sibi provideret priusquam foret eis graciam concessurus."—Letter Book H, fo. 215b.

678. Higden, Polychron. ix, 93.

679. Letter Book H, fo. 222.

680. The oath as set out in the letter to the king differs from another copy of the oath, which immediately precedes the letter in Letter Book H, fos. 220b, 221; a clause having been subsequently added to the latter to the effect that the swearer abjured the opinions of Northampton and his followers, and would oppose their return within the bounds and limits set out in the king's letters patent.

681. Letter Book H, fo. 222.

682. Letter Book H, fo. 223b.

683. Walsingham, ii, 150.

684. Higden, Polychron. ix, 104.

685. Letter Book H, fo. 223b.

686. Higden, Polychron. ix, 106; Walsingham, ii, 166.

687. Letter Book H, fo. 223b. (Memorials, p. 449.)

688. Higden, Polychron. ix, 108-109.

689. "Londonienses ... mobiles erant ut arundo, et nunc cum Dominis, nunc cum Rege, sentiebant, nusquam stabiles sed fallaces."—Hist. Angliæ, ii, 161.

690. Higden, Polychron. ix, 108; Walsingham, ii, 169.

691. Pleas and Mem., Roll A, membr. 7.

692. Higden, ix, 111-114; Walsingham, ii, 170, 171; Engl. Chron. (Camd. Soc. No. 64), p. 5.

693. Higden, ix, 117, 118.

694. Howell's State Trials, i, 115.

695. Higden, Polychron. ix, 168.

696. State Trials, i, 118, 119.

697. Walsingham, ii, 165-174.

698. Higden, ix, 167-169.

699. Letter Book H, fo. 228.

700. Letter Book H, fo, 161.

701. -Id., fo. 126; Higden ix, 179.

702. Letter Book H, fos. 234, 234b.

703. Higden ix, 217.

704. Higden ix, 238, 239.

705. Letters patent, date, 2 Dec, 1390.—Letter Book H, fo. 255; Higden ix, 243.

706. Letter Book H, fo. 259. (Memorials, p. 526.).

707. -Id., fo. 300.

708. -Id., fo. 270.

709. Higden, ix, 270. According to Walsingham (Hist. Angl. ii, 208), the Lombard failed to get the money from the citizens, who nearly killed him when they learnt his purpose.

710. The names of the citizens chosen for the occasion are given by Higden (Polychron. ix, 269, 270), and in Letter Book H, fo. 270.

711.   The reason given in the City Records for the dismissals which followed is stated to be "certain defects in a commission under the common seal and other causes." —Letter Book H, fo. 270b.

712.   Higden, Polychron. ix, 272; Walsingham, ii, 208-209.

713.   Higden, ix, 273; Letter Book H, fo. 270b.

714.   Letter Book H, fo. 275b.

715.   -Id., fo. 273.

716.   Letter Book H, fo. 269b; Higden, ix, 267. Walsingham (ii, 213) suggests that this was done at the instance of the Archbishop of York, the Chancellor.

717.   "Putabant isti officiarii per hoc non modicum damnificare civitatem Lundoniæ, sed potius hoc multo majora damna intulerunt regi et hominibus regni quam jam dictæ civitati." —Higden, ix, 267-268.

718.   Walsingham, ii, 210.

719.   Higden, ix, 273.

720.   Letters Patent of pardon, dated Woodstock, 19 September, 1392. Preserved at the Guildhall (Box No. 6).

721.   Higden. ix, 274, 276, 278; Letter Book H, fos. 271b, 272, 274. Notwithstanding these remissions, the city was mulcted, according to Waisingham (ii, 211), in no less a sum than £10,000 before it received its liberties. —Cf. Chron. of London, 1089-1483 (ed. by Sir H. Nicolas, sometimes called "Tyrrell's Chronicle," from a City Remembrancer of that name), p. 80.

722.   Stat. 17, Ric. II, c. 13; Letter Book H, fos. 290b, 291.; Bohun, "Privilegia Londini" (ed. 1723), p. 57.

723.   Higden, ix, 274.

724.   Stubbs, Const. Hist., ii, 489-490.

725.   Letter Book H, fo. 314.

726.   Engl. Chron. (Camd. Soc. No. 64), p. 12.

727. "Also this yere (1397-8), by selying of blank chartres, the Citie of London paied to the kyng a ml li."—Chron. of London (ed. by Sir H. Nicolas); p. 83.

728. Letters Patent, dat. 9 May, 1399.—Letter Book H, fo. 326. Richard set sail on the 29th.

729. "Douze cent hommes de Londres, tous armés et montés à cheval."—Froissart (ed. Lyon, 1559), vol. iv, c. 108, p. 328. In Lord Berner's translation of Froissart (iv, 566), the number is wrongly given as 12,000.

730. Walsingham, ii, 245, 246.

731. Walsingham, ii, 262-264. Serle's Christian name is given elsewhere as John.—Eng. Chron. (Camd. Soc., No. 64), p. 30. The writ for his execution is dated 5 August, 1404.—Letter Book I, fo. 31b.

732. Letter Book I, fo. 180b. (Memorials, pp. 638-641). Walsingham, ii, 317.

733. City Records Journal, I, fo. 83b. We have now a series of MS. Volumes among the City's archives known as "Journals" to assist us. They contain minutes of proceedings of the Court of Common Council, just as the "Repertories" (which we shall have occasion to consult later on), contain a record of the proceedings of the Court of Aldermen. The Letter Books may now be regarded as "fair copies" of the more important of the proceedings of both Courts.

734. Letter Book H, fo. 307b. The Lollards are said to have derived their name from a low German word *lollen*, to sing or chant, from their habit of chanting, but their clerical opponents affected to derive it from the Latin *lolium*, as if this sect were as tares among the true wheat of the church.

735. Letter Book I, fo. 125b-132.

736. -*Id.*, fo. 130b.

737. -*Ibid.*

738. Letter Book I, fo. 11b.

739. He appears, however, to have burnt by a special order of the king, before the passing of the statute.—See Fasc. Zizan. (Rolls Series No. 5), Introd. p. lxix.

740. A curious story is told of boys in the streets playing at England and Scotland at this time, with the result that what began in play ended in fighting and loss of life.—See Chron. Mon. S. Albani (Rolls Series No. 28, 3), p. 332.

741. Letter Book I, fo. 16.

742. Letter Book I, fo. 27; Chron. Mon. S. Albani (Rolls Series No. 28, 3), p. 379.

743. Letter Book I, fo. 89b.

744. -Id., fo. 113.

745. -Id., fo. 108b.

746. Letter Book I, fo. 112b.

747. Exchequer Roll, Lay Subsidy, 144-20.—See Archæological Journal, vol. xliv, 56-82.

748. Letter Book I, fo. 54. (Memorials pp. 563-564.)

749. License, dated Westminster, 29 May, 12 Henry IV (A.D. 1411).— Letter Book I, fo. 103b. In 1417 the mayor and aldermen ordained that the rector of St. Peter's for the time being should in future take precedence of the rectors of all other city churches, on the ground that Saint Peter's was the first church founded in the city of London, having been built in 199 by King Lucius, and for 400 years or more held the metropolitan chair.—Letter Book I, fo. 203. (Memorials, pp. 651-653.) Cf. Journal 1, fo. 21b.

750. "Eminentissima turris Ecclesiæ Anglicanæ et pugil invictus Dominus Thomas de Arundelia."—Hist. Angl. ii, 300.

751. A certain William Fyssher, a *parchemyner* or parchment-maker of London, was afterwards (1416) convicted of assisting in Oldcastle's escape, and was executed at Tyburn.—Letter Book I, fo. 181b. (Memorials, p. 641.)

752. Walsingham, ii, 292-299; Fasc. Zizan. (Rolls Series No. 5), 433-449; Chron. of London (ed. by Sir H. Nicolas), p. 97.

753. Letter Book I, fos. 286-290.

754. 2 Hen. V. Stat. i, c. 7.

755. It was not, however, the last occasion upon which parliamentary action was attempted. In 1422, and again in 1425, the Lollards were formidable in London, and parliament on both occasions ordered that those who were in prison should be delivered at once to the Ordinary, in accordance with the provisions of this Statute.—Stubbs, Const. Hist., iii, 81, 363.

756. Letter Book I, fo. 147.

757. Walsingham, ii, 306, 307.

758. Hist. Angl., ii, 307.

759. Letter Book I, fol. 154.

760. See letter from the mayor to the king, giving an account of Cleydon's trial, 22nd August, 1415.—Letter Book I, fo. 155. (Memorials, p. 617). Foxe, "Acts and Monuments," iii, 531-534.

761. Walsingham, ii, 327, 328.

762. Engl. Chron. (Camd. Soc., No. 64), p. 46; Chron. of London (Nicolas), p. 106.

763. Stubbs, Const. Hist., iii., 363, 364.

764. Letter Book I, fo. 150. This "very antient memorandum" of the Lord Mayor's precedence in the City was submitted to Charles II in 1670, when that monarch insisted upon Sir Richard Ford, the Lord Mayor of the day, giving "the hand and the place" to the Prince of Orange (afterwards William III of England), on the occasion of the prince being entertained by the City.—Repertory, 76, fos. 28b, 29.

765. Letter Book I, fo. 158b. (Memorials, p. 613).

766. -Id., fo. 157.

767. Gregory's Chron. (Camd. Soc, N.S., No. 17), pp. 108-109. Gregory was an alderman of the City, and an eye-witness of much that he relates.

768. Letter dated 2nd August—the day on which Sir Thomas Grey, one of the chief conspiritors was executed.—Letter Book I, fo. 180.

769. Letter Book I, fo. 143. (Memorials, p. 619).

770. Letter Book I, fo. 177.

771. Letter Book I, fo. 159. (Memorials, pp. 620, 622).

772. "Quali gaudio, quali tripudio, quali denique triumpho, sit acceptus a Londoniensibus, dicere prætermitto. Quia revera curiositas apparatumn, nimietas expensarum, varietates spectaculorum, tractatus exigerent merito speciales." —Walsingham, ii, 314.

773. Chron. of London (Nicolas), p. 103.

774. Letter Book I, fo. 178b. Other proclamations on the same subject are recorded in the same place, most of which will be found in "Memorials" (pp. 627-629).

775. Letter Book I, fo. 190b.

776. -Id., fos. 188, 188b.

777. Letter Book I, fo. 191b.

778. Letter Book I, fo. 218b. In May, 1419, the sword was surrendered, and the security changed to one on wool, woolfells, &c. —Id., fo. 227b.

779. Letter Book I, fo. 229. (Memorials, p. 654.)

780. Journal 1, fo. 30b.

781. Letter Book I, fo. 200b. (Memorials, p. 657.)

782. Letter, dated Caen, 11 September. —Letter Book I, fo. 200b.

783. Writ, dated 18th Oct. —Letter Book I, fo. 203.

784. Stubbs, Const. Hist., iii, 89.

785. Letter Book I, fo. 222.

786. Letter Book I, fos. 211b, 212b, 217. Proclamations made by the civic authorities at this time were subscribed "Carpenter" —the name of the Common Clerk or Town Clerk of the City. The custom of the Town Clerk of London for the time being, signing official documents of this kind with his surname alone, continues at the present day.

787. Letter Book I, fo. 215b.

788. Letter Book I, fo. 216. (Memorials, p. 664).

789. Letter Book I, fo. 216. On the 15th September the question of payment to the brewers, wine drawers and turners of the cups was considered.—Journal I, fo. 48. (Memorials, pp. 665, 666).

790. Gregory's Chron. (Camd. Soc, N.S., No. 17), 1222.

791. Letter Book I, fos. 236, 236b.

792. Letter Book I, fo. 237. (Memorials, p. 674).

793. -Id., fo. 241b.

794. Letter Book I, fo. 252.

795. Walsingham, ii, 335.

796. Letter Book I, fo. 263.

797. Letter Book I, fo. 259. According to Walsingham (ii, 336), the ceremony took place on the *first* Sunday in Lent.

798. Walsingham, ii, 336, 337.

799. Parliament voted a fifteenth and a tenth to assist the king in his necessities; John Gedney, alderman, John Perneys, John Bacon, grocer, and John Patesley, goldsmith, being appointed commissioners to levy the same within the City.—Letter Book I, fo. 277b.

800. Letter Book K, fo. 1b.

801. Letter Book I, fo. 282b.

802. Letter Book I, fo. 282b; Letter Book K, fo. 12.

803. Letter Book K, fo. 2.

804. Stubbs, Const. Hist., iii, 97.

805. Letter Book K, fos. 10, 10b.

806. -Id., fo. 15b.

807. Letter Book K, fos. 10-18.

808. Chron. London (Nicolas), p. 114; Gregory's Chron. (Camd. Soc., N.S., No. 17), p. 159; Engl. Chron. (Camd. Soc., No. 64), pp. 53, 54.

809. See two letters from the mayor.—Letter Book K, fos. 18b, 21.

810. Gregory's Chron., p. 160.

811. -Id., p. 162.

812. Journal 2, fos. 22b, 64b (new pagination).

813. Letter Book K, fo. 50b.

814. Gregory's Chron., p. 161.

815. Letter Book K, fo. 55b.

816. Letter Book K, fos. 62, 63b; Gregory's Chron., p. 164.

817. Letter Book K, fo. 66b; Gregory's Chron., p. 164.

818. Letter Book K, fo. 68b. In 1443 the Common Council agreed to allow the City members their reasonable expenses out of the chamber (Journal 5, fo. 129b), but when parliament met at Coventry in 1459, the City members were allowed 40s. a day, besides any disbursements they might make in the City's honour (Journal 6, fo. 166b), and the same allowance was made in 1464, when parliament sat at York (Journal 7, fos. 52, 54).

819. -Id., fo. 69b.

820. Gregory's Chron., pp. 164-168.

821. City Records, Liber Dunthorn, fo. 61b; Letter Book K, fo. 70.

822. Cal. of Wills, Court of Husting, London, ii, 509.

823. Letter Book K, fo. 84.

824. A long account of his entry into the French capital, and of the pageantry in honour of the occasion, is set out in full in the City's Records.—Letter Book K, fos. 101b-103.

825. A full descriptive account of Henry's reception on his return from France is set out in the City Records (Letter Book K, fos. 103b-104b). It purports to be an account sent by John Carpenter, the Town Clerk, to a friend,

and has been printed at the end of the *Liber Albus* (Rolls Series); *Cf.* Gregory's Chron., pp. 173-175.

826.   He informed the City of his intention by letter, dated from Ghent the 13th April.—Letter Book K, fo. 105.

827.   Stubbs, Const. Hist., iii, 114-117.

828.   Letter Book K, fo. 137b.

829.   Letter Book K, fo. 138.

830.   Gregory's Chron., p. 177.

831.   Letter Book K, fo. 148.

832.   "And that same yere (1437), the Mayre of London sende, by the good a-vyse and consent of craftys, sent sowdyers to Calys, for hyt was sayde that the Duke of Burgone lay sege unto Calis."—Gregory's Chron. p. 178.

833.   Letter Book K, fos. 160-162.

834.   Gregory's Chron. p. 179.

835.   Letter Book K. fo. 183b. The tax was found to be so successful that it was subsequently renewed. In 1453 it was renewed for the king's life.— *Id.*, fo. 280b.

836.   Journal 3, fo. 103b.

837.   Chron. of London (Nicolas), p. 129.

838.   The validity as well as the effect of this charter (which is preserved in the Town Clerk's office) has been made the subject of much controversy, some contending that it is in effect a grant of the soil of the river from Staines to Yantlet, that being the extent of the City's liberties on the Thames, whilst others restrict the grant to the City's territorial limits, *i.e.*, from Temple Bar to the Tower.

839.   Letter Book K, fo. 220b.

840.   Chron. of London (Nicholas), p. 134.

841. See "Historical Memoranda," by Stow, printed in "Three Fifteenth Cent. Chron." (Camd. Soc., N.S., No. 28), pp. 94-99.

842. "And the Meire of London with the comynes of the city came to the kynge besekynge him that he wolde tarye in the cite, and they wolde lyve and dye with him, and pay for his costes of householde an halff yere; but he wold nott, but toke his journey to Kyllyngworthe."—"Three Fifteenth Cent. Chronicles" (Camd. Soc.), p. 67.

843. Journal 5, fo. 36b.

844. Journal 5, fo. 39.

845. He had been admitted alderman of Lime Street ward in 1448, at the king's special request, and had only recently been discharged.—Journal 4, fo. 213b; Journal 5, fo. 38b. In 1461 he left England, but was captured at sea by the French and put to ransom for 4,000 marks.—Fabyan, p. 638.

846. Holinshed, iii, 224.

847. Gregory's Chron., p. 192.

848. Journal 5, fo. 40b.

849. Alexander Iden, who appears to have pursued Cade beyond the limits of his own jurisdiction, as Sheriff of Kent, into the neighbouring county of Sussex, where the rebel was apprehended in a garden at Heathfield.—"Three Fifteenth Cent. Chron.," preface, p. vii.

850. The exclusion of the Duke and other nobles from the king's council had been made an express ground of complaint by the Kentish insurgents.

851. Chron., p. 196.

852. "And so thei brought (the duke) ungirt thurgh London bitwene ij bisshoppes ridyng unto his place; and after that made hym swere at Paulis after theire entent, and put him frome his good peticions which were for the comoen wele of the realme."—Chron. of London (Nicolas), p. 138.

853. Journal 5, fos. 131, 132b, 133b.

854. Journal 5, fos. 134b, 135b, 136.

855. -Id., fo. 148.

856. -*Id.*, fo. 152.

857. -*Id.*, fo. 152b.

858. -*Id.*, fos. 183, 184.

859. Journal 5, fo. 206.

860. Report of City Chamberlain to the Court of Common Council.— Journal 5, fos. 227-228b.

861. News-letter of John Stodeley, 19 Jan., 1454; Paston Letters (Gairdner), i, 265, 266.

862. Journal 5, fos 143, 145b, 152, 152b-160b.

863. Journal 5, fo. 150.

864. -*Id.*, fos. 162, 162b.

865. -*Id.*, fo. 164b.

866. Booking to Paston, 15 May; Paston Letters (Gairdner), i, 387; *Cf.* Chron. of London (Nicolas), p. 139; Gregory's Chron., p. 199.

867. William Cantelowe, alderman of Cripplegate and Billingsgate wards, from the latter of which he was discharged in October, 1461, on the score of old age and infirmity (Journal 6, fo. 81b). He appears in his time to have had financial dealings with the crown, on one occasion conveying money over sea for bringing Queen Margaret to England, and on another supplying gunpowder to the castle of Cherbourg, when it was in the hands of the English. He is thought by some to be identical with the William Cantelowe who afterwards (in 1464) captured Henry VI in a wood in the North of England.—"Three Fifteenth Cent. Chron." (Camd. Soc, N.S., No. 28), Preface, p. viii.

868. Short English Chron. (Camd. Soc., N.S., No. 28), p. 70.

869. Letter Book K, fo. 287.

870. -*Id.*, fo. 288b.

871. Cotton MS., Vitell. A, xvi, fo. 114.

872. Engl. Chron., 1377-1461 (Camd. Soc., No. 64), p. 77.

873. Fabyan, Chron. (ed. 1811), p. 633; *Cf.* Chron. of London (Nicolas), p. 139.

874. Journal 6, fos. 138, 138b, 139.

875. Engl. Chron., 1377-1461 (Camd. Soc., No. 64), p. 78; *Cf.* Fabyan, p. 633; Holinshed, iii, 249.

876. Short Engl. Chron. (Camd. Soc., N.S., No. 28), p. 71; Chron. of London (Nicolas), p. 140.

877. Journal 6, fo. 166.

878. *-Id.*, fo. 145.

879. *-Id.*, fo. 163.

880. English Chron., 1377-1461 (Camd. Soc., No. 64), p. 179.

881. Journal 6, fo. 224b.

882. William Paston, writing to his brother John, under date 28th January, 1460, remarks, "Item, the kyng cometh to London ward, and, as it is seyd, rereth the pepyll as he come; but it is certayn ther be comyssyons made in to dyvers schyres that every man be redy in his best aray to com when the kyng send for hem." —Paston Letters (Gairdner), i, 506.

883. Paston Letters (Gairdner), Introd., p. cxl.

884. The king's letter, dated 2 Feb., was read before the Common Council on the 5 Feb. —Letter Book K, fo. 313b; Journal 6, fo. 196b.

885. Journal 6, fo. 197b.

886. *-Id.*, fo. 203b.

887. *-Id.*, fo. 158.

888. Journal 6, fo. 237.

889. It had been destroyed by fire during the Kentish outbreak. —Gregory's Chron., p. 193.

890. Journal 6, fo. 237b.

891.   Journal 6, fo. 238.

892.   -*Id.*, fo. 238b.

893.   Journal 6, fos. 239, 239b; Eng. Chron., 1377-1461 (Camd. Soc. No. 64), p. 94.

894.   Journal 6, fo. 252b.

895.   Eo quod nullus alius modus videtur esse tutus pro civitate.—*Id.*, fo. 251.

896.   Journal 6, fo. 251b.

897.   -*Id.*, fo. 250b.

898.   Eng. Chron. (Camd. Soc., No. 64), p. 98. The Thames boatmen and sailors were almost as powerful and troublesome a body of men as the London apprentices. The Common Council had recently (11th July) endeavoured to subdue their turbulent spirit by the distribution among them of a large sum of money (£100).—Journal 6, fo. 254.

899.   On the 4th July the Common Council voted the earls the sum of £1,000 by way of loan.—Journal 6, fo. 253.

900.   Journal 6, fo. 256. By some inadvertence two copies of the agreement were sealed, one of which was returned to the mayor to be cancelled.

901.   Journal 6, fo. 257.

902.   Gregory's Chron., p. 208; Engl. Chron., pp, 99-100; Short Engl. Chron., p. 75.

903.   The interview with the wardens of the companies took place at a Common Council held on the 13th December, 1460.—Journal 6, fo. 282b.

904.   Journal 6, fo. 13.

905.   The governing body in the city was still Lancastrian at heart. On the 13th Feb. the Common Council had voted Henry, at that time in the hands of Warwick, a loan of 1,000 marks, and a further sum of 500 marks (making in all £1,000) for the purpose of *garnysshyng* and safeguarding the city. On the 24th a certain number of aldermen and commoners were deputed to answer for the safe custody of the Tower, and on the following

day (25 Feb.) the mayor forbade, by public proclamation, any insult being offered to Sir Edmund Hampden and others, who had been despatched by the king and queen to London for the purpose of ascertaining "the true and faithful disposition" of the city.—Journal 6, fos. 35, 35b, 40.

906.   Gregory's Chron., p. 215.

907.   Stubbs, Const. Hist., iii, 189.

908.   Journal 6, fo. 37b.

909.   Letter Book L, fo. 4; Lib. Dunthorn, fo. 62; Journal 7, fo. 98.

910.   Short English Chron. (Camd. Soc., N.S., No. 28), p. 80.

911.   Journal 7, fos. 97b, 98.

912.   Charter, dat. Winchecombe, 26 Aug., 1461. Preserved at the Guildhall (Box No. 28).

913.   Inspeximus charter, dated Westminster, 25 March, 1462. Preserved at the Guildhall (Box No. 13).

914.   Journal 7, fo. 8.

915.   -Id., fo. 15.

916.   See Inspeximus charter 15 Charles II.

917.   Journal 7, fo. 21b.

918.   Journal 7, fo. 175.

919.   Ancestor of Lord Bacon and others of the nobility.—See Orridge "Citizens and their Rulers," p. 222.

920.   Fabyan, p. 656. He was deprived of his aldermanry (Broad Street Ward) by the king's orders.—Journal 7, fo. 128.

921.   Journal 7, fos. 196, 198, 199.

922.   Journal 7, fos. 215b, 222b.

923.   -Id., fos. 229b, 230b.

924.   -*Id.*, fo. 222b.

925.   A record of what took place in the city between the 1st and 6th October is set out in Journal 7, fo. 223b.

926.   -*Id.*, fo. 225.

927.   He had, after Warwick's flight to France in March of this year, put to death and impaled twenty of the earl's followers.—Warkworth's Chron. (Camd. Soc., No. 10), p. 9.

928.   Journal 7, fo. 225.

929.   Fabyan Chron., p. 660.

930.   Warkworth's Chron. (Camd. Soc., No. 10), p. 15.—According to the chronicler, the *Commons* of the city were still loyal to Henry, whom Archbishop Nevill had carried through the streets, weak and sickly as he was, in the hope of exciting the sympathy of the burgesses. Had the archbishop been a true man, "as the Commons of London were," Edward would not have gained an entry into the city until after the victory of Barnet-field.

931.   Journal 5, fos. 152, 175.

932.   The "bastard's" letter and the reply of the mayor and aldermen are set out in Journal 8, fos. 4b-6b, and Letter Book L, fo. 78.

933.   Holinshed, iii, 323; Fabyan, p. 662.—According to Warkworth (p. 19), the *Commons* would willingly have admitted the rebels had the latter not attempted to fire Aldgate and London Bridge.

934.   Paston Letters, iii, 17.

935.   The 21st May is the day usually given as that on which Edward returned. The City's Journal, however, gives the day as the Eve of the Ascension, that festival falling on May the 23rd.—Journal 8, fo. 7.

936.   Warkworth's Chron., p. 21.

937.   Namely, Richard Lee, Matthew Philip, Ralph Verney, John Young, William Tailour, George Irlond, William Hampton, Bartholomew James, Thomas Stalbrok, and William Stokker.—Journal 8, fo. 7.

938.   Journal 7, fo. 246.

939. *-Id.*, 8, fo. 98.

940. *-Id.*, fo. 101.

941. Journal 8, fo. 110b.

942. Preserved at the Guildhall (Box No. 28).

943. Journal 8, fo. 244.

944. Fabyan, p. 667.

945. Proclamation, dated 21 Nov., 22 Edw. IV.—Letter Book L, fo. 281b; Journal 9, fo. 2.

946. Journal 9, fo. 12.

947. *-Id.*, fo. 14.

948. *-Id.*, fo. 14b.

949. *-Id.*, fos. 18, 18b.

950. Journal 9, fo. 21b.

951. The oath taken by Gloucester to King Edward V, as well as the oath which he was willing to take to the queen, if she consented to quit Westminster, were read before the Common Council on the 23rd March.— Journal 9, fo. 23b.

952. Wife of Matthew Shore, a respectable goldsmith of Lombard Street:—

> "In Lombard-street, I once did dwelle,
> As London yet can witness welle;
> Where many gallants did beholde
> My beautye in a shop of golde."

(Percy Reliques).

She had recently been made to do penance by Gloucester in a white sheet for practising witchcraft upon him; but her unhappy position, as well as her well-known charity in better days, gained for her much sympathy and respect.

953. The duke's speech, interesting as it is, as showing the importance attached to gaining the favour of the City, cannot be regarded as historical.— Stubbs, Const. Hist., iii, 224 note.

954. Journal 9, fo. 27.

955. Journal 9, fo. 33b. The names of the citizens selected for that honour are recorded.—*Id.*, fo. 21b. The names also of those who attended coronations in the same capacity down to the time of George IV are, with one exception (the coronation of Charles I), entered in the City's archives.— (See Report on Coronations, presented to Co. Co., 18 Aug., 1831. *Printed.*)

956. -*Id.*, fo. 43.

957. -*Id.*, fo. 114b.

958. Journal 9, fo. 39.

959. Green, Hist. of the English People, ii, 63.

960. Stat. 1 Richard III, c. 9.

961. -*Id.*, c. 2.

962. Journal 9, fo. 43b.

963. Journal 9, fo. 56.

964. Cotton MS. Vitellius A, xvi, fo. 140.

965. Journal 9, fos. 78b, 81. Richard issued a proclamation against Henry "Tydder" on the 23 June, calling upon his subjects to defend themselves against his proposed attack.—Paston Letters (Gairdner), iii, 316-320.

966. Journal 9, fos. 81b-83b.

967. Journal 9, fos. 84, 85b, 86b; *Cf.* "Materials illustrative of the reign of Henry VII" (Rolls Series, No. 60), i, 4-6.

968. Holinshed, iii, 479.

969. Hecker's "Epidemics of the Middle Ages," p. 168.

970. Journal 9, fo. 87b.

971. The day for election of mayor varied; at one time it was the Feast of the Translation of S. Edward (13 Oct.), at another the Feast of SS. Simon and Jude (28 Oct.).

972. Journal 9, fo. 88.

973. -Id., fo. 78b.

974. -Id., fo. 89b.

975. Holinshed, iii, 482, 483; Cotton MS. Vitellius A, xvi, fo. 141b. According to Fabyan (p. 683), the Mercers, Grocers and Drapers subscribed nearly one half of the loan.

976. Pol. Verg., 717; "Materials illustrative of the reign of Henry VII" (Rolls Series, No. 60), i, 3.

977. Gairdner's "Henry the Seventh" (Twelve English Statesmen Series), p. 47. No record of this appears in the City's archives.

978. Journal 9, fos. 150b, 151.

979. -Id., fo. 151.

980. He arrived on the 3rd Nov.—Gairdner, p. 57.

981. Journal 9, fos. 157b, 158.

982. -Id., fo. 161.

983. Journal 9, fo. 223b; Cotton MS. Vitellius A, xvi, fo. 142b; Fabyan, p. 683; Holinshed, iii, 492.

984. Henry's second parliament was summoned to meet the 9th Nov., 1487. The names of the City's representatives have not come down to us, but we know that William White, an alderman, was elected one or the members in the place of Thomas Fitz-William, who was chosen member for Lincolnshire, and we have the names of six men chosen to superintend the City's affairs in this parliament (*ad prosequendum in parliamento pro negociis civitatis*), viz:—William Capell, alderman, Thomas Bullesdon, Nicholas Alwyn, Simon Harrys, William Brogreve, and Thomas Grafton.—Journal 9, fo. 224.

985. Holinshed, iii, 492.

986. Journal 9, fo. 273b.

987. Fabyan, p. 684.

988. Journal 10, fos. 80b, 83; Repertory 1, fos. 10b, 13. The "Repertories" — containing minutes of the proceedings of the Court of Aldermen, distinct from those of the Common Council — commence in 1495.

989. Repertory 1, fo. 19b.

990. Two years later, when the post was held by Arnold Babyngton, complaint being made of the noisome smell arising from the burning of bones, horns, shavings of leather, &c., in preparing food for the City's hounds, near Moorgate, the Common Hunt was allowed a sum of 26s. 8d. in addition to his customary fees for the purpose of supplying wood for the purpose. — Repertory 1, fo. 70. The office was maintained as late as the year 1807, when it was abolished by order of the Common Council. — Journal 84, fo. 135b.

991. Repertory 1, fo. 20b.

992. -Id., fos. 20, 20b.

993. Journal 10, fo. 104b.

994. -Id., fo. 105.

995. -Id., fo. 108.

996. Fabyan, p. 687.

997. Cotton MS. Vitellius A, xvi, fo. 176.

998. Repertory 1, fo. 41b.

999. Repertory 1, fo. 62.

1000. Journal 10, fo. 187b.

1001. Journal 10, fo. 190b.

1002. -Id., fo. 191.

1003. This is the date given by Gairdner (p. 198). According to Fabyan (p. 687) she arrived on the 4th Oct.

1004. Journal 10, fos. 238, 238b.

1005. Repertory 1, fos. 122b-126. The account will be found in Archæol., vol. xxxii, p. 126.

1006. Repertory 1, fos. 130, 130b.

1007. By Stat. 19 Henry VII, c. 7, annulling Stat. 15 Henry VI, c. 6.

1008. Repertory 2, fo. 146.

1009. Charter dated 23 July, 1505, preserved at the Guildhall (Box No. 15).

1010. Repertory 1, fo. 175.

1011. Strype, Stow's "Survey" (1720), bk. ii, p. 193.

1012. Repertory 2, fos. 12, 14; Grey Friars Chron. (Camd. Soc., No. 53), p. 29.

1013. The sum mentioned by Holinshed (iii. 539), is £1,400; *Cf.* Fabyan, p. 689.

1014. Baker, in his Chronicle (ed. 1674), p. 248, puts Capel's fine at £1,400; *Cf.* Fabyan, p. 689; Holinshed, iii, 530; Journal 11, fo. 94.

1015. Fabyan, p. 690.

1016. Letter Book M, fo. 138; Journal 11, fo. 28.

1017. Journal 11, fos. 37-39.

1018. Gairdner's "Henry the Seventh," p. 206.

1019. Journal 10, fos. 318, 318b; Repertory 2, fos. 10b-11b. A list of "such places as have charged themself and promysed to kepe the yerely obit" of Henry VII, as well as a copy of indentures made for the assurance of the same obit, with schedule of sums paid to various religious houses for the observance of the same, are entered in the City's Records.—Repertory 1. fo. 167b; Letter Book P, fo. 186b.

1020. The generally accepted day of his death, although the City's Archives in one place record it as having taken place on the 21st.—Journal 2, fo. 67b; *Cf.* Fabyan, 690.

1021. Holinshed, iii, 541.

1022. Journal 11, fos. 67b-69.

1023. "Aldermen barons and presenting barons astate whiche hath been Maires."

1024. Journal 2, fo. 69.

1025. Repertory 11, fo. 68b.

1026. Letters Patent, dated 9 June, 1509, preserved at the Guildhall (Box No. 29).

1027. Letter Book M, fo. 159; Journal 11, fo. 74b.

1028. Repertory 2, fo. 68.

1029. Journal 11, fos. 80, 81b, 82; Letter Book M, fo. 160.

1030. Journal 11, fo. 80.

1031. Holinshed, iii, 547.

1032. According to Holinshed (iii, 567), Parliament opened on the 25th Jan., 1512. The Parliamentary Returns give the date as the 4th Feb. with "no returns found." The names of the City's members, however, are recorded in the City's Archives. They were Alderman Sir William Capell, who had suffered so much at the close of the last reign, Richard Broke, the City's new Recorder, William Cawle or Calley, draper, and John Kyme, mercer, commoners.—Journal 11, fo. 147b; Repertory 2, fo. 125b.

1033. The Act for levying the necessary subsidy ordained that every alien made a denizen should be rated like a native, but that aliens who had not become denizens should be assessed at double the amount at which natives were assessed.—See "Historical Introd. to Cal. of Denizations and Naturalizations of Aliens in England, 1509-1603." (Huguenot Soc.), viii, 7.

1034. Journal 11, fo. 1.

1035. -Id., fo. 1b.

1036. Journal 11, fo. 171; Repertory 2, fos. 150b, 172.

1037. Repertory 2, fos. 151b-152.

1038. Journal 11, fo. 2.

1039. Repertory 2, fo. 153.

1040. Letter Book M., fo. 257; Repertory 3, fo. 221. In July, 1517, the Fellowship of Saddlers of London consented, on the recommendation of Archbishop Warham, to refer a matter of dispute between it and the parishioners of St. Vedast to the Recorder and Thomas More, gentleman, for settlement (Repertory 3, fo. 149); and in Aug., 1521, "Thomas More, late of London, gentleman," was bound over, in the sum of £20, to appear before the mayor for the time being, to answer such charges as might be made against him.—Journal 12, fo. 123.

1041. Roper's Life of Sir Thomas More, pp. 3, 5, 6.

1042. Journal 8, fo. 144; Journal 9, fos. 13, 142b.

1043. William Lichfield, rector of All Hallows the Great, Gilbert Worthington, rector of St. Andrew's, Holborn, John Cote, rector of St. Peter's, Cornhill, and John Nigel or Neel, master of the hospital of St. Thomas de Acon and parson of St. Mary Colechurch.—Rot. Parl. v, 137.

1044. Stow's Survey (Thoms's ed., 1876), p. 42.

1045. Chamber Accounts (Town Clerk's office), i, fos. 202b, 203.

1046. Repertory 2, fos. 121b, 123.

1047. -Id., fo. 126b; Journal 11, fo. 147b.

1048. Journal 11, fo. 163; Repertory 2, fos. 133b, 142.

1049. Letter of Erasmus to Justus Jonas quoted in Lupton's Life of Colet, pp. 166, 167.

1050. Survey (Thoms's ed., 1876), p. 28.

1051. "The number of grammar schools, in various parts of the country, which owe their foundation and endowment to the piety and liberality of citizens of London ... far exceeds what might be supposed, approaching as it does nearly to a hundred."—Preface to Brewer's Life of Carpenter, p. xi.

1052. Repertory 3, fo. 46.

1053. -Id., fos. 70b, 71.

1054.   -*Id.*, fos. 86, 86b, 88.

1055.   Repertory 3, fos. 116, 116b.

1056.   Wares bought and sold between strangers—"foreign bought and sold"—were declared forfeited to the City by Letters Patent of Henry VII, 23 July. 1505, confirmed by Henry VIII, 12 July, 1523.

1057.   In 1500, and again in 1516, orders were issued for all freemen to return with their families to the city on pain of losing their freedom.—Journal 10. fos. 181b, 259.

1058.   Repertory 3, fos. 141b, 142.

1059.   Holinshed, iii, 618.

1060.   Or Munday; the name is said to appear in twenty-seven different forms. He was a goldsmith by trade, and was appointed (among others) by Cardinal Wolsey to report upon the assay of gold and silver coinage in 1526.—Journal 13, fo. 45b; Letter Book O, fo. 71b. He served sheriff, 1514; and was mayor in 1522.

1061.   In 1462 the Common Council ordered basket-makers, gold wire-drawers, and other foreigners plying a craft within the city, to reside at Blanchappleton—a manor in the vicinity of Mark Lane—and not elsewhere.

1062.   Repertory 3, fo. 55b.

1063.   For an account of the riot and subsequent proceedings, see Holinshed, iii, 621-623, and the Grey Friars Chron. (Camd. Soc., No. 53). p. 30.

1064.   Repertory 3, fos. 143, 143b.

1065.   Holinshed, iii, 624.

1066.   Repertory 3, fo. 144b.

1067.   -*Id.*, fo. 143b.

1068.   Holinshed, 624.

1069.   Repertory 3, fo. 145b.

1070.   -*Id.*, fo. 145.

1071. Repertory 3, fo. 165.

1072. -*Id.*, fo. 166.

1073. "Thys yere was much a doo in the yelde-halle for the mayer for the comyns wold not have had Semer, for be cause of yell May-day." — Grey Friars Chron. (Camd. Soc., No. 53), p. 33.

1074. Repertory 11, fo. 351b.

1075. Cal. Letters and Papers, For. and Dom. (Henry VIII), vol. ii, pt. i, Pref., p. ccxxi.

1076. -*Id.*, vol. ii, pt. ii, p. 1276.

1077. Repertory 3, fos. 184b, 189b, 191, 192.

1078. Letter Book N, fo. 95b.

1079. Repertory 3, fos. 192, 194; Letter Book N, fos. 63b, 74.

1080. Repertory 3, fo. 197.

1081. Hall's Chron., pp. 593, 594.

1082. Holinshed, iii, 632.

1083. Cal. Letters and Papers, For. and Dom. (Henry VIII), vol. ii. pt. i, Pref., pp. clx, clxi.

1084. "An order devysed by the Mayer and hys brethrern the aldremen by the Kynges commandment for a Tryumphe to be done in the Citie of London at the Request of the Right honorable ambassadors of the Kynge of Romayns." — 10 July, Journal 12, fo. 9.

1085. Hall, pp. 592, 593.

1086. Holinshed, iii, 639.

1087. Journal 12, fos. 125, 172b, 173b; Letter Book N, fo. 194b.

1088. Knighted the next day at Greenwich. — Repertory 5, fo. 295.

1089. Repertory 5, fo. 294.

1090. *-Id.* 4, fo. 134b.

1091. *-Id.* 5, fo. 293.

1092. Journal 12, fos. 75b-76; Letter Book N, fos. 142-143.

1093. Grey Friars Chron., p. 30; Repertory 4, fo. 71b.

1094. Repertory 4, fos. 1b, 12, 13.

1095. Journal 12, fo. 136.

1096. *-Id.*, fo. 144.

1097. Journal 12, fos. 158, 161, 163b; Letter Book N, fos. 187b, 190b.

1098. Holinshed, iii, 675.

1099. Shakespere mentions the Duke's manor thus:—

"Not long before your highness sped to France,

The duke being at the Rose, within the parish

St. Laurence Poultney, did of me demand

What was the speech among the Londoners

Concerning the French journey."

—Henry VIII, act 1, sc. 2.

1100. Cal. Letters and Papers, For. and Dom. (Henry VIII), vol. iii, pt. i, Pref., pp. cxxv, cxxvi, cxxxv, cxxxvi.

1101. On the 5th July steps were taken by the Court of Aldermen for putting a stop to the mutinous and seditious words that were current in the city "concerning the lamenting and sorrowing of the death of the duke"— men saying that he was guiltless—and special precautions were taken for the safe custody of weapons and harness for fear of an outbreak. The scribe evinced his loyalty by heading the page of the record with *Lex domini immaculata: Vivat Rex Currat L.*—Repertory 5, fo. 204.

1102. Repertory 5, fo. 288.

1103. Journal 12, fos. 187b, 188b, 195; Letter Book N, fos. 203b, 204, 208.

1104. Repertory 5, fo. 292.

1105. Journal 12, fo. 187b.

1106. Repertory 5, fos. 289, 290.

1107. *-Id.*, fo. 291.

1108. Repertory 5, fos. 296b, 297.

1109. *-Id.*, fo. 294.

1110. A portion remained unpaid on 16 August.—Journal 12, fo. 195.

1111. Letter dated 3 Sept.—Journal 12, fo. 196b. On 28 Sept. Wolsey asked for more time to repay the loan.—Repertory 5, fo. 326.

1112. Journal 12, fo. 200.

1113. Journal 12, fo. 210.

1114. See Green's "Hist. of the English People," ii, 121. 122.

1115. Grey Friars Chron., p. 31.

1116. Repertory 4, fo. 144; *Cf.* Repertory 6, fo. 20b; Letter Book N, fo. 222.

1117. Repertory 4, fo. 145b.

1118. Roper's "Life of More," pp. 17-20.

1119. Repertory 4, fos. 152, 168; *Cf.* Repertory 6, fo. 38.

1120. Repertory 4, fos. 144b, 145, 146, 150; *Cf.* Repertory 6, fos. 22b, 29, 32b.

1121. Grey Friars Chron. pp. 30, 31.

1122. Repertory 4, fos. 153b-154; *Cf.* Repertory 6, fo. 42.

1123. Repertory 6, fo. 61b.

1124. Holinshed, iii, 692, 693.

1125. Journal 12, fos. 249-250.

1126. Journal 12, fos. 287-288.

1127. -*Id.*, fo. 276.

1128. -*Id.*, fo. 284.

1129. Letter Book N, fo. 280; Journal 12, fo. 329.

1130. Grey Friars Chron., p. 32.

1131. Hall's Chron., p. 695.

1132. Journal 12, fo. 331; Letter Book N. fo. 278.

1133. Journal 12, fo. 331b.

1134. Hall's Chron., p. 701.

1135. The truce was to last from 14 August to 1 December.—Letter Book N, fos. 291, 293; Journal 12, fos. 300, 305.

1136. "Item in lyke wyse the Chamberleyn shall have allowance of and for suche gyftes and presentes as were geven presentyd on Sonday laste passyd at the Bysshoppes palace at Paules to the Ambassadours of Fraunce devysed and appoynted by my lorde Cardynalles Grace and most specyally at his contemplacioun geven for asmoch as lyke precedent in so ample maner hath not afore tyme be seen; the presents ensue etc."—Repertory 7, fo. 225.

1137. He had been one of the commoners sent to confer with Wolsey touching the amicable loan (Journal 12, fo. 331b). He attended the coronation banquet of Anne Boleyn in 1533 (Repertory 9, fo. 2), and was M.P. for the city from 1529-1536 (Letter Book O, fo. 157). His daughter Elizabeth married Emanuel Lucar, also a merchant-tailor.—Repertory 9, fos. 139. 140.

1138. Repertory 7, fos. 171b, 172, 174b, 179.

1139. Repertory 7, fos. 179b, 180.

1140. To the effect that he was not worth £1,000.—Journal 7, fo. 198.

1141. Repertory 7, fos. 238b, 240, 240b.

1142. -*Id.*, fo. 243b.

1143. Repertory 7, fo. 206. The Common Council assessed the fine at £100.—Journal 13, fo. 61b; Letter Book O, fo. 80b.

1144. Repertory 7, fo. 264.

1145. Journal 13, fo. 184b.

1146. Letter Book O, fos. 88b, 89b.

1147. Cal. Letters and Papers For. and Dom. (Henry VIII), vol. iv, Introd., p. cccclxv.

1148. Letter Book O, fos. 174b-175; Journal 13, fo. 180b.

1149. Letter Book O, fo. 157.

1150. About the year 1522 Cromwell was living in the city, near Fenchurch, combining the business of a merchant with that of a money-lender. He sat in the parliament of 1523, and towards the close of that year served on a wardmote inquest for Bread Street Ward. In 1524 he entered Wolsey's service.—Cal. Letters and Papers For. and Dom. (Henry VIII.), vol. iii, pt. i, Introd., pp. cclvi, cclvii.

1151. Cal. Letters and Papers For. and Dom. (Henry VIII), vol. iv, Introd., pp. dliii-dlvi.

1152. Stat. 21, Henry VIII, caps. 5, 6 and 13.

1153. Proclamation, 12 Sept., 1530.—Letter Book O, fo. 199b.

1154. Burnell, "London (City) Tithes Act, 1879," Introd., pp. 1, 2.

1155. Letter Book O, fos. 47, *seq.*

1156. A list of these, comprising seven churches, was submitted to the Court of Aldermen, 23 Feb., 1528.—Repertory 8, fo. 21.

1157. Letter Book O, fos. 140b, 141b.

1158. Repertory 8, fo. 27b.

1159. Letter Book O, fos. 145, 145b; Journal 13, fo. 125b.

1160. Letter book P, fos. 31, 34, 41b; Journal 13, fo. 417b.

1161. This order was confirmed by stat. 27, Henry VIII, cap. 21. Ten years later a decree was made pursuant to stat. 37, Henry VIII, cap. 12, regulating the whole subject of tithes, but owing to the decree not having been enrolled in accordance with the terms of the statute, much litigation has in recent times arisen.—Burnell, "London (City) Tithes Act, 1879," Introd., p. 3.

1162. The well-known and somewhat romantic account of the origin of the priory and of its connection with the city cnihten-guild is given in Letter Book C, fos. 134b, *seq.*; *Cf.* Liber Dunthorn, fo. 79.

1163. Grey Friars Chron. (Camd. Soc., No. 53), p. 35. Three years later (30 March, 1534) the Court of Aldermen resolved to wait upon the chancellor "to know his mind for the office concerning the lands" belonging to the late priory.—Repertory 9, fo. 53b.

1164. By letters patent dated 13 April, 1531 (preserved at the Guildhall, Box No. 16).

1165. Henry Lumnore, Lumnar or Lomner, a grocer by guild as well as calling (see Cal. Letters and Papers For. and Dom. (Henry VIII), vol. iii, pt. ii, p. 879), was associated with Sidney in holding the beam. The City offered to buy him out either by bestowing on him an annuity of £10 during the joint lives of himself and Sidney, or else by paying him a lump sum of £100.—Repertory 8, fo. 218b.

1166. Anne Boleyn.

1167. Repertory 8, fo. 131.

1168. *-Id.*, fos. 142b. 202b.

1169. Chapuys to the emperor.—Cal. State Papers (Spanish), vol. iv., pt. ii, p. 646.

1170. Repertory 9, fo. 1b. There is a fine drawing at Berlin by Holbein which is thought to be the original design for the triumphal arch erected by the merchants of the Steelyard on this occasion.

1171. Journal 13, fo. 371b. According to Wriothesley (Camd. Soc., N.S., No. 11, p. 19) the present to the queen was made to her in a purse of cloth of gold on the occasion of her passing through the city on the 31st May, the day before her coronation.

1172. Repertory 2, fo. 70b; Repertory 9, fo. 2.

1173. Letter Book P, fos. 37-37b; Journal 13, fo. 408b.

1174.   Letter to Lord Lisle.—Cal. Letters and Papers For. and Dom. (Henry VIII), vol. vii, p. 208.

1175.   Repertory 9, fo. 57b. "Allso the same day [20 April] all the craftes in London were called to their halls, and there were sworne on a booke to be true to Queene Anne and to believe and take her for lawfull wife of the Kinge and rightfull Queene of Englande, and utterlie to thincke the Lady Marie, daughter to the Kinge by Queene Katherin, but as a bastarde, and thus to doe without any scrupulositie of conscience."—Wriothesley's Chron., i, 24.

1176.   Grey Friars Chron., p. 37. In November of the last year they had been made to do penance at Paul's Cross and afterwards at Canterbury.

1177.   "Historia aliquot nostri sæculi martyrum," 1583. Much of it is quoted by Father Gasquet in his work on "Henry VIII and the English Monasteries" (cap. vi), and also by Mr. Froude ("Hist. of England," vol. ii, cap. ix).

1178.   Cal. Letters and Papers For. and Dom. (Henry VIII), vol. vii, p. 283.

1179.   This convent—the most virtuous house of religion in England—was of the Order of St. Bridget, and received an annual visit from the mayor and aldermen of the City of London at what was known as "the pardon time of Sion," in the month of August. In return for the hospitality bestowed by the lady abbess on these occasions the Court of Aldermen occasionally made her presents of wine (Repertories 3, fo. 94b; 7, fo. 275). In 1517 the court instructed the chamberlain to avoid excess of diet on the customary visit. There was to be no breakfast on the barge and no swans at dinner (Repertory 3, fo. 154b). In 1825 the Court of Common Council decreed (*inter alia*) that "as tonchyng the goyng of my lord mayre and my masters his brethern the aldermen [to] Syon, yt is sett at large and to be in case as it was before the Restreynt" (Journal 12, fo. 302). It was suppressed 25 Nov., 1539.—Wriothesley's Chron., i, 109.

1180.   The Act of Supremacy was passed in 1534, but the king's new title as Supreme Head of the Church was not incorporated in his style before the 15 Jan., 1535.

1181.   Cal. Letters and Papers For. and Dom. (Henry VIII), vol. viii, p. 321.

1182.   -*Id.*, p. 354.

1183. Repertory 9, fo. 145.

1184. -Id., fo. 199.

1185. He had been elected mayor for the second time in October last (1535), much against his own wish, at the king's express desire.—Journal 13, fo. 452b; Wriothesley, i, 31. He presented the City with a collar of SS. to be worn by the mayor for the time being.—Repertory 11, fo. 238.

1186. Repertory 9, fos. 199, 199b.

1187. Repertory 9, fo. 200.

1188. -Id., fo. 200b.

1189. Son of Thomas Warren, fuller; grandson of William Warren, of Fering, co. Sussex. He was knighted on the day that his election was confirmed by the king (Wriothesley. i, 59). His daughter Joan (by his second wife Joan, daughter of John Lake, of London) married Sir Henry Williams, *alias* Cromwell (Repertory 14, fo. 180; Journal 17. fo. 137b), by whom she had issue Robert Cromwell, father of the Protector. Warren died 11 July, 1533, and his widow married Alderman Sir Thomas White.—See notes to Machyn's Diary, p. 330.

1190. Repertory 9, fo. 209b.

1191. Henry attributed her miscarriage to licentiousness; others to her having received a shock at seeing her royal husband thrown from his horse whilst tilting at the ring.—Wriothesley, i, 33.

1192. Chapuys to [Granvelle] 25 Aug., 1536.—Cal. Letters and Papers For. and Dom. (Henry VIII), vol. xi., p. 145.

1193. Wriothesley, i, 52-53.

1194. Letter Book P, fo. 103b.

1195. Wriothesley, i, 69.

1196. Letter Book P, fo. 135b; Wriothesley, i, 71, 72.

1197. Repertory 10, fos. 152b, 153; Wriothesley, i, 109, 111.

1198. Repertory 10, fo. 161. The circumstance that Henry carried his new bride to Westminster by water instead of conducting her thither through the streets of the city has been considered a proof of his want of regard for her.

1199. Holinshed, iii. 807.

1200. Letter Book P, fo. 113; Journal 14, fo. 30b.

1201. Stow's "Survey" (Thoms's ed., 1876), p. 68.

1202. The Mercers' Company applied for a grant of the chapel and other property of the hospital; and this was conceded by letters patent, 21 April, 1542, upon payment of the sum of £969 17s. 6d., subject to a reserved rent of £7 8s. 10d., which was redeemed by the company in 1560.—Livery Comp. Com. (1880), Append. to Report, 1884, vol. ii, p. 9.

1203. On the re-establishment of the Dutch or Mother Strangers' Church, at Elizabeth's accession, it was declared by the Privy Council to be under the superintendence of the Bishop of London (Cal. State Papers Dom., Feb., 1560). Hence it was that Dr. Temple, Bishop of London, was memorialised in March, 1888, as superintendent of the French Church in London.—See "Eng. Hist. Review," April, 1891, pp. 388-389.

1204. Stow's "Survey" (Thoms's ed., 1876), p. 67.

1205. Nichols' "Progresses of Queen Eliz.," iii. 598. For particulars of Swinnerton see Clode's "Early Hist. of the Merchant Taylors' Company," i, 262, etc.

1206. Strype's Stow, bk. ii, pp. 114, 115.

1207. Remembrancia (Analytical Index), pp. 133, 134.

1208. In 1439 Reginald Kentwode, Dean of St. Paul's, having in a recent visitation discovered "many defaults and excesses," drew up a schedule of injunctions for their better regulation.—Printed in London and Middlesex Archæol. Soc. Transactions, ii, 200-203.

1209. Journal 12, fo. 75.

1210. Repertory 2, fo. 185b.

1211. Repertory 5, fos. 15, 15b, 82b.

1212. Repertory 2, fo. 185; Grey Friars Chron., pp. 29, 31.

1213. Sixteen other registers for city parishes commence in 1538, and four in 1539.—See Paper on St. James Garlickhithe, by W. D. Cooper, F.S.A. (London and Middlesex Arch. Soc. Trans., vol. iii, p. 392, note).

1214. Wriothesley's Chron. (Camd. Soc, N.S., No. 11), i, 77, 78.

1215. Descended from a Norfolk family. Apprenticed to John Middleton, mercer, of London, and admitted to the freedom of the Mercers' Company in 1507. Alderman of Walbrook and Cheap Wards successively. Sheriff 1531-2. Married (1) Audrey, daughter of William Lynne, of Southwick, co. Northampton, (2) Isabella Taverson, *née* Worpfall. Was the father of Sir Thomas Gresham, the founder of the Royal Exchange and of the college which bears his name.—*Ob.*, 21 Feb., 1549. Buried in the church of St. Laurence Jewry.

1216. Cott. MS., Cleop. E., iv, fo. 222.—Printed in Burgon's "Life of Gresham," i, 26-29.

1217. Journal 14, fo. 129; Letter Book P, fo. 178.

1218. Journal 14, fo. 216b; Letter Book P, fo. 220b.

1219. Repertory 10, fo. 200.

1220. Journal 14, fo. 269.

1221. Wriothesley, i, 129.

1222. Son of Thomas Hill, of Hodnet, co. Salop. He devoted large sums of money to building causeways and bridges, and erected a grammar school at Drayton-in-Hales, otherwise Market Drayton, in his native county, which he endowed by will, dated 6 April, 1551 (Cal. of Wills, Court of Hust., London, part ii, p. 651). See also Holinshed, iii, 1021.

1223. Holinshed, iii, 824; Wriothesley, i, 135. According to the Grey Friars Chron. (p. 45), it was the sergeant-at-arms himself whom the sheriffs detained.

1224. Proclamation dated 13 Aug., 1543.—Journal 15, fo. 48b.

1225. Journal 15, fo. 55; Letter Book Q, fo. 93.

1226. Letter Book Q, fo. 92b; Grey Friars Chron., p. 45.

1227. Writ to mayor and sheriffs for proclamation of war, dat. 2 Aug., 1543.—Journal 15, fo. 46b.

1228. Repertory 11, fo. 32b.

1229. Repertory 11, fo. 65b.

1230. Journal 15, fo. 95; Repertory 11, fo. 74; Letter Book Q, fo. 109.

1231. "Memoranda ... relating to the Royal Hospitals," 1863, pp. 4-7.

1232. Repertory 11, fo. 106; Letter Book Q, fo. 116b.

1233. Repertory, 11, fo. 118b; Letter Book Q, fo. 120b.

1234. Journal 15, fo. 123; Letter Book Q, fo. 119.

1235. Journal 15, fo. 124; Letter Book Q, fo. 122.

1236. Letter Book Q, fo. 120b.

1237. Wriothesley, i, 151, 153; Grey Friars Chron., p. 48.

1238. Holinshed, iii, 346.

1239. Wriothesley, i, 151, 152.

1240. Journal 15, fo. 239b; Letter Book Q, fo. 167b.

1241. Journal 15, fo. 240.; Letter Book Q, fo. 168; Wriothesley, i, 154.

1242. "A coarse frieze was so called from a small town in the West Riding of Yorkshire. An Act of 5 and 6 Edward VI (1551-2) provided that all "clothes commonly called Pennystones or Forest Whites ... shall conteyne in length beinge wett betwixt twelve and thirtene yardes."

1243. Repertory 11, fo. 193b; Letter Book Q, fo. 133; Wriothesley, i, 154.

1244. Wriothesley, i, 155.

1245. Repertory 11, fos. 203, 212b.

1246. 30 July.—Repertory 11, fo. 215b. The Midsummer watch had not been kept this year.—Wriothesley, i, 156.

1247. Repertory 11, fo. 213.

1248. Wriothesley, i, 58.

1249. Repertory 11, fo. 216b.

1250. Stat. 37, Henry VIII, c. 4.

1251. Repertory 11, fo. 299b; Letter Book Q, fo. 181; Journal 15, fo. 270; Wriothesley, i, 165.

1252. Holinshed, iii, 856; Grey Friars Chron., p. 50.

1253. Holinshed, iii, 847.

1254. Letter Book Q, fo. 181.

1255. Repertory 11, fo. 247.

1256. Journal 15, fo. 213b.

1257. Wriothesley, i, 162, 175.

1258. Journal 15, fos. 245, 399b, *seq.*

1259. "Memoranda ... Royal Hospitals," pp. 20-45.

1260. Repertory 11, fo. 349b.

1261. In Sept., 1547, the citizens were called upon to contribute half a fifteenth for the maintenance of the poor of St. Bartholomew's.—Journal 15, fo. 325b. In Dec, 1548, an annual sum of 500 marks out of the profits of Blackwell, and in 1557 the whole of the same profits were set aside for the poor.—Journal 15, fos. 398, *seq.*; Repertory 13, pt. ii, fo. 512.

1262. Royal proclamation, 7 July, 1545, forbidding all pursuit of game in Westminster, Islington, Highgate, Hornsey and elsewhere in the suburbs of London.—Journal 15, fo. 240b.

1263. Son of Christopher Huberthorne, of Waddington, co. Lane, Alderman of Farringdon Within. His mansion adjoined the Leadenhall. *Ob.,* Oct., 1556. Buried in the church of St. Peter, Cornhill.—Machyn. 115, 352. It was in Huberthorne's mayoralty that the customary banquet to the aldermen, the "officers lerned" and the commoners of the city, on Monday next after the Feast of Epiphany, known as "Plow Monday," was discontinued.—Letter Book Q, fo. 191b. It was afterwards renewed and continues to this day in the form of a dinner given by the new mayor to the officers of his household and clerks engaged in various departments of the service of the Corporation. An attempt was at the same time made to put down the lord mayor's banquet also.—Wriothesley, i, 176.

1264. Journal 15. fos. 303b, 305b; Letter Book Q, os. 192b, 194; Wriothesley. i, 178.

1265. Journal 15, fo. 304; Letter Book Q, fo. 195; Repertory 11, fo. 335b.

1266. "The lord mayor of London, Henry Hobulthorne, was called fourth, who kneeling before the king, his majestie tooke the sworde of the Lord Protector and made him knight, which was the first that eaver he made."—Wriothesley's Chron. (Camd. Soc, N.S., No. 11.), i, 181.

1267. This mace is still in possession of the Corporation. It is only brought out for use on such occasions as a coronation, when it is carried by the lord mayor as on the occasion narrated above, and at the annual election of the chief magistrate of the city, when it is formally handed by the Chamberlain to the lord mayor elect. The mace consists of a tapering shaft of rock crystal mounted in gold, with a coroneted head also of gold, adorned with pearls and large jewels. Its age is uncertain. Whilst some hazard the conjecture that it may be of Saxon origin, there are others who are of opinion that the head of it at least cannot be earlier than the 15th century.

1268. Journal 15, fo. 305; Letter Book Q, fos. 195b-196; Repertory 11, fo. 334b.

1269. "All these chyldren shall every Chyldermasse day come to Paulis Church and here the chylde bisshoppis sermon, and after be at the hye masse, and eche of them offer a 1d. to the childe bisshop and with theme the maisters and surveyors of the scole."—Statutes of St. Paul's School, printed in Lupton's "Life of Dean Colet," p. 278b.

1270. Letter Book P, fo. 172b.

1271. Journal 14, fo. 158b; Letter Book P, fo. 197.

1272. See Brewer's Introd. to Cal. Letters and Papers For. and Dom., vol. iv, pp. dcli-dcliii.

1273. Letter Book P, fo. 153.

1274. Letter Book Q, fo. 102.

1275. "Also this same tyme [Nov., 1547] was moche spekying agayne the sacrament of the auter, that some callyd it Jacke of the boxe, with divers other shamefulle names... And at this tyme [Easter, 1548] was more prechyng agayne the masse." —Grey Friars Chron., p. 55.

1276. Letter Book Q, fo. 250b.

1277. Repertory 11, fo. 423.

1278. "After the redyng of the preposycioun made yesterday in the Sterre Chamber by the lorde chaunceler and ye declaracioun made by my lorde mayer of suche comunicacioun as his lordshyp had wt the Bysshop of Caunterburye concernyng the demeanor of certein prechers and other dysobedyent persones yt was ordered and agreyd that my lorde mayer and all my maisters thaldermen shall this afternone att ij of ye clok repayre to my lorde protectors grace and the hole counseill and declare unto theim the seid mysdemeanor and that thei shall mete att Saint Martyns in the Vyntrey att one of the clok." —Repertory 11, fo. 456b.

1279. Repertory 11, fo. 465.

1280. A proclamation against the evil behaviour of citizens and others against priests, 12 Nov., 1547.—Letter Book Q. fo. 218; Journal 15, fo. 335b.

1281. By letters patent dated 14 July, 1550 (preserved at the Guildhall, Box 17).

1282. Letter Book R, fo. 166b; Wriothesley's Chron. (Camden Soc., N.S., No. 20), ii, 35. See also exemplification of Act of Parl. passed a° 5 Edward VI, in accordance with the terms of this petition (Box 29).

1283. Journal 15, fo. 322; Letter Book Q, fo. 210b.

1284. Repertory 11. fo. 373; Letter Book Q, fo. 214.

1285. Grey Friars Chron., 54, 55; Wriothesley. ii, 1.

1286. Grey Friars Chron., p. 58. In May (1548) the duke applied to the City for water to be laid on to Stronde House, afterwards known as Somerset House.—Repertory 11, fos. 462b, 484; Journal 15. fo. 383b; Letter Book Q, fo. 253b.

1287. Grey Friars Chron., p. 55.

1288. Wriothesley, ii, 29. Touching the ceremony of visiting the tomb of the Bishop of London, to whom the citizens were indebted for the charter of William the Conqueror, see chap. i, p. 35.

1289. Letter Book Q, fos. 232, 234b; Repertory 11, fos. 356, 415, 431, 444b, 511b.

1290. "Item, at this same tyme [*circ.* Sept., 1547] was pullyd up alle the tomes, grett stones, alle the auteres, with stalles and walles of the qweer and auters in the church that was some tyme the Gray freeres, and solde and the qweer made smaller." — Grey Friars Chron., p. 54.

1291. "At Ester followyng there began the commonion, and confession but of thoys that wolde, as the boke dothe specifythe." — Grey Friars Chron., p. 55; *Cf.* Wriothesley (Camd. Soc, N.S., No. 20), ii, 2.

1292. The Guildhall college, chapel and library were restored to the City in 1550, by Edward VI, on payment of £456 13s. 4d., — Pat. Roll 4 Edward VI, p. 9m. (32) 20; Letter Book R, fo. 64b.

1293. Repertory 11, fo. 493b.

1294. -*Id.,* fo. 455. (431 pencil mark); Letter Book Q, fo. 237. "This yeare in the Whitson holidaies my lord maior [Sir John Gresham] caused three notable sermons to be made at Sainct Marie Spittell, according as they are kept at Easter.... And the sensing in Poules cleene put downe." — Wriothesley, ii, 2, 3. The processions were kept up in 1554, "but there was no sensynge." — Grey Friars Chron., p. 89.

1295. -*Cf.* Journal 15, fo. 352b; Letter Book Q, fos. 230-252b. "This yeare [1548] the xxviiith daie of September, proclamation was made to inhibite all preachers generallie till the kinges further pleasure. After which daie all sermons seasede at Poules Crosse and in all other places." — Wriothesley, ii, 6.

1296. Grey Friars Chron., pp. 59, 62. Occasionally the chronicler is overcome by his feelings, and cries out, "Almyghty God helpe it whan hys wylle ys!" *Id.*, p. 67.

1297. In some cases the new owners may have experienced some difficulty in fixing a fair rent, as appears to have been the case with the City of London and its recently acquired property of Bethlehem. When the Chamberlain reported that the rents demanded for houses in the precincts of the hospital were far too high, he was at once authorised to reduce them at discretion.—Letter Book R, fo. 10b.

1298. Letter Book R, fo. 11b.

1299. Grey Friars Chron., p. 60; Wriothesley, ii, 15, 16.

1300. Wriothesley, ii, 16, 17; Grey Friars Chron., p. 60.

1301. Wriothesley, ii, 19.

1302. Wriothesley, ii, 20; Grey Friars Chron., p. 61.

1303. Holinshed, iii, 982-984.

1304. Letter Book R, fo. 40; Journal 16, fo. 36.

1305. Letter Book R, fo. 39b.

1306. Acts of the Privy Council, ii, 331-332; Wriothesley, ii, 24-25; Holinshed, iii, 1014; Repertory 12, pt. i, fos. 149-150.

1307. Holinshed, iii, 1014-1015; Acts of Privy Council, ii, 333.

1308. Acts of Privy Council, ii, fos. 333-336.

1309. Repertory 12, pt. i, fo. 150b.

1310. Letter Book R, fo. 40b.

1311. -Id., fos. 43-43b.

1312. Acts of Privy Council, ii, 336, 337.

1313. Wriothesley, ii, 26.

1314. Acts of Privy Council, ii, 337-342.

1315. Letter Book R, fos. 41-42; Journal 16, fos. 37, 37b. According to Holinshed (iii, 1017, 1018), considerable opposition was made by a member of the Common Council named George Stadlow to any force at all being sent by the city. He reminded the court of the evils that had arisen in former times from the city rendering support to the barons against Henry III, and how the city lost its liberties in consequence. The course he recommended was that the city should join the lords in making a humble representation to the king as to the Protector's conduct.

1316. Wriothesley, ii, 26, 27.

1317. Letter Book R, fo. 37; Journal 16, fo. 34; Wriothesley, ii, 26.

1318. Stow's "Summarie of the Chronicles of England" (ed. 1590), p. 545; Wriothesley, ii, 27, 28. The names are given differently in the Acts of the Privy Council, ii, 344.

1319. Grey Friars Chron., pp. 63, 64; Cf. Wriothesley, ii, 24.

1320. Wriothesley, ii, 28.

1321. Acts of Privy Council, ii, 384; Wriothesley, ii, 33.

1322. For more than a week he had been compelled to lie on nothing but straw, his bed having been taken away by order of the knight marshal for refusing to pay an extortionate fee.—Grey Friars Chron., p. 65.

1323. Thomas Thurlby, the last abbot of Westminster, became the first and only bishop of the see. Upon the union of the see with that of London Thurlby became bishop of Norwich. Among the archives of the city there is a release by him, in his capacity as bishop of Westminster, and the dean and chapter of the same, to the City of London of the parish church of St. Nicholas, Shambles. The document is dated 14 March, 1549, and has the seals of the bishopric and of the dean and chapter, in excellent preservation, appended.

1324. For objecting to the prescribed vestments, he was committed to the Fleet by order of the Privy Council, 27 Jan., 1551, and was not consecrated until the following 8th March.—Hooper to Bullinger, 1 Aug., 1551 ("Original Letters relative to the English Reformation." ed. for Parker Society, 1846, p. 91).

1325. Their respective boundaries are set out in the Report of Commissioners on Municipal Corporations (1837), p. 3.

1326. Charter dated 6 March, 1 Edward III.

1327. Charter dated 9 Nov., 2 Edward IV.

1328. Letter Book Q, fos. 239b-241b.

1329. Letter Book R, fo. 58b.

1330. Dated 23 April, 1550. A fee of £6 "and odde money" was paid for the enrolment of this charter in the Exchequer.—Repertory 12, pt. ii, fo. 458. This fee appears to have been paid, notwithstanding the express terms of the charter that no fee great or small should be paid or made or by any means given to the hanaper to the king's use. According to Wriothesley (ii, 36), the "purchase" of Southwark cost the city 1,000 marks, "so that nowe they shall have all the whole towne of Southwarke by letters patent as free as they have the City of London, the Kinges Place [*i.e.* Southwark Place or Suffolk House] and the two prison houses of the Kinges Bench and the Marshalsea excepted."

1331. Wriothesley, ii, 38.

1332. Letter Book R, fo. 80; Journal 16, fo. 82b.

1333. The custom in the city was for the inhabitants of a vacant ward to nominate four persons for the Court of Aldermen to select one. As there were no means of enforcing the above ordinance it was repealed by Act of Co. Co., 16 June, 1558.—Letter Book S., fo. 167b.

1334. Letter Book R, fo. 71b. The following particulars of Aylyff and his family are drawn from the city's archives. From Bridge Ward Without he removed to Dowgate Ward. At the time of his death, in 1556, he was keeper of the clothmarket at Blackwell Hall. His widow was allowed to take the issues and profits of her late husband's place for one week, and was forgiven a quarter's rent. Aylyff's son Erkenwald succeeded him at Blackwell Hall. The son died in 1561. After his decease he was convicted of having forged a deed. His widow, Dorothy, married Henry Butler, "gentleman."—Repertory 13, pt. ii, fos. 442b, 443, 461; Repertory 14, fos. 446b, 477b, 478; Repertory 16, fo. 6b.

1335. Printed Report. Co. Co., 20 May, 1836.

1336. See Report Committee of the whole Court for General Purposes, with Appendix, 31 May, 1892 (*Printed*).

1337. Grey Friars Chron., p. 66. The surrender of Boulogne was "sore lamented of all Englishmen."—Wriothesley, ii, 37.

1338. Repertory 12, pt. ii, fo. 271b; Letter Book R, fos. 74, 85b; Journal 16, fos. 66b, 91b.

1339. Letter Book R, fo. 115; Journal 16, fo. 118.

1340. Wriothesley, ii, 48. The price of living became so dear that the town clerk and the under-sheriffs asked for and obtained from the Common Council an increase of emoluments.—Letter Book R, fo. 117b.

1341. Wriothesley, ii, 54.

1342. Grey Friars Chron., p. 72.

1343. Wriothesley, ii, 56; Grey Friars Chron., p. 71.

1344. Grey Friars Chron., pp. 72, 73.

1345. -Id., pp. 71, 72.

1346. Wriothesley, ii, 57.

1347. Repertory 12, pt. ii, fo. 426; Letter Book R, fo. 157b.

1348. Wriothesley, ii, 63.

1349. Holinshed, iii, 1032.

1350. Journal 15, fo. 325b; Letter Book Q, fo. 214b.

1351. Letter Book Q, fo. 237; Repertory 11, fo. 445b.

1352. Journal 15, fo. 384.

1353. Letter Book Q, fo. 261b; Journal 15, fos. 398, 401; Appendix vii to "Memoranda of the Royal Hospitals," pp. 46-51.

1354. Repertory 12, pt. ii., fos. 311, 312b.

1355. Both deeds are printed in Supplement to Memoranda relating to Royal Hospitals, pp. 15-32.

1356. Son of Robert Dobbs, of Batley, Yorks. Alderman of Tower Ward. Knighted 8 May, 1552. Ob. 1556. Buried in Church of St. Margaret Moses.—Machyn, pp. 105, 269, 349; Wriothesley, ii, 69.

1357. Report, Charity Commissioners, No. 32, pt. vi, p. 75; Strype, Stow's "Survey," bk. i, p. 176.

1358. Among the names of those forming the deputation appears that of Richard Grafton, whose printing house, from which issued "The Prymer"—one of the earliest books of private devotion printed in English as well as Latin—was situate within the precinct of the Old Grey Friars.—Repertory 12, p. ii., fos. 271b, 272b.

1359. Strype, Stow's "Survey," bk. i, p. 176.

1360. Wriothesley, 83; Repertory 13, fo. 60.

1361. Charter dated 26 June, 1553.

1362. "Letters Patent for the limitation of the Crown," sometimes called the "counterfeit will" of King Edward VI.—Chron. of Q. Jane and Q. Mary (Camd. Soc., No. 48), pp. 91-100.

1363. Richard Hilles to Henry Bullinger, 9 July, 1553.—"Original letters relative to the English Reformation" (Parker Soc.), pp. 272-274.

1364. Grey Friars Chron., pp. 78, 79.

1365. Wriothesley, ii, 88-90.

1366. Letter Book R, fo. 262b; Repertory 13, pt. i, fo. 68.

1367. Wriothesley, ii, 90, 91; Grey Friars Chron., p. 81.

1368. Repertory 13, pt. i, fo. 69.

1369. -Id., fo. 70b.

1370. Repertory 13, pt. i, fo. 69b.

1371. Wriothesley, 93-95.

1372. Chron. of Q. Jane and Q. Mary, p. 14; Wriothesley, ii, 95.

1373. Grey Friars Chron., p. 83; Wriothesley, ii, 96-98.

1374. Chron. of Q. Jane and Q. Mary, p. 24.

1375. Letter Book R, fo. 270; Journal 16, fo. 261b.

1376. Wriothesley, ii, 99, 100; Holinshed, iv, 3.

1377.   Citizen and Merchant Taylor. Son of William White, of Reading, and formerly of Rickmansworth. Founder of St. John's College, Oxford, and principal benefactor of Merchant Taylors' School. Alderman of Cornhill Ward; when first elected alderman he declined to accept office and was committed to Newgate for contumacy (Letter Book Q, fo. 109b; Repertory 11, fo. 80b). Sheriff 1547. Knighted at Whitehall 10 Dec., 1553 (Wriothesley, ii, 105). His first wife, Avice (surname unknown), died 26 Feb., 1588, and was buried in the church of St. Mary Aldermary. He afterwards married Joan, daughter of John Lake and widow of Sir Ralph Warren, twice Mayor of London. *Ob.* 11 Feb., 1566, at Oxford, aged 72.—Clode, "Early Hist. Guild of Merchant Taylors," pt. ii, chaps. x-xii; Machyn's Diary, pp. 167, 330, 363.

1378.   Journal 16, fo. 261; Repertory 13, pt. i, fo. 74b.

1379.   Grey Friars Chron., p. 84.

1380.   Met in October, 1553. The names of the city's representatives are not recorded. The Court of Aldermen, according to a custom then prevalent, authorized the city chamberlain to make a gift of £6 13s. 4d. to Sir John Pollard, the Speaker, "for his lawfull favor to be borne and shewed in the parlyment howse towardes this cytie and theyre affayres theire."—Repertory 13, pt. i, fo. 92.

1381.   Grey Friars Chron., p. 85; Wriothesley, ii, 104; Chron. Q. Jane and Q. Mary, p. 32. There is preserved in the British Museum a small manual of prayers believed to have been used by Lady Jane Grey on the scaffold. The tiny volume (Harl. MS., 2342) measures only 3-1/2 inches by 2-3/4 inches, and contains on the margin lines addressed to Sir John Gage, lieutenant of the Tower, and to her father, the Duke of Suffolk.

1382.   Journal 16, fo. 283.

1383.   Chron. of Q. Jane and Q. Mary, 35.

1384.   Wriothesley, ii, 106.

1385.   Repertory 13, pt. i, fos. 116, 116b, 117, 117b, 119-122b.

1386.   Wriothesley, ii, 107.

1387.   Repertory 13, pt. i, fo. 121.

1388.   Foxe's "Acts and Monuments," vi, 414-415; Holinshed, iv, 16.

1389. Holinshed, iv, 15.

1390. Repertory 13, pt. i, fo. 124.

1391. Wriothesley, iii, 109.

1392. Stow.

1393. Foxe's "Acts and Monuments," vi, 415.

1394. Grey Friars Chron., p. 87.

1395. Chron. of Q. Jane and Q. Mary, p. 43; Wriothesley, iii, 107, 108.

1396. Grey Friars Chron., p. 87.

1397.   Machyn, 45. The gibbets remained standing till the following June, when they were taken down in anticipation of Philip's public entry into London.—Chron. of Q. Jane and Q. Mary, 76.

1398. Grey Friars Chron., p. 89.

1399. Journal 16, fo. 283; Letter Book R, fo. 288.

1400. Repertory 13, pt. i, fo. 131.

1401. Holinshed, iv, 26.

1402. Repertory 13, pt. i, fo. 153; Letter Book R, fo. 293.

1403. Repertory 13, pt. i, fo. 130; Journal 16, fo. 284b.

1404. Repertory 13, pt. i, fo. 138b.

1405. -Id., fos. 142b, 146b.

1406. -Id., fo. 147.

1407. Wriothesley, ii, 115.

1408. Repertory 13, pt. i, fo. 186b.

1409. -Id., fo. 190b.

1410.   Howell's "State Trials," i, 901, 902; Chron. of Q. Jane and Q. Mary, p. 75.

1411.   It sat from 2 April until 5 May.—Wriothesley, ii, 114, 115. The city returned the same members that had served in the last parliament of Edward VI, namely, Martin Bowes, Broke the Recorder, John Marsh and John Blundell.

1412.   Journal 16, fo. 295b.

1413.   Repertory 13, pt. i, fos. 165, 166, 166b, 170.

1414.   Chron. of Q. Jane and Q. Mary, p. 77.

1415.   -Id., p. 78.

1416.   Journal 16, fo. 263.

1417.   Repertory 13, pt. i, fo. 191. A full account of the pageants, etc., will be found in John Elder's letter.—Chron. of Q. Jane and Q. Mary, Appendix X.

1418.   Chron. of Q. Jane and Q. Mary, pp. 78-79.

1419.   Martin Bowes, of the old members, alone continued to sit for the city, the places of the other members being taken by Ralph Cholmeley, who had succeeded Broke as Recorder; Richard Grafton, the printer; and Richard Burnell.

1420.   Chron. of Q. Jane and Q. Mary, 82; Wriothesley, 122.

1421.   Repertory 13, part i, fo. 111b.

1422.   -Id., fo. 193.

1423.   Journal 16, fo. 300. Bishop Braybroke, nearly two centuries before, had done all he could to put down marketing within the sacred precincts, and to render "Paul's Walk"—as the great nave of the cathedral was called—less a scene of barter and frivolity.

1424.   Repertory 13, pt. i, fo. 251b.

1425.   In 1558, a man convicted of breaking this law was ordered to ride through the public market places of the city, his face towards the horse's tail, with a piece of beef hanging before and behind him, and a paper on his head setting forth his offence.—Repertory 13, fo. 12b.

1426.   Repertory 13, pt. i, fo. 193; Letter Book S, fo. 119b.

1427. Journal 16, fo. 285b; Letter Book R, fo. 290b; Repertory 13, pt. i, fo. 147; Wriothesley, ii, 114.

1428. Grey Friars Chron., p. 89.

1429. -Id., p. 95.

1430. -Id., ibid.

1431. -Id., p. 78n.

1432. Journal 16, fo. 321b.

1433. Wriothesley, ii, 126; Grey Friars Chron., p. 94.

1434. Wriothesley, ii, 126n; Grey Friars Chron., pp. 56, 57, 95.

1435. Foxe's "Acts and Monuments," vi, 717, 737, 740, vii, 114, 115.

1436. "Item the vth day of September [1556], was browte thorrow Cheppesyde teyd in ropes xxiijti tayd together as herreytkes, and soo unto the Lowlers tower." — Grey Friars Chron., p. 98.

1437. "At this time [Aug., 1554] there was so many Spanyerdes in London that a man shoulde have mett in the stretes for one Inglisheman above iiij Spanyerdes, to the great discomfort of the Inglishe nation. The halles taken up for Spanyerdes." — Chron. Q. Jane and Q. Mary, p. 81.

1438. -Id., ibid.

1439. Repertory 13, pt. i, fo. 205b.

1440. By an order in council, dated Greenwich, 13 March, 1555, the merchants of the Steelyard were thenceforth to be allowed to buy cloth in warehouses adjoining the Steelyard, without hindrance from the mayor. The mayor was ordered to give up cloth that had been seized as foreign bought and sold at Blackwell Hall. He was, moreover, not to demand *quotam salis* of the merchants, who were to be allowed to import into the city fish, corn and other provisions free of import. — Repertory 13, pt. ii, fo. 384b; Letter Book S, fo. 76.

1441. Repertory 13, pt. ii, fos. 399b, 404, 406; Letter Book S, fos. 70, 93b.

1442. Repertory 13, pt. ii, fo. 508b.

1443.   Wheeler's "Treatise of Commerce" (ed. 1601), p. 100.

1444.   Repertory 13, pt. ii, fos. 507b, 520b, 540.

1445.   Repertory 13, pt. ii, fo. 529.

1446.   -Id., fo. 526b.

1447.   -Id., fo. 534b.

1448.   Repertory 13, pt. ii, fo. 420.

1449.   Stafford had issued a proclamation from Scarborough Castle declaiming against Philip for introducing 12,000 foreigners into the country, and announcing himself as protector and governor of the realm. He was captured by the Earl of Westmoreland and executed on Tower Hill 28 May.—Journal 17, fo. 34b; Letter Book S, fo. 127b; Holinshed. iv, 87; Machyn's Diary, p. 137.

1450.   Journal 17, fo. 37b; Letter Book S, fo. 131.

1451.   Journal 17, fos. 37b, 38; Letter Book S, fo. 131b.

1452.   Machyn, p. 142.

1453.   Repertory 13, pt. ii, fo. 517.

1454.   "London fond v.c. men all in bluw cassokes, sum by shyppes and sum to Dover by land, the goodlyst men that ever whent, and best be-sene in change (of) apprelle."—Diary, p. 143.

1455.   Merchant Taylor, son of William Offley, of Chester; alderman of Portsoken and Aldgate Wards. Was one of the signatories to the document nominating Lady Jane Grey successor to Edward VI, and was within a few weeks (1 Aug.) elected sheriff. Knighted with alderman William Chester, 7 Feb., 1557. His mansion-house was in Lime Street, near the Church of St. Andrew Undershaft. Ob. 29 Aug, 1582.—Machyn, pp. 125, 353; Index to Remembrancia, p. 37, note. Fuller, who erroneously places his death in 1580, describes him as the "Zaccheus of London" not "on account of his low stature, but his great charity in bestowing half of his estate on the poor." — Fuller's "Worthies," p. 191.

1456.   Repertory 13, pt. ii, fos. 521b, 522; Letter Book S, fo. 134.

1457. Journal 17, fo. 54b.

1458. Repertory 13, pt. ii, fo. 530.

1459. Repertory 13, pt. ii, fos. 530, 532, 522b, 535; Journal 17, fo. 54.

1460. Machyn, p. 147.

1461. Repertory 13, pt. ii, fo. 571.

1462. Journal 17, fo. 55. See Appendix. They were ordered in the first instance to be forwarded to Dover by the 19th Jan. at the latest, but on the 6th Jan. the Privy Council sent a letter to the mayor to the effect that "albeit he was willed to send the vc men levied in London to Dover, forasmuch as it is sithence considered here that they may with best speede be brought to the place of service by seas, he is willen to sende them with all speede by hoyes to Queenburgh, where order is given for the receavinge and placing of them in the shippes, to be transported with all speede possible." — Harl. MS. 643, fo. 198; Notes to Machyn's Diary, p. 362.

1463. Journal 17, fo. 56.

1464. Wriothesley, ii, 140.

1465. Order of the Court of Aldermen, 10 Jan. — Repertory 13, pt. ii, fo. 582.

1466. Repertory 13, pt. ii, fo. 582b; Precept to the Companies. — Journal 17, fo. 56b.

1467. Journal 17, fo. 57. So furious was this storm, lasting four or five days, that "some said that the same came to passe through necromancie, and that the diuell was raised vp and become French, the truth whereof is known (saith Master Grafton) to God." — Holinshed, iv, 93.

1468. Journal 17, fo. 7.

1469. Repertory 14, fo. 1b; Journal 17, fo. 58; Machyn, 164.

1470. Journal 17, fos. 59, 59b; Letter Book S, fos. 154b, 155.

1471. Cal. State Papers Dom. (1547-1580), p. 100; Wriothesley, ii, 140, 141.

1472. Stat. 5 and 6, Edward VI, c. 20, which repealed Stat. *37*, Henry VIII, c. 9 (allowing interest to be taken on loans at the rate of ten per cent.) and forbade all usury. This Statute was afterwards repealed (Stat. 13, Eliz., c. 8) and the Statute of Henry VIII re-enacted. The dispensation granted by Mary was confirmed in 1560 by Elizabeth.—Repertory 14, fo. 404b.

1473. Repertory 14, fo. 15b; Journal 17, fo. 63. A large portion of this loan was repaid by Elizabeth soon after her accession.—Repertory 14, fos. 236b, 289.

1474. Repertory 14, fos. 94b, 96b.

1475. The commemoration was eventually put down by the Stuarts as giving rise to tumults and disorders.—Journal 49, fo. 270b; Luttrell's Diary, 17 Nov., 1682.

1476. Son of Roger Leigh, of Wellington, co. Salop, an apprentice of Sir Rowland Hill, whose niece, Alice Barker, he married. Buried in the Mercers' Chapel. By his second son, William, he was ancestor of the Lords Leigh, of Stoneleigh, and by his third son William, grandfather of Francis Leigh, Earl of Chichester.—Notes to Machyn's Diary, p. 407.

1477. "The order of the sheryfes at the receyvyng of the quenes highenes in to Myddlesex."—Letter Book S, fo. 183; Repertory 14, fo. 90b.

1478. Letter Book S, fo. 182b; Journal 7, fo. 101b.

1479. Repertory 14, fos. 97, 98.

1480. -*Id.*, fo. 99.

1481. -*Id.*, fo. 102b.

1482. Repertory 14, fo. 103b.

1483. Dated 27 Dec., 1558.—Journal 17, fo. 106b.

1484. Wriothesley, ii, 145.

1485. -*Id. ibid.*

1486. Repertory 4, fo. 213b.

1487. Journal 17, fos. 120b, 168; Repertory 14, fo. 152; Letter Book T, fo. 82b.

1488. "In some places the coapes, vestments, and aulter clothes, bookes, banners, sepulchers and other ornaments of the churches were burned, which cost above £2,000 renuinge agayne in Queen Maries time" (Wriothesley, ii, 146; Cf. Machyn, p. 298). Among the churchwarden accounts of the parish of St. Mary-at-Hill for the year 1558-1559 there is a payment of one shilling for "bringing down ymages to Romeland (near Billingsgate) to be burnt."

1489. Proclamation, dated 19 Sept., 1559.—Journal 17, fo. 267; Letter Book T, fo. 5b.

1490. Journal 17, fo. 184b.

1491. Proclamation, dated 24 March, 1560.—Journal 17, fo. 223b.

1492. In April the city was called upon to furnish 900 soldiers, in May 250 seamen, and in June 200 soldiers.—Repertory 14, fos. 323, 336, 339b, 340, 340b, 344b; Journal 17, fos. 238b, 244. It is noteworthy that the number of able men in the city at this time serviceable for war, although untrained, was estimated to amount to no more than 5,000.—Journal 17, fo. 244b.

1493. Journal 18, fos. 57-60b. The livery companies furnished the men according to allotment. The barber-surgeons claimed exemption by statute (32 Henry VIII, c. 42), but subsequently consented to waive their claim. The city also objected to supplying the soldiers with cloaks.—Repertory 15, fos. 110b, 113.

1494. Journal 18, fo. 66; Machyn, pp. 292, 293.

1495. Journal 18, fo. 71.

1496. The queen to the mayor and corporation of London, 30 June, 1563.—Journal 18, fo. 124.

1497. Repertory 15, fo. 258.

1498. -Id., fo. 259.

1499. -Id., fo. 263.

1500. The queen to the mayor, 2 Aug., 1563.—Journal 18, fo. 140. Precept of the mayor.—Id., fo. 136; Repertory 15, fo. 279b; Machyn's Diary, p. 312.

1501. Journal 18, fo. 128.

1502. -*Id.*, fo. 119b.

1503. Repertory 15, fo. 265b.

1504. Machyn, 312.

1505. Journal 18, fos. 139, 139b, 142, 151b, 152b, 154, 156b, 184, 189b. With the sickness was associated, as was so often the case, a scarcity of food.—Repertory 15, fos. 127, 133b, 138, 168, 178, 179b, etc. The rate of mortality increased to such an extent that a committee was appointed for the purpose of procuring more burial accommodation.—Repertory 15, fos. 311b, 313b, 333.

1506. Proclamation dated 1 Aug., 1563.—Journal 18, fo. 141.

1507. Repertory 15, fo. 284b.

1508. Journal 18, fo. 249.

1509. -*Id.*, fo. 190b.

1510. Journal 18, fos. 214, 215, 227, 291b, 354b; Holinshed, iv, 224.

1511. Journal 17, fos. 320, 321, 331b; Letter Book T, fos. 42, 42b; Repertory 14, fo. 491b. The fire caused by the lightning threatened the neighbouring shops, and their contents were therefore removed to Christchurch, Newgate and elsewhere for safety.—Journal 17, fo. 319b; Letter Book T, fo. 42.

1512. Repertory 15, fos. 474, 478.

1513. Repertory 16, fos. 227, 241b, 274; Letter Book V, fo. 108b.

1514. Repertory 16, fos. 303b, 448. Among the Chamber Accounts of this period we find an item of a sum exceeding £4 paid for "Cusshens to be occupied at Powles by my L. Maior and thaldermen, vz:—for cloth for the uttorside lyning of leather feathers and for making of theym as by a bill appearth."—Chamber Accounts, Town Clerk's Office, vol. i, fo. 50b.

1515. Journal 13, fos. 417, 420, 435, 442b, 443.

1516. Cotton MS., Otho E, x. fo. 45; *Cf.* Burgon's "Life of Gresham," i, 31-33.

1517. Journal 14, fos. 124, 124b.

1518. By Sir Richard's first wife Audrey, daughter of William Lynne, of Southwick, co. Northampton. Sir Thomas is supposed to have been born in London in 1519. Having been bound apprentice to his uncle, Sir John Gresham, he was admitted to the freedom of the Mercers' Company in 1543. Married Anne, daughter of William Ferneley, of West Creting, co. Suffolk, widow of William Read, mercer.

1519. The queen's business kept him so much abroad that her majesty wrote to the Common Council (7 March, 1563) desiring that he might be discharged from all municipal duties.—Journal 18, fo. 137.

1520. Printed in Burgon's "Life of Gresham," i, 409.

1521. Repertory 15, fo. 237b.

1522. Burgon, ii, 30-40.

1523. Repertory 15, fos. 406b, 407.

1524. Repertory 15, fos. 410b, 412.

1525. -Id., fos. 417b, 431.

1526. Repertory 16, fos. 31b, 32b, 43b; Letter Book V, fos. 5, 7b, 8, 17, 21b.

1527. The amount of subscriptions and charges is set out in a "booke" and entered on the City's Journal (No. 19, fos. 12-20; *Cf.* Letter Book V, fos. 70b-79); see also Repertory 16, fo. 126.

1528. Journal 18. fo. 398.

1529. Repertory 16, fo. 316.

1530. Repertory 16, fo. 406b.

1531. Repertory 15, fo. 268b.

1532. Repertory 16, fo. 229.

1533. "A proclamacioun concernyng the cutting of the crest conyzans and mantell of the arms of Sr Thomas Gresham."—Journal 19, fo. 150b; Letter Book V, fo. 222.

1534. Journal 20, pt. ii, fo. 341.

1535. Repertory 18, fo. 362.

1536. "Law and Practice of Marine Insurance," by John Duer, LL.D. (New York, 1845), Lecture ii, p. 33.

1537. At the present day the form of policy used at Lloyds and commonly called the "Lloyd's policy" contains the following clause:—"and it is agreed by us the insurers, that this writing or policy of assurance shall be of as much force and effect as the surest writing or policy of assurance heretofore made in Lombard Street or in the Royal Exchange or elsewhere in London."—Arnould, "Marine Insurance" (6th ed.), i, 230.

1538. Repertory 18, fo. 362b.

1539. Cal. State Papers Dom. (1547-1580), p. 523.

1540. Repertory 19, fos. 166b, 168.

1541. The reader is here reminded that there is an essential difference between life policies and fire or marine policies of assurance. The latter, being policies of indemnity, recovery can be had at law only to the extent of the actual damage done, whereas in life policies the whole amount of the policy can be recovered.

1542. Repertory 17, fo. 300.

1543. Repertory 19, fo. 150.

1544. Cal. Wills, Court of Hust., London, ii, 698.

1545. Printed Report "Gresham College Trust," 29 Oct., 1885.

1546. A return made in 1567 by the livery companies of foreigners residing in the city and liberties gives the number as 3,562.—Repertory 16, fo. 202. Another authority gives the number as 4,851, of which 3,838 were Dutch.—Burgon's "Life of Gresham," ii, 242, citing Haynes, p. 461.

1547. Burgon's "Life of Gresham," ii, 271-275.

1548. Repertory 16, fo. 164.

1549. Journal 19, fo. 116.

1550. Precept of the mayor to that effect, 19 Oct., 1568.-*Id.*, fo. 132b.

1551.   Repertory 16, fo. 451.

1552.   Journal 19, fo. 180; Letter Book V, fo. 245.

1553.   Letter Book V, fo. 246. Holinshed (iv, 234) and others give the whole credit of providing the cemetery to the liberality of Sir Thomas Rowe, the mayor.

1554.   Proclamation (15 July, 1568) against suspected persons landing in England or returning "with any furniture for mayntenaunce of ther rebellion or other lyke cryme" against the King of Spain.—Journal 18, fo. 115; Cf. Letter Book V, fos. 181, 246b.

1555.   Green, "Hist. of the English People," ii, 418.

1556.   Repertory 15, fos. 162, 164, 166b, 241b, 258, 267b, 297, etc.

1557.   Strype, Stow's "Survey" (ed. 1720), bk. i, p. 283.

1558.   Journal II, fo. 253.

1559.   Journal 19, fos. 55-58; Letter Book V, fos. 115b-117b.

1560.   Price's "London Bankers" (enlarged edition), p. 51.

1561.   Letter Book V, fo. 139.

1562.   Cal. State Papers Dom. (1547-1580), p. 314.

1563.   Clode, "Early Hist. of the Guild of Merchant Taylors," pt. ii, pp. 229-230.

1564.   Journal 19, fo. 133b.

1565.   Holinshed, iv, 234.

1566.   "Mesmes j'entendz que de la blanque, qu'on a tirée ces jours passés en ceste ville, ceste Royne retirera pour elle plus de cent mille livres esterlin, qui sont 33,000 escuz; de quoy le monde murumre assés pour la diminution qu'ilz trouvent aulx bénéfices qu'ilz esperoient de leurs billetz"—wrote De la Motlie Fénélon, the French ambassador in London.—Cooper's "Recueil des Dépéches, etc., des Ambassadeurs de France (Paris and London, 1838-1840)," i, 155.

1567.   Proclamation, 6 Jan., 1569.—Journal 19, fo. 139; Letter Book V, fo. 210.

1568.   See letter from Sir Arthur Champernowne, William Hawkins and others to the lords of the council. 1 Jan., 1569.—Cal. State Papers Dom. (1547-1580), p. 326.

1569.   Cal. State Papers Dom. (1547-1580), p. 326.

1570.   Cotton MS., Galba C, iii, fo. 151b. This letter was signed by John Gresham, Thomas Offley, John White, Roger Martyn, Leonell Duckett, Thomas Heaton, Richard Wheler, Thomas Aldersey and Francis Beinson.

1571.   Citizen and Merchant Taylor: Alderman of the Wards of Portsoken and Bishopsgate; Sheriff, 1560-61. *Ob.* 2 Sept., 1570. Buried in Hackney Church. He bestowed the sum of £100 for the relief of members of his company "usinge the brode shire or ell rowinge of the pearch or making of garmentes" during his lifetime, and some landed estate in the city by his will for like purpose.—Letter Book V, fo. 274b; Cal. of Wills, Court of Husting, ii, 686.

1572.   Letter printed (from original among State Papers Dom.) in Burgon's "Life of Gresham," ii, 287.

1573.   Sir Thomas Rowe, mayor, to Secretary Cecil. 23 Jan., 1569.—Cal. State Papers Dom. (1547-1580), p. 329; Burgon's "Life of Gresham," ii, 295-296.

1574.   -*Id.,* 25 Jan.

1575.   Cooper's "Dépêches, etc., des Ambassadeurs de France," i, 176-177.

1576.   Burgon's "Life of Gresham," ii, 297.

1577.   Lansd. MS., No. xii, fo. 16b.

1578.   -*Id.,* fo. 22.

1579.   Repertory 17, fo. 36b.

1580.   Journal 19, fo. 247b; Letter Book V, fo. 301.

1581.   Journal 19, fo. 257.

1582. -*Id.*, fo. 390b.

1583. Journal 19, fo. 390b.

1584. Add. MS., No. 5, 755, fo. 58.

1585. In the following year he was removed to the Charterhouse, but being discovered in correspondence with the deposed Queen of Scots was again placed in the Tower. He was tried and convicted of treason, and after some delay executed on Tower Hill.—Holinshed, iv, 254, 262, 264, 267.

1586. The proclamation, which is set out in Journal 19, fo. 202b (*Cf.* Letter Book V, fo. 267b), gives in detail the rise and progress of the rebellion.

1587. Journal 19, fo. 202; Letter Book V, fo. 267.

1588. Journal 19, fo. 202; Letter Book V, fo. 267.

1589. Letter Book V, fo. 269.

1590. Journal 19, fo. 206b; Letter Book V, fo. 270b; Repertory 16, fo. 522b.

1591. Holinshed, iv, 254.

1592. -*Id.*, 262.

1593. From Hertfordshire, alderman of Billingsgate Ward.

1594. Dated 8 Nov.—Journal 19, fo. 370b.

1595. Holinshed, iv, 263.

1596. Repertory 17, fos. 8b, 23, 27b, 29. 243, etc.; Repertory 19, fos. 24b, 154, etc.; City Records known as "Remembrancia" (Analytical Index), pp. 51-55.

1597. Stranger denizens, carrying on a handicraft in the city, had recently preferred a Bill in Parliament against several of the livery companies. They were persuaded, however, to drop it, and refer their grievance to the Court of Aldermen.—Repertory 17, fos. 302b, 335, 337. A return made by the mayor (10 Nov., 1571) of the strangers then living in London and Southwark and liberties thereof gives the total number as 4,631.—Cal. State Papers Dom. (1547-1580), p. 427.

1598. Repertory 17, fo. 372.

1599. Journal 19, fos. 407-408b, 417-417b; Repertory 17, fos. 292, 298b, 307, 308.

1600. Journal 20, pt. i, fos. 133b, 143b; Repertory 18, fo. 224b.

1601. Journal 20, pt. i, fo. 156b.

1602. Journal 20, pt. i, fo. 252; *Id.*, pt. ii, fo. 280b.

1603. Journal 20, pt. i, fos. 228b, 239.

1604. Repertory 19, fo. 98.

1605. Journal 20, pt. ii, fo. 371.

1606. He was removed by order of Common Council, 13 Dec., *pre diversis magnis rebus dictam civitatem et negotia ejusdem tangentibus.*—Journal 20, pt. ii, fo. 376b.

1607. Journal 20, pt. ii, fos. 388b, 389, 394-395b. The queen to the mayor, etc., of London, 12 March.—Cal. State Papers Dom. (1547-1580), p. 586.

1608. Journal 20, pt. ii, fo. 409b.

1609. *-Id.*, fos. 404, 408b, 412.

1610. Repertory 19, fo. 346b.

1611. This conjecture is made from the fact of a precept having been issued on the 20th Jan. for certain persons to furnish themselves with velvet coats, chains and horses, and a suitable suite, to wait upon the lord mayor on the following Saturday.—Journal 20, pt. ii, fo. 404b.

1612. Burgon's "Life of Gresham," ii, 451-452.

1613. Journal 20, pt. ii, fos. 464, 480.

1614. Continuation of Holinshed, iv, 315.

1615. City Records known as "Remembrancia" (Printed Analytical Index), pp. 306, 330, 331, 350-352; Journal 20, pt. ii, fos. 373, 379, 407.

1616. Remembrancia (Index), pp. 207, 331, 334; Journal 21, fo. 235b.

1617. Remembrancia, vol. i, No. 331.

1618. A reference to this defeat is to be found in the Dublin Assembly Roll under the year 1581.—"Cal. of Ancient Records of Dublin" (ed. by John T. Gilbert, 1891), ii, 155.

1619. Bright, "Hist. of England," ii, 539.

1620. Journal 21, fos. 19, 34, 52, 53, 69b-71b, 78b, etc.; Repertory 20, fos. 90, 117, 117b, 119b, etc.; Remembrancia (Analytical Index), pp. 230-236.

1621. Journal 21, fo. 329b.

1622. Among Chamber Accounts *circa* 1585 we find the following:—"Pd. the x of Dec. by order of Courte to Roger Warffeld Treasuror of Bridewell towards the conveyinge of all the Irishe begging people in and nere London to the Citie of Bristowe v1."—Chamber Accounts, Town Clerk's Office, vol. ii, fo. 17.

1623. Repertory 16, fo. 350.

1624. Repertory 18, fo. 167.

1625. Journal 20, fo. 219b.

1626. Journal 21, fo. 81b; Repertory 20, fo. 1b.

1627. Journal 21, fo. 90.

1628. -*Id.*, fos. 114b, 135, 290, 322.

1629. Remembrancia (Analytical Index), pp. 364, 365.

1630. As early as 1554 students had been supported by the Corporation and the Companies at the Universities.—Repertory 13, fos. 144b, 148, 150b.

1631. Rembrancia, i, 250, 256 (Analytical Index, pp. 365, 366). Another difference shortly occurred between the corporation and the Bishop of London in October of this year. A dispute arose between them as to who was responsible for keeping St. Paul's Cathedral in repair, each party endeavouring to throw the burden upon the other (*Id.*, Analytical Index, pp. 323-327); and in the following March (1582) Bishop Aylmer found cause to complain by letter of unbecoming treatment by the mayor, both of the bishop and his clergy, and threatened, unless matters changed for the better, to admonish the mayor publicly at Paul's Cross, "where the lord mayor must sit, not as a judge to control, but as a scholar to learn, and the writer, not as John Aylmer to be thwarted, but as John London, to teach him and all London." — (*Id.*, *ibid.*, pp. 128-129).

1632. Repertory 20, fo. 282.

1633. Son of Richard Osborne, of Ashford, co. Kent. The story goes that he was apprenticed to Sir William Hewet, clothworker, and that he married his master's daughter, whom he had rescued from a watery grave in the Thames at London Bridge. His son, Sir Edward Osborne, was created a baronet by Charles I, and his grandson, Sir Thomas, made Duke of Leeds in 1692 by King William III.

1634. Cal. State Papers Dom. (1581-1590), p. 157. The right of holding musters in Southwark was again questioned; and the claim of the city was upheld by Sir Francis Walsingham. For this he received the thanks of the lord mayor by letter dated 15 Feb. — *Id.*, p. 159.

1635. "A lettre from the quenes maty for ye mustringe of 4000 men, and also for the shewes on the evens of St. John Baptist and St. Peter thapostles." — Journal 21, fo. 421b.

1636. Contin. of Holinshed, v, 599, 600.

1637. Journal 21, fo. 388b.

1638. Stow's Annals (ed. 1592), pp. 1198-1201.

1639. Motley, "United Netherlands," i, pp. 318-324.

1640. For particulars of his life see Remembrancia (Analytical Index), p. 284, note.

1641. Journal 21, fo. 448b.

1642. "Thaccompte of the saide chamberlyn for the transportacioun and necessary provision of MMCCCCXX soldiers into the lowe countryes of Flaunders." — Chamber Accounts, vol. ii, fos. 56-58b.

1643. Motley, "United Netherlands," i, 340.

1644. Chamber Accounts, ii, 134. The earl's honor of Denbigh, North Wales, was mortgaged to certain citizens of London, and not being redeemed, was afterwards purchased by the queen herself.—Repertory 22, fo. 287.

1645. Repertory 21, fos. 308-311.

1646. For many years after the passing of the Act (1 Edw. VI, c. 14) confiscating property devoted to "superstitious uses," the corporation and the livery companies were the objects of suspicion of holding "concealed lands," *i.e.* lands held charged for superstitious uses, which they had failed to divulge. The appointment of a royal commission to search for such lands was submitted to the law officers of the city for consideration, 9 Sept., 1567.— Repertory 16, fo. 276b. Vexatious proceedings continued to be taken under the Act until the year 1623, when a Statute was passed, entitled "An Act for the General Quiet of the Subjects against all Pretences of Concealment whatsoever."—Stat. 21, James I, c. ii.

1647. Journal 22, fo. 1.

1648. *-Id.*, fos. 26, 29.

1649. Journal 22, fo. 37b; Repertory 21, fo. 288b.

1650. Journal 22, fos. 52-53. Both the queen's letter and Dalton's speech are printed in Stow's Continuation of Holinshed, iv, 902-904.

1651. Journal 22, fos. 48, 57b, 58; Repertory 21, fo. 327.

1652. Proclamation, dated Richmond, 4 Dec., 1586.—Journal 22, fo. 67b.

1653. Royal Proclamation against engrossers of corn, 2 Jan., 1587.— Journal 22, fo. 74.

1654. Journal 22, fo. 64.

1655. Repertory 21, fo. 370b.

1656. Journal 21, fo. 136b.

1657. Motley, "United Netherlands," ii, 281.

1658. Journal 22, fos. 144, 161b, 166-167b, 170b.

1659. Journal 22, fo. 190.

1660. Only 1,000 men out of the force raised by the city went to Tilbury, and the earl only consented to receive this small contingent on condition they brought their own provisions with them, so scantily was the camp supplied with victuals through the queen's parsimony.—Remembrancia (Analytical Index), p. 244. Letter from Leicester to Walsingham, 26 July.—Cal. State Papers Dom. (1581-1590), p. 513.

1661. Leicester to Walsingham, 28 July, 1588.—State Papers Dom., vol. ccxiii, No. 55.

1662. William of Malmesbury bears similar testimony to the courage of Londoners under good leadership: *Laudandi prorsus viri et quos Mars ipse collata non sperneret hasta si ducem habuissent.*—Gesta Regum (Rolls Series, No. 90), i, 208.

1663. Repertory 22, fo. 148b.

1664. A list of "the London shippes" (including pinnaces), dated 19 July, 1588, is preserved among the State Papers (Domestic) at the Public Record Office (vol. ccxii, No. 68), and is set out in the Appendix to this work. Two other lists, dated 24 July, giving the names of the ships (exclusive of pinnaces) are also preserved (State Papers Dom., vol. ccxiii, Nos. 15, 16). Each of these lists give the number of vessels supplied by the city against the Armada as sixteen ships and four pinnaces, or as twenty ships (inclusive of pinnaces). It is not clear what was the authority of Stow (Howes's Chron., p. 743) for stating that the city, having been requested to furnish fifteen ships of war and 5,000 men, asked for two days to deliberate, and then furnished thirty ships and 10,000 men. At the same time there does exist a list of "shipps set forth and payde upon ye charge of ye city of London, anno 1588" (that is to say, the ships furnished by the city for that whole year), and that list contains the names of thirty ships, with the number of men on board each vessel and the names of the commanders.—State Papers Dom., vol. ccxxxii, fos. 16, 16b.

1665. Journal 22, fo. 173. The assessment was afterwards (19 April) settled at three shillings in the pound.—*Id.*, fo. 175.

1666. Journal 22, fos. 193, 200b.

1667. Richard Tomson to Walsingham, 30 July, 1588.—Cal. State Papers Dom. (1581-1590), p. 517.

1668. Hawkins to Walsingham, 31 July, 1588.—Cal. State Papers Dom. (1581-1590), p. 517.

1669. Howard to the same, 21 July.—*Id.*, p. 507.

1670. Sir William Wynter to Walsingham, 1 Aug., 1588.—Cal. State Papers Dom. (1581-1590), p. 521.

1671. Journal 22, fo. 196b.

1672. -*Id.*, fo. 196.

1673. Tomson to Walsingham, 30 July, 1588.—State Papers Dom., vol. ccxiii, No. 67.

1674. Repertory 21, fo. 578.

1675. Journal 22, fo. 200b; Cal. State Papers Dom. (1581-1590), p. 510.

1676. Journal 22, fo. 197.

1677. -*Id.*, fo. 199b.

1678. Journal 22, fo. 200.

1679. Nichols' "Progresses of Q. Elizabeth," ii, 537.

1680. Journal 22, fos. 233, 235.

1681. Nichols' "Progresses of Q. Elizabeth," ii, 538, 539.

1682. On the 7th Feb., 1583, previously to setting out on his last ill-fated expedition, Gilbert addressed a letter to Walsingham from "his house in Redcross Street."—Cal. State Papers Dom. (1581-1590), p. 95.

1683. See the will of Dame Margaret Hawkins, dated 23 April, 1619.—Cal. of Wills, Court of Hust., London, ii, 745. The will contains many bequests of articles which savour of Spanish loot.

1684. Strype, Stow's "Survey" (1720), bk. ii, p. 44.

1685. Journal 22, fo. 202b.

1686. Journal 22, fo. 210; Repertory 21, fos. 590b, 593; Repertory 22, fos. 15, 26b, 27; Cal. State Papers Dom. (1581-1590), p. 471.

1687. Journal 22, fo. 252; Repertory 22, fo. 16b.

1688. Journal 22, fos. 227b, 278.

1689. Burghley and others to the mayor, 26 July, 1589.—Journal 22, fo. 312.

1690. -Id., fo. 316b.

1691. Journal 22, fo. 345b; Journal 23, fo. 79.

1692. Journal 22, fo. 314.

1693. Journal 22, fo. 321b.

1694. -Id., fo. 326.

1695. -Id., fo. 321.

1696. Journal 23, fos. 35, 38.

1697. July 24, 1591.—Remembrancia. i, 599 (Analytical Index, p. 408).

1698. Journal 23, fos. 31, 43b, 48b; Repertory 22, fo. 284b.

1699. Journal 23, fos. 68, 68b; *Cf.* Cal. State Papers Dom. (1591-1594), p. 48, where the date of the letter is given as "May."

1700. Journal 23, fos. 325b, 383b.

1701. Journal 23, fos. 45-46b.

1702. Journal 24, fo. 86.

1703. Proclamation, dated 16 Sept., 1591.—Journal 23, fo. 47.

1704. Journal 23, fo. 73.

1705. -Id., fo. 71.

1706. Proclamations, dated 8 Jan. and 26 Sept., 1592.—Journal 23, fos. 78b, 136.

1707. The queen to the lord mayor, 6 Jan., 1592.—Cal. State Papers Dom. (1591-1594), p. 168. The same to the same, 25 Jan.—Journal 23, fo. 87.

1708. Journal 23, fos. 157, 167, 174, 224b; Repertory 23, fo. 29.

1709. It was in 1592 that bills of mortality, kept by the parish clerks, were for the first time published.

1710. Journal 23, fo. 204b.

1711. Journal 23, fo. 266.

1712. -*Id.*, fos. 400, 402.

1713. -*Id.*, fo. 153.

1714. Journal 23, fo. 290b. The number was afterwards reduced to 350 men.—*Id.*, fo. 296b; Remembrancia, ii, 3, 27, 30.

1715. Journal 23, fo. 290.

1716. -*Id.*, fo. 289.

1717. Journal 23, fo. 293. The names, tonnage and crews of the ships are thus given (Remembrancia, ii, 26):—The Assention, 400 tons, 100 mariners; The Consent, 350 tons, 100 mariners; The Susan Bonadventure, 300 tons, 70 mariners; The Cherubim, 300 tons, 70 mariners; The Minion, 180 tons, 50 mariners; and The Primrose, 180 tons, 50 mariners. Only one pinnace is mentioned, of 50 tons, with 20 mariners.

1718. Journal 23, fo. 323b.

1719. Chamberlain's Letters, *temp.*, Eliz. (Camd. Soc., No. 79), p. 50. The writer was a son of Richard Chamberlain, a city alderman.

1720. Alderman of Tower Ward; Sheriff 1584-5; Mayor 1597.

1721. Repertory 24, fo. 410b.

1722. Repertory 25, fo. 216b.

1723. The letter is printed *in extenso* in Chambers' "Book of Days," i, 464, and in Goodman's "Court of James I," ii, 127.

1724. Journal 24, fos. 79b, 81, 82, 82b.

1725. -*Id.*, fo. 85b.

1726. Journal 24, fos. 105, 144.

1727. -*Id*., fo. 84b.

1728. Macaulay's "Essay on Lord Bacon."

1729. Journal 24, fo. 145.

1730. -*Id*., fos. 146b, 149.

1731. Journal 24, fos. 110-111, 129b.; Repertory 23, fo. 594b.

1732. Journal 24, fos. 124, 154b, 157b.

1733. The queen to the mayor, 25 July; the lords of the council to the same, 26 July.—Journal 24, fo. 142.

1734. Journal 24, fos. 173, 175.

1735. The same dissatisfaction at the result of the Cadiz expedition so far as it affected the citizens of London was displayed in a previous letter from the mayor to the lords of the Privy Council (3 Nov.) in answer to a demand for 3,000 men and three ships to ride at Tilbury Hope and give notice of the approach of the Spanish fleet.—Remembrancia (Analytical Index), pp. 243, 244.

1736. Repertory 24, fo. 60b.

1737. Journal 24, fos. 210b-213b, 216, 217.

1738. Journal 24, fos. 324b, 325, 329b; Repertory 24, fos. 268, 287, 306; *Id*. 25, fo. 4b. Elizabeth asked for £40,000, but only succeeded in getting half that sum.—Chamberlain's Letters, p. 15.

1739. Journal 25, fos. 34, 47b, 48; Repertory 24, fo. 352b. In July, 1600, a deputation was appointed to wait upon the lords of the council touching the repayment of this loan.—Repertory 25, fo. 119b. It still remained unpaid in Feb., 1604.—Journal 26, fo. 163b. By the end of 1606 £20,000 had been paid off.—Remembrancia (Analytical Index), p. 188; Repertory 27, fo. 278. And by July, 1607, the whole was repaid.—Howes's Chron., p. 890.

1740. Journal 25, fos. 74b, 75, 77b-78b, 81, 81b, 82b-84, etc.

1741. Chamberlain's Letters, p. 59.

1742. Journal 25, fo. 79b.

1743. -*Id.*, fos. 80, 80b.

1744. Chamberlain's Letters, p. 59.

1745. Chamberlain's Letters, p. 61; Journal 25, fos. 81, 84b.

1746. Journal 25, fo. 238.

1747. Journal 25. fo. 245; Letter Book BB, fo. 85. He was deprived of his aldermanry of the Ward of Farringdon Without and debarred from ever becoming alderman of any other ward "for causes sufficiently made known" to the Court of Aldermen.

1748. Repertory 25, fos. 209b, 213.

1749. Cal. State Papers Dom. (1598-1601), p. 546.

1750. Secretary Cecil to the Lord Lieutenant of Ireland and others, 10 Feb., 1601.—Cal. State Papers Dom. (1598-1601), p. 547.

1751. Proclamation, dated 9 Feb., 1601.—Journal 25, fo. 240b.

1752. Repertory 25, fos. 213, 246.

1753. Journal 25, fos. 242, 243, 243b.

1754. Cal. State Papers Dom. (1601-1603), pp. 16, 26, 89, 90.

1755. Journal 25, fos. 137, 161b, 166, 179, 189, 190, 218b, 223, 237, 237b, 262b-265b, 293, 295, 301, 302b, 313b, 315; Journal 26, fos. 16b-19.

1756. Repertory 25, fo. 296b.

1757. Repertory 24, fos. 343, 354; Repertory 25, fos. 165-175. The Steelyard was re-opened in 1606.—Journal 27, fo. 66.

1758. Letter from Sir Christopher Hatton to the mayor, 27 Nov., 1583.— Remembrancia (Analytical Index), p. 407.

1759. Journal 26, fo. 42.